COMPETITION FOR EMPIRE

THE RISE OF MODERN EUROPE
Edited by William L. Langer

COMPETITION FOR EMPIRE

1740-1763

BY

WALTER L. DORN
Ohio State University

ILLUSTRATED

NEW YORK
HARPER & ROW, PUBLISHERS

To

OTTO HINTZE

FERDINAND SCHEVILL

TABLE OF CONTENTS

INTRODUCTION

Our age of specialization produces an almost incredible amount of monographic research in all fields of human knowledge. So great is the mass of this material that even the professional scholar cannot keep abreast of the contributions in anything but a restricted part of his general subject. In all branches of learning the need for intelligent synthesis is now more urgent than ever before, and this need is felt by the layman even more acutely than by the scholar. He cannot hope to read the products of microscopic research or to keep up with the changing interpretations of experts, unless new knowledge and new viewpoints are made accessible to him by those who make it their business to be informed and who are competent to speak with authority.

These volumes, published under the general title of *The Rise of Modern Europe* are designed primarily to give the general reader and student a reliable survey of European history written by experts in various branches of that vast subject. In consonance with the current broad conception of the scope of history, they attempt to go beyond a merely political-military narrative, and to lay stress upon social, economic, religious, scientific and artistic developments. The minutely detailed, chronological approach is to some extent sacrificed in the effort to emphasize the dominant factors and to set forth their interrelationships. At the same time the division of European history into national histories has been abandoned and wherever possible attention has been focussed upon larger forces common to the whole of European civilization. These are the broad lines on which this history as a whole has been laid out. The individual volumes are integral parts of the larger scheme, but they are intended also to stand as independent units, each the work of a scholar well qualified to treat the period covered by his book. Each volume contains about fifty illustrations selected from the mass of contemporary pictorial material. All non-contemporary illustrations have been excluded on principle. The bibliographical note appended to each volume is designed to facilitate further study of special aspects touched upon in the text. In general every effort has been made to give the reader a clear idea of the main movements in European history, to embody the monographic contributions of research workers, and to present the material in a forceful and vivid manner.

The period covered by Professor Dorn's volume was taken up very largely by two great wars, both of them fought out on the continent of Europe but also in the remoteness of America and India. The author, however, has eschewed a detailed, conventional narrative of military and naval operations and exploits. In keeping with the spirit of the series, he has instead attempted to analyze and explain the nature of the continental conflicts and the struggle for overseas empire by examining the dynamics of the eighteenth-century state. His chapters on economic trends and administration are, to my knowledge, quite unique, while his account of the military organizations of the various states and his study of the peculiar limitations of military action in that period serve to throw a great deal of light on the actual developments of the two great wars. But apart from the treatment of political and military affairs, Professor Dorn is, in my opinion, to be congratulated particularly for the altogether admirable chapter in which he attempts to draw together the intellectual, scientific, religious and artistic currents of these years. He makes the Age of Reason comprehensible and, in a really masterly synthesis, demonstrates the relationship of the Enlightenment to the other forces operative during the mid-century.

WILLIAM L. LANGER

PREFACE

It requires no very intensive scrutiny to perceive that the twenty-three years which form the subject of this volume, though punctuated by no spectacular revolution, have left a legacy which still continually attracts our attention. The peculiar interest of these decades lies in the fact that war and politics had lost all their imaginative idealism. They provide an exceptional opportunity for a study of the functioning of the competitive state system of Europe at a time before liberal criticism began materially to affect social and political life. Accordingly, a discussion of the social foundations of politics, militarism and culture, a comparative examination of the constitutional structures of the principal countries of Europe, the permutations of their diplomatic combinations and military conflicts command the center of the stage. Together with these things the Enlightenment which in these years burst into full vigor constitutes the central theme of this volume. To do justice to these great subjects it has been imperative to make a number of painful excisions, particularly a separate consideration of the Scandinavian countries and the Ottoman Empire which in these years played a distinctly subordinate role in the large affairs of Europe. Moreover, the dedication of a separate volume in this series to the general phenomenon of enlightened despotism makes it advisable to exclude this subject from a specific discussion in this volume, all the more since there is no essential difference between the domestic policy of Marquis of Pombal in Portugal or Frederick the Great in Prussia before and after the Seven Years' War.

It is impossible to write a book on so ambitious a scale without a heavy debt of gratitude to the work of others. The author gratefully acknowledges his indebtedness to the editor, Professor William L. Langer, who has given his time and good counsel without stint; to Professors Leo Gershoy and Robert Binkley who have given large sections of the manuscript the benefit of intelligent criticism; to

Professor Dietrich Gerhard who has gone over much of the manuscript and whose knowledge of economic and diplomatic history has been a source of constant amazement; to my colleagues, Professor Warner Woodring for his unrivaled knowledge of British naval history and Professor George Havens for his thoughtful Voltaire studies; above all to the courtesy of the Harvard Library and the Library of Congress in placing their vast collections at the disposal of the author. My wife has collaborated with me in revising the manuscript.

W. L. D.

October 9, 1939

COMPETITION FOR EMPIRE

Chapter One

THE COMPETITIVE STATE SYSTEM

I. THE BALANCE OF POWER SYSTEM

IN 1740 Europe was in a state of equilibrium. The years before had been a time of lull in political aspirations. Great national passions seemed to have run underground. There was nothing to disturb the peace of Europe nor yet to encourage the hope that the world was changing for the better. There were no great popular ferments to bedevil the lives of statesmen. Religion was no longer and modern liberal ideals were not yet the mainspring of political action. But then as before the equilibrium was unstable, affected by the unequal development of competing units or by diplomatic combinations. The fluctuations of economic prosperity and military power were bound to reassert themselves sooner or later. Power politics pure and simple dominated the scene, and to grasp the full import of the two great wars which, with but a short interval between them, fill the middle decades of the century it is imperative to cast a brief glance at the competitive state system of Europe.

It is this very competitive character of the state system of modern Europe that distinguishes it from the political life of all previous and non-European civilizations of the world. Its essence lies in the coexistence of independent and co-ordinate states, whose expansionist drive provoked incessant military conflicts and periodical reshufflings of the territorial and political map, and above all in the prevention of any single power from reducing the others to a state of permanent subjection. But to be a great power in 1740 signified the pursuit of an expansionist or imperialistic foreign policy. Every great power was a potential aggressor to its neighbor and, since it knew this neighbor to be inspired by similar motives, it could not but regard every subtle maneuver of the latter as a potential aggression. An incorrigible distrust had taken possession of the statesmen of Europe and this mutual distrust necessitated a reciprocal vigilance with regard to power in territory, inhabitants and wealth, in a word with regard to all the means of economic, political and military strength, without which they felt themselves threatened with conquest. But, despite the appalling waste of energy and human lives caused by incessant wars, this competitive state system exercised a dynamic function. It communicated a stimulus to intensive economic enterprise and forced upon statesmen an ever greater rationalization and modernization of their political and military mechanisms. The spirit of enterprise which lay at the root of early modern capitalism had its counterpart in the enterprise and competition of the statesmen of this epoch of state-building.

Eighteenth-century wars had not yet ceased to be waged for the development of states, but they tended more and more to become wars for the balance of power. Such wars presupposed highly organized states with nearly equal forces and with a systematized political and military tradition behind them. They further presupposed an anarchic international society in which expansion was left free until it was checked by conflicting ambitions, expressed in terms of the balance of power. This principle of the balance of power was one of the essential conditions of the sovereign independence of the nations of Europe. The historian of the eighteenth century would do wrong either to deride it as a scarecrow or to worship it as a totem. As a restraining influence it was even more useful than international law, which, in this epoch at least, was nothing more than a war code. Like private persons engaged in a duel, the states of Europe created this war code to govern their international relations, a code which they invoked prior to an appeal to arms, and reaffirmed or modified after a fight. This code laid down the principles and rules, but never quite obtained the force of law, because legal procedure and penalties were utterly lacking. The principle of balance of power, too, was not an end in itself, but only a means to an end and as such necessarily imperfect. At its best it created a certain common consciousness, a certain feeling of solidarity among the peoples of Europe. In spite of their babel of tongues, their bloody and endless quarrels, Europe still remained a vital and organic unity. The wrongs and injuries which these peoples had done one another in the past, their conquests and reconquests, groupings and regroupings, their occasional fierce hatreds arising from balked ambitions, had welded them into a kind of union from which even Englishmen, in spite of their insularity, have been unable to escape to this day.

Since the Peace of Utrecht international affairs had been controlled by a small group of great powers which applied the doctrine of the balance of power only to themselves, not to their relations with smaller and weaker states. Moreover, the Peace of Utrecht, with its territorial partition and partition treaties, set the pattern for the eighteenth century and by so doing created a general feeling of insecurity of territorial possession. The principle of partition or the doctrine that the interests of Europe at large were to be placed above the interests of individual monarchs had triumphed. Now that the empire of the Spanish Hapsburgs had been broken up in the name of the European balance, any kind of redivision of territory seemed possible. No war had yet succeeded in producing a permanent equilibrium. It was apparent that the balance of power system, though intended as an instrument of peace, might easily be invoked to justify the absorption of smaller states or an attack upon a great one. While seeking to limit and check the others, each great power strove for a supremacy difficult to achieve and still more difficult to maintain.

II. SOCIAL STRUCTURE AND POLITICS

In 1740 the states of Europe still exhibited the characteristic features of the old feudal society. They were states in which social classes were more or less sharply defined, polities of superior and inferior groups, based on inherited privilege, birth and property. The great days of the nobility were over, yet the laws which protected their estates and their fortunes continued to be enforced. Despite the legal, fiscal and administrative absolutism of the monarch, the typical state of the Continent was still a *Herrenstaat*, that is to say, a state whose foreign and domestic policies were dominated by the feudal aristocracy. For the eighteenth-century monarchy, however progressive or enlightened, never made a determined or systematic effort to balance social classes and never permitted the free play of social and economic forces.[1] The nobility, like the other classes, had bowed before the absolute king; they had surrendered their independence and their political rights. But this subjection was more in the nature of a compromise than of an abject surrender. The French aristocracy retained inheritable privileges which had pecuniary value, while in northern and eastern Europe aristocrats lived on their estates like miniature kings, endowed with complete economic and legal authority over their serfs. Notwithstanding their absolutism the rulers of France, Austria, Russia and Prussia were essentially the executive agents of their feudal aristocracies. Not even an energetic autocrat like Frederick the Great could emancipate the serfs in the teeth of the opposition of the landed proprietors of Prussia. When the Russian tsar failed to rule in accordance with the wishes of the nobility, he was removed through the instrumentality of the palace guards. In Sweden both the parliament and the crown were dominated by the nobles in the middle decades of the eighteenth century.

So long as the monarchs of the Continent did essentially what the magnates wanted them to do, so long as they placed the wealth and the power of the state at the disposal of the aristocracy, they got on magnificently with them. This was natural enough, for it was the king's function to be the apex of the social pyramid. *"Je suis aristocrate, c'est mon métier,"* said Catherine the Great. The nobility had powers and privileges, inherited feudal relics precisely like those pertaining to the sovereign himself. This was notably true of France where, in the time of Louis XV, the king was scarcely more than an agent of the nobility, which ruled much more effectively through the king than in opposition to him. At a time when, as de Tocqueville pointed out, the progressive impoverishment of the nobility became strikingly apparent, they attached all the more importance to forming the immediate entourage of the king, commanding the fleets, officering the armies and filling the higher posts in the civil service and in the church. Many were paid pensions outright from the royal treasury.[2] Only the noblemen who had been presented at court, the *gens de la cour*, could hope to play

---

[1] See the illuminating essay by Fritz Kern, "Vom Herrenstaat zum Wohlfahrtsstaat," *Schmollers Jahrbuch*, vol. LII (1928), 398.
[2] Alexis de Tocqueville, *France Before the Revolution of 1789* (London, 1873), 98.

an important political role. They engaged in perpetual intrigue to obtain from the king or queen profitable sinecures or gifts of land or money; and those in favor at court were expected to provide for their relatives and friends. What historians used to criticize as a reckless mismanagement of public finance was in large measure the natural result of the social system. The real master of the French state was not the king, but a class. The vast income of the crown belonged to the king only in a nominal sense, for the crown shared this income with the feudal aristocracy.[3]

It is well known that the history of the European nobility was *par excellence* a military history. Since the Middle Ages their principal occupation had been warfare, a fact which the emergence of standing armies did not alter. In all the principal countries their psychological orientation, their traditions, their ambitions, their sense of honor, their very language were military. Everywhere they constituted a more or less highly integrated military caste, everywhere a considerable number of them found in military activity their only outlet and their natural source of political influence. It was a rooted tradition that the proper occupation of a nobleman was to serve as officer in the army. Throughout Europe diplomatic officials came from the same class and all of them accepted war as a necessary part of the system. In this sense warfare became a function, if not an actual necessity, of the structure of European society. For the aristocracy an extension of frontiers signified a multiplication of offices and an improvement of their chances of advancement. Nobles were in need of occasional wars to distinguish themselves; their class interests coincided with the tradition of the crown, which had made warfare a legitimate and necessary occupation of kings. The crown itself needed occasional foreign triumphs, if only for the sake of security and the splendor of the monarchy at home. The specific causes for which the monarchy went to war were often indifferent enough, for the nobility and ruling classes were satisfied with any war.

Politically and socially the peasantry and artisans were negligible; they were exclusively occupied with their own peculiar interests

---

[3] See the brilliant and penetrating, but sometimes historically inaccurate and erratic comments by J. Schumpeter, "Zur Soziologie der Imperialismen," *Archiv für Sozialwissenschaft und Sozialpolitik*, XLVI (1918), 275.

and took no active share in the life of the community at large. They
were the helots of the social order, whom the nobility exploited
and whom the king enrolled in his army. Even the capitalist
bourgeoisie, in spite of their growing strength, commanded little
political influence in the absolute monarchies of the Continent.
They had long ceased to be necessary allies against the nobility,
and the monarch's interest in them was largely fiscal. It must also
be remembered that as one traveled eastward the middle classes
shrank in number and importance even in the economic sense.
Before the nineteenth century the states of eastern Europe scarcely
possessed a bourgeoisie worthy of the name. These states were all
more or less feudal societies. According to Hungarian law the nobles
alone constituted the nation, while the remainder of the inhabitants
were the *misera plebs contribuens*.[4] Even in France, which had the
largest and most progressive bourgeoisie of any continental power,
they had no means of forcing the state to orient its policy in conformity with their interests. King Louis XV, preoccupied as he was
with dynastic politics, accorded but indifferent support to commercial interests.[5] He encouraged trade, of course, but only because and
in so far as the royal treasury profited from it. In spite of the prevalence of mercantilist theories, commercial interests rarely played a
decisive role in politics. On the Continent at least, outspokenly
commercial or mercantilist wars were unknown in the middle
decades of the eighteenth century. Modern industry was still in its
swaddling clothes and production was quantitatively so small that
exportation was not and could not be a controlling factor in foreign
affairs.

It was impossible, of course, for the absolute monarchies to wage
war without hard money, particularly in countries of undeveloped
credit economy. In states like Prussia and Russia the monarch was
constantly in need of cash to pay for his military establishment. If
his supply of ready money ran short while he was engaged in war,
mass desertion of his troops and the end of the conflict were inevitable. In this sense alone were all wars waged with mercenary

4 H. Marczali, *Hungary in the Eighteenth Century* (Cambridge, 1910), 110. Bohemia,
economically the most advanced state of the Hapsburg empire, had an urban population
of less than eighteen per cent. The actual bourgeoisie constituted no more than five per
cent at most. R. J. Kerner, *Bohemia in the Eighteenth Century* (New York, 1932), 76.

5 H. Sée, *Esquisse d'une histoire économique et sociale de la France* (Paris, 1929), 322.

armies economic or mercantilist wars, for this kind of army had no other basis than the economic. The intelligent monarch, there-fore, assiduously supported the business interests of the middle classes, because he saw in them the surest guarantee of his own financial solvency. But it is important to remember that mer-cantilism was not in the first instance a policy designed to promote the interests of the middle classes. Indeed, mercantilism becomes fully intelligible, as Heckscher has again pointed out, only when it is understood that its supreme aim was to place the entire economic life of the people in the service of the power politics of the state, a state which, as we have seen, was dominated socially and polit-ically by the feudal aristocracy.[6] Despite the fact that in these years the French philosopher-critics opened the barrage of their criticism on the old state, on its social structure and its mercantilism, the vast majority of the French middle classes was still securely anchored in its traditional moorings. Because the king needed soldiers and tax-payers, the middle classes were populationist; because the king found treasure necessary for his wars, they, too, were bullionist. In the absolute monarchy the traders and manufacturers were of all capitalist groups the most useful, for they paid taxes and were a source of credit—and they, too, regarded international commerce from the exporter's rather than from the consumer's point of view.

Somewhat different was the case of the maritime powers, Great Britain and Holland, where the middle classes had attained a rela-tively high stage of maturity. Whereas the barrier that divided the nobility of France from the other classes was always clear and mani-fested itself to those who remained outside the charmed circle by striking and odious tokens, the outline of the British aristocracy remained indistinct. Political power in Britain was divided among the monarch, the aristocracy and the landed gentry. But there was never an impassable gulf between the upper and middle classes. The house of commons, though at this time a bulwark of inherited privilege, maintained at least a façade of popular government. In English society the middle class occupied so large a place that it is almost impossible to give it a sharp definition. It already colored the entire national outlook and indirectly controlled policy. Admin-

[6] Eli Heckscher, *Mercantilism* (London, 1934), Vol. II, 12.

istration and government policy were in the hands, or at least at the service, of the masters of trade and industry. Nowhere on the Continent was the landed aristocracy so closely allied with commercial and manufacturing interests as in Great Britain. As a class it was made up of families that had risen in the first great land speculation after the destruction of the monasteries in Tudor times. In other words, the aristocracy of eighteenth-century England was really little more than a wealthier middle class. Notwithstanding their attachment to their landed estates and to the social and political privileges that went with them, the British nobility had become largely middle class in substance. The increasing scale of their private expenditures had made them in effect dependent on trade and speculation. If a British nobleman found the income from his rent rolls inadequate, he could and did invest in the great joint-stock enterprises to secure profits without the stigma of trade.[7] The aristocracy combined landowning with membership in the privileged mercantile companies. There was no difference between Whigs and Tories in this respect, for both directed foreign policy to support and enlarge their trading interests. If the nobility enriched themselves, it was in the middle-class spirit of speculation and investment.

Unlike France, Austria and Prussia, Britain possessed no military aristocracy; on the other hand, she had an aggressive commercial community. Now so long as the policy of trade restriction is pursued in any form, so long will the support given to individual commercial interests be liable to lead countries into war, even though the economic interests of the nation as a whole are bound up with the preservation of peace. In these years the great maritime powers on the Atlantic seaboard were still rooted in mercantilist traditions, and trade wars were regarded as a legitimate and necessary function of the state. These commercial wars were in the final analysis the result not only of an attempt to maintain a trade monopoly in a given area, but also of the mercantilist conception of the static nature of commerce, of the notion that the world could support only a definite volume of commerce and shipping, and that if

[7] R. H. Gretton, *The English Middle Class* (London, 1917), 166.

one nation desired to increase its commerce it could do so only at the expense of another.[8]

In spite of this doctrine of the limited market—or rather because of it—the mercantilists of Great Britain and France attempted with fanatical zeal to assure to their nation the largest possible share in this unchanging volume of the world's trade. The whole mercantilist theory rested on the basis of exclusive exploitation rather than of mutual advantage. Those were the days when Beckford, a great London merchant, could say of France in parliament, "Our trade will improve by the total extinction of theirs." The brilliant and skeptical David Hume, who in 1752 tossed this mercantilist illusion overboard, may have prayed, as he said he did, for the prosperity of Spain and even of France in the interest of British subjects, but that was not the policy on which the government acted.[9] Moreover, Hume forgot, as sometimes modern economists forget, that even in Britain mercantilism was not merely an economic policy but a weapon of power politics, and that what appears absurd as an economic measure may be sound common sense from the point of view of military strategy. Great Britain and France fought each other with Navigation Acts and the "Exclusif," with navies and privateers, by keeping their respective trade routes and markets open and closing those of their rival, but they fought also with normal peacetime commerce and shipping, with trade monopoly and the economic self-sufficiency of their respective colonial empires. Thus power politics and economic policy became interchangeable terms.

The agrarian and feudal states of the Continent were powerful because of their ownership of land and people. Conversely the masters of the maritime commonwealths were powerful chiefly because of their trade. The continental monarch could maintain his domination over the state only by means of a large army. In order to have as large an army as possible, he must, since the process of industrialization was too slow for him, seek to increase his territory. The rulers of the maritime powers, on the other hand, could control their states and their policies by means of movable wealth, with

[8] Eli Heckscher, *Mercantilism* (London, 1934), Vol. II, 14, 260.
[9] D. Hume, "Of the Jealousy of Trade," *Essays, Moral, Political and Literary* (London, 1898), Vol. II, 348.

which they could hire soldiers and pay subsidies to their allies. What the conquest of a wealthy contiguous province meant to land powers like Prussia and Austria, the expansion of commerce meant to a maritime power like Great Britain. The acquisition of Silesia by Prussia produced an increment of wealth and power, much as the dislodgment of the French from the slave-trading stations of the African Gold Coast signified an expansion of British commerce and sea power. In both cases the policy was essentially predatory.

There was, of course, the important difference that in an absolute monarchy like France, which had a foothold in both systems, the king held all the levers and handles that operated the political machine and the aristocracy could share in power only through intrigue and corruption; while in parliamentary England the aristocracy held all the controls and it was the king who had to work behind the scenes to influence policy. But in considering the relation between the ruling classes and government policy this difference in constitutional structure is less material than may appear at first glance. The continental monarch might proclaim ever so stridently that the kingdom was the private possession of his dynasty, that his private interests were the interests of the state, that the framing of policy was the exclusive business of the king, that as the anointed and crowned head of the kingdom he was exempt from the organized scrutiny and criticism of public opinion; at bottom he was nevertheless a slave to tradition, to the bureaucracy, and to the nobility. If we were to apply the scalpel of scientific psychological dissection even to a genuine autocrat like Frederick the Great, a man of fire and resolution and capable of independent action, we should find characteristics which were individual and personal, but also a mass of others which, as we have seen, were the reflection of the ideas, ideals, traditions, beliefs, aims, and desires of the military and feudal aristocracy of Prussia.

But in the Europe of 1740 not only did the social system influence and often control politics; international politics, in turn, reacted upon the state and its social system.[10] A state that was simply and

[10] See the suggestive essay by Otto Hintze, *Staatsverfassung und Heeresverfassung* (Dresden, 1906); also the able discussion of Arthur Salz, *Das Wesen des Imperialismus* (Tübingen, 1932), 23.

solely consecrated to the economic prosperity of its citizens, a state in which domestic and cultural issues were paramount in public life, did not and could not exist on the Continent during the old regime. To be sure, there were already a thousand roads that led from the crown to the third estate. The masses had always desired a political despot who could keep the anarchic forces of the feudality in leash. From the very nature of the case they were anti-feudal and monarchist—as long as they could not be democratic. Asked to choose between the feudal state and absolute monarchy, the vast majority of the people would have sided with the monarchy. A ruler who wished to restrain the feudal aristocracy always had an unorganized but still powerful ally in the sympathy of the middle classes, not to mention the servile peasantry, who preferred a remote central despot to a feudal oppressor in the immediate neighborhood. Cases were not rare of monarchs who relaxed the bonds uniting them with the nobility in order to seek their welfare in the welfare of the masses. They gave them public order and a certain economic and legal security, they mitigated the worst brutalities of the rule of the feudal aristocracy.

In the class conflicts between the nobility, peasantry and middle classes the bureaucracy constituted a neutral force. It represented the foundation of order and regularity in the administration of public affairs. The more active, efficient and adaptable this bureaucratic organization, the greater were the returns which the monarch could offer his subjects for the heavy taxes he imposed upon them. These returns were often substantial enough. But when a king of the old regime spoke of public welfare, he did not and could not mean the happiness of his subjects as individuals, but only the growth and power of the state as a collective unit. The incessant rivalries among the powers of the European state system, the permanent pressure that came from their conflicting territorial ambitions, obliged European statesmen to focus their unremitting attention on their military machine. By some tragic destiny the European state never succeeded in escaping from its military origin. Power politics had laid the foundations of the modern state in Europe and, once begun, they continued to dictate the economic, administrative and financial policies of the absolute monarchy. Power politics continued to inspire the diplomacy of the state system which they had produced. Only in the parliamentary and anti-militarist England of the Revolution Settlement of 1688 did political evolution proceed on different lines. For the states of the Continent there was no escape from the coercive force of the militarist tradition. Absolutism, mercantilism, fiscalism and militarism were so closely interdependent that they were blended into a single political phenomenon.

III. WAR AND PROGRESS

Among recent historians, especially in Great Britain and America, a tendency has arisen to belittle the importance of war as a contributory force in the building up of modern nations, to divert attention from battles, sieges and campaigns and concentrate it, rather, on the peaceful evolution of science, literature, art, thought, industry, political government and domestic life. Much can be said in defense of this tendency, and yet, though the importance of war was exaggerated by an older school of historians, to overlook it altogether or to belittle it is an even greater mistake. With a social structure designed to keep alive a military temper, and with a competitive state system which never completely emerged from the psychology of war, war itself became a basic ingredient of European civilization, and, paradoxically enough, military organization became in some quarters a veritable barometer of cultural and social progress.

At first glance the mercenary army appeared to be an alien body in the state. It was not an institution of the people but the personal instrument of the absolute monarch. It had developed quite apart from the state. It possessed its own police power, its own religious institutions and its own jurisdiction, which exempted it from every civil authority in the realm. None the less, the standing army became an organic feature of the continental state. It is quite impossible to imagine the old regime without it. It was the symbol of the unity and power of the modern centralized state. It dominated economic policy, controlled public finance, and necessitated an ever increasing volume of taxation; it was a guarantee against sedition at home and an instrument of defense and expansion abroad.

In the history of modern Europe the progress of military science and technique depended entirely on the mercenary or professional army. The dilettante soldiering of the citizen militia was no longer suited to the new weapons, the use of which required constant training and drill. It was the professional army that converted these military possibilities into a system, reduced casual experience to a science, and raised warfare to the level of an art. Under the compelling influence of this refinement in the art of warfare all armies became professional or, where internal difficulties presented themselves, professional at least at the core. Modern discipline and order on the Continent were the creations of the professional soldier. He, too, created that phenomenon in European history which we have come to call militarism.[11] Under his influence the entire structure of the state took on a military slant. In spite of the fact that armies were essentially parasitic and non-productive organisms, militarism introduced new blood, new motor energies into the state and its society. For good or for evil, militarism became one of the constituent elements of European civilization at the very time when European influence was being extended over the rest of the world. It is a notorious fact that the history of colonial expansion is also the history of incessant warfare. Militarism and its matrix, the standing professional army, have left their indelible impress on every state of the Continent.

But the influence of the mercenary army did not end at the walls of the garrison town. Militarism, with its insistence on iron discipline, punctilious regularity, promptitude and precision, cultivated traits and virtues that exerted an influence on culture in general, even on the larger business world of the new capitalism, particularly in the more strictly agricultural countries where medieval tradition and feudal custom still continued in full vigor. Through the gradual introduction of the principle of military conscription in one form or another these military traits were diffused by imperceptible degrees among ever larger social groups. Militarism left its mark on the discipline of the continental family, and especially on the economic life of this epoch. There may be no direct historical continuity between the organization of labor in the early modern mining industry, the regime of slave labor on a colonial plantation and that of the

---

11 Paul Schmitthenner, *Europäische Geschichte und Söldnertum* (Berlin, 1933), 17; Alfred Vagts, *A History of Militarism* (New York, 1937).

modern industrial production unit. What is common to them all, however, is discipline, and nowhere could this discipline, so necessary to capitalistic society, be found in a more highly rationalized form than in the professional army. Somewhat less rigid, because stereotyped by feudal tradition, was the discipline of servile labor on the nobleman's landed estate. One need not have read very extensively in the agricultural history of Prussia and Austria to discover unmistakable evidence of military discipline even there. It is obvious, in any event, that military discipline served as the model pattern for the organization of labor in the modern factory system. Here, as in the army, discipline was placed on a rational basis; it was calculated to achieve certain specific ends, which could be measured in terms of speed, precision and quantity of production. More palpable still was the influence of military discipline and subordination on the bureaucracies of continental monarchies. It is one of the significant traits of the eighteenth century that all armies were more or less highly bureaucratized and that all bureaucracies absorbed more or less of the spirit and discipline of the army. In this sense, then, the standing army became an instrument of social efficiency and discipline or at least supplied the pattern for such discipline. It materially assisted in destroying the feudal individual ruled by immemorial custom and usage, and in creating the calculating, disciplined individual of modern capitalistic society. So comprehensive was this influence that in many countries of Europe it was less capitalism that called into being the standing army than the standing army that paved the way for modern capitalism.

It was one of the distinguishing features of the professional army that its size grew with its success. There were regions in Europe where the extent of the state's territory literally depended on the size of the army. The professional army was inherently dynamic and expansive in a sense that was true neither of the medieval host nor of the burgher militia of early modern times. Indeed, the mercenary or professional army was the first institution of western civilization which showed an inherent tendency to expand. Like leaven transforming the whole mass, it transmitted this dynamism to all the other factors of government. It was the standing army that first introduced this dynamic element into the otherwise static and feudal economy of states like Prussia and Russia.

The dominant influence of the army in the public life of Europe may be seen at a glance by demonstrating its central position in public finance. The king of Prussia in 1752 spent approximately ninety per cent of his total revenues for military purposes. He augmented his army as fast as he found the means to support an increase.[12] According to Necker's calculation France spent roughly two thirds of her total income on the army alone in 1784. Great Britain appropriated more to her army and navy than any country on the Continent.

These vast European armies, ranging in size from one to three hundred thousand men, had to be equipped, armed, clothed, fed and housed. The stimulating effect of the enormous purchasing power of the army can readily be imagined, particularly in countries where the majority of the population had hitherto lived in a subsistence economy. In these years armies were of overwhelming importance for the development of capitalism, while later in the century a thousand other factors complicated its growth. Sombart argues with some plausibility that capitalism would have come to Prussia a century later than it actually did but for the standing army.[13] Armies supplied the first great markets for mass consumption in modern times. They also facilitated the accumulation of great fortunes by army contractors in all the countries of Europe. King Frederick William I of Prussia contended that the income from the excise or sales tax dropped to one third of the normal sum whenever the army was out of the country. In most Prussian towns the army was the only buyer of importance. Frederick William, the originator of Prussian militarism, never wearied of emphasizing the close connection between industrial prosperity and the increase of the army.

Armies were by far the greatest consumers of such raw materials as copper, tin and iron; indeed, they were the only large-scale purchasers of iron products in the middle of the eighteenth century. Sweden was still the leading iron-producing country of Europe, and the new iron cannon was Sweden's chief article of export. The development of the English and Scottish iron industry also bore

12 See his *Testament Politique* of 1752 printed in G. B. Volz, *Die politischen Testamente Friedrichs des Grossen* (Berlin, 1920), 4-27.
13 W. Sombart, *Krieg und Kapitalismus* (Leipzig, 1913), 132.

a demonstrable relation to the military needs of English and continental armies. The same was true of the Upper Silesian iron industry of Prussia. Every major military state possessed its own munition industries, which, because of the enormous quantities produced, were usually already organized on a factory basis. Up to the middle of the eighteenth century English rifle factories were generally regarded as the most efficient in Europe, but after 1750 France created her own foundries at Ruelle, Montcenis, Sedan, Verdun and a score of other places.[14] Armies not only stimulated quantitative production, but through their requirements for uniformity and precision in the product forced on the merchant a mechanization of the processes of labor which was impossible under the old domestic system. If the merchant wanted to retain his market, he had perforce to organize his business on a capitalistic and factory basis.

Scarcely less significant was the impulse which army provisions gave to agricultural production. According to Dupré d'Aulnay, who gives us the figures for France, an army of one hundred fifty thousand men consumed thirty thousand tons of grain annually.[15] With an eye to this vast market the landed nobility of central and eastern Europe proceeded to enlarge and reorganize their estates so as to be able to produce grain on a quantitative basis. In this sense army grain purchases had a vitalizing influence on the countryside. The new market had a stimulating effect on international trade. The great distributing centers of the grain trade, Danzig, Amsterdam, Basel, served largely to supply the armies of Europe, for in the middle of the century large cities like London and Paris were still supplied by home production. Even shipbuilding came under military influence. In these years the British fleet possessed almost two thirds the tonnage of the entire world's shipping. Ship construction was designed largely for naval purposes and such construction of merchant vessels as there was, was done under naval stimulus, for shipwrights were awarded government premiums whenever they built large vessels that might be converted into ships of war.

14 H. Carré in Lavisse, *Histoire de France* (1909), VIII, part 2, 377.
15 Dupré d'Aulnay, *Traité générale, etc.* I, 165, quoted in W. Sombart, *Der moderne Kapitalismus* (1928), I, part 2, 756. What this meant may be seen from the fact that Danzig, one of the great grain ports of Europe, exported approximately fifty thousand tons of grain annually. See also Richard Lewinsohn, *Les profits de guerre à travers les siècles* (Paris, 1935), 33 ff.

Chapter Two

THE LEVIATHAN STATE

I. FEUDAL VERSUS BUREAUCRATIC OFFICIALISM

THE stimulating effect of the interrelationship between the competitive state system, militarism and capitalism on the one hand and the progressive development of the instrumentalities of the modern state on the other, which was pointed out in the first chapter, was assuredly no novel discovery of the statesmen of 1740. But never before in the history of Europe had the knowledge of the close correlation between these forces become the common possession of so many statesmen in all countries as during the generation that came to power in the middle decades of the eighteenth century. With an intensity hitherto unprecedented the spirit of competition and enterprise in the state no less than in economic life permeated almost the whole of Europe. The more generally and insistently the important states were drawn into the orbit of this competitive process, the more plainly the inequalities among the various countries were dragged into the light of day, the more imperative became the necessity for statesmen to devote their best attention to the problems of internal government and administration. It is no accident that the terrible blows of the War of the Austrian Succession, which unbalanced the budgets of nearly all the states of Europe, witnessed the beginning of the golden age of administrative achievement. From one end of the Continent to the other intensified preoccupation with administrative problems became all but universal. The building of dams, reservoirs, canals, roads, bridges, drainage projects, the rebuilding of towns, the altering of rivers to make them navigable demanded a new type of engineering official; new government departments were created for registration, land, mortgages, postal service, forests, agriculture, stud farms and stock raising, internal colonization and a score of other pressing problems. This was as true of the France of Machault and Tourny, in spite of the debility of the monarchy, as it was of the Spain of Ensenada, the Austria of Maria Theresa and Count Haugwitz, the Prussia of Frederick the Great, and even the Russia of Count Peter Shuvalov.

Nothing can be more instructive, therefore, than a comparative analysis of the principal governments of Europe on the eve of this epoch of invigorated administrative action. In spite of the great contrasts between east and west, north and south in economic structure, social stratification and cultural levels, there was an unmistakable parallelism running through the evolution of the principal states of the Continent which makes certain generalizations possible. The day had long passed when these states, though still essentially dynastic, were no more than appendages of the courts of their absolute sovereigns. Confronted with a vast and complicated network of institutions, the absolutism of the monarch, not unlike leadership in a modern private business firm in the second or third generation, tended to become more institutional than personal, and, often enough, it was a pure fiction. In the entire company of mid-century kings, Frederick the Great was the sole authentic autocrat. Almost everywhere else royal absolutism had assumed the character of a bureaucracy, although the crown retained, and often exercised, the right of ultimate decision. This modern bureaucratic state, however, had been imposed upon a society still suffused with a thousand feudal and traditional remnants, which the absolute monarchy did not remove and perhaps could not remove without committing suicide. Thus, like an old Gothic cathedral, which, rebuilt at different epochs, presents strange incongruities of style, royal government everywhere on the Continent in 1750 was a hybrid mechanism compounded of elements that were bureaucratic and modern and others that were feudal and patrimonial.

This paradoxical combination of apparently contradictory elements requires a word of explanation. It will be recalled that the feudal state was federalist, not unitary. It was dualistic, not absolutistic; that is to say, its authority was divided between the ruling dynasty and the estates. It was patrimonial; in other words, it drew no distinction between public and private affairs, nor did it separate public from private property. Offices, outside the municipalities, were the hereditary property of feudal families and their incumbents were irremovable. Public authority, such as it was, was dispersed among a host of chartered corporations, orders, classes, professions, families and individuals. The modern concept of public office as an accountable authority appointed to perform specific functions on the basis of an objective legal norm was utterly alien to the feudal state.

Now everywhere on the Continent, from Spain to Russia, the modern state, proceeding from the household of the sovereign as the point of crystallization, advanced from a loose federation of provinces, joined together by the personal union of the monarch, to actual territorial incorporation by means of institutional unification and administrative centralization. Nowhere, however, had the state of the absolute monarchy completely lost its original federalist character. Nowhere had this process of incorporation advanced to the point of complete assimilation of all its component territorial units. In 1750 every great continental state was still composite in structure, a complex aggregate of provinces and territories, brought together by inheritance, contractual agreement or military conquest. There is no need to emphasize the special position of Alsace and later of Lorraine in the kingdom of France. The distinction between the *pays d'élections* and the *pays d'états* in historic France itself is familiar. Together with their estates the latter provinces retained certain vestiges of autonomy which the Bourbon kings, bound by contractual agreements, had left inviolate. Nor had all the institutional peculiarities of the ancient kingdoms of Spain been completely obliterated. In the Danubian monarchy of 1740 the Hapsburgs had not yet incorporated even Bohemia with Austria, let alone Hungary. While the rest of Europe spoke of Prussia as a single unit, Frederick the Great constantly referred to *mes états*. In Russia the Ukraine and the Baltic provinces occupied a similar position. It is true that in each case these federated provinces had grown together by a process that may be described as one of diosmosis, and that everywhere they had yielded to the financial, legal and military necessities of an absolute monarchy, but the final result was neither a feudal, nor a federal, nor a completely integrated modern national state. It was still a state reared on dynastic foundations in which the sovereign had acquired absolute hegemony over his incorporated territories.[1]

In England this territorial unification had been achieved once for all times by the Norman Conquest and thereafter it was parliament that proved to be the strongest unifying and nationalizing agency in the kingdom. On the Continent, however, territorial unification came too late for the estates, whether general or provincial, rooted as they were in cultural regionalism and feudal localism, to perform a similar function. After a few faltering efforts to employ the Estates General for this purpose the attempt to do so in France was abandoned. In Spain and Prussia no such experiments were ever made. Only in Hungary, Poland and Sweden, all more or less agrarian communities, did the general estates possess any capacity to survive, in Poland at least, with disastrous results. Provincial estates were equally impervious to the needs of the modern state and they were either shorn of their political functions as in France or completely destroyed as in Prussia.

In their efforts at legal and administrative consolidation kings were not equally successful in all countries, nor were they equally successful in all the branches of royal government. The obstacles that stood in the way of a concentration of national resources were great everywhere, but greater in the agrarian east than in the more advanced commercial and capitalistic west. Much depended upon the countless uncertainties of dynastic succession. Under a feeble monarch the administrative progress of generations might be quickly undone. The shortsighted practice of selling judicial, financial and military offices frequently reduced impecunious monarchs, as in France, to renewed dependence on their own creatures. Generally it may be said that so long as the social system of continental Europe was founded on the feudal principle of heredity, it was impossible for even the most progressive monarch completely to defeudalize his state or administrative mechanism. But when that social system fell, the institution of the absolute monarchy fell with it.

In spite of these imperfections, the absolute monarchy has left its indelible impress upon the government of every great continental

[1] O. Hoetzsch prefers to call it a "Hegemonialer Gesamtstaat," *Osteuropa und Deutscher Osten* (Berlin, 1934); O. Hintze, "Staatsverfassung und Staatsentwicklung," *Historische und Politische Aufsätze*, IV, 25.

state. Bureaucracy was its answer to the feudal parochialism of the nobility and simplification, economy and efficiency its reply to the fossilized pluralism of the estates. The patrimonial official of the pre-bureaucratic state, the favorite, the courtier, the priest, the princely father confessor, had received no fixed salary. He exploited his office as a source of perquisites, snapped up vacant fiefs and sine-cures and regarded the duties of office as a matter of incidental concern. As an instrument of government the new bureaucratic civil servant was incomparably more efficient, more precise and depend-able, and far less expensive. The word bureaucracy is employed here not in the derogatory sense current among the English-speaking peoples of today, but in the sense of a hierarchy of appointed, paid and removable civil servants, equipped with definite commissions to perform certain special functions. Its essence is accountability and control. It implies a complicated administrative mechanism based on the principles of division of labor and specialized technical skill. It was possible only in countries with a fully developed money economy and a fixed system of taxation. It was inevitable, therefore, that the transition from the feudal or patrimonial to the bureaucratic con-ception of office should be a fluid one and that bureaucracy should be more fully matured in some countries than in others, or in one branch of the service than in another. At his best, the eighteenth-century civil servant was an expert; he brought to his office a special training and a professional sense of duty. Sheltered by anonymity from public criticism and guided by his inflexible bureaucratic *règlement*, he could apply royal decrees without respect of persons to nobleman and serf alike.[2]

Looking back over the past two and a half centuries of continental history the bureaucratic civil service may well pass as the greatest and most enduring achievement of the absolute monarchy, an achievement which, *mutatis mutandis,* survived all the revolutionary changes of the nineteenth century. Even the members of the feudal aristocracy who entered the civil service were affected by the new standards of professional probity and devotion to public service. It is true that where civil servants were corrupt, as in Russia, their

[2] Historical students are still indebted to Max Weber, *Wirtschaft und Gesellschaft* (1925), Vol. II, 650 ff. for the best discussion of this much neglected field of historical inquiry.

influence was vicious and destructive; but wherever they represented a tradition of service rather than a class, they habituated all classes to a regular discharge of public obligations and in their daily contact with peasants, merchants and feudal lords evoked a sentiment of common statehood. In this way they fulfilled a function not altogether unlike that of the British parliament.

Although creatures of the monarchy, the new officials reacted on the absolute monarch himself. The cult of royalty was receding and the cult of peoples by their kings was slowly taking its place. If the older notion of kingship as the patrimonial property of the dynasty was gradually yielding to the idea of kingship as a public trust, this was in large measure due to the new professional standards of bureaucratic officialism. Mid-century monarchs had by no means completely emancipated themselves from a dynastic outlook, but when the ablest of them, Frederick the Great, remarked, "It appears that God has created me, pack-horses, Doric columns and us kings generally to carry the burdens of the world in order that others might enjoy its fruits," he expressed a sentiment which Ferdinand VI of Spain, Maria Theresa and even the dissipated Louis XV shared with him.

But there is another aspect of bureaucratic government that cannot be ignored. Quantitatively, progressive bureaucratization was accompanied by an unprecedented expansion of administrative action, never again equalled until the modern social service state came into existence. Mercantilist legislation with its multitude of regulations, orders and prohibitions, its complicated mechanisms for supervising and controlling every trade, every industry, every class, even the nobility itself, pointed in the same direction. The more energetic and intelligent the monarch, the more resolutely he was bent on dragging his people out of the quagmire of immobile feudal traditionalism, the more formidable and comprehensive became what Germans picturesquely call the *Polizeistaat*. Indeed, this authoritarian, paternalistic, bureaucratic state acquired so terrible a momentum that it threatened, in the phrase of de Tocqueville, to transform society into a house of correction. More significant still was the fact that everywhere authority fled from the law courts into the administrative *bureaux*, and the new administrative law, replacing the old and

inadequate *jus quaesitum*, recognized but one supreme principle—
that of *raison d'état*. The sanctity of law anchored in fixed principles
had given way to the administrative necessities of the modern state.
The chaotic confusion of legal systems everywhere forced the administrative official with his wide powers of arbitrary discretion to
invade the judicial process ever more deeply.

II. FRANCE

At first view France, the historic center of continental statecraft,
presents the picture of a clear, homogeneous and consistent governmental structure. The king was the sole legislator, the supreme chief
of the administrative hierarchy and the source of all justice. He
exercised this absolute authority through the various divisions of
the council of state and through his ministers, the departmental
chiefs. All authority was delegated by the crown, and its agents,
whether ministers, provincial intendants or subdelegates, were its
mandataries. This implied that they were appointed, paid, controlled and subject to recall and dismissal. In the matter of justice
the council of state, acting as the king's private court, could override
judgments of all ordinary courts. The sovereign *parlements*, the
intermediary and lower courts pronounced justice in the king's
name, and even the seigneurial, municipal and ecclesiastical courts
were subject to his control, were, indeed, an integral part of the
hierarchy of royal justices. The Estates General were no more and
the few remaining provincial estates were reduced to pure administrative bodies. The Church paid its regular *don gratuit*, and when it
resisted Machault's plan of taxation, at least it made no effort to
influence the general affairs of the kingdom.

Yet this picture is deceptive. Quite apart from the personality of
Louis XV, it must be said that the old French monarchy was never
thoroughly despotic, never quite absolute. The theoretical absolutism
of the crown was modified by the remarkably independent position
of the French judiciary which, basing its claim on the right to register
royal edicts, required that these edicts and ordinances be promulgated in the forms of judicial procedure and further demanded ad-
herence to juristic usages and formalities which were so many
barriers to the arbitrary authority of the sovereign. This authority

was further modified by two other sets of circumstances: first by the absence of any clear and sharp distinction between judicial and administrative authority, the first condition of any sound system of administration; second by the proprietary or patrimonial conception of office which, one may safely say, permeated the entire system.

In an absolute monarchy it is the duty of the king himself to provide the unity of policy and exercise supreme control over administration—or he must appoint a prime minister to do these things. After the death of Cardinal Fleury in 1743 Louis XV was advised by sycophant courtiers not to appoint another prime minister, lest this should diminish his glory and power. The only alternative was personal government. But Louis XV did neither the one nor the other. By character and temperament he was unsuited to the role of an autocrat. Grown up under the majestic shadow of Louis XIV, he was paralyzed by timidity and handicapped by a sense of inferiority. He had intelligence, dignity, good sense, discrimination, but, perpetually afraid of making mistakes and excessively respectful of the opinions of his ministers, he lacked the force to assert a will of his own. That he had plans of his own and knew how to support them with arguments, we know from his correspondence with the Duc de Noailles; but he had no courage to put them into execution.[3] He had the mentality of a bureaucrat rather than that of a king. For Louis XIV the essence of kingship was government through the council, where every decision was arrived at by means of discussion; Louis XV was really at home only in his secret retreat, where he was surrounded by filing cases, notes and dockets. It is slightly ironical to call despotic this king who, appearing to agree with his ministers in council, secretly conspired against these same official agents, men of his own choice, because he did not have the steadfast brow and unflinching gaze to oppose them in public. Bored, sunk in debauchery, Louis XV's interest in public affairs was at best spasmodic and intermittent. Since the king left to others the direction of affairs much of the time, there was no firm hand to maintain the unity and tradition of the French monarchy.

The king's irregular procedure of delegating his power without official act had a confusing effect on the government of the kingdom.

3 *Correspondence de Louis XV et du Maréchal de Noailles* (Paris, 1865), 2 vols.

It had the inevitable consequence of bringing into political prominence the coteries of a court divided by jealous clans. When a
minister or general wished to make himself independent, he protested that he had received special orders from the court. But the
court was nothing more than the influence which for the moment
happened to be dominant, the Marquise de Pompadour, Cardinal
Bernis, Duc de Choiseul, the entourage of the queen or that of the
dauphin, or perhaps, most important of all, the financier, Pâris
Duverney. He who desires to discover the motives for appointments
and dismissals in the France of 1750 must penetrate the maze of
intrigue among these coteries of the court.

This is no place to discuss Louis XV's liaison with the charming
and vivacious Marquise de Pompadour, whose influence upon affairs
after 1745 was both real and important. She generally passed as a
friend of the philosophers and an enemy of the church, but she was
above all the creature of finance, particularly of the Pâris brothers,
the early ancestors of Balzac's Gobseck. With the Pâris brothers the
entire band of farmers-general forced the portals of the court.
Thanks to the persistent favor of the Marquise, Pâris Duverney
brought a steady pressure to bear upon administrative, military and
foreign affairs. Controller-General Orry had to go in 1745 because
he refused to co-operate with these Pâris brothers. Thereafter the
controller-general and the secretary of state for war were largely
dependent upon these bankers of the kingdom. During the Seven
Years' War they made and unmade ministers and generals and
often dictated military operations.[4] It was inevitable that these
coteries of the court should have their supporters in the council,
which was no longer a homogeneous body. It became all but impossible for ministers to govern and maintain themselves in this
atmosphere at one and the same time. The consequence was an
appallingly rapid turnover in the personnel of the ministry. Louis
XV had no less than eighteen foreign secretaries and fourteen con-
trollers-general.[5] It cannot be surprising, therefore, that the central
government was the weakest point in the entire French administrative system.

[4] A. Dussauge, *Le ministère de Belle-Isle* (Paris, 1914), 45.
[5] F. Piétri, *La réforme de l'état au XVIIIe siècle* (Paris, 1935), 17.

No examination of this system as a going concern, however cursory, can avoid the delicate problem of judicial control over administration by the magistracy of the *parlements*. Nowhere on the Continent was there a more fearless and intrepid magistracy than that of the French *parlements*. The French monarchy never remedied its fatal error of having sold judicial offices just at the moment when it became master of the political machine. The monarch was almost completely powerless in the face of his judges, whom he could not dismiss, transfer or promote. Even his punishments, such as temporary exile, were singularly ineffective. But, admitting that the stability of the magistracy was a sound principle and that through their right of remonstrance and frequent refusal to register royal edicts the *parlements* exercised a salutary restraint on the despotism of the crown, no one can seriously contend that their relation to the administrative system was a healthy one. The entire reign of Louis XV was a prolonged conflict between crown and *parlements*, the crown appealing to one kind of absolute law and the *parlements* to another. Each continuously encroached on the domain of the other. Because of the independence of the magistrates, the administrative officers, intendants and the royal council withdrew, by a process called evocation, from the jurisdiction of the *parlements* not only suits in which the authority of the crown was directly concerned, such as matters of the fisc and the royal domains, but private suits which properly belonged to the law courts. This administrative justice was not unpopular. Administrative officers expedited suits with intelligence, speed and equity, above all without expense to the parties, for the justice of the intendant was gratuitous, at least in principle.[6] The *parlements* on the other hand interfered at every turn in the administrative process by enacting regulations which were manifestly beyond their proper jurisdiction.

It must be admitted that the role of the *parlements* as the guardians of the fundamental laws of the realm, whatever these may have been, was generally recognized. That the monarch himself acknowledged their right to control the crown by means of judicial review is apparent from a study of the normal functioning of their

6 P. Ardascheff, *Les intendants de province sous Louis XVI* (Paris, 1909), vol. I, XVIII.

practice of registering royal edicts. Legislation in France was a complicated procedure. The necessary preliminary step to the execution of any royal edict was its registration by the *parlements*, which in case these bodies proved recalcitrant, could be obtained only by a *lettre de jussion* or by a formal royal command to register the edict, the *lit de justice*. But the *parlements* deduced from this right of registration not only the right of judicial review, but the power to amend edicts and even to co-operate in legislation. When in 1750 they objected to the edicts of the *Bureau de Bertin* (Agriculture) not merely on the ground of their legality but on the ground that they were inopportune, they sought to reduce the legislative power of the crown to one of mere proposal. That in their resistance to the crown the *parlements* often passed beyond the limits of legality is certain; that they were retrograde defenders of a superannuated tradition and set against progress is undeniable; that in exceeding their legitimate powers they sometimes employed revolutionary means is also beyond question. It may well be argued, however, that if the crown had the right to set aside the ancient constitution of the kingdom, which, as the *parlements* contended and the king agreed, gave them the right to control the crown, then their resistance may be said to have been inspired by a concern for constitutional legality.[7]

Whatever the legal merits of the contest, this confusion of powers was destructive of good administration. Due to the encouragement of the *parlements*, administrative commands were given but disobeyed. Even after royal orders had been posted in the streets the *parlements* often tore them down and replaced them with orders of their own. In 1756 the *parlement* of Besançon is said to have hanged a high royal tax official because he had collected the *vingtième* before the local court had registered the edict in question. When, as frequently happened under Louis XV, the crown was in need of money, the *parlement* of Paris issued proclamations which ruined the credit of the crown. Laws were promulgated, but they were not executed. "No land," said Fontanieu, "where laws are so perfect as in France, but none where their execution is more neglected."[8]

[7] V. de Marcé, *Le contrôle des finances* (Paris, 1928), 161; R. Villers, *L'organisation du parlement de Paris et des conseils d'après la réforme de Maupeou* (Paris, 1937), 14; E. Glasson, *Le parlement de Paris* (Paris, 1901), Vol. II, 69 ff.

[8] Mention, *L'armée de l'ancien régime*, 37.

There were two other characteristics that placed their stamp upon
the French administrative mechanism. The first was the principle
of the venality of offices. All the members of the bench and bar of the
parlements, the masters of requests, the financial, road, forestry,
postal and customs officials, the inspectors of industry and commerce,
the mayors and police officers had all acquired their offices by private
purchase or inheritance. The principle of venality converted offices
into a species of property the transmission of which was governed
by an elaborate jurisprudence. Once the government had embarked
upon the policy of selling offices, it created offices in such prodigal
profusion, that old offices were divided and subdivided to the point
where the profits from the sale of each were materially reduced.
By selling offices it thus had created a rival power that shackled
government initiative and impeded the freedom of administrative
action. It had in large measure renounced the right of appointing
its own officials, for it could remove them only by a process of
judicial condemnation.[9]

No less important in its ultimate consequences was another characteristic. It was from the magistracy of the *parlements* that the
French administrative personnel, ministers, councillors of state, intendants and masters of requests were recruited. Taking them all
together they constituted that state nobility which passed under
the general designation of the *noblesse de robe*. Since time immemorial the channel through which officials passed from the magistracy
of the *parlements* into the central or provincial administrative
service had been the office of master of requests. To provide a steady
supply of candidates for these administrative positions the law of
1751 fixed the number of these masters of requests at eighty. "Long
usage," says Necker, "has called to the position of intendant only
masters of requests."[10] These masters of requests were usually attached to the council, but before they became members of the
council, they had climbed several rungs in the ladder of the *parlements*. Thus every intendant had once been a magistrate and he did

9 Louis-Lucas, *Étude sur la venalité des charges depuis l'antiquité romaine jusqu'à nos
jours* (Paris, 1883), Voɪ. II; A. Maury, "L'administration française avant la Revolution," *Revue des deux mondes*, CVII (1873), 832.
10 Necker, *De l'administration des finances*, III, 379.

not lose the character of a magistrate when he became an intendant. Like the councillors of *parlement* the masters of requests had acquired their office by wealth or inheritance and their office was their property. There was, however, an essential difference in the way both were recruited. The *parlements* chose their councillors by co-option, but in the administrative service the principle of appointment prevailed. So long as the magistrate was a member of *parlement* he was part of an independent chartered corporation, but once he had entered the administrative service he was subject to the principle of bureaucratic subordination.

That so large a section of the French administrative personnel had originated in the magistracy of the *parlements* carried with it certain significant implications. First, the men who issued from the *parlements* brought with them into the administrative service the spirit of independence which they had inherited with their offices and which they had breathed in the atmosphere of the *parlements*. Second, ministers, councillors of state, intendants, and the entire higher personnel of the administration were all men of wealth and social position who belonged to the same social class and shared a common education and cultural outlook. There were dynasties of administrative officials just as there were dynasties among the members of the *parlements*. To cite but a single example: Orry, the controller-general, had a brother who was an intendant of finance; one of his sisters had married the intendant of Lorraine; she in turn was the wife, the mother and grandmother of intendants. In other words, this personnel was that of a thoroughly plutocratic, patrimonial nobility. Now a patrimonial aristocracy is no congenial soil for the growth of a fully developed bureaucracy. The office of the provincial intendant was nothing if not bureaucratic: it was appointive, paid, revocable, subordinated and accountable to the central authorities. But intendants lacked one essential quality of bureaucrats: they were not dependent on their salaries for a livelihood. They were all men of wealth who before their appointment had purchased the office of master of requests for 200,000 livres and whose wealth, derived from land or finance, made them too independent to resign themselves to that degree of subordination characteristic of ordinary bureaucrats.[11] The office of the intendant may have increased their authority, but it scarcely improved their social rank and often added little or nothing to their income.

Compared with the Prussian system the French administrative mechanism was freer, less rigid and precise, less dragooned by discipline and military subordination, less bureaucratic in the popular sense of the term. The single, responsible functionary predominated throughout the French system. There were no collective boards, no exhaustive regulations to fetter the initiative of the able and the ambitious. But it was also more disjointed, less uniform, less effectively geared by control devices, above all less firmly co-ordinated by a single driving purpose penetrating the entire administrative hierarchy.

This was, no doubt, due in the first instance to the void, as d'Argenson calls it, caused by the apathetic indifference of Louis XV; but it was also due to the confusion which arose from the co-ordinate authority of two distinct central organs, the council of state and the individual ministers at the head of the several department *bureaux*. Theoretically the council of state was the brain of the vast organism of which the king was the heart. Theoretically all important legislative and administrative measures were enacted by the "King in Council," whence they emerged in the form of *arrêts du conseil*, which, duly registered by the *parlements*, had the force of law.[12] But, despite the theory of the omnipotence of the council, the great volume of public business was transacted by the incumbents of the six "ministerial" posts: the chancellor at the head of justice, the controller-general of finance, and the four secretaries of state, for war, for the navy, for foreign affairs, and for the king's household. In view of the steadily expanding authority of these ministerial *bureaux*, in which already most of the labor was done by senior clerks, the council suffered a relative eclipse.[13] These ministers could work through the council, if they chose, but they could also avoid collaboration with that body by issuing a simple ministerial letter,

[11] Aucoc, *Le conseil d'état avant et depuis 1789* (Paris, 1876), 74; P. Ardascheff, *Les intendants de province sous Louis XVI* (Paris, 1909), vol. I, 73.

[12] E. Chénon, *Histoire générale du droit publique et privé des origines à 1815* (Paris, 1929), II, 416; Aucoc, *Le conseil d'état etc.* (Paris, 1876).

[13] De Luçay, *Les secrétaires d'état depuis leur institution jusqu'à la mort de Louis XV* (Paris, 1881), 149, 573.

which had the additional advantage that it did not have to be formally registered by the *parlements*. Ardascheff has cited instances in which individual ministers by means of such ministerial letters revoked royal edicts solemnly registered by *parlement*.[14] Indeed, under Louis XV it was less the *lettre de cachet* than the ministerial letter that was the symbol of arbitrary government. By means of it ministers made themselves independent not only of the council but of one another.[15] Frederick the Great, who had a keen eye for the governmental processes of his French ally, spoke ironically of France as being governed by four independent kings who were unable to understand each other's language. Even the controller-general of finance who, after the death of Cardinal Fleury became the directing intelligence of the central government, could not remedy the appalling dispersion of effort which in these years left such unhappy memories in the minds of the French people. So precarious, in fact, had the office of controller-general already become that chancellors offered it to rivals whom they sought to ruin.

John Law's familiar statement that it was upon the thirty intendants that the happiness and misery, the abundance and sterility of France depended, was rhetorical exaggeration, but it contained a substantial truth. Even on the surface the contrast between central and provincial government leaps to the eye. At the center an idle king who, if he had a fitful interest in affairs, never had the courage to direct them; a badly jointed mechanism of central government in which one wheel obstructed the other; ephemeral ministers, perpetually at the mercy of favorites at the court, with an average tenure of office which did not exceed two or three years—all this contrasted sharply with the remarkable permanence, stability and efficiency of provincial and local government in the hands of intendants who remained in their generalities for fifteen, twenty or thirty years and were seldom recalled. For roughly a hundred years these intendants had been sent into the provinces as the special commissioners of the crown to supervise and control police, justice and finance, words which comprehended all law, all administration and the entire system of taxation. They were in a position to repair

[14] P. Ardascheff, "Les intendants de province etc.," *Revue d'histoire moderne et contemporaine*, Vol. V (1903), 9.
[15] P. Viollet, *Le roi et ses ministres* (Paris, 1912), 280.

some of the worst faults of the monarchy, to harmonize and humanize administrative processes and to mitigate the worst evils of a barbarous legal and an inequitable financial system.

It must be emphasized, of course, that the intendant was preeminently the king's man, who exercised his authority under the council and was subordinated above all to the controller-general who had secured his appointment. As the special commissioner of the crown he was bound to refer all important matters to the council for final decision. The council could accept and reject his advice or modify his measures. But it is less the subordination than the tone of urbanity, mutual respect and consideration that characterizes the correspondence between ministers and their provincial intendant. The latter was the collaborator rather than the slave of the central authority. If he represented the interests of the crown in the province, he also frequently represented the province against the encroachments of the central authority. If he received his orders from above, he was not forever begging for instructions. No specific instructions defined his powers, and these powers, being elastic, expanded or contracted in accordance with the personality of the intendant. In a score of matters he could proceed without control. His authority was absolute where administration touched most people—in the apportionment of the *taille*, the *corvée*, militia duty, security and the police of local commerce. The council divided the taxes by generalities but the intendant apportioned them among the parishes and in so doing he could improve the incidence of the *taille*. Not infrequently he modified the character of the *taille* itself and sometimes made it an almost acceptable fiscal instrument. In some provinces he mitigated the *corvée*, the forced road service, and replaced it by a general property tax. He often humanized the obligation of militia service by sparing married men. If he was intelligent and active, as many of them were, his influence might extend to the central authority. The council decided few matters without previous consultation with intendants. Very often the advice of the intendant determined the contents and even the form of a ministerial letter, an order in council, or an edict of the king. Often his initiative underlay legislation on a national scale. On occasion he might oppose and even refuse to execute formal ministerial orders.

Opposing the excessive centralization which de Tocqueville attributed to them, intendants like Aubert de Tourny at Bordeaux established in their generalities something like a centralized regionalism.[16]

The intendants touched too many vested interests not to find themselves exposed to frequent criticism. When they interfered in the government of corrupt municipal oligarchies, protected peasants against extortionate seigneurial justices or intervened in the affairs of the *parlements*, they encountered a coalition of interests that were quick to raise the cry of despotism. There were more criticisms than eulogies. It must not be forgotten that the intendants were trained in the principles of Roman law, which demanded the subordination of private to public interests. Those among them who, like the ancient legists, were no more than bureaucrats of the crown, still made no distinction between public interests and the special interests of the monarch. What is significant, however, is the fact that a growing number among them, under the influence of the mental climate of the epoch, helped to change this concept of the sovereign from that of the old legists into that of the modern public servant who feels a sense of responsibility to the interests of the nation at large. These men, like Tourny at Bordeaux, Brissac at Poitiers, Montyon at Auvergne, d'Étigny at Pau, assuredly did not deserve Taine's condemnation as the passive instruments of fiscal tyranny who exhausted their provinces.[17]

The intendants were hamstrung, no doubt, by being forced to accept the services of that countless host of useless officials who had purchased their offices. Their principal aids, the subdelegates, who represented them in the local government units, also inspired little confidence. The meager salary attached to this office was insufficient to support a man of education and social position and the intendants were compelled to avail themselves of such local talent as they could find. They usually appointed some member of the local bench or bar to serve as subdelegate in addition to his other offices. Completely under the thumb of the intendant and utterly devoid

16 M. Lhéritier, *Tourny, intendant de Bordeaux* (Paris, 1920), 774.
17 M. Marion, *Dictionnaire des institutions de la France au XVIIe et XVIIIe siècle* (Paris, 1923), 293; *Études sur l'histoire administrative et sociale de l'ancien régime*, ed. by G. Pagès (Paris, 1938), 52.

of scientific knowledge, these subdelegates were an unimpressive lot. It is only fair to add, however, that it was unreasonable to expect expert service from agents whose official duties were smothered in a flock of other irrelevant and often incompatible occupations. For the more technical tasks of building roads, canals, reservoirs and bridges the intendants were compelled to turn elsewhere. To meet the accumulated pressure of such tasks, which were multiplying from day to day, the intendants proceeded to gather about them a staff of specialist collaborators, engineers, architects and physicians, which ultimately made their bureaus no less important than those of Versailles. Thanks to the farsighted Trudaine, who in 1750 obtained a charter for the Corporation of Roads and Bridges and later for the Corporation of Mines, government training schools were opened where the young engineer might study geometry, trigonometry, land surveying, draughtsmanship, mechanics, hydraulics and architecture. Here in the intendant's bureau we find the first representatives of the modern French civil servant proper. They owed their positions neither to patronage nor purchase but to competitive examinations and technical skill. They were no longer a magistracy or a delegation. Their occupation was already a profession.

A final judgment on French administration in the mid-century remains almost as difficult today as it was in the days of de Tocqueville. Until French historians present us with a comprehensive documentary study on every branch of the service comparable to the Prussian *Acta Borussica*, every judgment must remain incomplete and tentative, which, of course, includes the one offered here. That in its broad structural pattern the system was sound enough is apparent from the survival of so many of its essential features. Of its salient traits, centralization, *étatisme*, caste differentiation of officials, popular detestation and hostility to public administration, the system of administrative law, the maladjustment between justice and administration, the sale of offices, all but the last two are still present in modern France. The perpetual warfare between judges and administrative officers, the venality of offices, both relics of the prebureaucratic patrimonial state, are impossible to defend on any grounds. But the Achilles heel of the French system was its administration of finance. While Prussia already possessed a fixed budget

system, France had no budget because the accounts of past years
were not completely closed. With a system of taxation neither more
scientific nor socially more just Prussia managed better. Finally,
France was neither so highly centralized, particularly after 1760, as
de Tocqueville contended, nor was centralization as such the worst
of evils. It became, indeed, an evil under Louis XV when the king
failed to supply the necessary leadership to guarantee both effective
coordination and scientific division of labor among the central governing agencies. That this could be done even within the framework
of the old monarchy is apparent from the reorganization of Austria
under Maria Theresa. That this was not done in the culturally and
technologically more advanced France was chiefly the fault of
Louis XV.

III. SPAIN

The change from Hapsburg to Bourbon in Spain signified more
than a change of dynasty; it meant a change of spirit, of ideas and
political direction. Catholic Spain, which had been on the verge of
falling into the condition of those oriental peoples who, like the
Tibetans, have become fossilized, henceforth felt the salutary stimu-
lant of French influence. The French monarchs, horrified by the
multitude of councils, *fueros* and local liberties, introduced the
spirit of reform, order and activism into the sluggish movements of
the Spanish *covachuela* (bureaucracy), which had become the symbol of indecision, inefficiency and procrastination. Thanks to the
slow and cautious but continuous transformation of this administrative system, the introduction of characteristic French institutions
such as the departmental ministries, the superintendent of finance,
the provincial intendants, by the first two Bourbon monarchs and
their able ministers, Spain was prepared once more to re-enter the
arena of European struggles without having to make any further
retreat.

Under the protection of the Bourbon kings there had been formed
the *"Regalista"* party, composed of lawyers and public officials,
whose members vigorously defended the use of the regalities—the
superior rights of the crown or the lay state—to suppress further
encroachments of the church. This task was both difficult and dan-

gerous, for, despite the favorable Concordat of 1754 which placed the church of Spain under the authority of the king, the peculiar symbiosis between church and state which had grown up during the *Reconquista* still persisted. The clergy still controlled the kings through their father confessors. The Jesuit confessor of Ferdinand VI, Ravago, still regularly transmitted to the king the advice of a junta of his Order. The clergy still dominated Spanish intellectual life through the Inquisition, which inquired into the orthodoxy of every official who was known to hold *regalista* opinions. Representing some 200,000 persons in a total Spanish population of ten million, the church still held one fifth of the wealth of the nation immobilized and largely withdrawn from public authority.[18] Menaced in its traditional privileges by the Bourbons, the hostile church discovered in these kings the devil who was leading the people astray. The church thus became a serious obstacle to reform.[19]

But the greatest obstacle to social and political progress lay in the feudal economy and the moral stagnation of the Spanish people themselves. In spite of its limitless colonial domains, Spanish economic life was still pre-capitalistic to its roots.[20] The wealth of the Spaniard was seigneurial wealth, the wealth of the *rentier*, of the exploiters of colonial mines. While Adam Smith was meditating his *Wealth of Nations*, Spaniards were still debating the question whether a commercial career could be honorable. The notion that economic success was the mark of divine favor may have been approved Puritan doctrine, but it was utterly alien to Spanish Catholicism. In England and France wealth guaranteed a place of prestige in the social hierarchy, but in Spain beggary brought no dishonor on the beggar. All attempts to emancipate the commerce of America from foreign enterprise had failed, though Philip V lowered the customs duties which Spanish merchandise had to pay. Trading companies such as the Caracas Company attained only a factitious prosperity. It is not surprising that under these circumstances Span-

18 A. Girard, *La repartition de la population en Espagne dans les temps modernes* (Paris, 1929).

19 C. de Mazade, "La monarchie absolue en Espagne," *Revue des deux mondes*, XVIII (1860), 704; A. Ferrer del Rio, *Historia reynado de Carlos IIIo en Espana* (Madrid, 1856), Vol. I.

20 G. Briefs, "Ueber den Wirtschaftsgeist Spaniens," *Gesammelte Aufsätze zur Kulturgeschichte Spaniens*, ed. by H. Finke (Muenster, 1931), Vol. III, 238.

ish foreign commerce had passed almost entirely into the hands of foreigners. Spain was no more than the channel by which the products of the mines and the wealth of the Indies were distributed over Europe. The Spanish population actually lacked capital.[21]

No people of western Europe carried its poverty with greater dignity and pride and none guarded so jealously the inviolability of its hereditary inertia. Spaniards were naturally lazy, and centuries of clerical education had made them timid, over-scrupulous and irresolute. Even the introduction of French institutions and ideas could not shake Spaniards out of this static ataxia. The obvious Spanish preference for bureaucratic juntas and commissions was merely a means of escaping from individual responsibility. Officials who profited by old familiar abuses met every proposal for improvement with endless *mémoires* or by acting in the spirit of the old formula that his majesty's instructions should be "obeyed but not carried out" (*obedicidas y no cumplidas*). An absolute monarch who could send any man to the penal settlement at Ceuta, as the Prussian king sent corrupt officials to the Spandau prison, could soon have brought his officials to heel. But Spanish absolutism was too benign for such vigorous action. Nothing could be more expressive of the temper of Spanish bureaucracy than the report of the commission appointed in the early days of Charles III and charged with the task of making the Tagus navigable. The reply stated that if God, who was omnipotent, had intended to make the Tagus navigable, he would indubitably have done so, but the fact that he had not done so was sufficient reason for believing that it should not be done. So long as this temper prevailed, every partial revival, carefully nursed by a benevolent monarch, was quickly compromised.

Since neither Philip V nor Ferdinand VI possessed the vigor to govern in person, the supreme direction of affairs was lodged in the hands of the incumbents of the six ministerial posts, foreign affairs, justice, the navy, the Indies, war and finance. From 1742 onward the superintendent of finance, like the controller-general in France, was the chief master of the administrative machine; he used

21 H. Berindoague, *Le mercantilisme en Espagne* (Paris, 1929), 164; R. D. Hussey, *The Caracas Company* (Cambridge [Mass.], 1934), 51.

the provincial intendants and the local corregidors as his special agents and reduced the council of Castile to a purely consultative role.[22] Whenever these six departments were distributed among individual ministers, each minister dealt separately with the monarch, and, since there was no collective cabinet council, usually worked at cross purposes with his colleagues. Vigor of direction and co-ordination in central affairs, therefore, invariably improved when several departments were united in a single hand. Between 1743 and 1754 such supreme authority was entrusted to the Marquis Ensenada who, in addition to controlling finance, war, navy and the Indies, held the important office of president of the council of Castile. During these years when Ensenada was the *privado*, the special confidant of the monarch, there was no limit to his authority. Yet even Ensenada, who occupies a place of honor in the history of Spanish economy, could not reform the outrageous fiscal system which lay at the bottom of most of the difficulties of Spanish economic life. He did, indeed, suppress the tax farmers and replace them with responsible royal agents, but in spite of these reforms the deficit continued as a general rule. It was not until 1751 that he succeeded for a short spell in balancing the budget.

What gave to the Spanish government its special national character, however, were the boards, councils and commissions of every variety and importance which functioned at the center of affairs. The Spaniard had not yet learned the meaning of the French proverb that, had God turned the creation of the world over to a commission, chaos would still reign supreme. So inbred was this tradition of government by council that whenever a reform was proposed, this reform usually ended in the creation of another commission. It was a curious contradiction that this strange Spanish monarchy, so despotic in theory and actually so ineffective, should possess more deliberative bodies than any contemporary republic. The division of labor among the numerous councils and countless commissions was haphazard and corresponded to no rational plan. The council of Castile was engaged in perpetual jurisdictional disputes with every other council in the kingdom. The method of conducting business

22 G. Desdevises du Dezert, "Les institutions de l'Espagne," *Revue Hispanique*, LXX (1927), 303.

was woefully ineffective. The rigid ceremonial, reminiscent of a sacramental ritual, the cumbersome and minutely prescribed bureaucratic procedure, the solemn gravity of discussion, the extreme variety and complexity of the services they were expected to perform— all these things retarded decision and added the arrears of today to the unfinished business of yesterday. Nothing was so rare in Spain as a measure taken betimes.

These councils were not all of equal importance. Some of them, the council of finance, the council of war, the council of the military orders, were the advisory agencies of the new departmental ministries, while others, the council of Castile, the council of the Indies and the council of the Inquisition, were institutions of great national importance. The council of Castile was the real heart of the monarchy. It was the highest legislative body, the supreme court and chief administrative center of the kingdom, the vehicle through which royal edicts were transmitted to provincial intendants, corregidors and alcaldes. It was an omnicompetent body, for, besides acting as the highest judicial and administrative tribunal, it supervised the church, regulated economic and military affairs, controlled provincial and local officials by a system of organized espionage that was as detestable as it was ineffective, approved the curricula of the universities and appointed their professors. No matter was too important, no bagatelle too insignificant for its attention. It granted permission to the butchers of Madrid to cut mutton tongues in two parts and market them separately, regulated municipal finances, and allowed the publication of a novel. This reckless concentration of business in the hands of thirty councillors whose powers had no serious limits defeated its own ends. The council of Castile may have been a suitable administrative agency in the days of the Catholic monarchs, but in the reign of Ferdinand VI, with functions multiplied a hundredfold, it was a hopelessly antiquated institution. It lost even the illusion of objectivity in its decisions when it permitted grandees, provinces and cities to employ paid lobbyists at court to look after their interests and distribute gratifications in quarters where they might be most effective.[23]

[23] G. D. du Dezert, "Le conseil de Castile," *Revue Historique* (1902); and by the same author, "Le conseil de Castile," *Revue Hispanique* (1907).

Faithful to its principle of absolute uniformity, the Spanish monarchy had transplanted the same regime that prevailed in Spain to its overseas colonies. The council of the Indies with its two administrative bodies, one for the kingdoms of New Spain, the other for those of Peru, and its supreme court of justice, was the perfect image of the council of Castile. The two viceroys, the one in Mexico, the other in Lima, had their counterpart in the Spanish monarch. The colonial intendants, corregidors, and municipal institutions were also analogous to those of Spain. The council of the Indies, like that of Castile, pretended to regulate all the details of colonial administration and, like the latter, was guilty of the same intolerable delays. Castillian despotism has left an imprint on Spanish America which more than a century of independence has been unable to blot out. But in spite of the continuous stream of instructions which the council sent out to the viceroys and captains-general in Porto Rico, Cuba, Guatemala and Chile and its secret correspondence with members of the colonial *audiencias*, the viceroys were generally masters of their own household. In time of war when all communications with Spain were cut off their powers were unlimited. Humboldt contended, "If a viceroy is wealthy, adroit, sustained by courgeous assistants in America and at Madrid by powerful friends, he can govern arbitrarily and without fear of accountability."[24] The efficient, disinterested viceroy was a rare phenomenon in Spanish colonial administration. Most of them sold titles to Creoles, took a personal interest in the contraband trade, drew enormous profits from the distribution of mercury among the owners of silver mines—acts which justified the evil reputation of the Spanish colonial regime in the eyes of contemporaries. As England was to discover, however, they had succeeded in organizing colonial armies and in fortifying America at almost all strategical points. This Spanish system of colonial defense was no doubt their greatest achievement.

While this regime of the councils at the center of affairs reduced the departmental minister to the position of a mere mouthpiece of a collective board, the provinces and the local districts of Spain were placed under the control of single, responsible and revocable officials, the intendants and corregidors. At first glance this concentration of

[24] W. v. Humboldt, *Éssai sur Nouvelle-Espagne*, IV, 245.

authority in the single monocratic official appears to have been prompted by the sound principle of improving speed and account-ability and of guaranteeing greater effectiveness of execution. It ap-pears that the Bourbon monarchs sought an escape, at least in the provinces, from the appalling anarchy and lack of co-ordination produced at the center by the regime of the councils. Unfortunately, this transplantation of the French intendant to Spanish soil was merely administrative tinkering unaccompanied by any comprehen-sive plan of reorganizing the Spanish administrative system. It can occasion no surprise, therefore, that the French system of provin-cial intendants, introduced in 1718, then suppressed, and finally re-introduced by Ferdinand VI in 1747, did not function in Spain as it did in France. From the evidence at our disposal Spanish intend-ants were not equal to the variety and volume of affairs they were expected to discharge. Campomanes, who had every reason to know them, contended that "the instructions for provincial intendants are admirable, but in large provinces they are comparable to the dreams of Plato and Thomas More. How is it possible for the intendant of Andalusia to be accurately informed on all his functions? I imagine him to be endowed with divine intelligence, but, if he is human, these superb instructions must remain an agreeable ro-mance."[25]

More deeply rooted in Spanish soil were the corregidors, who administered the one hundred and four districts into which the provinces of Spain were divided. They were the true symbols of the centralization of Spanish absolutism and their functions embraced the entire range of activities of the Spanish bureaucracy itself. Hon-ored and highly respected in their districts, they exercised a certain control over the multitude of corporate jurisdictions that still pre-vailed in semi-feudal Spain, those of the church, the military orders, the feudal nobles and the municipalities. Strangers to the districts which they governed, they still combined judicial with administra-tive functions and exercised, in particular, a severe surveillance over the cities. There was still an endless variety of municipal institutions. The great free cities of medieval Spain had shrunk into small towns governed by hereditary noble coteries. While in Aragon the *regidores*

[25] D. G. du Dezert, *Revue Hispanique*, LXX (1927), 168.

of the cities were appointed by the crown, in *fuerist* lands their ancient liberties had continued intact. But everywhere financial control of the cities had passed into the hands of the central authority.

It was a contemporary who said that in Spain "absolutism is the synonym of poverty, misery, ferocity, fanaticism, ignorance and degradation."[26] It would have been more truthful to say that Spanish absolutism was less creative than elsewhere because Spanish sovereigns lacked genius and audacity. Monarchical leadership was still indispensable, because the Spanish bureaucracy was not yet settled on a sufficiently modern basis to proceed on its own momentum, and no initiative, as Campomanes, who knew his compatriots well, emphatically believed, was for the moment to be expected from the Spanish people themselves. Yet the Bourbon monarchy, however timidly, had entered the current of movement. Never had Spanish kingship enjoyed greater authority at home. With its numerous army and formidable fleet Spain was once more a power. The church had been placed under the control of the crown. The new intendants and the multiplication of corregidors made royal authority everywhere effective. But really incisive changes came only with Charles III.

IV. THE HAPSBURG MONARCHY

There is no more striking illustration of the process of integrating a number of disparate patrimonial entails with feudal and agrarian foundations into a modern state by means of a bureaucracy than the Hapsburg monarchy. Until the middle of the eighteenth century all the traditional devices which the Hapsburg monarchs had employed to consolidate the loosely agglomerated mass of their kingdoms, crown lands and provinces into a political and administrative unit had failed. Such measures as the brutal re-Catholicization of Bohemia, Hungary and Austria during the Counter Reformation, the dispossession of the native feudal aristocracies and their partial replacement with a specifically Hapsburg nobility entirely dependent on the throne, the policy of holding these countries together by purely military force or keeping them under the constant pressure of wars against Turkey and France—these and other devices had

26 Amiral, *L'Espagne telle qu'elle est* (Paris, 1886), 58.

contributed to make the Hapsburg rulers absolute but they brought them no nearer their ideal of state unity. To have accomplished this, at least temporarily, was the great achievement of Maria Theresa, the real founder of the unified Austrian state. It was Maria Theresa who first converted the federative union of dominions into a unitary modern state. She applied to the multiplicity of peoples, provinces and cultures of the Hapsburg monarchy the uniform norm of her enlightened absolutism.

We are not here concerned with the political structure of the Hapsburg monarchy in 1740, which can best be considered in connection with the War of the Austrian Succession, but rather with that profound transformation of the Austrian administrative system which began in 1749. This reorganization was dictated by the stern necessity of self-preservation and the system that emerged from it continued roughly down to the dissolution of the monarchy. Maria Theresa and her principal advisers, Counts Haugwitz and Kaunitz, agreed in attributing the catastrophe of 1741 and the loss of Silesia to a defective and antiquated administrative mechanism which had been unable to tap, let alone organize or develop the vast financial and military resources of the Hapsburg dominions. In this matter, indeed, Austria was an entire century behind France and Prussia. If Austria was to survive, its military forces and public revenues had to be increased and the administrative inequality with the states of western Europe had to be quickly and thoroughly removed. This could be done only by embarking upon the course that France had entered since the days of Richelieu and Prussia since Frederick William I: the creation of a centralized bureaucratic system that would enable the controlling executive arm of the government to reach deep into the provincial and local affairs of all the various sections of the monarchy.

Such a drastic defeudalization of the entire governing machine could not, in the very nature of the case, be effected through the agency of the estates of the various countries, much as one may be inclined to sympathize with the modern Czech and Magyar historians who deplore this aspect of the Theresan reforms.[27] The nu-

[27] K. Krofka, *A Short History of Czechoslovakia* (New York, 1934); F. Eckhart, *Short History of Hungarian People* (London, 1931); J. E. Denis, *La Bohème depuis la Montagne Blanche* (Paris, 1910), Vol. II.

merous estates of the Hapsburg dominions were without exception
retrograde bodies whose sole interest was to preserve a superannuated
past. Dominated by noble families, rooted in feudal localism, they
exhibited little concern for the problems of the Hapsburg monarchy
as a whole. Everywhere they still exercised the right of voting direct
taxes. Almost everywhere during the War of the Austrian Succession
the financial and military administration by permanent committees
of these estates had broken down. It was a humiliating experience
for Maria Theresa to find at the beginning of the war that she could
not secure in all Silesia the means to support two cavalry regiments,
whereas Frederick II kept an entire army adequately and abundantly supplied at a considerable distance from Prussia. With this
defective apparatus of permanent committees of the estates, which
might send two thirds, more or less, of all the taxes collected to the
central treasury, it was impossible to set up a military budget. Moreover, so long as these permanent committees of the estates had charge
of provincial and local administration, it was impossible to apply
effectively a uniform economic policy throughout the monarchy.[28]
The situation at the center of affairs in Vienna was no better. The
bewildering number and variety of central governing bodies whose
functions overlapped and conflicted with one another had caused
a frightful confusion in the last war. Some of these central institutions still betrayed their patrimonial origin. It was useless to
expect the two supreme administrative authorities of the monarchy,
the Bohemian and Austrian court chancelleries, to exercise any
effective control over the permanent committees of the estates in
the separate dominions so long as they themselves were honey-
combed with feudal and local interests which regularly exerted their
influence at the center of affairs to obtain special favors and privileges for the dominant groups of their respective home provinces.

The statesman to whom Maria Theresa committed the task of
reorganizing the government of Austria, Count Haugwitz, was an
inflexible enemy of regional traditionalism anywhere, in Vienna or
in the various countries of the Hapsburg monarchy. Profoundly
impressed with the efficiency of the Prussian civil service, he con-

---

[28] K. Uhlirtz, *Handbuch der Geschichte Österreichs und seiner Nachbarländer Böhmen
und Ungarn* (Vienna, 1930), II, 343.

THE LEVIATHAN STATE

ceived the plan of reorganizing the entire Austrian administrative system, outside of Hungary, Milan and the Austrian Netherlands, more or less according to the Prussian pattern. His plan implied a double metamorphosis: it meant, first, that henceforth the estates of the various countries, though not completely suppressed as in Prussia, would be deprived of their administrative functions; second, the creation of a specifically Hapsburg bureaucratic system in central, provincial and local administration, which, divorced from local and feudal interests, henceforth would stand above the separate nations, classes and countries. From this time onward the Hapsburg dynastic state and the bureaucratic hierarchy were synonymous terms. That such a thorough bureaucratization involved a still further Germanization of the Slavic sections of the Hapsburg monarchy even Austrian historians no longer deny. It must be said, however, that this was not Maria Theresa's prime inspiration. The crucial issue in the Hapsburg monarchy of 1750 was less the opposition between the Hapsburg dynasty and the German element on the one hand and the Slavonic and Magyar elements on the other than the opposition between Hapsburg bureaucratic absolutism and the centrifugal tendencies of the feudal estates of the component parts, the German sections not excepted, of the monarchy. Germanization was the natural consequence of administrative uniformity. The vast majority of the new civil servants were of German origin and German became the natural langauge of this bureaucracy, though it should be said that important laws were also published in the languages of the various localities.[29] In the eighteenth century this was the less surprising, since the language of practically the entire bourgeoisie, even of the Slavonic sections and Hungary, was German. Only the servile peasants of the western and southern Slav regions used their national idioms and only slowly did they learn to see in the noble lord not only a social but a national oppressor.

Maria Theresa was the first Hapsburg monarch to organize her central government on the western European principle of specialization and division of labor. To each of the five important departments—foreign affairs, commerce, war, justice, internal affairs—she

[29] *Das Nationalitätenrecht des alten Oesterreich,* ed. by K. Kugelmann (Vienna, 1934), 22; J. Redlich, *Das oesterreichische Staats-und Reichsproblem* (Vienna, 1920), I, 36; R. J. Kerner, *Bohemia in the Eighteenth Century* (New York, 1932), 345.

assigned a special administrative body. The upshot, it must be admitted, was still no rationally constructed edifice of central government. But in spite of all the curious complexities, compromises, and contradictions that were dragged along as the result of immediate political necessities, the reform settled the administration of Austria upon an effective and enduring foundation. Succeeding Hapsburg monarchs have but worked the mechanism they inherited from Maria Theresa.

The moving principle of this mechanism can best be described as a bureaucratic rather than a royal absolutism. Austrian royalty, while theoretically absolute, as a rule accepted the dictates of its civil servants. Nothing illustrates this feature of the system more trenchantly than the peculiar position of the council of state (*Staatsrat*), the *deus ex machina* of the Austrian government. Like the Napoleonic *conseil d'état*, it possessed neither executive nor administrative authority. Its authority was extrinsic. Its functions were those of an advisory council, a committee of experts or, more correctly, a parliament of bureaucrats, which discussed all the affairs of the monarchy, both internal and foreign, including those of Hungary, examined all projects of reform and made its recommendations to the sovereign. These recommendations were to remain as binding on the administrative authorities as on the monarch himself. It goes without saying that such an institution was incompatible with autocracy as we find it exemplified in the Prussia of Frederick the Great. The Austrian foreign office, reorganized under the name of the state chancellery (*Staatskanzlei*), was placed under the direction of Count Kaunitz in 1753. The council of war (*Hofkriegsrat*) was reconstituted and its authority extended to all parts of the monarchy. The new directory of commerce (*Kommerzdirektorium*), modeled on a similar institution in Prussia, became the special agency of a vigorous mercantilist economic policy in all the Hapsburg dominions. More significant still was the suppression of the archaic Bohemian and Austrian court chancelleries and the establishment in their stead of a single *Directorium in publicis et cameralibus* as a ministry of the interior and finance for all Hapsburg dominions with the exception of Hungary, Milan and the Austrian Netherlands. This formidable body, again modeled on the Prussian

General Directory, was designed to organize and develop all the economic and financial resources of the monarchy. Count Haugwitz took special care to place this *Directorium* under his own energetic leadership. The work of reorganizing the central government was completed by the creation of a supreme court for the entire monarchy. By this clean cut divorce of the judicial from the administrative process, Count Haugwitz executed a reform demanded by Montesquieu in his *Spirit of Laws*, published the year before. The reform, we may be certain, was not inspired by the doctrine of the separation of powers, but suggested itself as a practical means of improving both the quality of justice and of administration. If any theory may be said to have suggested the measure, it was rather the liberal mercantilism of the enlightened Austrian cameralists, Wilhelm von Schroeder and Justi, whom Haugwitz pressed into the service of invigorating the economic life of Austria and for whose opinions he exhibited a warm enthusiasm.[30]

Yet, important as these changes in Vienna were, the cornerstone of the entire reform was the reorganization of provincial government. Here the pivotal issue was the political and administrative authority of the estates which, due to the peculiar composition of the Hapsburg dominions, had exhibited a greater vitality than in other monarchies of western Europe. Convinced that they were the greatest stumbling block to efficient administration, Count Haugwitz was determined on a drastic reduction of their historic privileges. He took the first step toward this end in 1748 when he persuaded all the estates of the lands of the Bohemian and Austrian crown to sign contracts for increased taxation for a ten-year period, thus rendering their immemorial right to grant taxes illusory. Though they continued to meet almost annually, their legislative activity soon fell into abeyance. Important laws were henceforth promulgated by the crown without the participation of the estates. A peculiar combination of factors deprived these estates of all power of offering effective resistance to these measures. The issue between the Hapsburg dynasty and the estates was no longer, as in the preceding century, one of religion, but one of modernizing the administrative system, the necessity of which was generally conceded in view of the recent

[30] Louise Sommer, *Die oesterreichischen Kameralisten* (Vienna, 1920).

military disasters. The estates of Bohemia were in no position to argue the matter with Maria Theresa, who had just pardoned them for having treasonably sworn homage to Charles Albert of Bavaria, the pretender to the Bohemian crown in 1741.[31]

Having thus cleared the road for a reorganization of provincial administration, Haugwitz proceeded to divide the western half of the monarchy into ten provincial units, and, faithful to his principle of separating justice from administration, imposed on each unit a superior court and an administrative board. This administrative authority, called Representation and Treasury and generally known as the *Gubernium*, operated under the direction and control of the central *Directorium* in Vienna. Everywhere the ancient deputies of the estates now surrendered their administrative functions to this new bureaucracy, which was imposed in a uniform manner on all the *Gubernia* of the monarchy. Thus with a single stroke of the pen Maria had effected a political, constitutional and administrative revolution. This marks the end of Bohemia as an independent state. Amalgamated administratively with the other German dominions, Bohemia was henceforth a province like the Tyrol or Carniola. No doubt this measure, since it was executed without the consent of the estates, constituted a violation of the Bohemian constitution, but it was only with these changes that Austria became a modern unitary state.[32]

The exclusion of the estates from the field of provincial administration had the result of bringing the Austrian civil service into close and daily contact with the great masses of servile peasants. The greater the burdens of taxation and military service that were now imposed upon the peasantry, the more solicitous did the Austrian government become of the economic welfare of its subjects. Much, therefore, depended on the character of the local *Kreishauptmann* or district officer, who became the executor of this progressive social policy. This office, which had originated in Bohemia, was now extended to the entire western half of the monarchy. Formerly a deputy of the estates, the *Kreishauptmann* now became a royal and

[31] I. Beidtel, *Geschichte der oesterreichischen Staatsverwaltung* (Innsbruck, 1896), Vol. II; A. von Luschin, *Oesterreichische Reichsgeschichte* (Bamberg, 1896), 523-541.
[32] Kramarsch, *Das Böhmische Staatsrecht*, 25; O. Hintze, "Der oesterreichische und der preussische Beamtenstaat," *Historische Zeitschrift* (1901), Vol. 86, 432.

bureaucratic functionary, subject to the instructions and control of the *Gubernium*. He concentrated in his hands all those functions which in Prussia were divided between the local commissary and the *Landrat*, and occupied a position not unlike that of the French intendant. Whatever his other tasks, vigorous intervention in the patrimonial affairs of the landed nobility of Austria and Bohemia was one of his cardinal duties.

It is instructive to compare the role of this district officer in adjusting the lord-serf relationship to the new needs of the Austrian state with the similar role of the Prussian bureaucracy. Frederick the Great and the Prussian civil servants were prevented from advancing very far toward emancipating the serfs because the junker landowners, poor to begin with, occupied a commanding position in the Prussian army and civil service. In the eyes of Frederick the military nobility were as much in need of state protection in the ownership of their estates as were the peasants in the security of their holdings. Austria, however, possessed no military nobility comparable to that of Prussia. The great Bohemian magnates, too wealthy and too independent to be forced to enter the army and civil service in large numbers, were less indispensable to Hapsburg absolutism than the junkers were to Prussia. This may explain the sharper anti-feudal edge given to the institution of the Austrian district officer. The Austrian serf had a clear advantage over his Prussian brother in that his quarrels with his feudal lord were carried before this bureaucratic district officer, not, as in Prussia, before the ordinary law courts, which were dominated by the landed nobility. In his effort to prevent peasant evictions and the engrossing of peasant land, in restricting feudal payments and servile labor so as to make them compatible with the peasant's capacity to pay taxes to the state, the district officer became a terror of the nobility and monasteries, who waged a silent and stubborn warfare against the new social policy of the Austrian government.

Thus it was in competitive rivalry with Prussia that Austria exchanged her feudal and corporate structure for that of a modern military and bureaucratic state. All the logical implications of this reconstruction of the administrative mechanism, however, can be fully understood only when it is remembered that it was accom-

panied by a series of fiscal reforms between 1748 and 1760 which
for the first time subjected the nobility and clergy to a systematic
property and income tax and transformed the taxes on the servile
classes from personal into income taxes. This progressive measure
signified not merely a greater equalization in the distribution of
public burdens, but gave Austria a more enlightened system of
taxation than Prussia possessed.[33] Financial burdens, to be sure, were
still not equally divided either among classes or among the crown
lands of the monarchy. The peasant still paid twice as much as the
nobleman and Bohemia contributed twice as much as Hungary to
the Hapsburg treasury.

The autonomous kingdom of Hungary, in spite of the renewed
assurance of its independence given at the Diet of Pressburg in
1741, was now also to have its first experience of royal absolutism.
Without altering the dualistic structure of Austria-Hungary, without laying violent hands on the sacrosanct institutions of her
Magyar subjects, Maria Theresa succeeded in devitalizing almost
all the constitutional limitations that hedged in the crown of St.
Stephen. An ever growing volume of Hungarian business was
transacted in Vienna, which now for the first time became the capital
of Hungary also. Theoretically the reorganization in Vienna was
adapted to the special position of Hungary, but in actual fact all the
important functions of the Hungarian state were subordinated to
the new authorities in Vienna. Not only did these Viennese authorities, the councils of state, of war and of commerce, extend their
jurisdiction over Hungary as over the rest of the monarchy, but they
governed directly entire sections of Hungary, such as the defensive
zone along the southern frontier, called the Military Border, and the
extensive Banat of Temesvar. Transylvania also, still separated from
the mother country, was governed by authorities responsible to
Vienna rather than to Budapest. Even the important Hungarian
central officers, the Palatine, the *personalis*, the Lord Chief Justice,
the Ban of Croatia, became functionaries of the crown rather than
agents of the diet, or were deprived of all political authority. This
was notably true of the Palatine, who, as president of the governor's
council sitting in Budapest, directed all internal affairs, and of the

personalis who, as director of the meetings of the diets, used his influence in the interests of the dynasty.[34] In a word, Maria Theresa
succeeded in exercising an absolute royal power over the rebellious
kingdom of Hungary, a thing that Charles VI had no longer
attempted.

How did she accomplish this miracle? Briefly, by what Jászi, not
inaptly, describes as a system of *douce violence*.[35] In Hungary every
instrument of power and influence—the estates, offices, church, local
government—was in the hands of the nobility. All the authority
which elsewhere was exercised by an official bureaucracy was
wielded in Hungary by the landed gentry and the magnates. Elsewhere the nobility was a leading privileged order, but in Hungary
it was the ruling nation itself. Hungary, it will be remembered,
produced neither an independent national middle class nor an independent and wealthy peasantry such as we find in western Europe.
The German and Slavic burghers of the small towns led a separate
existence both as a class and as nationalities. Possessed of four fifths
of the soil of the country, these Magyar nobles enjoyed absolute
fiscal immunity. The entire weight of public burdens fell upon the
burghers and the servile masses, who owned but one fifth of the
land and were utterly destitute of political rights. Against the
wealthy Magyar aristocrats, some of whom owned estates equal in
size to a German principality, the Hapsburg monarchs had always
exhibited a deep-seated hostility and distrust. Maria Theresa now
lured them into the imperial service of the Hapsburg monarchy,
conferring upon them offices as diplomats, ambassadors, privy coun-
cilors, generals and court dignitaries. Attracted by titles and the
prospect of rewards in the form of Hungarian estates, the Magyar
aristocracy responded with enthusiasm. In growing numbers they
went to Vienna, the splendors of which they enhanced with their
great wealth and lavish expenditures. They intermarried with the
high aristocracy of Austria and Bohemia, and learned to utter their
gallantries in German. Maria Theresa showered honors upon them,
surrounded herself with a bodyguard of Hungarian nobles,
founded a special Hungarian order—the Order of St. Stephen—and

[34] F. Eckhart, *Short History of Hungary* (London, 1931), 121.
[35] O. Jászi, *The Dissolution of the Hapsburg Monarchy* (Chicago, 1929), 61; H. Marczali, *Hungary in the Eighteenth Century* (Cambridge, 1910), 119.

established for their sons an educational institution, the *Theresianum*, where they were educated together with the children of the sovereign. Thus arose a new Hungarian office-holding aristocracy, a court nobility, which accepted the permanence of the Hapsburg empire, that is to say, recognized that higher dynastic unit created by the Pragmatic Sanction. Thanks to their constant political and cultural association with Vienna, the Hungarian magnates prevailed over the protests and opposition of the other orders in the diet.

The more denationalized the higher nobility became, the more did the gentry of the countries become the defenders of the manners, customs and independence of an older Hungary. Over these subordinate county units the crown could exercise no effective authority. In their county assemblies the gentry elected their own officers and judges, sent protests to Vienna, deferred the execution or blunted the edge of royal edicts. But so long as they held to their formalized and meager Latin culture, their contracted political outlook, they were at a great disadvantage in defending the independence of Hungary. In upholding the regime of the diets they were also defending their own exaggerated privileges, which were an impediment to further progress. Due to this stubborn and unenlightened opposition Maria Theresa rarely called a meeting of the diet and preferred to act on her own authority.

V. PRUSSIA

The unique role of Prussia among the states of Europe lay not so much in its peculiar mixture of despotism and feudalism, but in the fact that it accomplished the impossible. A small, poor, still half-feudal and notoriously underpopulated country that was neither a geographic nor racial unit, with a retarded middle class that suffered from both lack of enterprise and capital, Prussia was suddenly thrust into the position of a European power. After his Silesian Wars it was no longer possible for Frederick to retreat from this European position. His only alternative to destruction by stronger neighbors was to mobilize the resources necessary to support his ever growing army, without which his European influence was utterly negligible, by means of superior organization and an unprecedented degree of social discipline. Whatever the cost, the experiment proved successful. In 1750 Prussia was the only larger continental state which managed not only to balance its budget but to produce a steady surplus of income over expenditures. This was not due to an equitable distribution of financial burdens among the various classes of Prussian society nor to an intelligent system of taxation. In these matters Prussia was not more advanced than other continental states. The Prussian peasant, who paid about forty per cent of his net income to the state and owed often unlimited services to his feudal lord, had no advantage over the Austrian or French peasant. What made the difference between Prussia and other continental states was the moral force that emanated from the greatest of the Hohenzollern and the superb quality of the Prussian bureaucracy, one of the first great modern civil service systems of Europe.[36]

The principle, *le roi fait tout,* elsewhere an empty symbolic formula which concealed a government by bureaucrats, was an accurate description of the Prussian administrative process. The unity of leadership, the clocklike precision and co-ordination of central government agencies which Prussia possessed to a superior degree, are not to be found in Prussian institutions, but in the person of the monarch. King Frederick was literally the only central co-ordinating organ of the monarchy, and the peculiar scaffolding of the Prussian bureaucratic mechanism—the central General Directory, the provincial chambers, the local commissaries and the *Landräte*—becomes intelligible only when it is understood that the king alone came into daily and continuous contact with all the branches of government and administration. The excellence of the system consisted in the combination of a single person with the wide knowledge of large affairs which is gained only by diversified action, and the specialized skill of individual bureaucrats. The king alone formulated policy and laid down directives; the ministers were not, as in France, the vehicles of opinions and programs, but royal clerks, the *Bedienten* of His Prussian Majesty. There was a foreign office, the *Cabinetsministerium*, with two ministers, but since Frederick carried on his foreign policy by means of a direct personal correspondence with

---

[36] To avoid cluttering up the page with numerous references the author may be permitted to refer for a complete bibliography to his series of articles on "The Prussian Bureaucracy in the Eighteenth Century," *Political Science Quarterly,* 46 (1931), 403-423; 47 (1932), 75-94, 259-273.

every Prussian ambassador abroad, these ministers might or might not know what the foreign policy of the king actually was. It will be pointed out in a later chapter that Frederick performed all the functions of a modern general staff of the army. But this applied also to his conduct of domestic affairs. From the day when he withdrew entire departments and whole provinces from the jurisdiction of the General Directory, only the king possessed complete information of the total financial resources of the kingdom and of the way in which money was disbursed. Convinced that foreign policy, military affairs, economic policy and finance were closely interdependent upon one another, he made himself the actual master of every department of government. Only in this way did he believe himself to be in a position to set up and pursue a consistent and rational system of politics which, he once said, must spring from a single rapid intelligence like Newton's law of gravity. It was impossible to carry the principle of autocracy to a greater extreme.

Such a personal autocracy may well appear to be a contradiction in terms in a modern bureaucratic state with its persistent urge to expand the area and intensity of its activities. Even for a man of large intellect and consummate ability like Frederick, ruling over a relatively simple and undifferentiated society such as that of Prussia, the problem presented almost insuperable difficulties. Frederick kept insisting that all impulses must proceed from him alone and yet he had to deal with a trained bureaucracy whose specialized functions and mastery of detail gave them the same kind of advantage over the king which the modern expert has over the dilettante legislator. A perpetual silent competition between the monarch and his bureaucracy for initiative was inevitable. This was not in itself an evil; in fact, it made the Prussian administrative process all the more precise and effective.

But how did the king maintain his ascendancy? First, by withdrawing himself from personal contact with his officials and negotiating with them only in writing from his Potsdam residence. Sitting in Berlin, the ministers prepared all the materials. From there they sent him their statistical reports, memorials and recommendations, and he replied by means of "cabinet orders" expedited through his private secretary Eichel, a mysterious personage, who was incorruptible and invisible to anyone but the monarch himself. The great merit of the system was the rapidity with which all public business was dispatched. Since everything was done by letter and the king's mind worked with extraordinary speed, there was no reason for delay. Nowhere in the entire Prussian bureaucratic system was there such impeccable order as in the cabinet of the king. Just as each hour of the day, each week and month, so the entire year was arranged in such a manner that no business crowded on the heels of another. A calendar on the king's table indicated not only the duties of each day and week, but reminded him when all outstanding reports, replies and other matters were due. Any official who addressed himself to the king could expect an immediate answer. The military precision of the king's life in Potsdam, where he had neither wife nor family, neither court nor French court etiquette, where he never observed a religious holiday and was never distracted by undesired interruptions, was conducive to hard work. He was the essence of practicality and good sense and he knew his kingdom like an open page. If Frederick can be said to have possessed a *faculté maitresse*, it was his moral energy and his unremitting application to work. When he called himself the first servant of the state, it was no empty phrase. What Prussia lacked in *force intrinsèque*, as he called it, was to be supplied by the moral drive of the monarch and his bureaucracy.

Frederick regarded his civil servants with an ineradicable distrust. Proceeding on the assumption that no official, however honest, was incorruptible, he provided some control device for every task which he committed to him. Dependent, as he was, upon written reports, he was forever suspecting his officials of bureaucratic inertia, of a propensity to interpret royal orders generously enough to suit the circumstances or their private convenience, of deceiving him, of deceiving him often, as he once admitted, with the best intentions. The means he employed to guarantee the honesty and integrity of his civil service may not meet the approval of a modern efficiency expert, but it cannot be denied that they were remarkably effective. At strategic points throughout the entire system, from the General Directory down to the local commissary, he placed a special royal agent, called the *Fiscal*, a curious combination of a royal scrutineer or spy and a modern prosecuting attorney, to guarantee the execution of royal orders and to report every suspicion of irregularity directly to the king. Wherever there was a responsible civil servant there was also the watchful eye of the *Fiscal* to pursue him in every official act. Although instances of actual corruption were rare, summary dismissals, whether for incompetence or negligence, were frequent. The Prussian civil servant was the galley slave of the state; he was utterly without legal rights and, unlike the Prussian citizen, could be sent to the Spandau prison without a trial. To control his ministers, the king regularly corresponded with their subordinates or with the presidents of the provincial chambers; and to assure himself of the veracity of the latter he dealt with individual members of these provincial bodies. Every year between May and August he journeyed through the provinces of his kingdom, examining his officials and interviewing private citizens, personally inspecting local conditions and consulting with burgomasters, merchants and manufacturers. In this way he tapped extraordinary sources of information which, besides the normal channels of reporting, acquainted him with everything he seriously wanted to know. Now and then he might be the dupe of bureaucratic hoodwinking, but the lynx-eyed vigilance of the king sooner or later discovered almost everything.

From what has already been said it is apparent that what distinguished the Prussian from the French bureaucracy was greater centralization and uniformity, a more effective subordination, a severe military discipline and a more precise system of accountability. To this must be added an important difference in recruiting the bureaucratic personnel. While in France offices were purchased or inherited, in Prussia the merit system had already become the fixed and universal rule for admitting candidates to public office, a rule that was not relaxed even in the case of an aspirant of noble extraction. The ability to pass several examinations was the only portal to the Prussian civil service and most officials had previously attended one or more of the Prussian universities, where in addition to jurisprudence they studied cameralism, a synthetic branch of academic studies which embraced government finance, agriculture and public administration. But the Prussian monarchs never regarded a university education as the final solution of the problem of training an efficient civil servant. It was a universal practice for every candidate, before presenting himself for his final examination, to spend one or two years on a royal farm to familiarize himself with the practical details of agriculture and the management of the royal domains. This experience brought the future official into personal contact with some of the most important problems of the Prussian monarchy: enlightened agricultural methods, the financial problems involved in drawing up a contract for leasing the royal domains, which amounted to one fourth of all the arable land of Prussia, and the realities of the lord-serf relationship. In France civil servants were for the most part jurists, in Prussia they were practical economists.

It was a matter of vast importance for the future of the Prussian monarchy that it developed a modern civil service before it produced a class of enterprising capitalists. The merit system had the effect of attracting and absorbing into the service of the monarchy the most industrious and intelligent elements of the population. Frederick encouraged the sons of his officials to follow in the footsteps of their fathers, a fact which could not fail to enhance the homogeneity and *esprit de corps* of the service. Since noble and bourgeois officials faced each other in the General Directory and the provincial chambers in approximately equal numbers, the Prussian bureaucracy was not the special instrument of a particular social class, although it is true that nobles occupied most of the higher positions. The devotion to the commonweal with which Frederick succeeded in impregnating his officials won for them the respect and confidence of all classes of Prussian society, and the deep-seated suspicion and distrust between the public and the "bureaucracy," which is so conspicuous in Anglo-Saxon countries, never arose in Prussia.

Whereas in the French system all authority was vested in the single, responsible, ministerial *chef de ressort* with a wide berth for individual initiative, the Prussian system was calculated to eliminate all personal influence whatsoever, first by binding the individual official to a collective board, then by subjecting both, the individual and the board, to an authoritative bureaucratic *règlement* which minutely prescribed every detail of the service. Not only were there no Prussian equivalents for the French functional ministries in 1740, but the four ministers of the supreme Prussian administrative authority, the General Directory, exercised identical functions, each in his special group of provinces, in such a manner that all four shared a collective responsibility for decisions in all four territorial departments. The General Directory was indubitably the weakest cog in the Prussian bureaucratic mechanism. This was in some measure due to its lumbering procedure. But it was chiefly due to the fact that Frederick incorporated with it two functional ministries of the French type, one for commerce in 1741 and one for the army in 1746, which were ill-adapted to the general scheme of the collective solidarity of the General Directory. When in 1742 Frederick established another special ministry for Silesia, which had no connection with the General Directory at all, autocracy became an absolute necessity of the system.

This lack of unity among the central institutions would have been disastrous to the efficiency of the Prussian bureaucracy had it not been for the industry of the king on the one hand and the energy and dependability of the fifteen provincial chambers (*Kriegs-und Domänen Kammern*) on the other. These provincial chambers were the vital centers of the bureaucracy. They were the classic workshops of the Prussian mercantilist state, through which the inhabitants of Prussia were galvanized into an active, thrifty people—the most highly disciplined people of modern Europe. Impatient of the obstructionist delays of the General Directory, Frederick negotiated with these provincial chambers directly, over the heads of the central authorities, issuing orders and receiving reports of which the General Directory might or might not be informed. Though sharply subordinated to the General Directory, the provincial chambers in this way acquired a certain discretionary authority which enabled them to defend their provinces against the exacting demands of the central government. An excellent opportunity for this presented itself when, beginning with 1748, Frederick annually convoked all the presidents of these provincial chambers in Berlin to discuss common measures for the prosperity of the kingdom.

The provincial chambers were pre-eminently financial organs, and their pivotal function was the prompt and accurate collection of the budgetary income. There was, however, a distinct advantage in the circumstance that the fiscalism which they represented was combined with a responsibility for the economic welfare of their provinces. They stimulated enterprise among the people, reclaimed sandy wastes, drained swamps, and made internal colonization one of their major activities. They inspected the private husbandry of peasants and the countinghouses of merchants and made indolence and shiftlessness a public offense. Their members journeyed through England and Holland to study improved agricultural and commercial methods, went out in search of markets for Prussian manufacturers, and superintended the fairs of the larger cities. There was not a phase of urban or rural life that escaped their regulating ordinances. Their ultimate aim was always to achieve that substantial "plus" in revenues which the king never ceased to demand from them and which he regarded as the only compelling proof of their efficiency.

In keeping with the collective principle, the provincial chamber was a body in which one official controlled another and all must answer for the actions of each individual member. Although each one of the fifteen or twenty members had his allotted duties, nothing was done save by common deliberation and decision. This made the grosser forms of corruption, errors of inadvertence or ignorance difficult, if not impossible. But their procedure was cumbersome and slow. The numerous control devices, the countless bureaucratic formalities commonly known as red tape, the exaggerated prominence given to the written documents which they produced in appalling quantities, slowed down the speed of the administrative process. The heroic efforts to simplify this process and to reduce the number of written documents, which run through the middle decades of the century, were only partially successful. But if their slow motions often exasperated the impatient Frederick, it should be stated that they were punctiliously exact in the impersonal application of the directives given to them from above.

The distinct and separate systems of taxation which prevailed in the towns and rural districts of Prussia required two different sets of local authorities. The local commissary or *Steuerrat*, a traveling official who supervised from six to ten towns, was a far more formidable officer than the rural *Landrat*, although both labored under the direction and scrutiny of the provincial chamber. The office of the local commissary was one of the key positions in the entire bureaucratic hierarchy. He was the executive organ of royal absolutism in the municipalities of Prussia and, with the local *gendarmerie* at his disposal, he possessed enormous executive powers. To achieve the prompt and effective execution of royal orders he might even call upon the local military commandant. Military execution by Prussian grenadiers, it should not be forgotten, always remained the *ultima ratio* of Prussian administration. The redoubtable, paternalistic tutelage of the local commissaries deprived Prussian municipalities of every vestige of local autonomy. The commissaries managed towns as though they were an integral part of the royal domains. They determined municipal budgets, fixed the local price of food and other commodities, enforced the mercantilist industrial and commercial legislation, regulated the guilds and adapted them to the needs of capitalistic enterprise, and saw to it that the local military garrison was properly billeted. Doubtless they conferred numerous blessings upon Prussian towns by guaranteeing religious toleration and freedom of thought, by improving urban sanitation, by providing the population with apothecaries and physicians, and by promoting vaccination. If Prussia did not remain a purely agricultural country but developed a commerce and industry, which, though not great, were sufficient to supply its own needs, this was largely due to the local commissaries and their superiors. Yet the exaggerated thrift of Prussian administration rested heavily on these cities; every *groschen* that was not indispensable for urgent municipal needs was syphoned from the urban treasuries to meet the larger needs of the Prussian state.[37]

Compared with the local commissary, the *Landrat* could hardly be classified as a bureaucratic official. Always a nobleman and the owner of a landed estate, he was as often elected by the local nobility as appointed by the king, though he, too, had to pass an examination in cameralism. As the executive organ of the provincial chamber he was charged with publishing royal edicts, regulating military conscription, exercising rural police power and enforcing laws designed to protect the peasant against exploitation by his noble

37 J. Ziekursch, *Das Ergebnis der friderizianischen Städteverwaltung* (Jena, 1908).

landlord. Representing the interests of the landowning nobility, the office of the *Landrat* lacked a bureaucratic edge. The actual unit of local government in Prussia was in reality the nobleman's patrimonial estate. The Prussian junker exercised all the vital functions of local government on his private estate, including the lower forms of justice and police power. He also collected the taxes from his peasants and supplied the army with recruits. So long as the Prussian landlord did not undermine the capacity of his peasants to discharge their fiscal and military obligations to the state, flagrantly abuse his peasants or reduce the total number of peasant holdings, he was relatively free from bureaucratic interference. Since Frederick lacked the financial resources to pay for local government authorities, he had no choice but to employ the unremunerated public service of the nobility in this capacity. In his special sphere the Prussian landlord exercised functions not unlike those of the English justices of the peace.

The boundless industry of Frederick the Great for the moment concealed the structural flaws in the Prussian bureaucracy. Even his own genius did not extend to the realm of public finance. He left unaltered the faulty excise tax, which proved to be a dead weight on Prussian commerce. He did not revise the antiquated *Kataster* or assessment rolls which served as the basis for the tax on the peasantry. For reasons best known to himself he made no effort to tax the landed nobility of the central provinces as he did those of Silesia and East Prussia. Yet despite its defective structure and its outmoded system of taxation, the management of public finance was easily the most brilliant achievement of the Prussian bureaucracy. By means of its effective system of accounting, its close-fisted parsimony, its unsparing severity against every extravagance with public funds, the Prussian civil service succeeded in making the most of the slender financial resources of Prussia. These resources supported Prussia's European position, the army and the bureaucratic machine, and enabled the king to sustain three wars in two decades without contracting a public debt worth mentioning. It is no explanation to say that in the Seven Years' War he received British subsidies; they were a mere pittance beside what he actually spent. Nor is it an explanation to say that Frederick cut his policy to suit his financial cloth. In view of the steady expansion of the army the contrary is rather the case.

In this Prussia, devoid of wealth and prosperity, the burdens and obligations of the masses stood in inverse proportion to their economic circumstances. Indeed, it was from the very poverty of its inhabitants that the Prussian state drew its greatest strength. The proud junker, living on an estate too diminutive for a decent standard of life, was constrained to seek public employment, notwithstanding the forbidding severity of its discipline. The ambitious bourgeois intellectual discovered in the Prussian civil service his best, indeed his only, opportunity for advancement. It was not wealth but connection with the army and civil service that guaranteed social position. It was the general poverty that produced the unprecedented concentration of resources, the furor, as Mirabeau was later to call it, of regulating and regimenting every aspect of public and private life, the one-sided emphasis on Spartan virtues and social discipline, in a word, what we generally call Prussianism. It is unthinkable that this Prussianism could ever have sprung from the soil of free, wealthy, parliamentary England. In England the island, as it were, replaced the state; in Prussia the state of the old regime attained its maximum expansion. While England was becoming constantly more individualistic, Prussia remained a collectivist state in which the individual was expected to sacrifice himself for the whole. The only freedom for the eighteenth-century Prussian was the *libertas oboedientiae*—the freedom to obey.

VI. RUSSIA

It might well appear that the Russia of 1750 is not comparable to the states of western Europe. Her prolonged isolation from the cultural centers and movements of western society, the fossilized Greek Orthodox Church and her ancient relations with Byzantium, then the protracted struggle with the Asiatic Tartars and Turks, had left an indelible impress on the cultural, economic and political life of the Russian people. Yet the process of Europeanization was already well under way and the decisive turning point came in these years under Elizabeth, when the upper classes ceased to be Muscovite and became European in their outlook. With the secularization of the state, the Orthodox Church ceased to be the sole depository of culture. Peter the Great's conquest of the Baltic provinces had been followed by intensified commercial contacts with the west, which were accompanied by corresponding changes in the structure of the state. Russia's influence in Sweden and Poland was rapidly becoming paramount and her alliances with England and Austria drew her still farther into the western orbit. Russia had become a member of the competitive state system of Europe and this circumstance imposed upon her the necessity of still further Europeanization.

If the administrative structure of Russia in 1750 is to be made intelligible, it must be examined against the background of the social and institutional antecedents of the Muscovite state. This amorphous state, created literally as an instrument of defense against the Tartars, necessitated an extreme concentration of public authority and immense efforts on the part of the Russian people. In the process of its formation the tsar became the theoretical owner of the land and he impressed into the service of the Russian state all the classes of Russian society. The ancient Muscovite polity was *par excellence* a service-state such as we find nowhere in western Europe. It rested on the twin foundation of a serving nobility, the *pomiestchiki*, and peasant serfdom, which, though far from being universal, gave its coloring to the entire social system. The military landowners and servitors of the tsar collected the taxes, administered justice and maintained a police system. The prevailing system of conditional landowning required the periodical registration of the servitors of the tsar in every region, on which occasion they were re-fitted with land according to their rank and deserts. Even the owners of hereditary estates, the *votchiniki*, were held liable to the discharge of military and other service. In this manner the formation of the Muscovite state was accompanied by the destruction of the concept of private property in land. Private property rights in land were based not on the sanctions of civil but of public law.[38]

The great administrative reforms of Peter the Great had not materially altered this situation. To be sure, Peter went far in the direction of meeting the wishes of his noble servitors when in 1714 he

[38] Boris Brutzkus, "Die historischen Eigentümlichkeiten der wirtschaftlichen und sozialen Entwicklung Russlands," *Jahrbücher für die Kultur und Geschichte der Slaven,* (1934) X, 62.

placed their service-estates on the same footing of hereditability with those of the *votchiniki*, who held their estates unconditionally. Henceforth the two classes of landowners were merged into the single class of *pomiestchiki*. But Peter had no intention of emancipating his servitors from their obligation to serve in the army, navy or civil service. He maintained the system of conditional land tenure and punished brutally all those who sought to escape from their duties. The great change came during the frequent palace revolutions of the eighteenth century, in which the regiments of the guards became a mechanism to safeguard the interests of the nobility. These guards, among whom even the private soldiers were largely nobles, intervened only in exceptional cases, but their presence was a constant reminder to the sovereign of those whose nominee he was. In the long intervals of peace after 1721 the obligation of service was observed with increasing slackness. This was all the more possible, since the Russian state had now progressed sufficiently in the economic sense to be able to pay its servants in money.

The Russian nobility had every reason to glorify the reign of the "good and joyous" Tsarina Elizabeth, who did so much to please them. She issued a series of ukases in which she progressively alleviated their obligation to serve, granted them an exclusive monopoly in the possession of "inhabited" estates, extended their economic and social privileges and increased their control over peasant serfs.[39] The upshot of all this legislation was to transform the Russian nobles into local government authorities much in the manner of the Prussian junkers. They collected the capitation tax in the name of the fisc, supervised the conduct of their peasants and punished them in case of desertion. From this time also dates that unique Russian practice of periodically redividing the land among the members of the peasant communities on the domains of the state as well as on the estates of the nobility. These periodical land divisions were a result of the Russian system of taxation and their primary purpose was to enable each peasant to pay his capitation tax. They had the further effect of bringing the views of nobles and peasants with regard to the soil into sharp contradiction with one another. While

[39] M. Kizevetter, *Histoire de Russie,* ed. by P. Milioukov, Ch. Seignobos, L. Eisenmann (Paris, 1932), II, 469; Mirsky, *History of Russia* (1934).

the nobles, thanks to Elizabeth's legislation, henceforth regarded
their landed possessions as their private property within the meaning
of Roman law, the periodical land divisions destroyed every notion
of private property in land among the servile peasantry. Their notion, not unnaturally, was that the possession of land was an institution of public law which gave the appearance of guaranteeing
them sufficient land to live and meet their obligations to the tsar.
This public-legal character of Russian serfdom found its classic expression not so much in the fact that the peasant was regarded as
the private property of his lord, but in the circumstance that he was
a member of an organized village community which owed obedience to its master for the sole reason that the latter was charged by
the central government with the exercise of certain local administrative functions. Henceforth every peasant who for one reason or
another had no master must choose one or have one imposed upon
him by government authorities. The result of this social and administrative legislation of Elizabeth was to create that fatal cleavage in
Russian society which progressively alienated the nobility and the
peasantry from one another for all time to come.

Elizabeth left the complete suppression of the obligatory service
of the nobility to her successor, Peter III. Together these sovereigns
endowed the Russian nobles with legal independence and wealth,
made them masters of the labor resources of the nation and solidified among them the spirit of caste. With the suppression of obligatory service one of the foundation stones of the ancient Muscovite
state had been removed. Henceforth, there was nothing to distinguish the Russian nobility from the nobility of the countries of central Europe. Little by little they ceased to participate in the central
administration and exhibited a marked tendency to seize the centers
of provincial and local authority, which were more useful for the
promotion of their special interests.

It might well be supposed that this overwhelming supremacy of
the nobility exposed the Russian state, ruled as it was by a succession
of weak women and foreigners, to the same danger of political
anarchy and administrative paralysis which ultimately destroyed the
Polish republic. But between Russia and Poland there was an important difference. The powerful impulses which drew Russia ever

deeper into the current of western capitalism were almost entirely absent in Poland. Whereas the Polish *Szlachta* oppressed its middle classes and restricted their commerce by a thousand trammels, Russia possessed fairs and markets of great national importance.[40] The backwardness and immobility of economic life was in no small measure responsible for the disintegration of the Polish state. But in Russia the administrative reforms of Peter the Great had given the autocratic caesarism of the tsar a new momentum. Having once shifted the center of gravity of the Russian empire to the Baltic coast, Peter proceeded to develop the vast economic resources of the Russian plain by the systematic application of the maxims of western mercantilism and by a vigorous promotion of foreign trade, particularly with England. Capitalism and the modern state, correlative phenomena in western Europe, made their simultaneous appearance in Russia also. The magnificent possibilities of capitalist enterprise, opened up by the expanded needs of the new army, the new administrative apparatus and public finance, had a stimulating effect on many aspects of Russian economic life.[41] New industries with western technique planted some of the most valuable seeds of occidental culture in this alien Russian soil. Everywhere the state established textile, metal and munition industries and then proceeded to turn them over to the management of private individuals. These industries, whether owned by bourgeois merchants or noblemen, worked mainly for the state, the army and navy being the principal consumers of iron, cloth and cordage. It was quite in keeping with the traditions of the Muscovite state that these industries were operated with unpaid, forced or servile labor. Compared with similar establishments in the west the Russian factories were large-scale enterprises. Some factories already employed a thousand workmen and occupied a not unimportant position in the economic life of western Europe. Indeed, the iron industry of the Ural area was the largest in the world. Russia remained overwhelmingly agricultural and feudal, yet this early and partial industrialization not

40 D. Gerhard, *England und der Aufstieg Russlands* (Berlin, 1933), 278; J. Rutkowski, *Histoire économique de la Pologne avant les partages* (Paris, 1927), 196.
41 J. Kulischer, "Die Kapitalistischen Unternehmer in Russland in den Anfangsstadien des Kapitalismus," *Archiv für Sozialwissenschaft und Sozialpolitik*, 65 (1931), 309; by the same author, *Russische Wirtschaftsgeschichte* (Jena, 1925), I, 387; Tugan-Baranowsky, *Geschichte der Russischen Fabrik* (German trans.), Berlin, 1900.

merely increased the taxpaying capacity of the Russian people but constituted the material foundation for the growing military influence of Russia in the affairs of western Europe.

This brief sketch of the social evolution of Russia may serve to explain the partial failure of Peter the Great's administrative reforms. If we accept the interpretation placed on these reforms by the Russian historian Kluchevsky, Peter sought to effect a double amalgam: first, between the old Muscovite system of the servitor class, the *dvoriané*, which resembled both a bureaucracy and a feudal aristocracy, and the western bureaucratic system borrowed from Sweden; second, between this *dvorianin* class and the class of superior urban merchants, the social groups which held concentrated in their hands the country's landed wealth and industry, the two fundamental forms of capital lying at the base of Russian national economy.[42] But this attempted amalgam proved unsuccessful. Peter expected better bread than could be made of wheat. To staff his new institutions he needed a body of trained and disciplined officials such as was not to be found in Russia. Contrary to Peter's expectations, native Russian institutions assimilated those that were introduced from the west, not vice versa. There were detailed instructions and bureaucratic regulations for governing bodies and individual officials, but their significance was largely academic. More important still was the fact that Peter's ideal of a bureaucratic civil service was ruined by his immediate successors. When Elizabeth set about emancipating nobles from the obligation of service, she deprived them of their bureaucratic character and transformed them into a class that was patrimonial, pure and simple. Their patrimonial conception of office was incompatible with the principle of rigorous bureaucratic accountability. Somehow the machine worked, but with such a dislocation of its parts, such a dispersion of human effort as would appall a western statesman. Again, the new patrimonial aristocrats had no further use for their bourgeois partners, whom they relegated to their former political insignificance. Thus the most autocratic empire in the world, which could dispose of persons and property in the manner of an Asiatic despotism, had, in spite of its European façade, capitulated to the nobles, to whom,

[42] V. O. Kluchevsky, *A History of Russia* (1926), IV, 199.

in the meantime, it had also surrendered the peasants. In other words, that class which Peter the Great had used as an instrument of government now employed the tsar and his government as the instruments of their interests. Yet they never attained nor, for that matter, needed to attain a position comparable to that of the Polish *Szlachta*.

Although her reign was not devoid of a certain luster, Empress Elizabeth contributed very little to it. The enormous vitality which she inherited from her great father she spent in seeking the distractions of a private life rather than in the service of Russia. Incredibly ignorant, she persisted till her death in the belief that England could be reached by land. She had neither capacity nor taste for public affairs. She allowed important diplomatic documents to go unsigned for weeks. Months might elapse before she granted her ministers an audience. Though she kept a jealous watch over her autocracy, she turned the burden of actual government over to an ill-defined group of "supreme lords," among whom Peter and Ivan Shuvalov stood out above all others. Peter Shuvalov, at least, merits the title of a major economic reformer for his courageous removal of internal customs frontiers in 1754; the resulting activity of internal trade increased the volume of exports through the Baltic ports, which enabled him to raise the tariff and thus increase public revenues. For the rest, the "supreme lords" ruled the country with little formality and less responsibility, increasing their fortunes by more or less open peculation.

What distinguishes the central administrative mechanism of Elizabeth from that of her predecessors was the fact that both the "supreme lords" and the presidents of the collegia now sat in the senate, thus making that body once more the supreme authority for all the internal, financial and economic affairs of the empire. At the zenith of its power under Elizabeth, the senate now began to issue laws in its own right. Subject to its authority were the collegia or *bureaux* (for commerce, finance, audit, mines, manufacture, justice and the chief pay office), which corresponded to ministerial departments in the countries of western Europe. The principle of collective responsibility, which Peter the Great had prescribed for these collegia as a guaranty against corruption and ignorance, had meanwhile become an empty form. The "supreme lords" had made themselves the absolute masters of these collegia, appointing their own plebeian clerks to do the work. Between the chief administrators and the clerks there was a social gulf almost as great as between the lord and his serf. Uneducated, unrespected, underpaid, forced by circumstances to live on bribes, this army of the *podiachie* was a universal pest. The fact that the collegia for foreign affairs, the army and the admiralty enjoyed a certain pre-eminence over the others and over the senate created no little confusion. This lack of co-ordination in the agencies of the central government was only partially remedied when in March, 1756 Elizabeth united all the superior functionaries connected with the army and foreign affairs into a special council and gave it a certain superior authority over the senate.

As soon as we descend the ladder of the administrative hierarchy to the governors of the twelve immense regional *gubernii* and their councils, staffed with the *Landräte* who were elected by the local nobility, and then to the *voevodi* of the provinces, who after 1761 were also elected by the local nobility, and finally to the dense ranks of local manorial lords, we breathe an atmosphere that grows progressively less bureaucratic and more thoroughly feudal and patrimonial. It is true, the *voevodi* and the *Landräte* were subordinated to their governors, and these governors in turn to the senate, but in reality the governors, who, like the leading personalities in St. Petersburg, belonged to the "supreme lords," tended to take a self-interested view of their authority and govern with the independence of autonomous rulers who could defy the central authorities.

There was, of course, that dreaded system of the *Fiscale*, familiar to us from Prussia, which in Russia became an instrument of senatorial supervision.[43] The *Ober-Fiscal* and his corps of five hundred subordinate *Fiscale*, whom we find in all the collegia, the councils of the governors and among the cities and *voevodi*, were authentically bureaucratic officials. As in Prussia, the Russian *Fiscal* combined the functions of the public prosecutor with those of the secret investigator; his principal duty was to keep an eye on public funds,

43 M. N. Pokrovsky, *History of Russia from Earliest Times to the Rise of Commercial Capitalism* (1931), 298.

report every irregularity and hale the guilty peculators before the senate "no matter how eminent they were." These senatorial *Fiscale* were part of an elaborate system which encouraged delation by informers who were entitled to a fourth of the property of the officials against whom they reported. In some cases informers were given the right to the estates, rank and office of their victims. However demoralizing such a system of organized espionage may appear to have been, it proved to be a singularly ineffective device to suppress corruption. Confronted with the unbroken array of patrimonial officials from the senate down to the *voevoda*, the despised bourgeois *Fiscale* were utterly powerless. Government brigandage was universal, provoking incessant complaints but never any effective repression.[44] Perhaps the most eloquent description of Russian administration is to be found in the ukase, issued by Empress Elizabeth on August 16, 1760. It was not a law, it was a diatribe. Here Elizabeth denounced the general contempt for the law among those whose duty it was to enforce it, the disorder and chaos in all branches of administration, the tribunals converted into markets, the negligence and greed of judges who denied justice, the systematic pilfering of public funds in the state monopolies, in the recruiting centers and in the collection of taxes.

Two simple facts may serve to summarize the upshot of this regime. The first is that scarcely one third of the income collected ever reached the central treasury. The second is that Prussia under Frederick the Great produced a larger total in public revenues than Russia on the accession of Catherine II in 1762.[45]

VII. ENGLAND

Montesquieu, publishing his *Spirit of Laws* in 1748, held up the English constitution as the most perfect instrument of government in Europe. It is not improbable that, had he made a more penetrating study of the realities of English constitutional practice instead of taking his ideas from the pages of John Locke, he would have admired it less. As it was, he thought he had discovered in England what was utterly lacking on the Continent, the separation

44 K. Waliszewski, *La dernière des Romanov: Elisabeth Ière* (1900), 161.
45 G. Schmoller, "Historische Betrachtungen über Staatenbildung und Finanzentwicklung," *Jahrbücher für Gesetzgebung und Verwaltung*, XXXIII (1909), 2.

of powers, and by focusing the attention of Europe on England he was responsible for creating that legend which, as it gathered in volume, had a potent influence in remodeling the constitutional systems of Europe within the following century. However erroneous the legend, Montesquieu was right in drawing a sharp contrast between England and the administrative Leviathan state of the Continent.

Mid-century travelers from the mainland generally regarded England as the home of ordered liberty, the land of individual freedom in speech, press and person. Even Frederick the Great spoke of the breath of freedom that reached the very foot of the British throne and referred to England as a country where kings were free to do good but could do no harm.[46] Most conspicuous of all was the absence in England of that centralized bureaucratic officialism which elsewhere made every policeman and tax collector look upon himself as the incarnation of the state. The English government staff was of the most rudimentary sort, and much had to be done by parliamentary statute that elsewhere was a matter of administrative routine. In this compact island, bounded by the inviolable sea, administration itself was a very simple thing compared with what it was in France or Prussia. This was in large measure due to England's insular position and her freedom from frontier problems. Here *raison d'état*, at bottom only another phrase for the problem of frontiers, required no executive equipped with extraordinary powers.[47] While everywhere on the Continent emphasis had shifted from the law courts to the administrative bureaus, the English state had taken a form which gave power to judges rather than to officials, which guaranteed civil rights rather than the authority of the state. On the Continent different layers and regions of separate jurisdictions still continued to bar the way to complete state unity, while England constituted a single jurisdiction in which the common law was a law for all, for the soldier and the official no less than for the citizen, for the noble as much as for the commoner. This law, it is true, was neither rational nor humane, and in some respects it was inferior to that of continental countries, but parlia-

[46] *Oeuvres de Frédéric le Grand*, XII, 195.
[47] Ernest Barker, *National Character and the Factors in Its Formation* (1927), 142.

ment sought to bring it into harmony with its interests by constant legislation. It was a cardinal feature of this system of common law that English judges, irremovable since the Bill of Rights, were vested with the power to interpret the entire law and to enforce it in all cases and upon all persons. It was this "rule of law" that preserved Englishmen from the rigors of the continental police-state. A separate body of administrative law, administered by separate administrative courts such as France and Prussia possessed, did not exist in England. If Louis XV still made extensive use of the *lettre de cachet*, freedom from such arbitrary arrest was assured in England by the writ of habeas corpus.

But if there was no administrative absolutism in England under George II, there was an oligarchy of the landed nobility as complete as that of any country on the Continent. It was the Augustan age of the English squirearchy, which was entrenched at every focal point in the British constitutional system. This system was based on the ownership of land and on the land rents; the close connection between the ownership of land and participation in public affairs was one of the axioms of British politics. The apparent harmony of English public life, the conspicuous smoothness with which all the wheels of government ran, the complete absence of social reform, were due to the circumstance that cabinet and parliament, local government in town and county, the control and supervision even over the parishes, the entire machinery of the constitution was controlled and directed by one and the same class in one and the same interest. In the counties landed proprietors supplied the justices of the peace. In the boroughs the select bodies had come under the influence of the noble patrons on whom they lived. Parliament itself had become a close corporation of landed and rich men, and if many of them were commoners, they were the nominees of men still richer than themselves. A few great "Revolution families," the Russels, the Cavendishes, and the Pelhams, had succeeded in adding to the influence which they already possessed as borough proprietors and great landowners the enormous resources of royal patronage, thus making the crown their accomplice rather than their competitor.

Nowhere was there a rival power in sight to challenge their supremacy. The genteel British custom which made the holding of public office non-remunerative was sufficient to exclude the lower classes from politics. The liberal professions were a monopoly of the wealthy or their friends and no opposition was to be expected from this quarter. The chartered corporations of English public life, the Established Church and the universities, had become an integral feature of the squirearchy. Education was the nursery not of society but of an order, not of the state but of the ruling classes. Since all universities and most of the higher schools stood under the control of the Established Church, clerics, physicians, jurists had to be Anglican, which is equivalent to saying that they came from the ruling classes or enjoyed their patronage.

But so mild and tolerant was this oligarchy that in these years it was scarcely felt to be an oligarchy at all. Selection and assimilation, not exclusion, were the means by which the British landowning aristocracy maintained its monopoly of power. The very fact that the parliamentary franchise was attached to the ownership of land had the effect of forcing the ambitious merchant into the landlord class. Once the owner of an estate, he too was enveloped in a land-lord atmosphere. Once the gifted son of an artisan subscribed to the Thirty-Nine Articles, the universities did not exclude him, and from the university he might ascend to the highest positions in the king-dom. Again, though it is true enough that the great prelates of the church owed their positions to their noble birth, divines of humble extraction could and did rise to the highest ecclesiastical offices. Above all, the Latitudinarian beliefs of this Established Church were so generous as to tend to obliterate the differences alike in creed and ecclesiastical polity which divided the sectarian churches of England.[48] It is well to remember, that in these years of the growing influence of the Methodism of John Wesley there was no persecution of Dissenters. Thus while in France men of letters were engaged in an intellectual rebellion against state and society, the England that read Hume, admired Reynolds, or listened to Dr. Johnson was immensely satisfied with itself.

The first half of the eighteenth century is commonly regarded as a decisive epoch in the development of the English system of cabi-

---

[48] N. Sykes, *The English Church in the Eighteenth Century* (1936); by the same au-thor, the article on "The Church" in A. S. Turberville's *Johnson's England* (1933), I, 16.

net and parliamentary government. At first glance all the essential factors of this modern English system appear to have been present in the government of George II: the limited monarchy; the cabinet as the core of the system, the supreme directing authority, integrating a heterogeneous collection of ministers and secretaries of state and providing unity to the entire system; the two-party system of Whigs and Tories, based on the voting electorate, which, though not fully representative, was not entirely unrepresentative; the parliament representing this electorate and exercising the sole power of legislation and control over finance, army, foreign and domestic policy. That some of these factors were actually present and operative is indubitable. By encroaching steadily on the power of the crown and transferring that power into the hands of the cabinet, the Whig oligarchy increased the authority of both the cabinet and the parliament over the policy of the country. In the first half of the century power had passed from the privy council, which was independent of parliament, to a committee of ministers and officers of state, the cabinet, "responsible" to parliament, whose authority ultimately rested on the house of commons.[49] The presence of ministers, nominally the king's servants, in both houses of parliament, which had been still resented early in the century, had become securely established and completed their "responsibility." There was still to be evolved in its final form the corporate responsibility of the cabinet as a whole. Ministers could still oppose each other in parliament, speak and vote on opposite sides. The greater initiative which parliament had meanwhile acquired reduced the role of the crown in legislation to simple assent or dissent. Even in this matter, however, the cabinet already knew the king's constitutional mind better than the king did himself.

Although on the surface this may look like parliamentary government, there were certain inherent weaknesses in the system, for the other factors of parliamentary government had not kept pace with the development of the cabinet. There was still no conception of party government independent of the king and, therefore, none of a constitutional parliamentary opposition. But there is a more

49 R. Lucas, *George II and His Ministers*, p. 11; H. W. V. Temperley, "Inner and Outer Cabinet and Privy Council," *Eng. Hist. Rev.*, 27, 683; E. H. Turner, *The Cabinet Council of England* (1932), Vol. II.

important objection to calling the system as it worked in 1750 parliamentary government. To characterize a system by which the cabinet produced its own parliamentary majorities as one of ministerial responsibility is surely a misuse of terms. In actual practice the system, as Mr. Namier puts it, was neither the old royal government nor parliamentary government as we know it, but one which combined the disadvantages of both.[50]

The truth is that the English kingship had not lost its meaning, nor technically its powers. The constitutional limitations placed on the power of the crown by the Bill of Rights and the Act of Settlement were very slight indeed. It is true that the personality of George II had next to no political importance. He was indifferent toward England and his attitude may be summarized in the following statement: "I am sick to death of all this foolish stuff, and wish with all my heart that the devil may take all your Bishops, and the devil take your Ministers, and the devil take the Parliament, and the devil take the whole island, provided I can get out of it and go to Hanover."[51] But he was indispensable. It was still his prerogative to choose his own ministers freely. These ministers were still ministers of the crown and their power was the crown's power, not that of parliament, even in these years of undisputed Whig ascendancy.[52] This right to choose his ministers was, of course, restricted by the practical necessity of gaining the support of the house of commons. George II stubbornly selected his ministers from the leaders of the Whig party alone, who had placed his dynasty on the throne and defended it against Jacobites. Thus arose his complete dependence upon a single set of politicians, who forced him to part with Walpole and then with Carteret, the two great humiliations of his life, and finally even to admit Pitt into his counsels. These events are sometimes cited as constitutional precedents, but, as Mr. Namier suggests, they were accidents rather than necessary consequences of constitutional ideas. George III could act with greater freedom than his predecessor at the moment when he decided to break the chains which bound him to a single party and to assume personal control

[50] L. B. Namier, *England in the Age of the American Revolution* (1930), 66.
[51] E. Charteris, *William Augustus, The Duke of Cumberland* (London, 1914), 47.
[52] R. H. Gretton, *The King's Majesty, a Study in the Historical Philosophy of Modern Kingship* (London, 1930), 119.

of royal patronage, which George II had yielded up to the leaders of the Whig party. By doing so George III was to prove that the English kingship still had a very effective meaning.

A rapid glance at the composition of parliament in these middle decades leads to the same conclusion. The successive ministries of George II, which chose and bought the majorities in parliament without which they could not govern, can scarcely be said to have regarded that body as an alternate sovereign. Under the Duke of Newcastle co-operation with parliament had become a mere matter of manipulation. The large and constant government majorities in the house of commons were the crowning achievement of this great master of patronage. With all his personal connections added to the vast patronage of the crown in the army, church, civil service and the government boroughs, Newcastle acquired an all but complete control of the house of commons. There still remained some few members of that body who, like Colonel Barré, regarded the presence of ministers in the house as a skillful means of enslaving the house of commons. In fact, ministers sat there to see that their majority, built up by patronage and influence, did what it was expected to do. They saw in it a means, not of controlling the crown, but of controlling parliament. Pitt might complain that the house of commons tended "to degenerate into a little assembly serving no other purpose than to register the edicts of one too powerful subject."[53] But Pitt himself was to discover in the autumn of 1756 that, however strong might be the support which he had in the nation at large, he could not pursue his policy without Newcastle's majority.

When George III ascended the throne in 1760 he merely needed to continue the system devised by Walpole and the Pelhams with this difference, that the government party was now called Tory instead of Whig. His task was greatly facilitated by the fact that he did not have to deal with the organized and disciplined parties of later times.[54] There is a certain unreality about party names in the middle of the century and the parties, such as they were, did not function as parties normally do in a system of parliamentary government. So long as the Whigs held virtual monopoly of office every

53 B. Williams, *The Life of William Pitt, Earl of Chatham* (1914), I, 256.
54 G. M. Trevelyan, *The Two-Party System in English Political History* (Oxford, 1926), 19; W. E. Lecky, *History of England in the Eighteenth Century* (1883), II, 505; L. B. Namier, *England in the Age of the American Revolution* (1930), 128, 217.

ambitious or interested politician called himself a Whig. Thus the Whigs became in reality a court party, "because they did not consider the king's interference in the least unconstitutional when it worked in their favor." The only cement that bound the members of the Whig party together were the places and profits dispensed by Newcastle. There was an all but complete absence of party principle. Tories were simply those who never asked for favors, kept away from court or refused to attend the levees of Newcastle. There was no Tory program and no Tory party organization. What survived of the old Toryism in this period retreated to the manor houses and cathedral cloisters. All that one can discover of it is in literature—in Squire Western, who represents the old fashioned squirearchy, and in Dr. Johnson, who represents the church, the two pillars of the Tory edifice that was deluged by the tidal wave of Whig ascendancy which ended in 1760.

In the eyes of the British governing class the government of England began and ended with the king and parliament and with the official dignitaries of the county, among whom the justices of the peace were the most important. London, of course, was wholly exempt from county control, and the cities and boroughs had franchises which exempted them from county jurisdiction. On the other hand, the officers of the parish, the constable, the overseers of the poor, the surveyors of highways, were subject to the orders of the justices of the peace. It is one of the curious facts of this British system that neither ministries nor parliaments exhibited the slightest concern for the structure of the local government of the kingdom. The Rebellion had broken the bond between the justice of the peace and the monarch, whose officer he originally was, and the squires saw to it that central supervision and control were not restored. The Webbs and Redlich and Hirst have described the incompetence and corruption, the misery and waste suffered by the people of the parishes and towns of England, because there was no central officer to supervise and control the behavior of the select bodies and the justices of the peace.[55] The system of local autonomy had, no doubt,

[55] Sidney and Beatrice Webb, *English Local Government from the Revolution to the Municipal Corporations Act* (1906), Vol. I; J. Redlich and F. Hirst, *The Local Government of England* (1903), Vol. I; John and Barbara Hammond, *The Village Laborer* (1920); G. Slater, *The Growth of Modern England* (1933), 29

certain distinct advantages. It fostered a sturdy self-reliant governing class and taught the arts of self-government at least to the squire-archy. But it is an exaggerated idealization to see in this system, as Gneist did, the matrix of modern democratic self-government.

The laws made by parliament were carried out not by the pro-fessional agents of the central authority but by those picturesque officials, the justices of the peace, who were co-opted from the landed proprietors of the county. They were a remarkably homo-geneous group, whose fathers and grandfathers had held both their estates and the commission of the peace before them. As members of the county oligarchy they were nearly all men of high standing and personal honor, though often narrow in opinion and prejudice. Unpaid and non-professional, though scarcely disinterested, they may be regarded as typical of the society that preceded the age of modern industrialism. No qualifications of literacy or study were required. Common sense was their guide and what little legal knowledge they possessed they acquired from the justice's manual. The necessary accommodation between governor and governed, in which public opinion played a not unimportant role, produced an occasional administration that was at once successful and liberal. Like other similar semi-feudal officials of the Continent they com-bined judicial and administrative functions. In some cases they could administer the law individually, in others the law required the co-operation of their fellow justices. The most important of these joint sessions, the court of the quarter sessions, was the ultimate judicial and administrative authority of county and parish affairs.

Originally this court received "presentments," or complaints, from numerous juries, each one of which represented some area of public opinion. The grand juries "presented" such matters as rates and wages, bridges, highways or prisons in need of repairs. But by 1750 most of these democratic methods had been abandoned. "Present-ment" by justices had supplanted "presentments" by juries and the administrative business of quarter sessions was no longer discussed in open court. More important still was the delegation of a large part of the county business from quarter sessions to petty sessions or even to single justices out of sessions. Statute after statute en-dowed the justice with the widest discretionary power of arrest and commitment. In this way the single justice could administer the draconic code for punishment of vagrants and poachers without a jury and without publicity. But the powers of the justices went even beyond this. They became, as the Webbs have pointed out, an advisory body for the legislature, for parliament generally regarded the opinion of the justices as conclusive on matters of social legislation. Thus this non-elected authority of the justices of the peace virtually controlled the decisions of parliament itself. It is not unnatural that such extensive powers, uncontrolled from above or by publicity, should produce some of the ugly features which the satirical novels of Fielding and Smollett have introduced into their portraits of justices of the peace. Richardson, who cannot be accused of harboring any animus against the justices in his *Pamela*, merely records the fact that Mr. B. was a magistrate for two counties and that, therefore, it was hopeless for Pamela, whom he wished to seduce, to elude his pursuit. But even these contemporary satirical novels introduce us to a better type of justice, found among the simple country gentlemen, who combined integrity and kindliness with largeness of view and devotion to the interests of their counties.

There is a curious irony in the circumstance that while the system of the justices of the peace enabled England to rid herself of feudalism an entire century earlier than the states of the mainland, this same system gave back to English landlords in another form the power they had lost when feudalism vanished.

Chapter Three

EIGHTEENTH-CENTURY MILITARISM

I. ARMIES

MILITARY students of the nineteenth century, nourished on the theory of Napoleon and Clausewitz, have generally shown little respect for eighteenth-century warfare. They have accused eighteenth-century generals of fencing instead of fighting, of artfully maneuvering instead of seeking decision by battle. They have derided their pedantic regard for petrified military rules and conventions. The charge is not altogether unjust. The art of warfare had become mechanical, precise and rational. Operations were confined to little more than half of the calendar year; a victory was seldom pushed to the complete destruction of the beaten force; and demoralized armies could restore their discipline and renew their equipment in the security of winter quarters. Defense predominated over offense. Except for the campaigns of Marshal de Saxe and of Frederick the Great, battles were rare and campaigns indecisive. But nineteenth-century critics have misunderstood the cause for this system of strategy.[1] It will not do simply to point to the reduced mobility of eighteenth-century armies which, because of the absence of metaled roads, could march only at a lumbering pace, or to the great importance attached to fortresses, which was, after all, only the reflex side of the difficulties of transport. An explanation must be sought rather in the social composition and military structure of the armies themselves, in the narrowly political purpose of warfare, and in the social and economic milieu in which wars were fought.

The social structure of eighteenth-century militarism was as far removed from that of medieval feudal society, when to be a soldier was the privilege of a nobleman, as from the extreme militarism of modern European dictatorships, in which every citizen is a potential

1 Captain Liddell Hart, *The Ghost of Napoleon* (New Haven, 1934). The author has done much in this useful booklet to correct this error, yet he, too, falls short of an adequate explanation.

soldier. What was significant in the militarism of the continental monarchies of the eighteenth century was the fact that, corresponding to social stratification, a sharp distinction was drawn between the military and non-military elements of society. So long as legally unequal social classes were superimposed one upon the other, it was utterly impracticable to exact the obligation of military service from all citizens alike. Again, since mercantilist statesmen were everywhere concerned with raising agricultural and industrial production to a maximum level, their problem was to create a strong army without making excessive inroads on the productive elements of society. Because of the undeveloped state of industrial technique, the number of skilled artisans was everywhere insufficient to meet the demands of an expanding economy. So long as economy needed to be strengthened by all the means of governmental planning, it would have been absurd to import skilled workers from abroad at great expense and upon their arrival force them into the army. Statesmen, therefore, had to make the effort to recruit their armies so far as possible from among those elements which stood outside the productive organization of society, to take their officers from the nobility who stood above it and their soldiers from the unemployed, vagabonds and beggars who stood below it. The middle classes, as a unit, did not participate in military action. Their prime function within the framework of the mercantilist state was to pay taxes. For the rest they were left relatively unmolested. The armies of the old regime, therefore, were composed as much as possible of the economically unproductive elements of society. This social structure of armies corresponded to the prevalent political system. The coalition wars of the middle of the century were wars between governments, not national wars such as have become familiar since the French Revolution. It was scarcely from want of imagination that statesmen failed to unchain the forces of sentiment and enlist the active participation of the masses. Such mass participation presupposed an entirely different social system no less than political objectives far different from those which the War of the Austrian Succession could provide.[2]

[2] H. Speier, "Militarism in the Eighteenth Century," *Social Research*, III (1936), 304.

This solicitude to exclude the mass of the population from military activity was reflected also in the actual conduct of war in the eighteenth century. If it can be said of any time in modern history that war resembled a gladiatorial combat witnessed by crowds seated in safety around a blood-stained arena, this can be said of the eighteenth century. Never, before or since, save perhaps in Renaissance Italy, was the civilian population more secure against wanton devastation, atrocities and the systematic plunder of requisition warfare. This was due less to the humanitarianism of the age than to elementary economic and military necessities. The greater numerical strength of armies, together with the means of recruiting them, had introduced into the ranks unreliable elements which could be kept with the colors only by the most rigorous discipline and supervision. To have permitted these armies to forage freely over the countryside for supplies would have encouraged wholesale desertion. Moreover, the wars of the seventeenth century had amply demonstrated that such systematic fleecing of civilian populations was wasteful and uneconomical.

It was, therefore, concern for effective discipline in the army as well as for the greater economic security of non-combatants that induced all military powers to establish a system of state magazines, from which in time of war troops could be regularly and adequately supplied, and which in time of peace might be used for regulating the price of grain. Before the opening of a campaign great stores were collected at certain points near the frontier and from there supplies were taken to the armies in the field. Two or three days' march from the magazine a number of ovens were built, and flour was brought to them by mule train. Each man could carry rations for four or six days. But there was a limit beyond which the army could not be supplied from the magazine. No army could safely advance beyond five days' march from its base of supplies. While this system reduced, if it did not completely abolish, the right of private plunder, armies were fettered to a chain of magazines which seriously reduced their mobility. But the civilian population had gained greater security. Frederick the Great remarked in his *Political Testament* that when he was engaged in war the civilian population should not be aware that a state of war existed. The order and stability of the bureaucratized monarchy and the disciplined and conventionalized warfare of professional armies flattered contemporaries into believing that they had attained a degree of humanity and moral sensibility that marked them off from all other epochs of history. Warfare was still destructive, but misery and death paraded, as it were, in the fancy costume of Rococo.

All armies, with the single exception of the Russian army, lacked homogeneity; that is to say, they represented an amalgam of national and foreign elements. Voluntary enrolments no longer produced the necessary numbers. Russia, Prussia and France had already introduced some form of conscription, and Austria and Spain were to do so after the Seven Years' War. But even in countries where conscript levies became a permanent institution it was only certain peasant and artisan groups who were drafted into the service. It was a common assumption that no army could dispense with foreign mercenaries. Their proportion varied from one-fourth to two-thirds of the entire army. Many of these had been kidnaped, forcibly dragged from taverns, swept up from the streets or released from the prisons. It was the pinch of poverty, however, that drove the great mass of mercenary soldiers into enlistment. No apprentice who received a decent wage exchanged his lot willingly for that of the soldier. The soldier's pay fluctuated with the supply and the supply was greatest in the most retrograde and indigent regions of Europe and correspondingly scarce in countries where industry and commerce absorbed the mass of the population. Everywhere, therefore, soldiers represented the dregs of society. It is not surprising, then, that the social attitude toward the soldier was one of universal contempt. In France as elsewhere a military career for anyone but a nobleman was considered degrading. In no country was the common soldier a national hero. The fighting quality of the human material thus assembled was something less than mediocre. It will explain the savage discipline and inhuman punishments characteristic of all armies of the old regime. The greater the proportion of mercenaries in an army, the more brutal was the discipline. Yet there were certain national differences. In Catholic countries discipline was less harsh but also less efficient than in Prussia. In France and Austria, where noblemen moved in the society of the court, the socially accepted behavior of an officer was that of the *honnête homme* who abhorred personal brutality.

There is no need to point out here that in all armies the upper ranks of the officers corps were invariably reserved for men of aristocratic origin. What requires emphasis is that, corresponding to the social progress of the European bourgeoisie, the number of middle-class officers was everywhere on the increase. In countries where military offices were sold it was impossible to keep the middle classes out of these positions. They varied in number from country to country; the percentage was considerable in France and Austria and almost negligible in Prussia. Strange as it may seem, this advance of the middle classes into the officers corps was not accompanied by any structural change in the army nor by any marked improvement in the professional capacity of the officer. For the moment at least quite the contrary was true. The Spanish army, in which bourgeois officers were already in the majority, was still the army it was at the time of the Thirty Years' War.[3]

As a comparative study of the principal armies of Europe will indicate, there were several types of military organization. Most of them corresponded to the older type represented by the French army. That the Prussian army exemplified a newer type is equally certain. There was nothing conspicuously unique about the Austrian army; in its composition and command it did not differ materially from the French army.[4] Only the Russian army was wholly national in character. It was levied by a system of conscription by which the burden fell upon the landed proprietors, who supplied one man for a stated number of serfs on their estates.[5] For the rest, it marked no departure from the armies of western Europe. It is really only the French and Prussian armies that require closer scrutiny.

3 G. Desdevises du Dezert, "Les institutions de l'Espagne au XVIII siècle," *Revue Hispanique*, LXX (1927), 365.

4 The fighting effectives of the principal belligerents in 1740 stood approximately as follows: France 190,000; Austria 108,000; Spain 67,000; Prussia 80,000; Russia 130,000; Bavaria 40,000; Saxony 34,000; Holland 30,000; Hanover 20,000; England 18,000. *Der Oesterreichische Erbfolgekrieg, bearbeitet von der kriegsgeschichtlichen Abteilung des Kriegsarchivs* (1896), I, 297; E. Guglia, *Maria Theresia* (1917), I, 48.

5 K. Waliszewski, *La dernière des Romanov, Elisabeth I* (Paris, 1902), 195.

II. THE FRENCH ARMY

At the beginning of the century, under Louis XIV, the French army was by common consent the most perfect military instrument in Europe. It was to have a still more brilliant career under Napoleon at the end of the century. All the more conspicuous was its unqualified mediocrity under Louis XV. It lacked cohesion and discipline. There was a general relaxation of the military spirit among its officers, and its commanders were for the most part incompetent. During the War of the Austrian Succession it acquitted itself well enough under the brilliant generalship of Marshal de Saxe. But Saxe had no following. It was no less than a disaster that France in the Seven Years' War, in spite of her numerical superiority, could gain no decisive victory over three diminutive German states, Hanover, Brunswick and Hesse, supported by a few Prussians and Englishmen.

There were many reasons for this decline: inadequate financial resources, a bitter class struggle between bourgeois and noble officers, excessive veneration for the traditions of the past, the indifference and neglect of Cardinal Fleury and later of the king, the control of the army by bureaucratic *gens de plume*, who opposed every innovation.[6] It was the old army of Louis XIV in a state of decay. But meanwhile a new military power had come forward and the conditions of war had changed. The Prussian army was a far more formidable opponent than the armies of Austria, the traditional enemy of France, had ever been. The severer methods of Frederick the Great demanded better instruction, greater mobility, greater endurance; they demanded that an army should seek out its enemy, harry him, strike him, defeat him in any season and on any terrain. To do this an army must learn to maneuver, to use each arm of the service at the right time and in the appropriate place, and to depend upon the initiative and sagacity of its subalterns. But all this was unknown in the French army of 1740. What made matters worse was that French generals were bound to the court in a way that frequently paralyzed initiative. They were

6 Col. F. Reboul in Hanotaux, *Histoire de la nation française, Histoire militaire et navale*, VII (Paris, 1925), 488.

compelled to make regular journeys to Versailles, contend with the intrigues of their detractors and suffer frequent intervention at the hand of the king in distant operations which he scarcely understood. Only the driving personality of a soldier of genius like Marshal de Saxe could brush aside the entire military hierarchy and sweep along the king, the court, the ministers and the army administration and make himself master of military operations. The French army was no longer adapted to the necessities of warfare against a formidable foe. The tardy reforms of Belle Isle at the end of the Seven Years' War came too late to make a difference. Except for the brief spell under Saxe the French army was unpopular, and after Rossbach this public disfavor hardened into contempt.

The French army was most wanting at the point where the Prussian army placed its strongest emphasis, in its officers corps. It suffered from a plethora of commanding officers.[7] In the lower ranks there was the same superabundance of officers. While in the Prussian army there was an average of one officer to thirty-seven men, in the French army the proportion was one for every fifteen men.[8] After the War of the Austrian Succession there were actually more noble officers than posts to which they might be appointed. Nobles were no longer created for commissions, but commissions for the nobility. This inflation of offices played havoc with discipline and was destructive of competent military leadership. The generals and colonels who lived in luxury at Paris or Versailles appeared only as rare meteors on the horizon of their regiments. They did not know their troops and their troops lacked confidence in commanders whom they saw only in camps and on the battlefield. The incredible number of officers with their staffs, their elaborate baggage and servants, who frequently became entangled with marching columns, reduced the mobility of the army in the field. The quartermaster-general had often to mobilize the resources of an entire city to provide for them. Actual service occupied only a small proportion of the officers. To create opportunities for all of them, one struck upon the expedient of rotating the command.

7 A. Dussauge, *Études sur la guerre de sept ans, Le ministère de Belle Isle* (Paris, 1914), 264.
8 In modern armies there is usually one officer to fifty men. Susane, *Histoire de l'infanterie*, I, 278; H. Delbrueck, *Geschichte der Kriegskunst* (Berlin, 1920), IV, 268.

Lieutenant-generals and marshals commanded "de jour," just for the day. The commands of the line and the flanks were passed on from one officer to another from one day to the next. That such a practice must destroy cohesion and undermine authority requires no further demonstration.

But this was scarcely the worst of evils. The general practice of purchasing military offices had the consequence of introducing into the army the class struggle between the nobility and the bourgeoisie that was rapidly assuming an acute form throughout the nation. The growth of speculative capitalism in French society and the financial needs of the government had transformed public administration into a banking house that was subject to all the fluctuations of the stock exchange. It will be recalled that the French government administered few affairs directly; judicial offices and the collection of taxes were farmed out to those who had the money to purchase the contracts. The army also had come under the influence of this system. Companies and regiments had been sold before, but in the preceding reigns the state confined these transactions to the nobility. The wave of speculation under Law had not reduced the prices for military offices. The army had increased in size, but the impoverished lower nobility could less than ever afford to purchase captaincies and colonelcies, when the price of a company stood at eight to ten thousand livres. The government, therefore, ignoring the protests of the nobility, opened army offices to the sons of wealthy merchants. By the middle of the century almost a third of the infantry officers were men of middle-class origin.[9] We find them chiefly in the lower ranks, for commissions from colonel upward were in the possession of companions and favorites of the king, of those who traveled in *carrosses* or had been "presented" at court. These offices were awarded without fixed rule and no other qualification was required beyond that of noble birth. In 1750 a royal edict created a military nobility which enabled the *roturier* to become noble by the simple purchase of a commission.

The older noble officers, for whom the officers corps was more a gentlemen's club than a closely integrated group of warriors, re-

[9] L. Tuetey, *Les officiers sous l'ancien régime, nobles et roturiers* (Paris, 1908); Dussauge, *Le ministère de Belle Isle*, 263.

garded these bourgeois intruders with unconcealed hostility. The
jealousy and quarrels between these two elements were fatal to
discipline, subordination and cohesion. Repeated legislative efforts
to efface the distinction between noble and bourgeois officers were
fruitless. The social cleavage remained.[10] More serious, however,
was the fact that it was not merit but birth and money that determined appointments to military positions.[11] Inexperienced titled
mediocrities without solid military education were present in alarming number and even the juvenile colonel of fourteen or sixteen
years—the *colonel à la bavette*—was not altogether unusual.[12]
"Colonels who are too young," wrote an officer to Choiseul in 1762,
"have been the ruin of the French army." When superannuated
colonels were permitted to sell their offices to the highest bidder,
all professional standards were thrown to the winds. It became painfully evident during the Seven Years' War that the professional
capacity of these officers, whether noble or bourgeois, was almost nil.

The French army was not wanting in able and resourceful generals, but court intrigue kept them out of responsible positions. Few
armies had at their disposal so much expert military intelligence.
Indeed, the eighteenth century was the most brilliant epoch in the
entire history of French military literature. Feuquière's *Mémoires
sur la guerre* became the standard work on the theory of war for all
the armies of Europe; Chevalier Folard's *Commentaires sur Polybe*
was, perhaps, the most discussed book on war in the middle of the
century. In his *Mes Rêveries* Maurice de Saxe proved himself to be
even more brilliant as a military writer than as a general. Guichard,
who revived classical military theory in his *Mémoires militaires sur
les Grecs et les Romains* (1757), became the boon companion of
Frederick the Great, who gave him a commission in the Prussian
army.[13]

The French army was recruited from three sources: by voluntary
enrolment, from foreign mercenaries, and from the militia. Because of the rising standard of living the captain, who did the

10 Mention, *L'armée sous l'ancien régime* (1900), 89.
11 H. Carré, *La noblesse de France et l'opinion publique au XVIIIe siècle* (Paris,
1920), 29.
12 M. Sautai, *Les débuts de la guerre de la Succession d'Autriche* (Paris, 1910), 9.
13 The best discussion of this military literature is found in Max Jaehns, *Geschichte
der Kriegswissenschaften* (1891), III.

recruiting for his company, found it progressively more difficult to collect his full quota of recruits even in time of peace. In time of war, when the army stood on the Rhine or on the Weser, it was altogether impossible to do so. Recruiting officers, therefore, had recourse to foreign mercenaries, who constituted about one-fourth, sometimes one half, of the entire regular army of the kingdom. But even this did not produce the necessary number of recruits. To find them the army administration began to draft men from the militia, a practice that, once it became a regular procedure, was equivalent to conscription, although there was a royal ordinance which declared that all enrolments should be voluntary. Theoretically, the militia in France as elsewhere was designed to defend the soil of the nation; practically, it served as a reservoir from which the troops in the field were reinforced. In the War of the Austrian Succession militiamen were retained as permanent units in the regular army and thus gradually amalgamated with the rest of the professional troops. Henceforth there was nothing to distinguish the militiaman from the regular soldier, although theoretically he was enrolled for no more than six years. From 1745 onward the principle of obligatory military service became a fixed French institution. This gave the French army a more strongly marked national character than the Prussian army.[14] This national character was not sufficiently developed to produce a definite military effect, yet the French element was considerable enough to prevent the introduction of the barbarous severity of Prussian discipline. Until the Seven Years' War the flogging penalty was unknown in the French army, while the Prussian officer's right to flog his half-foreign troops was unlimited.

In the matter of organization the French army lacked simplicity. There was a complex hierarchy of fighting units ranging all the way from the grenadiers to the militia, and everywhere there was a tendency to create an élite at the expense of the mass of fighting troops. This tendency to draw the best elements from each branch of the service to form a *corps d'élite* had the inevitable consequence of weakening the main fighting army. It often happened that the weakened front line cracked under the strain, while the excellent

[14] Dussauge, *Le ministère de Belle Isle*, 158.

troops held in reserve scarcely had an opportunity to get into play. The disastrous consequences of the ignorance of its officers were intensified by the lack of uniformity of drill and the total absence of maneuvering regulations. There were as many systems of drill as there were regiments, a circumstance which created no end of confusion in the field. Badly instructed, poorly drilled, wretchedly disciplined, inadequately officered, the French army in spite of its greater numbers was no longer the equal of the Prussian army.

III. THE PRUSSIAN ARMY

In 1740 most armies were still the same cumbersome machines they were in the days of Marlborough and Eugene. But this could no longer be said of the Prussian army. The old Prussian monarchy never had a better army than the army of Frederick the Great.[15] Its superiority over other armies was one of the causes of Frederick's victories. It was as national in composition as Prussia could afford to make it, it was admirably organized down to the minutest detail, its discipline was severe and effective, it was thoroughly trained and instructed, and it was equipped with weapons of exceptional quality. Regular drill gave to its movements a uniformity which other armies did not possess. It was as mobile as it was expert in maneuvers. No other army was more flexible and none could strike more quickly.[16]

There were good reasons for this pre-eminence. The army was Prussia's trump card, indeed, its only trump card in the international political game. Prussia's economic resources were inconsiderable, and in population she stood twelfth among the states of Europe in 1740. A national state like France could sustain military reverses and still remain a great power. For Prussia, however, a military defeat must always be disastrous, since Prussia was not a nation, but a purely artificial state. With an astonishing singleness of purpose all resources of the monarchy were concentrated on making the army an incomparable instrument of warfare. It is no exaggeration to say that it was not Prussia that made the army, but the army that made modern Prussia.

15 Gen. C. Jany, *Geschichte der Koeniglich-Preussischen Armee* (Berlin, 1928), II, 179.
16 This is also the judgment of an intelligent French military critic. R. Sauliol, *Frédéric II, La campagne de 1757* (Paris, 1924), Introduction.

But there was a more important reason. The Prussian monarch, Frederick II, was not merely a political autocrat; he was also the supreme commander of his army and, after the passing of Maurice de Saxe, the greatest general of his day. He gathered into his hands all the affairs which in our modern armies are divided between the ministry of war and the general staff. This concentration of power gave him an immense advantage over other generals who were forever dependent on their home governments. His position was comparable only to that of Alexander or Napoleon. There was no appeal from his orders, which were executed as quickly as they were conceived. This, in the last analysis, was the secret of Prussian success. It was Frederick's conviction that the Prussian monarch must be a soldier, and he never concealed his disdain for kings who trifled away their time in the agreeable inanities of court society. The inadequacy of his means did not permit him to revolutionize the tactics and strategy of his century. But he applied his resources with rare intelligence and exceptional finesse. In spite of his mastery of the military literature and science of his day and his accurate study of the strategy of the ancients, his art was above all personal and spontaneous. He was the embodiment of the ideal of stern living so peculiar to his own Prussian warrior state, and under his rigorous supervision his army took on the same Spartan character. All important instructions for every branch of the service issued from his headquarters, and his semiannual inspection journeys and maneuvers kept his army in perfect fighting trim. His discipline was brutal, but he knew on occasion how to recognize authentic military merit and reward it with open-handed generosity.

At bottom, Frederick had a contempt for the common soldier. He was firmly convinced that the quality of his army depended on the spirit and efficiency of his officers. The skill of his officers was to compensate the Prussian army for what it lacked in numbers and in the excellence of its soldier material. Frederick attributed his victories less to his soldiers than to his officers. The valor of the Austrian troops was certainly not inferior to that of the Prussian army; what made all the difference was the superiority of the Prussian officer.

Prussian officers, coming as they did almost exclusively from the rural nobility, constituted a closely integrated social unit.[17] The preference given the nobility was less the result of tradition as in France than of deliberate calculation. The intense social solidarity of the Prussian nobility was to be a guarantee for the spirit and discipline of both officers and men. Bound together by the ties of family kinship, alike in the economic foundations of their existence, occupation and mental outlook, nourished by the same feudal and warlike traditions, they became, perhaps, the most remarkable military class of modern Europe. Among no other class of Prussian society was military service so universal as among these landowning junkers. There was scarcely a noble family that did not have a father, several sons and cousins in the Prussian army. They were not permitted to take service in foreign armies. In responding to the military needs of the state they were, of course, serving their own interests, for the junkers were not as a body a wealthy nobility. The social uniformity of the Prussian officers corps was a distinct military advantage especially when compared with the motley composition of the Austrian corps.

At first glance it is surprising to learn that the enlightened philosopher-king Frederick entertained an ineradicable prejudice against bourgeois officers. The moral stamina and dash which he needed for his peculiar methods of warfare he thought he could find only among noblemen. He often repeated the remark that if a bourgeois officer were dismissed in disgrace he would simply turn to another profession without being mortally shaken, but that the disgrace of a noble officer left the latter no alternative but suicide.[18] He thought bourgeois officers obsequious, corruptible, and lamentably wanting in carriage and character. He employed them, but only when, as happened in the Seven Years' War, the scarcity of noble officers left no alternative. In the artillery, where a knowledge of technology and mathematics was indispensable, they were in the majority. Yet so rooted was his prejudice against them that on one occasion he transferred an officer from the field army to the inferior

[17] F. Pribatzsch, *Geschichte des Preussischen Offizierkorps* (Breslau, 1919); K. Demeter, *Das Deutsche Offizierkorps* (Berlin, 1930), 7.
[18] *Oeuvres de Frédéric le Grand*, ed. Preuss (Berlin, 1846), VI, 95; *Acta Borussica* (Berlin, 1909), IX, 673.

garrison troops because he harbored doubts as to the genuineness of the latter's noble pedigree.[19] It is not difficult to understand this prejudice. Frederick was an aristocrat to the bone and his code of honor was minted in the same feudal die as that of his junkers. The junkers suffered no insult even from the king. A General von Kleist drew his sword at the risk of his life when in an outburst of anger the king threatened to strike him with a swagger stick (he later came off with the mere trifle of two days' arrest)—but bourgeois officers presented him with no such examples of reckless courage in challenging fate.

It was not so much the higher standards of professional education that made the Prussian officers conspicuous among the armies of Europe. Frederick II encouraged study and many of his officers wrote treatises on military science and tactics, none of which survived the age for which they were written. Few Prussian generals, with the possible exception of Seydlitz, Winterfeld, and Schwerin, satisfied the exacting demands which the king placed upon them. But in the iron system of discipline that prevailed among Prussian officers there was scarcely a flaw. Their strenuous life began in early youth in the *Cadettenhaus*. Then came the years of active service which, with its incessant drill, the punctilious performance of the daily round of duties, the racking tension of the military review, was more exacting than in other armies by a good deal. The word *Service*, wrote one of them, rang in his ears like the Holy Inquisition. It would happen that officers guilty of negligence committed suicide before the review rather than face the angry king.[20] The king rarely forgot an error or the failure of a regiment in action. Officers of such regiments had their leaves canceled and received no promotion for years to come. The Prussian officer was almost never on leave. If he were young, he could not marry. Even among the older officers a surprisingly small number were married. The king wanted a celibate officers corps for a double reason: he could not afford to pay pensions to widows of officers killed in action, and he felt that marriage interfered with devotion to the

19 I. D. E. Preuss, *Friedrich der Grosse* (Berlin, 1832), III, 469.
20 M. Jaehns, *Geschichte der Kriegswissenschaften* (1891), III, 2123; K. Schmidt, *Dreissig Jahre am Hofe Friedrichs des Grossen* (1907), I, 328.

service. Voltaire, who had occasion to learn to know the Prussian army officer, described him in verse:

> *Aimer son roi, le dévoir et la patrie,*
> *Sacrifier son bien, sa santé et sa vie,*
> *Tourmenté par des fous, chicané pour un rien,*
> *Voilà la vrai portrait d'un officier prussien.*

There were compensations for this rigorous life. The Prussian officers corps was the first estate of the realm. Its members were the companions of the king and enjoyed absolute precedence over all court and civil officials. The king closed his eyes to duels among them over a *point d'honneur*, provided they made no noisy fuss about it. While any soldier who raised his hands against an officer was promptly condemned to death, the officer was entirely free from accountability for his conduct toward the soldier. Brutalities did occur. Yet it is not probable that many officers drew the bow too far, or Lessing, who had no special affection for Prussia, would not have given us the amiable figure of Major von Tellheim in his *Minna von Barnhelm*. The soldiers of Leuthen and Rossbach could not be so easily manhandled.

In his *Political Testament* of 1752 Frederick contended that it was impossible for Prussia to support a national army. Prussia was a thinly populated country. Her industries suffered from an inadequate supply of labor, and agriculture from a scarcity of peasant population. Even after the conquest of Silesia, with a population of four and a half millions, it was impossible to sustain a national army. The proportion of mercenaries was therefore appreciably larger than in the French army. In 1742 the proportion of native troops was only one-third. But it rose to one-half in 1750 and at the end of the Seven Years' War it had increased to two-thirds. This progressive increase of the national element was the result not of policy, but of the growing difficulty of recruiting abroad. As it was, the size of the army in relation to the total population surpassed all comparable figures in other countries. The French army in 1761 amounted to one and one-fifth per cent of the entire population; in Prussia it was four and four-tenths per cent.

The Prussian element was recruited by a system of conscription which divided the provinces of Prussia into cantons, each canton serving as the recruiting ground for the regiment assigned to it. To spare peasant families and industrialists the king allowed so many exemptions that the burden of obligatory service fell only on certain peasant and artisan groups. The area of the canton was so designed as to be large enough to recruit its regiment entirely three times. By filling the depleted ranks of their respective regiments after bloody battles, the cantons made each regiment, as it were, "immortal." Frederick called these cantonists the very substance of the Prussian monarchy. They constituted something like a national militia, a loyal nucleus within an army which, for the rest, was composed of dubious elements. The system represented as comprehensive a utilization of the agricultural population as the straitened economic circumstances of Prussia could bear and the privileged landowning class would tolerate. The system was inexpensive inasmuch as the cantonists, after their first year of service, could be sent home on leave for ten months in the year to engage in agricultural labor. It had the added advantage of facilitating rapid mobilization, for these cantonists lived in the immediate vicinity of their regiments.

But it was the methods for recruiting abroad that made Prussia the object of universal though impotent resentment among neighboring states. In Germany, the favorite recruiting ground, all the military powers of Europe were rival contenders and the general competition for soldiers compelled principality after principality to close its frontiers against alien recruiting officers. But as long as Prussia continued so largely dependent on foreign soldiers and the king persisted in increasing the size of his army, Prussian recruiting officers were compelled to take their men where they could find them and by any feasible method. The dukes of Mecklenburg, which supplied the Prussian army with the largest number of involuntary recruits, complained to the king of Prussia, appealed to the emperor, attempted to set the creaky punitive mechanism of the moribund Empire into motion, but without effect. The able-bodied men of entire Mecklenburg villages were carried off by Prussian press gangs. Flying squadrons of hussars surrounded churches on Sunday morning during divine worship, selected the men they wanted and passed on to the next church.[21] No one has ever described more trenchantly the devices of the eighteenth-century recruiting officer than Voltaire in the second chapter of his *Candide.*

Candide halted sadly at the door of an inn. Two men dressed in blue noticed him. "Comrade," said one, "there's a well-built young man of the right height." They went up to Candide and very civilly invited him to dinner. "Gentlemen," said Candide with charming modesty, "you do me a great honour, but I have no money to pay my share." "Ah, sir," said one of the men in blue, "persons of your figure and merit never pay anything; are you not five feet five tall?" "Yes, gentlemen," said he, bowing, "that is my height." "Ah, sir, come to table; we will not only pay your expenses, we will never allow a man like you to be short of money; men were only made to help each other." "You are in the right," said Candide, "that is what Doctor Pangloss was always telling me, and I see that everything is for the best." They begged him to accept a few crowns, he took them and wished to give them an I O U; they refused to take it and all sat down to table. "Do you not love tenderly . . ." "Oh, yes," said he. "I love Mademoiselle Cunegonde tenderly." "No," said one of the gentlemen. "We were asking if you do not tenderly love the King of the Bulgarians." "Not a bit," said he, "for I have never seen him." "What! He is the most charming of Kings, and you must drink his health." "Oh, gladly, gentlemen." And he drank. "That is sufficient," he was told. "You are now the support, the aid, the defender, the hero of the Bulgarians; your fortune is made and your glory assured." They immediately put irons on his legs and took him to a regiment.

These recruiting officers displayed an absolute indifference to the quality of prospective soldiers. In time of war they accepted deserters from other armies and even pressed war prisoners into service. There were entire battalions of Austrian deserters in the Prussian army. The crowning incident of this system of recruitment occurred at the beginning of the Seven Years' War, when the king conceived the fantastic notion of incorporating the entire Saxon army with his own. His tactics in the siege of Pirna were calculated to achieve this end without bloodshed.[22] Had this occurred one

21 E. Dette, *Friedrich der Grosse und sein Heer* (Halle, 1914), 54; W. Schultze, *Die Preussischen Werbungen unter Friedrich Wilhelm I und Friedrich dem Grossen* (1887), 56.
22 H. Hoehne, *Die Einstellung der saechsischen Regimenter in die preussische Armee im Jahre 1756* (Halle, 1926), 99.

hundred years before it would have excited little attention or criticism. But the armies of Europe were no longer the exclusively mercenary armies of the age of Wallenstein. The circumstance that this recruiting device no longer worked is indicative of the fact that the absolutistic system was already in process of disintegration. In spite of the mass desertions among these Saxons, Frederick persisted in the practice of recruiting on enemy territory and did not even hesitate to raise conscript levies in the Austrian crown lands. In order to alleviate the burden of his cantons at home this system of recruitment on foreign soil became an integral part of Prussian policy.

One might well ask, how was it possible with soldiers such as these, desperadoes and poor yokels, brought together indiscriminately and frequently against their will from the four corners of the compass and without any consideration of their moral fiber, to fight battles and even win them? The answer is that, within limits, it was possible, but it could be done only by means of the most rigid and exacting discipline and constant drill. Some military historians refer to this Prussian mania for drill with a spice of ironic ridicule, as though it were something worthy of Gilbert and Sullivan. Quite mistakenly. Military drill has a dual object: first, to instil obedience, self-control, cohesion, quickness and alertness; second, to develop the mobility and flexibility of fighting units for battle. The Prussian drill was no idle play on the parade ground. In the eighteenth century the column and close-order formations which armies used on the parade ground were the actual tactical formations and movements that were employed on the battlefield. In those days the drill system was fundamentally sound, because it fulfilled both objects of drill—the discipline of the individual soldier and the maneuvering flexibility of fighting units to meet battle conditions. Drill supported discipline and discipline rendered possible an exactitude and finesse in drilling which increased progressively. The more perfect the discipline and the more precise the drill, the less did the Prussian officer need to rely upon good will and other moral qualities which are required from every modern soldier. Even those who had been pressed into the army gradually accustomed themselves to the life and were more or less affected by the *esprit de corps* of their respective fighting units. The Prussian king and his officers were perpetually occupied with new experiments in drilling with a view to achieving ever greater perfection, speed and precision in their tactical movements. Herein lay the superiority of the Prussian army over its adversaries.

All this does not alter the fact, however, that contemporaries looked upon the Prussian army as a gigantic penal institute.[23] Fear and coercion alone, not love of country or personal ambition, it was thought, could move the soldier of the Prussian army. Frederick was fond of repeating the maxim that the Prussian soldier should stand in greater fear of his officer than of the enemy. In view of the elements of which his army was composed one can understand this extreme solicitude for discipline and drill. A long campaign that weakened both had a demoralizing effect on the army. Hence the Prussian doctrine that all wars must be short and decisive. At the end of the Seven Years' War the Prussian army had degenerated into a mere peasant mob, poorly disciplined and badly drilled. When this stage was reached it was absolutely necessary for the army to go into winter quarters in order to recover its ruined morale.

It is obvious that an army so composed and so controlled imposed certain limitations on the general who employed it. There was more desertion from the Prussian army than from any other army in Europe.[24] It was serious enough in time of peace, but a war multiplied opportunities a thousandfold. All the control mechanisms of the army were designed to reduce desertion to a minimum. Reading Frederick's *Principes générales de la guerre* one gains the impression that the prime function of an officer was to prevent desertion; that to fight the enemy was a secondary consideration. The French traveler, Toulongeon, perhaps the keenest observer of mid-century Prussia, put it aptly when he said that to the native half of the Prussian army was assigned the duty of preventing the foreign half from deserting.[25]

The problem of preventing desertion seriously affected the tactical movements of the Prussian army during a campaign. Precautions

---

23 I. D. E. Preuss, *Friedrich der Grosse, Urkundenbuch* (1832), IV, 226.

24 From 1713 to 1740, 30,216 men deserted from the Prussian army. P. Losch, *Soldatenhandel* (Kassel, 1933), 35.

25 Finot et Galmiche, *Une mission militaire* (1892), 292.

against desertion not infrequently paralyzed its activity. It was sometimes impossible, from fear of desertion, to accelerate a march, to make skirmishes in forests or villages or to attempt night attacks. After a victorious battle it was rarely possible for the king to pursue the enemy in order to annihilate him, because in the pursuit he would lose a considerable portion of his army. For the same reason Frederick never desired a hand-to-hand encounter with the enemy, such as developed in later wars. It is important to note this close correspondence between the composition of the Prussian army and its tactics on the battlefield. The eighteenth-century Prussian soldier was an automaton. He had nothing to do but obey commands and march forward. At his right and left were officers and behind him marched another firing company. In spite of the greater fire rapidity of the Prussian infantry, Frederick had no real confidence in the effectiveness of infantry fire. If he allowed his infantrymen to fire during an advance, it was rather to keep up their courage. He placed his confidence in the moral effect of the steady advance of his lines and columns upon the enemy. When they reached the enemy a serious struggle was no longer expected.

The lively controversy that has arisen among military critics over the strategy of Frederick the Great opens a number of problems which must be considered in another connection. It should be pointed out here, however, that the structure of the army was one of the factors that determined this strategy. While it is true that the Prussian army was more mobile, more flexible, better disciplined and better officered than other contemporary armies, Frederick could not expect to deal the annihilating blows with this army that Napoleon dealt with the armies of the French Revolution. In this sense the structure of his army shackled Frederick's talents as a general.

IV. THE DILEMMA OF THE ANTI-MILITARISTS IN ENGLAND AND ON THE CONTINENT

It is significant to note that the first serious challenge to the universal prevalence of standing professional armies was coincident with the growth of constitutional government. England was the home of the one as of the other. But this same England illustrates also the dilemma of eighteenth-century anti-militarists generally.

Here the rising bourgeoisie had succeeded in making an ally of the state. In the Revolution Settlement it had sought constitutional freedom as a means to the enjoyment of wealth and the opportunities that were open to it. Since the days of Oliver Cromwell the standing army had been an object of universal abhorrence among the English middle classes. Blackstone called professional soldiering a species of slavery; Hume contended that a country with a large standing army was at war with itself; and Pope in his *Essay on Man* had termed the militarist a madman. It was the haunting fear of military dictatorship that inspired parliament to oppose armies as a matter of principle. Standing armies, so ran the parliamentary doctrine, were a characteristic of continental absolute monarchies, where the military situation was different from that of Great Britain, whose shores were lapped by the waters of the ocean and whose natural defense was the navy. A standing army would be divorced from the rest of the nation. Created and controlled by the king, disciplined by him, it would be obedient only to his orders. So persistent was this jealousy of the army that when proposals were made in 1756 to reorganize the militia, the Duke of Newcastle wrote that the establishment of a militia would be the ruin of the constitution and the immediate destruction of the Whig party.[26]

England did in fact possess a militia, but it was neither a professional nor a standing army, nor yet separate from the rest of the nation. As an instrument of national defense it was utterly useless and it could not be called out for service overseas. The Militia Act of 1757, so warmly sponsored by Pitt, was really an attempt to translate into fact the theory held by parliament that it was possible to develop a force as a substitute for a regular army. But the mild form of conscription introduced by this act was made so ineffective by allowing those who had been chosen by lot to purchase substitutes, that the notion of a citizens' army became an illusion. The act required only twenty-eight days of drill in the year, yet the new militia was extremely unpopular. As a fighting force the troops so levied were ridiculously inadequate, and they were poorly disciplined and incompetently officered.

In reality the militia was no longer adequate to the political and

[26] L. B. Namier, *England in the Age of the American Revolution* (1930), 134.

economic needs of a great power. The militia presupposed a self-contained nation living in an agricultural economy; that such an economy was no longer possible scarcely needs discussion. If England wished to defend her imperialistic and colonial interests, if she wished to play an active role in continental politics, she had to accept the continental institution of the standing army. But the establishment of the standing army in England was not a triumph of the crown. It was really due to the bourgeoisie. What the crown could never have obtained for its own purposes was quietly brought about by the middle classes, who saw their own profit in it. A government that had become mainly commercial in composition and outlook found the new standing army neither wasteful, extravagant nor dangerous. Every year parliament passed the Mutiny Act, which fixed the number of men whom the executive could keep under arms.[27] According to the legal fiction this professional army was not strictly speaking a standing army, but engaged and paid for one year only. The soldiers, if they were not used to enforce the revenue laws and prevent smuggling, were sent out as colonial garrisons to New York, Gibraltar, Nova Scotia and the Antilles.

The predicament of the English Whigs was not so different from that of the only other anti-militarist critics of standing armies, the French philosophers. They opposed standing armies for substantially the same reasons, that is to say, their objections were political and constitutional. To Montesquieu, Voltaire, Rousseau and the Encyclopedists the standing army was an instrument of dynastic ambition and royal tyranny, for it gave sovereigns "the precious right of being unjust when they pleased." The remedy most of them proposed was to make the army an exact transposition of the social order. With Montesquieu at their head, most of them advocated the transformation of the regular army into a national militia after the manner of Machiavelli's proposal of several centuries before.[28] But they thought of a national militia less in terms of the nineteenth-century principle of universal conscription than in terms of those local militias which had thrived in the pre-absolutistic epoch, which were composed of free burghers and peasants, and some of which

[27] J. S. Omond, *Parliament and the Army* (Cambridge, 1933), 44. Sir John Fortescue, "The Army," in A. S. Turberville, *Johnson's England* (Oxford, 1933), vol. I, 67.
[28] Montesquieu, *De l'esprit des lois*, XI, chap. 6.

still existed in a degenerate form. What they did not see was that such a militia was suitable only to an agrarian and non-dynamic society which had no interests to defend outside of the national frontiers. One need only read Montesquieu's treatment of the problem to see that the philosophers were caught in the perennial dilemma of all anti-militarists and pacifists, that of offering a remedy in the efficacy of which they themselves only half believed.

V. NAVIES AND SEA POWER

While in the eighteenth century there was an apparent but by no means necessary correlation between national wealth, population and the size and efficiency of armies, there was a very palpable interdependence between navies on the one hand and the volume of seaborne commerce and merchant marine on the other. If Great Britain, France, Spain and Holland were the great sea powers of Europe in 1740, they held this position first and foremost because they were great overseas traders, for transmarine commerce was the prime foundation of naval strength. Merchant fleets were the mainspring of the British and French navies. They produced the wealth for building ships and the seamen to man the fighting vessels and transports that carried their troops to all parts of the world. There was no great difference in construction between large commercial ships and war vessels. The same rules of navigation applied to both and both needed similar repairs. Certain merchant ships could easily be transformed into war vessels and vice versa. So long as the principle of trade monopoly prevailed in each colonial empire, commerce was dependent on naval protection and naval strength rested on commerce. It was a great disadvantage to Spain that she was contented with a permanently organized navy, and failed to develop commercial shipping and industries which could support her transoceanic trade.[29] The reverse was true of the Dutch Republic. The peculiar geographical position of the United Provinces necessitated both a military and a naval defense. Always in fear of invasion, they were under compulsion to maintain an army of thirty thousand men to occupy the Barrier fortresses and defend their

29 The Spanish navy since the revival under Patiño in 1735 was far from contemptible. Spain had 34 line-of-battle ships of 60 to 114 guns. G. Desdevises du Dezert, "Les institutions de l'Espagne," *Revue Hispanique*, LXX (1927), 442.

territory. But at a time when they were rapidly losing their pre-eminent position in the commerce of Europe the Dutch could no longer stand the financial strain of supporting also a great navy. The time had come when it was no longer possible to improvise fleets. The permanent decay of the Dutch navy became so obvious that Lord Chesterfield wrote in 1745 that the United Provinces had no other title but courtesy to the name of a maritime power.

In the meantime commerce had everywhere established trading stations which in turn had become nurseries of colonies. It had become apparent to every commercial power that the relation between these scattered settlements and the navy was one of mutual dependence. It must be remembered that in the days of the sailing ship navies were not self-supporting; the sailing ship needed secure harbors and bases in which she could refresh and refit; she needed frequent replacement of her supplies. Again, these settlements, expanding into colonies, in their turn contributed to the sea power of the home country by developing a trade and seafaring population of their own. So long as these settlements and colonies were thinly populated, the number of men available for military service was definitely limited. The lack of easy means of communication between them made necessary the concentration of military resources in a few defended places, which were at the mercy of a comparatively small military force. Of course, colonies like Canada and those on the American seaboard, which could readily raise a limited military force, possessed certain facilities for defense and conquest, but any measurable increase of colonial troops had to be drawn from the mother country. Now because of the prevalent doctrine of trade monopoly, every trading station and every larger colony was a potential area of dispute. To be able to assert herself in such an area of dispute, the mother country had first to transport her military force by sea, and then had to feed this force, provision it and keep it supplied with reinforcements by way of the ocean. The home country being the source of power, the line of communication between the home country and the colony must be secure and only sea power could furnish this security.

Because of the technique of navigation and the necessity of seeking winter quarters, great naval powers as a rule concentrated their naval forces in metropolitan waters. Colonial interests, apart from actual settlements, being private in character, admiralties felt no need of establishing naval bases with permanent units in remote zones, even where important interests were concerned. At most they maintained fortified ports of war like Louisburg and Port Mahon to harbor squadrons when in colonial waters, to supply naval stores to fleets in need of refitting and to serve as bases near the theatre of action which might facilitate privateering operations.[30]

It was the British who first departed from this older system of colonial defense in time of war. While the French annually concentrated their fleets and redistributed them, sending out squadrons to the colonies for short periods as they were needed, the British kept small squadrons permanently stationed in the West Indies. They were in a position to do this, for the victuals and naval stores necessary for the upkeep of their squadrons were abundantly provided from North America. Nor were the English ships stationed in the West Indies obliged to go home to England to refit, since they had dockyards in Jamaica and Antigua where almost all repairs could be made. The question as to which of the two systems of colonial defense possessed superior merit is open to argument. The British station-system was very useful for the ordinary routine of defending or interrupting trade. But it was unequal to the major emergencies of war, for these small naval units were too weak to conquer a colony or to engage a powerful enemy fleet. Therefore Britain had to beat the enemy with his own weapons by hurrying ships to the colonies whenever the enemy did so.

In 1740 the principal contenders for the possession of the New World and for commercial and naval supremacy were still Great Britain and France. For more than fifty years they had been the most formidable competitors in maritime and colonial enterprise in every quarter of the globe: in the Mediterranean and the Levant, in India and the slave-trading stations on the coasts of Africa, in the West Indies and in North America. Both had had some successes and had suffered some failures; some areas had changed hands, but the entire naval strength of both countries had not yet come

30 D'Outre-Seille, "L'évolution du problème des bases navales," La Revue Maritime, CXLV (1932), 172.

into full play, for the conflicts were local and the results also were local. Beginning with 1744, however, the pacific commercial rivalry between them burst into a universal contest for colonial and naval supremacy.

In this conflict naval power, the merchant marine, the quality of officers and seamen were of decisive importance. Even before the war began Great Britain had a clear superiority on almost all counts. The British navy, though in a degenerate condition, was more than double that of France. The British merchant marine and the seamen who manned it were vastly superior in numbers to those of France—according to one contemporary writer no less than six and ten times respectively.[31] Half of the commerce of the world was done under the British flag. More satisfactory also was the relation between the British navy and the merchant fleet which, notwithstanding the use of the vicious system of the press to man the navy, could at least continue its normal business activity in time of war. When Adam Smith criticized the English Navigation Acts, condemning their monopolistic tendencies, he still described them as sound, because they created a strong merchant marine with numerous trained sailors which served as the recruiting ground for the navy.

On one count only, in naval architecture, did the French enjoy undisputed ascendancy. The French and Spaniards built better ships, stiffer in a breeze and more heavily armed. An English ship of seventy guns could not take a French or Spanish ship of the same class. A French ship of fifty-two guns was not inferior to a British ship of seventy-two.[32] Even in a light breeze English ships heeled so much that they could not open the lower deck of ports where the heaviest guns were mounted, thus having to fight thirty-two and forty pounders of the enemy with twelve and eighteen pounders of their own. Lord Anson said in 1744, "I have never seen or heard . . . that one of our ships, alone and singly opposed to one of the enemy's of equal force has taken her, and yet I have been in almost every action and skirmish since 1718, and yet we are daily boasting of the prowess of our Fleet." Indeed, British ships were

[31] W. H. Richmond, *National Policy and Naval Strength and other Essays* (London, 1928), 19.
[32] H. W. Hodges, *Select Naval Documents* (Cambridge, 1922), 122.

modeled on the vessels captured from the French.[33] British ships
were therefore inferior in make, not so well armed and not so
durable. The great majority of the one hundred and twenty line-of-
battle ships which Britain possessed under Lord Anson were
medium-sized vessels, only a small number being exceptionally
powerful ships of eighty, ninety, or one hundred guns. This circumstance was of some importance because of eighteenth-century naval
tactics. Two hostile fleets rarely joined in battle unless they could
oppose an equal number of ships of the same class. Usually drawn
up in two parallel lines, they maneuvered with a view to direct
collision. The naval battle was a series of single combats, ship-of-the-
line against ship-of-the-line and frigate against frigate. Battles were
decided by the numbers and quality of the ships, by luck, by the
order and discipline of the crews, and by the skill and energy of
individual captains.

A navy in sailing-ship days could not suddenly spring into existence when an emergency arose. At the beginning of every war the
navies were slow in getting into their stride. All navies alike deteri-
orated in time of peace for want of practical experience and regular
peace-time training in naval strategy. The lessons learned in previous
wars were invariably obliterated by the desire for economy when
peace came. In time of peace the British parliament reduced the navy
to the smallest number of ships compatible with its police duties.
Before a navy could embark on its work in war, ships had to be
built or purchased from merchants, manned and equipped with
stores and fitted out for the sea. The system of manning was defective. There was a good deal of corruption in British dockyards and
in the civil administration of the navy. Though there might be
enough ships, there were rarely sufficient large ships in readiness
when the demand for them arose. This will partially account for
the numerous indecisive encounters at the beginning of every war.

More serious still was the persistent interference of commercial
interests with naval strategy. At the beginning and during every
war a large part of the fleet had to be devoted to the protection of
commerce before any thought could be given to offensive action
against the enemy navy. Theoretically, naval strategy requires con-

33 J. Charnock, *History of Marine Architecture* (1802), III, 172.

centration on the major issues of the war, while defense of trade and attack on enemy commerce are secondary operations which must not interfere with the main strategic effort. But eighteenth century naval warfare was a branch of business and purely commercial considerations deflected strategy far more than they do in our own day. In England this excessive influence of the commercial and financial interests may be explained by the fact that, while among the landed aristocracy, clergy and country gentry there was a strong leaven of Jacobites, the resolute if interested devotion of the trading and mercantile classes to the Act of Settlement gave them an influence with the government which made it difficult to reject even their less reasonable demands. The merchants naturally wished to have the war conducted in accordance with their immediate interests and, if their advice had been consistently followed, there would have been no naval strategy at all, but merely a number of cruisers rigidly cantoned upon stations where trade was most active. It was only by ignoring the protests of the merchants that the British admiralty won some of its greatest victories. Even as it was the disposition of naval squadrons was often governed less by strategical considerations than by the desire to protect the movements of merchant shipping to and from the colonies.[34]

To do this effectively all naval powers employed the convoy system. Because of the prevalence of privateering the convoy system was a necessary evil. To be sure, sailing with convoy was not compulsory in the colonial trade, but it appears that almost all ships took convoy on their outward-bound voyage. Many merchants probably took convoy more for the sake of insurance than for the safe arrival of their ships, for the underwriters of maritime insurance companies returned a part of the premium for ships which sailed under convoy. On their homeward voyage masters of merchantmen were tempted to set out with convoys only to desert them as soon as they came so near home that the risk they ran was worth the advantage of arriving on the market two or three days in advance of the others. The indiscipline of merchant captains made

---

[34] B. Tunstall, *Admiral Byng* (London, 1928), 19; C. E. Fayle, "The Deflection of Strategy by Commerce in the Eighteenth Century," *Journal of the Royal United Service Institution*, LXIII (1923), 288.

the lot of convoy commanders in both the French and British navies an extremely unhappy one.

The importance attached to the defense of trade is forcibly illustrated by the instructions given to all commanders of escorts that the safety of the convoys was to be their first consideration and that even the pursuit of a defeated attacking force was to be subordinated to this end. French practice went further still and held the escort to a rigidly defensive role, which is all the more significant since the escort of French convoys frequently consisted of strong squadrons of ships-of-the-line. In the later years of the War of the Austrian Succession so large a proportion of the French fleet was employed in this way that it rendered all but impossible any concentrated offensive action against the enemy. When, during this war, the French merchants petitioned Maurepas for regular convoys and he found himself unable to afford them from lack of funds, he promised them the necessary convoys in return for a percentage commission on the value of cargoes safely brought in.[35] The subordination of the navy in time of war to purely commercial ends could scarcely be carried farther. That similar motives were at work on the other side of the Channel may be seen from the fact that Admiral Boscawen took out to India in 1747 a plan of operations drawn up by the English East India Company itself.

VI. BRITISH NAVAL OFFICERS AND CREWS

The British navy, like the Prussian army, owed its brilliant triumphs over the French chiefly to the superiority of its officers. Admiral Mahan contends that the professional competence of the average British naval officer in 1740 stood at a dangerously low level.[36] It is equally true, however, that at the end of the Seven Years' War they had no serious rivals in Europe. Although socially the majority of British naval officers belonged to the governing aristocracy or gentry, neither birth nor health was essential for a midshipman. Even promotion from the deck was fairly common. Cadets could enter the navy through the Royal Naval Academy at Portsmouth, opened in 1732, but most of them began their careers

[35] On Maurepas's convoy system see R. Pares, *War and Trade in the West Indies* (Oxford, 1936), 311-325.
[36] A. T. Mahan, *Types of Naval Officers* (Boston, 1901), 82.

between the ages of thirteen and sixteen as captain's servants. When the captain was a cultivated man like Collingwood, the boy started with a great advantage over others. Rooke, Anson, Hawke and Boscawen began in this way at the age of fifteen.[37] Promotion to the rank of midshipman depended entirely upon the captain. The school for young seamen was the sea. They were not to be commissioned before they had had six years as midshipman or mate and had passed the lieutenant's examination, usually not before they were twenty-one years of age. There was sharp competition for all these positions and along the whole line the duties were onerous. Before these young boys became officers they had acquired a professional knowledge and a sense of responsibility, and the life they led developed seamanship, which in turn bred confidence and self-reliance. It was a hard life, but they were well paid and the other rewards were great. A naval officer might make his fortune in a single day if in war time he met a French Indiaman or a Spanish vessel laden with gold from America.

Promotion from lieutenant to captain depended on many things. As was inevitable in eighteenth-century Britain, influence went very far, although merit might obtain recognition. The Duke of Newcastle made persistent efforts to use the navy as he used the army and the civil service, as an instrument of patronage, but as long as Lord Anson was at the admiralty his recommendations were usually rejected.[38] Neither Hyde Parker, Kempenfelt, Pellew nor Jervis—all great names—had family or political influence to support them. There were among the senior officers men who had begun in the merchant marine, for there was no lack of bold fighting seamen among the masters of merchant ships, as the privateer records amply show. Whatever else might be said of the system of promotion, it placed men in positions of responsibility while they were still young and ambitious. These men grew up in the habit of trusting their own judgment and of acting accordingly without waiting or asking for orders; and their seniors did not discourage them in this. In these years the British navy produced a considerable number of great commanders: Hawke, the greatest of them all;

[37] E. C. Millington, *Seamen in the Making, A Short History of Nautical Training* (London, 1935), 53.
[38] W. V. Anson, *The Life of Admiral Anson* (London, 1912), 112.

Vernon, Anson, Boscawen, Saunders, Rodney, Stevens, who clung to Pondichéry through the tempestuous weather of the monsoon; Watson, Clive's colleague in the retaking of Calcutta; and Kempenfelt, a great thinker and tactician.

Although British seamen and statesmen were acutely conscious of the general function of the navy within the scope of national policy, Admiral Richmond rightly emphasizes the absence of any systematic knowledge of naval strategy in the British admiralty in 1740.[39] In the early years of both wars the faulty disposition of English squadrons resulted in a whole series of indecisive engagements. It was only empirically and gradually that Great Britain came to adopt a strategy, which may be characterized as battle and blockade, as a means for gaining that supremacy of the sea upon which her colonial empire and national existence depended. The cardinal principle of this naval strategy was to seek out and destroy the naval forces of the enemy. Once the hostile fleet was destroyed and the enemy's trade, deprived of protection, collapsed, his troops could not venture out upon the seas. The doctrine was sound, and whenever they acted upon it the British won their greatest triumphs.

If, in the course of the war, the enemy was unwilling or unable to hazard all in a general engagement, his fleets had to be immobilized by a system of blockade. In general, the English were unable to keep up a permanent blockade, because their squadrons had too many duties for their size; besides occasional convoys, they had many cruising grounds to police and could not afford to keep their main blockading forces constantly relieved. They would stay as long as they could, but sooner or later they must go back unrelieved, and in the meantime the enemy could slip out to sea. It was not until such men as Anson, Vernon and Hawke came to realize the paramount importance of a strong Channel squadron as the bedrock foundation of British naval strategy that a blockade could be made effective by a system of organized reliefs. These men saw that the real defense of the colonies was in the Channel and in the Strait of Gibraltar, and that a government which could not keep up a proper system of blockade in Europe was naturally forced to

[39] W. H. Richmond, *The Navy in the War of 1738 to 1748* (Cambridge, 1920), I, Introduction.

send its fleets scurrying across the seas to relieve the colonies. The colonists in their turn contributed their share to make an effective blockade difficult, for, having no confidence in a blockade in Europe, they demanded that permanent naval units be stationed in colonial waters. This permanent detachment of naval units to colonial stations forced dispersion on the British admiralty and withdrew a considerable number of ships which would else have been available for service in Europe.[40]

Until recently no navy trained its own seamen in time of peace, for no state was sufficiently wealthy to stand the financial strain. At the outbreak of every war Great Britain was confronted with a fundamental difficulty in manning her fleet, because in time of peace she maintained no more than one-fifth of the men she needed in an emergency. The difficulty of expanding sixteen thousand men into sixty thousand was great enough. What made the difficulty greater still was that the admiralty could not simply transfer the crews from the merchant marine to the navy, for the uninterrupted flow of commerce in time of war was a matter of vital necessity. The British seafaring population had to perform two incompatible functions: to man the fleet and also supply the crews for the merchant ships. But the seafaring population was never numerous enough to do both. At the opening of the war with France in 1778 the British admiralty declared that the number of known seamen in the country was only sixty thousand (certainly an underestimation) and that a greater number of men had been carried as sailors in the navy alone during the Seven Years' War.

In Britain all vagabonds, sturdy beggars and idle apprentices were subject to impressment. Everyone has seen the plate in Hogarth's history of the *Idle Apprentice* in which the predestined gallows bird is seen in a boat on his way to a ship in the offing. But recruiting had to be done above all among the able seamen of the merchant fleet who could hand, reef, steer, set up rigging and repair it when damaged. Since sailors rarely or never entered a warship of their own free will, they were forced into the service by means of the press gang, the British equivalent of the Prussian recruiting officer.

[40] W. H. Hodges, *Select Naval Documents*, 139; R. Pares, *War and Trade in the West Indies* (Oxford, 1936), 284.

The right to impress seamen was, as Lord Mansfield put it, "founded on immemorial usage allowed for ages." While in France the law bound the entire body of seamen to serve in the navy, in England the sailor was personally liable and could be forced to serve whenever he could be caught. But he was under no obligation to come forward. The difference between the French system of conscription and the British press was that France sacrificed her merchant marine to her navy, while Britain, though pressing her merchant seamen, also maintained a great sea-borne commerce in her own ships in time of war.[41]

How was this done? Briefly, by suspending the manning clauses of the Navigation Acts whenever a war broke out and admitting foreigners into the merchant service. The Navigation Acts, which from first to last aimed at the promotion of English shipping, concern us here only insofar as they applied to the seafaring population. The Act of 1672 required that the master and three-fourths of the crew of a merchant vessel be drawn from England, Ireland and the Plantations. However, as commerce expanded and the size of the navy increased, it became necessary to liberalize the terms, which were wide enough for the England of Charles II but not for the eighteenth century. This was done by drawing more heavily on alien populations, especially on the seafaring populations of Scandinavia and the Baltic. The policy adopted under the new circumstances was summarized by the Act of 1755, passed by parliament on the eve of the Seven Years' War. This act not only suspended the manning clauses and the three-fourths rule of the previous acts but allowed all foreigners who had served on board any British ship for two years to be called British seamen.[42] It is apparent that the British government did not contemplate manning both its navy and its merchant fleet with even a majority of British seamen.

It must also be remembered that able seamen did not constitute the majority of a warship's crew. Rarely more than a third of a ship's crew was made up of men bred to the sea. When parliament called for fifty thousand men it did not expect that more than a third of them would be prime seamen. One-fifth were usually marines

41 D. Hannay, *The Sea Trader* (London, 1912), 267.
42 D. Hannay, *Short History of the British Navy* (1907), II, 143.

and the rest were landsmen, "waisters" and others who worked below under the mate of the hold, a subordinate kind of sea laborer. Even this third made a wide gap in the merchant marine. During a long war a merchant vessel's crew usually consisted of her master, two mates, one boatswain and a number of boys under eighteen. If there were more grown men, they were certain to be foreigners. Frequently even the master and mates were foreign.

Because prime seamen refused to come forward voluntarily, the bulk of them had to be swept into the navy by press gangs who operated in great drives at ports or on ships at sea. To try to get them on shore was almost useless. The gangs cruised about in tenders at the harbor's mouth or even farther out at sea to intercept home-coming ships, colliers and fishermen. Since trade was the one power which the admiralty respected, certain concessions had to be made to the merchants. Seamen in outward-bound ships were immune, though they might be snapped up at the other end of the voyage.[43]

The able seaman hated service in the navy, less because of the harsh discipline than because of the pay, the system of pay, and the life itself. Merchant ships paid prompt and good wages, and war risks sent up the pay for able seamen still higher. The navy, on the other hand, had not increased the pay for an able seaman since the days of Oliver Cromwell, and then often paid him only six months after his arrival in a home port.[44] Meanwhile, to the disgust of the sailor, the suspension of the manning clauses of the Navigation Acts had opened the merchant marine with its exorbitant wages to foreigners. He might have been seized as he entered home waters after a voyage abroad of two or three years—often without the pay due to him—and shipped from one warship to another without prospect of release until the end of the war, whenever that might be, and without hope of a holiday—since sailors on shore seldom came back. Seamen were, virtually, prisoners in their ships, huddled together in a fetid atmosphere with the sweepings of the docksides, the dregs from prisons, thieves and cardsharpers; and to increase the difficulty, ten per cent of them were foreigners. Again, there was the danger of scurvy, the losses from which were immense. To gain

43 J. R. Hutchinson, *The Press Gang* (New York, 1914).
44 G. E. Manwaring and B. Dobrée, *The Floating Republic* (London, 1935), 23 note.

some impression of the vile life of the 'tween decks one must read Smollett's terrible picture in *Roderick Random*. The *Annual Register* for 1763 records that in the Seven Years' War 1,512 seamen were killed in battle while 133,708 died of disease or were missing. One recalls Nelson's statement that the average able seaman was finished at forty-five.

VII. THE FRENCH NAVY

Whereas Great Britain, aided by her insular position, worked her way through to the clear view that her national interests lay in the direction of an unrivaled naval and commercial power, France was unable to make so definite a commitment. The amphibious geography of France, which made her at once the greatest land power and a great maritime power, was a serious handicap. Partly continental, partly maritime, she could not, like Great Britain, throw all her energies in one direction or the other; willy-nilly she had to attempt to do both. The result was that she was torn by conflicting interests and conflicting policies, a state of affairs reflected in a continually vacillating public opinion that was unable to arrive at a clean-cut solution of the problem in what direction her best interests lay. For every Frenchman who, like Maurepas and Choiseul, pressed for a strong navy there was a host of others whose sentiments were expressed by Louis XV when he said, "My dear Choiseul, you are as mad as your predecessors. They have all told me they want a navy. There will never be any other navies in France than those of Vernet, the artist." It may be true, as Gaxotte has pointed out, that it is upon land that France has staked her whole existence, but that was not necessarily true in 1740.[45]

This is not the place to discuss the role of foreign and colonial commerce in French national economy. It must be said, however, that France was no longer a self-contained nation, living peacefully on her own soil, exporting nothing to foreign countries but luxury goods and importing only exotic produce. The textile industries of southern France produced for the markets of the Levant, and the factories of Rouen, Amiens and Orleans were dependent on cotton that came from America. The same was true of a score of other

[45] P. Gaxotte, *Louis XV and His Times*, Engl. trans. (Philadelphia, 1934), 148.

industries. If it must be admitted that much of her vast colonial empire was nothing more than an immense façade, this cannot be said of her empire as a whole, for in the Antilles she possessed the richest colonies in the world. French foreign commerce, carefully fostered by Cardinal Fleury, was entering upon its period of maximum expansion. Here were solid national interests which only a navy could defend. Inasmuch as the growing French competition had already begun to excite the jealousy of the English, who attributed the sharp decline of their commerce to French encroachments, it might have appeared prudent statesmanship to construct a formidable navy.[46]

There were, however, certain obstacles which prevented France from becoming a truly great naval power. The French merchant marine had not kept pace with the enormous increase of French foreign commerce. If one excepts the Levant trade, which employed eight hundred French ships annually, the commerce of French ports and the coastwise trade were largely in the hands of British, Dutch and Hamburg shippers. Besides the Levant, it was only in Africa and in the Antilles that the French merchant fleet was exceptionally successful, but this trade occupied only from three hundred to five hundred ships, although the volume which they carried was enormous.[47] In the Orient the French East India Company with its thirty-five large vessels and frigates possessed a complete monopoly. In case of war the French fleet could count on the support of these ships.

Compared with her British competitor this inferiority of the French merchant fleet was a grave disadvantage. But there was another impediment. British statesmen measured their strength in terms of commerce and looked upon commercial problems as national problems. This was not the case in France, where policy, naturally enough, was frequently dominated by continental considerations. Like the British, the French merchants persistently complained of inadequate naval protection, and with better reason. The charge has frequently been made that, although Cardinal Fleury gave his wholehearted support to French commerce, he failed

[46] P. Vaucher, *Walpole et la politique de Fleury* (Paris, 1924), 297.
[47] Gaston-Martin, *Nantes au XVIIIième siècle; L'ère des négriers* (Paris, 1931), 215; J. Tramond, *Manuél d'histoire maritime de la France* (Paris, 1916), 374.

to provide this commerce with adequate security because he permitted the navy to atrophy from want of financial support. If by atrophy is meant the failure to maintain naval parity with Great Britain, the charge must be sustained. The French navy, which in the days of Tourville had equalled that of Great Britain, had fallen far behind, but the responsibility for this decline is scarcely to be laid at the door of Cardinal Fleury. Fleury gave his unstinted support to the navy and at the end of his administration allotted far greater sums to the navy than had any one of his immediate predecessors. He increased the naval budget from nine million livres in 1728 to twenty-seven millions in 1742.[48] It was only after the passing of Fleury in 1745 that naval appropriations were actually reduced to a sum slightly over nineteen millions. Such sums were sufficient to make France the strongest naval power of the Continent. But neither saturated Spain nor Holland were serious rivals. The dangerous competitor was Great Britain, and to compete with the latter it would have been necessary to double the budget. The average annual British expenditure for the navy from 1740 to 1744 was in excess of two and a quarter million pounds, while in the best years of the War of the Austrian Succession, Maurepas, the French minister of marine, could obtain no more than thirty million livres.[49]

Maurepas contended that France needed a minimum of sixty vessels, but in 1745 she had no more than forty-five ships and fifteen frigates in condition to put to sea. At no time during this period did France have more than seventy-two ships-of-the-line, while Great Britain had one hundred and twenty. In spite of Maurepas' strenuous efforts to build a formidable naval force, parity with Great Britain was not achieved. To do so was beyond French resources so long as France's continental commitments necessitated her maintaining numerically the strongest army in Europe. Maurepas described the naval problem that confronted France very clearly in a mildly ironical memorial which he sent to the king in the early years of the war with Great Britain:

48 A. M. Wilson, *French Foreign Policy During the Administration of Cardinal Fleury, Harvard Historical Studies* (Cambridge, 1936), 72-90 where the entire literature has been carefully examined.

49 G. Lacour-Gayet, *La marine militaire de la France sous le règne de Louis XV* (Paris, 1910), 102.

I submit that it is principally on the sea that one must make war on a maritime power . . . I agree that in France land forces are necessary and demand great expense in time of war, but are not naval forces equally so when the war is against a maritime power and should they not be given preference from the moment when they serve to procure by means of commerce public revenues without which land forces cannot be maintained? I have often heard foreign ministers say that our navy is too much neglected, that it would be better if the King had 50,000 troops less and 50 vessels more. One can imagine the effect which this augmentation would have upon foreign courts.[50]

He argued that a larger navy which kept pace with the growth of commerce might prevent foreign wars, while a chronic neglect of the navy would most certainly invite them. In view of what was transpiring across the Channel at this moment, it would have been impossible to put the situation better. Yet this man, who did so much to modernize the French navy, was disgraced by Madame de Pompadour. But French naval policy did not simply reduce itself to a question of finance. French naval experts themselves, as will be seen, encouraged the belief that even with a numerically inferior fleet France could carry on a successful maritime war against Great Britain.

Nor were French naval officers the equals of their British rivals. The French government had the opportunity of creating a really efficient body of naval officers, for unlike those of the army, naval commissions were not sold.[51] But French naval officers were quite as aristocratic and feudal as those of the army and even more exclusive. They constituted the aristocratic *Navy of the Red*, who held in contempt the bourgeois officers drawn from the merchant marine, usually only for the duration of the war. The latter, together with the captains of fireships, lieutenants of frigates and captains of the flute formed the small body of the *Officers of the Blue*. The perpetual quarrels between these two classes of naval officers frequently demoralized French tactics. The education of French naval officers also was a faulty one. They were trained almost exclusively in hydrography and theoretical nautical science. They may have been more scholarly and erudite than British officers, but they lacked the

[50] R. Jouan, *Histoire de la marine française* (Paris, 1932), I, 223.
[51] M. Loir, *La marine royale en 1789* (Paris, 1892), 102.

more practical experience in seamanship which could not be learned in port. Unlike their British rivals they were not in the first instance sailors. Among these officers, again, it was the bureaucratic element in charge of naval administration, men who rarely or never saw active service at sea and who were, therefore, least fitted for action, that dominated the French navy.[52] It had been the design of Louis XIV to give all authority in the navy to the fighting element, but now under Louis XV the situation was reversed. Thus to diminish the authority of the fighting element among officers was to reduce unreason to a system.

The French system of naval conscription, known since 1689 as "les classes" and applied to the entire seafaring population, had its official defenders in France and its ill-informed admirers abroad; yet it was vicious and had disastrous consequences. Under this system all the sailors of the maritime provinces were divided into three, four and five classes, each class serving one year out of four, five or ten according to the number of seamen in the particular locality. Theoretically, while one class was drafted for the navy, the others were free to serve as sailors in the merchant marine. The classes being staggered, they were to be called up in rotation and, when not needed, were to receive half pay; but while on service they could not go out on a merchant vessel. All sailors were to be at the disposal of the navy for their entire lives. This system operated well enough when the classes were asked to supply crews for a small navy, but when there was a great fleet to man and the war was a long one, it usually broke down. Then, as in England, the government was found trying to press the entire seafaring population into the fleet and, as in England, the men did their best to escape.

Discontent with this system was general, and the more so because the French government did not keep its engagements. The half pay was never paid. Because of the persistent tendency of the seamen to escape, it was thought necessary to employ such brutal measures as quartering *garnissaires* upon their families—soldiers who were lodged in their homes to be fed by them. This system was so revolting to the seamen of France that little by little it was responsible

---

[52] Lacour-Gayet, *La marine militaire de la France sous le règne de Louis XV* (Paris, 1910), 236.

for depopulating the coast. The French maritime population, so full of promise in the seventeenth century, actually declined in the eighteenth. The loss which this inflicted on the navy, the merchant fleet and the fishing industry was irreparable.[53] In all these wars there was a scarcity of French sailors and in the end the government had to seek foreigners in Genoa, Nice and other Mediterranean ports. When foreigners were not available it impressed peasants and artisans who had never seen the sea. In view of the devastating effect of this system of *classement* one is inclined to agree with the opinion of David Hannay that it was a patriotic delusion on the part of complacent Englishmen when they believed that it was the British navy that ruined French maritime activity.[54]

But one must go beyond the external organization of the French navy to explain its conduct in the wars that were to follow. French naval experts, conscious of the inferiority of their navy, accepted the doctrine that it was necessary to economize their forces. Flattering themselves that they could wage effective war without measuring themselves with the organized forces of the enemy, they were guilty of a fundamental misconception of the prime function of a navy in time of war. This function can be no other than the destruction of the enemy's navy. It is only when the hostile naval squadrons which protect enemy commerce and territory have been annihilated that a *guerre de course* or privateering and operations against the enemy's coasts can be fully effective. Admiral Castex rightly charges French seamen of the eighteenth century with placing these corollaries above the main premise.[55] French naval strategy did not seek the destruction of the British fleet but aimed at piratical raids on British commerce. The corsairs, as one French naval historian puts it, supplanted the admirals. The French kept their battle fleets in their harbors in order to compel the enemy to blockade them with a much larger force, thus giving their lighter squadrons an opportunity to prey on enemy commerce. They did not seek battle because they regarded it as a mere episode incapable of producing decisive results. They took it heroically when it came, but the naval engage-

[53] Loir, *La marine royale*, 40.
[54] D. Hannay, *The Sea Trader* (1912), 267.
[55] R. Castex, *Les idées militaires de la marine du XVIIIe siècle* (Paris, 1911), 30.

ment was not the supreme object on which all naval efforts were concentrated. Their real aim was privateering, the *guerre de course*. This doctrine, that the principal aim of naval warfare was to destroy enemy commerce, was an inheritance from Pontchartrain and continued to delude French seamen throughout this and later periods. One of the best expressions of it we find in a memorial of the Count of Toulouse, who died as Grand Admiral of France in 1737:

Divergent opinions have sometimes come into conflict on the most useful employment which can be made of warships; some have asserted that fleets were of great expense and little utility, because, they say, when a battle has been won, it is seldom that an immediate benefit is derived from it, and that it is not the case with sea-battles as it is with those fought on land, where a victory sometimes makes one master of a province or of some important place; that consequently it would be better to divide up the vessels into special squadrons, to cruise now in one place, now in another, depending upon the merchant fleets expected from distant countries or upon those which it is desired to convoy, upon leaving France, in order to conduct them to places where it is to be presumed that they will be in safety from privateers. They add that at the same time these squadrons would protect one's own individual privateers, and would make it possible to capture sufficient prizes so that the damage which the enemy would receive would dispose him to desire peace more than the loss of a sea-battle, of which the damage never appears to fall on individuals, and consequently does not give so much occasion for crying out and complaining; that besides these advantages, distant operations cannot be undertaken when fleets, which absorb all available vessels, are fitted out.[56]

These remarks betray a complete misunderstanding of the meaning and the possible results of a naval battle. The abiding faith of French seamen in the effectiveness of the *guerre de course* was destined to be brutally shattered. French privateers did, in fact, inflict heavy damage on British commerce, but since the British navy was intact, this commerce always remained strong and active, while French commerce was almost completely swept from the seas once the principal French naval squadrons were destroyed.[57] It was this

---

56 *Mémoires du marquis de Villette* (Paris, 1844), lxviii, quoted in A. M. Wilson, *French Foreign Policy During the Administration of Cardinal Fleury*, 84.
57 Leon Vignols, "La course maritime," *Revue d'histoire économique et sociale*, XV (1927), 207.

avoidance of the enemy fleet, this hesitation to seek battle, these geographical and commercial objectives, this absence of pursuit, that Admiral Suffren, a really great naval commander, meant when he spoke of the "feebleness and ineptitude" of the French navy of this period.

Chapter Four

THE BALANCE OF THE CONTINENTS

IN THE long perspective of two centuries the War of the Austrian Succession stands out less as an unholy raid by rapacious powers on the Hapsburg inheritance of Maria Theresa than as the first clear signal for a vaster struggle to overthrow a double equilibrium. In this war the rising power of Prussia permanently and irrevocably shattered the continental balance established by the Treaty of Utrecht. But it marks also the beginning of one of the great ages of modern imperialism, in which the attempt was made to overthrow the balance of rival colonial empires as also determined at Utrecht. Indeed, more than a year before the hands of death closed the eyes of Charles VI, the last male descendant of the most fortunate of German dynasties, the outbreak of the Anglo-Spanish war of 1739 had opened that prolonged and complex struggle between Great Britain, France and Spain for maritime and colonial dominion which was to reach its climax in the destruction of the major portion of the old French colonial empire. These two wars, the one dynastic and continental, the other commercial and colonial, proceeded in close parallelism with one another. They were fought simultaneously and to some extent by the same powers; their currents mingled, influenced and checked each other. Because of their essential unity and interdependence the historian can best hope to make them more readily intelligible by beginning with the Anglo-Spanish crisis which was swallowed up by the Austrian Succession War.

I. THE ANGLO-SPANISH WAR

The Anglo-Spanish crisis arose out of a situation which, while not in itself irremediable, could have been corrected only by a revolutionary statesmanship for which Spain, the greatest empire builder since Rome, was scarcely prepared. The great weakness of Spanish imperialism lay less in the decrepitude of the Spanish monarchy than in having attempted too much. In the case of Spain the preemption of an entire continent from Patagonia to Mexico defeated its own purpose. There was a glaring contradiction between Spain's claim to absolute trade monopoly, which led her to cling to a system of trade regulation disastrous to honest commerce, and her inability to enforce this system. There was a further irreconcilability between this system of trade monopoly and the grant of restricted trading privileges to the British South Sea Company under the Asiento Treaty of 1713, a shoe horn for a vast illicit commerce but the inescapable price which Spain had to pay to Great Britain at Utrecht for the reimposition of the old system of trade.[1] There was a manifest dislocation in a colonial system in which the Spanish government was solely preoccupied with the exploitation of the vast mines of America, while a Spanish American population scattered over a continent had needs which Spain could not supply. Spain possessed neither adequate shipping nor sufficient sailors, and no more than one twentieth of the products she exported to America were of Spanish origin.[2]

One naturally asks why the Spanish government kept up this strange and comical fiction, why it continued to regulate, limit, fix certain ports as the only places of trade, and enforce convoy? The answer lies largely in the vicious fiscal system of the Spanish monarchy. In its dire need for money the treasury could not dispense with the heavy taxes, the high export and import duties of the colonial trade. It was bound to maintain the old system of trade by which the Indies were kept as a special preserve for Spanish traders, and by which these traders paid for this boon by being outrageously fleeced in the mother country. Well might the Spanish minister Campillo write:

With such high duties and such restrictive rights, and other notable hindrances, it may be said that we have shut the door of the Indies on the manufactures of Spain, and invited other nations to supply those goods to the Spanish dominions, since every port in fourteen thousand leagues is open to them and those provinces must be supplied from somewhere.[3]

[1] A. Aiton, "The Asiento Treaty," *Hispanic-American Historical Review*, VIII (1928), 167.
[2] H. Berindoague, *Le mercantilisme en Espagne* (Paris, 1929), 162.
[3] Quoted from R. Pares, *War and Trade in the West Indies, 1739-1763* (Oxford, 1936), 4.

The Spanish system aimed at high prices, great profits, slow returns and small consumption, but it created a situation in which contraband trade and smuggling on a grand scale must inevitably arise. Compare with this system that of a country like England which in these years was becoming steadily more industrialized, with a vast commerce hungry for markets and Spanish colonists equally hungry for goods. British enterprise and the Spanish colonial system could hardly co-exist without conflict. Especially for the North American colonists trade with the Spanish settlements was imperative, as this trade furnished their main supply of ready money. They and British West India merchants could easily afford to undersell Spanish traders who must sell dear to cover the charges. But more than that, the whole Spanish colonial trade moved in a vicious circle. The less often the Spanish *flota* and the galleons sailed, the greater were the opportunities and the profits of the interlopers. The wholesale merchants of Mexico and Peru might well have preferred to deal with the regular Spanish fleets, but they could not afford to wait, and if some of them dealt with the smugglers, the others had to follow suit for fear of being undersold. The more the colonial markets, however, were stocked with smuggled goods, the less inducement was there to use the galleons. These galleon fleets became smaller and less frequent, in spite of repeated royal edicts which prescribed regular sailings.[4] In the 1730's there was an interval of seven years between sailings and when at last the galleons did appear at Cartagena in 1737, they found the market glutted with smuggled goods.

It was over the chronic mutual outrages on the Spanish Main arising from an attempt on the part of the insulted and defrauded Spanish government to stop this contraband trade by means of *guarda-costas*, that the Anglo-Spanish War broke out. The hectoring tactics employed by these *guarda-costas*, for the most part unpaid and private individuals or ruined merchants who had to rely on their prizes for their subsistence and profits, were strongly reminiscent of the days of the buccaneers. It was apparent that the Spanish

[4] G. D. du Dezert, "La richesse et la civilisation espagnoles au XVIIIᵉ siècle," *Revue Hispanique,* LXXIII (1928), 185. Vera L. Brown, "The South Sea Company and the Contraband Trade," *American Historical Review,* XXXI (1926), 671. By the same author, "The Contraband Trade, etc.," *Hispanic-American Historical Review,* VIII (1928), 178.

governors were either unwilling or unable to control them and sometimes shared in their takings. Ranging at large, often at some distance from the coast, they preyed upon all commerce, both lawful and illicit, particularly that of Jamaica, the headquarters of the British West Indian contraband trade. If the smugglers were blessed with British swagger and resorted to counter-piracy, they found this game scarcely profitable, for there were fifty British ships in the West Indies to one Spaniard. The depredations caused by the *guarda-costas* among traders, both legitimate and illegitimate, aroused such shrieks of resentment among British merchants that the cabinet took up the issue with the Spanish government.

From the very beginning the diplomatic discussions, in which Spain defended the right of search and Great Britain the right of free navigation, were complicated by British domestic politics. Walpole's conduct in the Spanish affair was that of a just, clear-headed man who saw that England had a bad case and wanted a settlement with Spain. Being a country squire without any imperial theory that we know of, he persisted in believing that such a settlement was possible. He did, in fact, arrange a partial settlement in the Convention of El Pardo (January 14, 1739), which involved concessions on both sides. But a settlement was the last thing the parliamentary opposition, composed of disappointed office seekers, wanted. It has recently been contended that the opposition forced war upon Walpole in order to throw him out of office.[5] This may be true. But it is also true that the opposition politicians did not create but merely exploited the wider discontent among the merchants of London and Bristol. The American planters noisily demanded that the right of search be abolished. The Lord Mayor of London, the various provincial municipalities, the merchants of Liverpool and Edinburgh insisted on vigorous measures against Spain. This decidedly bellicose temper of the English merchants, suggests M. Vaucher, was due to the pinch of a trade depression which whetted their desire for new markets.[6] Even if this was not the case, it is true that the quantity of British trade had remained almost stationary during the ten years preceding the crisis. Complaints abounded that British commerce

[5] G. R. Stirling Taylor, *Robert Walpole and His Age* (London, 1931), 299.
[6] P. Vaucher, *Robert Walpole et la politique de Fleury* (Paris, 1924), 301-302.

was declining. It was certain that it was not advancing as rapidly as that of France. Economists and politicians alike were frightened by the bugbear of increasing French competition, and the competition of French merchandise in the Spanish market was thought to be particularly serious.[7] In a frenzy of apprehension and jealousy English pamphleteers, egged on by the jingoism of the Boy Patriots, among whom the volcanic Pitt was already conspicuous, excited their countrymen to strike a blow at Spain in the hope of restoring their trade to its old pre-eminence. No historian interested in a judicial examination of the case between the two countries can deny the justice of the Spanish claim to the right of search in territorial waters. But men like Carteret wanted no judicial examination. "No search," he cried in the House of Lords, "is the only remedy for this case. No search, my Lords, is the cry that runs from the sailor to the merchant, from the merchant to the Parliament, and from Parliament, my Lords, it ought to reach the throne."[8]

England was spoiling for a fight and, after a laudable effort to settle the dispute amicably, Walpole gave way to the popular clamor. At last, on October 19, 1739, war was declared on Spain and England's purest trade war began.[9]

It was clear that a war with Spain must be fought in the West Indies, but what was such a war to accomplish? Was it to be simply the kind of trade attack which in the past hundred years had become an integral part of British national strategy? Or was it to be a war of conquest, a war for the possession of the American mines or the Spanish islands of the Caribbean? There were pamphlets, leading articles and anonymous letters enough which echoed Lord Carteret's demand for a war of conquest. That the British ministers were impressed by these demands may be seen from the instructions given to Admiral Cathcart, which aimed at the annexation of Spanish colonies by consent. There was, however, a genuine conflict of interest between those who wanted lands for new plantations and those who wanted only outposts for trade in the Spanish colonial

---

[7] R. Pares, *War and Trade in the West Indies*, 61.
[8] *Parliamentary History*, X, 745-754.
[9] For diplomatic details see R. Pares, *War and Trade in the West Indies*, 29-64; P. Vaucher, *Walpole et la politique de Fleury*, 228-288; H. Temperley, "The Causes of War of Jenkins' Ear," *Royal Historical Society Transactions* (1909), 235; G. B. Hertz, *British Imperialism in the XVIII Century* (Manchester, 1908), 47.

dominions. While the North American colonists were in favor of new conquests, the sugar planters of the British West Indies were resolutely opposed to a further extension of territory. The British sugar planters had lost the European market to the French and the Dutch, and they were now anxious to keep up the high price of sugar in the closed but expanding market of Great Britain. It would naturally be impossible to do this if the number of sugar planters and the area of production were to be vastly increased. But the economic balance between the British North American and the tropical colonies had become badly upset since the productive capacity of these northern colonies had far outrun the consuming capacity of the British West Indies. There were but two ways to restore the balance; either allow the North Americans to trade with the French and Spanish colonies, or acquire new territories in the West Indies. The West India interest opposed both solutions and, as previous legislation such as the Molasses Act of 1733 had shown, their influence with parliament and the ministry was often decisive. The sugar interest, particularly in Jamaica, supported plans which would not be likely to lead to an extension of territory but to create access to the forbidden regions of Spanish America. If such a strategy ultimately prevailed, it was due less, perhaps, to the influence of the West India interest than to the failure of the British navy. The fact remains, however, that the actual conduct of the war was in keeping with the wishes of the West India interest.

The main object of the British attacks on Port Bello, Cartagena, Chagres and La Guayra was to paralyze Spanish colonial trade by the destruction of its terminal ports. Their justification lay in the preponderant part played by the treasure fleets in Spanish finance. Had the execution of these attacks been as sound as their conception, the effect must have been decisive. But the attack on Cartagena, watched with agonized anxiety by both Spain and France, proved to be an ignominious failure.[10] With this failure the British offensive in the West Indies fizzled out.

Any war in the West Indies in which Great Britain sought to disturb the balance of power in America must stir two other com-

[10] M. Sautai, *Les préliminaires de la guerre de la Succession d'Autriche* (Paris, 1907), I, 360.

mercial nations, France and Holland, to vigilance and action. Holland was at this time so closely associated with England in European affairs, that it was customary to speak of them as the "Maritime Powers." The bond that united them was the Barrier Treaty of 1715, by which the two powers turned the Spanish Netherlands over to Austria on two conditions: that Austria should contribute to the support of the border fortresses occupied by the Dutch as security against French aggression; and, second, that the import duties of the Austrian Netherlands should not be altered except by the unanimous consent of all three states.[11] As a military defense against French aggression the border fortresses were then and later proved to be worthless, but they were an incomparable instrument for controlling Belgian economic life and the commercial policy of the emperor.[12] But however much Holland, because of the Barrier Treaty, consented to become the cockboat in the tow of the English frigate, to use the contemptuous phrase of Frederick the Great, the Dutch refused to become implicated in the West Indian dispute.

Quite different was the case of France. Great Britain's assault upon the Spanish empire found France in a position that was not merely advantageous but brilliant. Her diplomatic hegemony on the Continent was beyond question. On friendly terms with the Bourbons of Spain and Naples, she was allied with Sweden, Saxony Poland and Turkey, where the Capitulations of 1740 carried French prestige and commercial privileges to the highest point ever attained. With a whole shoal of German client princes dependent upon subsidies, France's influence upon purely German affairs had never been greater.[13] Above all, France had become reconciled with Austria, and the secular hostility between Bourbon and Hapsburg might be considered to have reached its term. With the French acquisition of Lorraine in the Treaty of Vienna in 1738, Austria had ceased to be a menace to French frontiers. One year later France had negotiated the Treaty of Belgrade, in which Austria was forced to hand back to the Sultan all the conquests of Prince Eugene (Serbia, Wallachia, Orsova and Belgrade). Further hostility to Austria would not only be without purpose but would only serve to play into the hands of

11 Sir Richard Lodge, "The Maritime Powers," *History*, 15 (1930), 246.
12 H. Pirenne, *Histoire de Belgique* (Brussels, 1926), V, 234.
13 G. Grosjean, *La politique rhénane de Vergennes* (Paris, 1925), 25.

England, ever alert to create a continental diversion when in conflict with France on the high seas. No one saw this more clearly than Cardinal Fleury, who instructed the Marquis de Mirepoix on his departure for Vienna to work "for the establishment of an understanding and union, both lasting and intimate, between the King and the Emperor."[14] Indeed, the shrewd, supple Fleury, who directed the destinies of France with the same caution with which he nursed his emaciated body, weighed down with his eighty-seven years, had succeeded in isolating Great Britain. The latter had not so much as a single trustworthy and useful ally on the Continent.[15] For the first time in her history France was in a position to co-ordinate her continental policy with her imperial and commercial interests—and these interests in the West Indies now hung in the balance.

France had few smugglers in the West Indies. Her principal stake was in the Cadiz trade. From one half to seven ninths of all the commodities which the galleons and the *flotas* regularly conveyed to Spanish America came from France.[16] France, therefore, had both commercial and political reasons for supporting Spain. If on commercial grounds alone she must attempt to prevent Great Britain from engrossing the entire trade of the Spanish West Indies, the overthrow of the balance in the Caribbean by British annexations would be altogether intolerable, unless the French colonies were to be written off as a loss. With ample evidence in hand that this was Britain's intention, Fleury resolved upon military intervention. He proceeded with caution and yet with audacity. He did nothing on the Continent that might arouse the suspicion of aggressive intentions or that might provoke a diversion in favor of England. He announced to the emperor and to Holland that he was acting without any collusion with Spain, simply to preserve the colonial balance established at Utrecht. With peace on the Continent assured,

[14] Quoted from P. Gaxotte, *Louis the Fifteenth and His Times* (English trans. [Philadelphia, 1934], 162).

[15] England could count on no active support from Austria. Charles VI was still very bitter over the Treaty of Vienna, whose unfavorable terms he attributed to the "treachery" of the English. K. Pribram, *Englische Staatsvertraege* (Vienna, 1907), I, 549; A. M. Wilson, *French Foreign Policy during the Administration of Cardinal Fleury* (Cambridge, 1936), 318.

[16] M. Sautai, *Les préliminaires, etc.*, I, 100; H. Sée, *Les armateurs de Saint-Malo* (Paris, 1929), 3; E. W. Dahlgren, "Voyages français à destination de la mer du Sud, 1695-1749," *Nouvelles archives des missions scientifiques*, XIV (1907), 423-554; R. Pares, *War and Trade in the West Indies*, 142-143.

he could concentrate all French resources on the struggle with England, which, he was convinced, must come. Then, at the end of August, 1740, he sent two powerful French battle squadrons, one under d'Antin with eighteen vessels and another under La Roche-Allard with fifteen vessels, to the West Indies. The instructions which he gave to d'Antin breathed aggression in every line. D'Antin was to unite with La Roche-Allard, attack and destroy the inferior British fleet, invade Jamaica, destroy its towns and carry off the greatest possible number of negroes from the plantations.[17] Had d'Antin done his duty, France would have been at war with Great Britain before the end of the year.

One month later the Emperor Charles VI died without a male heir. This unforeseen event led to the recall of d'Antin and threw France back into the vortex of European complications.

II. THE AUSTRIAN SUCCESSION

To outward appearances there was no more formidable power in Europe than the Hapsburg monarchy. Neither France nor Russia was more populous. Its resources seemed inexhaustible. It was, however, extremely vulnerable, not merely because, being a dynastic state of the purest type, it lacked the compact internal unity of the states of western Europe, but because since the Treaty of Utrecht its dominions lay dispersed over the map of Europe in a manner that made them difficult to defend. To protect the Austrian Netherlands against France and the Milanese with the Duchy of Parma against the restless ambition of the Spanish Queen, Elizabeth Farnese, Austria was dependent upon the alliance of the maritime powers, whose interest in the Hapsburg monarchy went no further than to maintain a potential enemy of France. It is not surprising that there were Austrian statesmen who regarded these outposts merely as transitory possessions.

But even the permanent units of the Hapsburg monarchy, the kingdom of Bohemia with Silesia and Moravia, the kingdom of Hungary with Transylvania and Croatia, and the various Austrias were bound together by only the loosest of dynastic ties. Almost one

17 For the best discussion of these instructions, see R. Pares, *War and Trade in the West Indies*, 164-178.

half of all the peoples thus brought together were Slavs and these Slavs were twice as numerous as the Hungarians. None the less, it was the Germans of Austria who dominated the Hapsburg monarchy. Whether or not one accepts the view of Hantsch, the latest historian of Austria, that a permanent union of Hungary, Bohemia and Austria under Hapsburg leadership was a political necessity as a measure of defense against the advance of Islam, the fact remains that the Austrian archdukes could never have succeeded in retaining and consolidating these divergent kingdoms and peoples into a permanent union, had they not at the same time been the bearers of the German imperial crown, which lent them a certain ideal dignity and enabled them at critical moments to draw upon the resources of Germany in the development of their Danubian monarchy.[18] It should not be forgotten that the destruction of the Czech constitution after the battle of the White Mountain in 1620 and the conquest of Hungary were effected largely with German arms. The dynasty was German; Austria, the core of the monarchy, was German; and the strongest cultural energies in the Danubian area were German. The closer the bond which the Hapsburgs cast about their hereditary dominions, the more thoroughly did they succeed in denationalizing and Germanizing at least the upper classes of the Slavic and Magyar sections of the monarchy.[19]

If they hoped to succeed in this policy, the Hapsburg rulers could not dispense with their German imperial connections.[20] Although the German Empire was nothing more than a bloodless anachronism after 1648, the Hapsburg emperors had managed to salvage enough fragments from the wreckage of the Thirty Years' War to make their possession very useful to the rulers of the Danubian monarchy. Before Frederick the Great did irreparable damage to it, the imperial authority was not an altogether negligible factor in the political life of central Europe. In the imperial court, the aulic council, which was predominantly Austrian in composition, the Hapsburgs had a pliable instrument, which might be depended upon

[18] H. Hantsch, *Die Entwicklung Österreich-Ungarns zur Grossmacht* (Freiburg, 1933), 36.

[19] H. Steinacker, "Die geschichtlichen Voraussetzungen des Nationalitätenproblems bis 1867," *Das Nationalitätenrecht im alten Österreich*, editor, K. G. Kugelmann (Vienna 1934), 6.

[20] H. Ritter von Srbik, *Deutsche Einheit* (Munich, 1935), I, 86.

to render decisions favorable to the House of Austria.[21] In two ecclesiastical electorates, Mainz and Trier, they were usually in a position to impose their candidates. Most important of all, the archbishops and canons, who formed the nucleus of the Catholic party among the princes of the Empire, were largely the creatures of the Hapsburg emperors. However insignificant the actual powers of the emperor, there were still levers enough which a shrewd Austrian statesman could employ to advantage.

Yet these imperial German connections could never be an adequate substitute for a well-integrated Danubian state. It is therefore all the more astonishing to learn that before the time of Maria Theresa so little had been accomplished in the way of unifying, centralizing and organizing as a modern state at least the central core of these extensive dominions. The Hapsburg monarchy of 1740 was an unfinished, ramshackle structure, which could not be called a state in the modern sense.[22] It was neither a commonwealth of self-governing dominions, nor yet a full-fledged royal autocracy, but a curious combination of a dynastic state and the dying remnants of the feudal *Staendestaat*, as represented by feudal corporations, the estates of Austria, Bohemia and Hungary. It is true that in the preceding century the estates of the lands of the Bohemian crown had been made more tractable by wholesale expulsion of the rebellious Czech nobles and their replacement by a nobility of German or international origin, but the administration of Bohemia was still in the hands of a few privileged noble families. Least of all had the principle of absolutism triumphed in Hungary, where the estates agreed to accept the Pragmatic Sanction in 1723 only after the solemn declaration of the independence of Hungary had been written into that document. The Hapsburg monarchy of 1740 was a mere congeries of units regarded by the dynasty as a family possession and employed by them as the basis for an imperialistic foreign policy. There was no common economic policy, no common political or military system. There was no common tradition of loyalty among its separate units. It was quite possible to lop off a province here, another there without affecting the rest of the organism.

21 G. Masur, "Deutsches Reich im 18. Jahrhundert," *Preussische Jahrbücher*, CCXXIX (1932), 5.
22 J. Redlich, *Das österreichische Staats-und Reichsproblem*, Leipzig (1920), 20.

Emperor Charles VI attempted to lay the ghost of the impending dissolution of the monarchy, which in the absence of a male heir frightened all Austrian statesmen, not by internal consolidation as Prince Eugene recommended, but by a measure more in keeping with his dynastic conception of politics. He drafted the Pragmatic Sanction of 1713. This document, which made over all the Hapsburg dominions to Maria Theresa, has rightly been called the first fundamental law of the Hapsburg monarchy. It was designed to transform what had hitherto been a merely personal union among the separate units of the monarchy into a real union.[23] This document, however, had merely a legal significance, for it altered nothing in the actual structure of the monarchy. Having thus appointed Maria Theresa to succeed him in all his dominions, Charles VI spent the second half of his reign in bringing the Pragmatic Sanction to the notice of all the parties concerned, beginning with his immediate kinsfolk and the estates of the various dominions and finishing up with all the principal powers of Europe. In exchange for concessions which were anything but negligible, all the powers had duly signified their concurrence. Leaving Austria without resources and without credit, this assiduous campaign for signatures does little credit to the political intelligence of the last male Hapsburger. When he died in 1740 both the army and civil service had been without pay for two years. The army was demoralized and under the command of superannuated generals. There were no provisions, no magazines, no serviceable fortresses.

At the age of twenty-three and utterly unprepared for a public career by education and experience, Maria Theresa ascended the most difficult throne in Europe. Neither her mediocre husband, Francis Stephen, nor her senescent ministry was of much assistance to her in these early critical years. Her strength lay in her good sense and in the undoubted feminine charm which she, as a sprightly and amiable Viennese woman, possessed in high degree. Entirely out of sympathy with the literary and intellectual currents of her day, her virtues were Christian and domestic, and in the midst of her large and ever growing family she became not unlike that

[23] W. Schüssler, *Das Verfassungsproblem im Habsburgerreich* (1918), 37; G. Turba, *Die Grundlagen der Pragmatischen Sanction* (Vienna, 1911).

bourgeois feminine type of the eighteenth century whom Goethe described in his *Hermann und Dorothea*. Her strongest impulses were maternal and her highest aspiration was to become "the universal mother" of all her people. Born to be happy and to please others, she had no grasp of foreign affairs, let alone the game of power politics as it was played in her century. Agreeing with Kant, though for different reasons, that politics should be moral, she could not look upon the war which broke upon her in 1740 as a clash of rival interests, but only as a conflict between her own sacred right and diabolical injustice. She lacked both the personal endowment and the knowledge of men and affairs to play the part of a genuine autocrat. She is scarcely comparable to her abler Prussian enemy, who attended to all affairs in person. She retained ultimate responsibility, upheld the prestige of the crown, inspired and encouraged, but she did not govern. Her government was the government of the "King in Council" and the Austrian *Staatskonferenz* was just as characteristic of Theresan Austria as autocracy was of Prussia.

Although the death of Charles VI sent a tremor through the chancelleries of Europe, there was no ground for immediate apprehension. Russia and England were old allies, and Spain, involved in a colonial war, for the moment remained silent. Fleury, on the verge of a maritime war with England and desiring no continental complications, hastened to recognize Maria Theresa and declared that in accordance with treaty obligations he would respect the Pragmatic Sanction. Charles Albert of Bavaria alone refused to recognize her, but Bavaria had no resources of its own and was, moreover, entirely dependent upon France. Fleury had examined the Bavarian pretensions to the Austrian throne and had found them wanting in adequate legal foundation. At most would he oppose the election of Francis Stephen to the German imperial crown, lest he might employ that office to recover his former Duchy of Lorraine. But even this had not yet become his settled policy.

III. THE PRUSSIAN INVASION OF SILESIA

The assault upon Austria came from an unexpected quarter—from Brandenburg-Prussia which, as the latest member to thrust its way into the company of the great powers, was to become a disturbing factor of incalculable importance in the affairs of continental Europe. The rise of Prussia marks the appearance on the European scene of a new and distinctive type of political structure. What gave force and individuality to eighteenth-century Prussia was not its resources in land, men and money. Austria was five times the size of Prussia in 1740, yet neither her public revenues nor her army greatly surpassed those of Prussia. The strength of the latter lay in the circumstance that it represented a system. This system, as it emerged from the iron age of Frederick William I in 1740, presented a peculiar and unique form of autocracy, a degree of economic paternalism and social discipline found nowhere else in Europe, a military organization which made every fifth inhabitant a soldier, and a civil service conspicuous among the bureaucracies of Europe for its integrity, economy and efficiency. Nature and geography alike conspired to place obstacles in the way of this hard and dour Prussian state, so sparingly furnished with cultural graces and amenities of life. It was only the thrift and frugality of a sturdy people that could extort from the infertile, sandy soil and the extensive swamp lands of Brandenburg a certain modest comfort. Prussian statesmanship also was engaged in an incessant struggle against the geographical dispersion of Prussian territories. These territories, scattered in three separate masses over the entire north German plain from Memel to the Rhine, formed neither a natural political nor a racial unit. But despite the fact that the commercial and industrial Rhineland had nothing in common, not even religion, with the agrarian and feudal economy of Prussia proper, which lay east of the Elbe river, these regions were organized into one of the most highly centralized states in Europe. Again, the king who ruled in Königsberg, Berlin and Wesel was constantly lifted out of the supine quietism of the normal German prince and driven into the brisker atmosphere of European power politics. And the Hohenzollern princes, one of the ablest ruling families of Europe, were never wanting in the ambition to play a European role.

The ancient and deep-seated hostility between Austria and Prussia was rooted in the difference between the imperial and Catholic power of the south and the rising Protestant state of northern Germany. Since the days of Leopold I the Austrian emperors had been placing obstacles in the way of the expansion of the Hohenzollern monarchy. Instead of openly throwing down the gauntlet to Prussia, however, they preferred, imprudently enough, the indirect tactics of mobilizing the judicial machinery of the Empire against their potential rival, thus dressing up a perfectly natural antagonism in the guise of a legal discrimination against Prussia. Only grudgingly and against his better judgment had Charles VI recognized the Prussian acquisition of Swedish Pomerania in 1721 and the Prussian claims to the Rhenish provinces of Jülich and Berg. Least felicitous of all was Charles VI's conduct in this latter affair. When in 1728 Charles VI sought Prussian support for the Pragmatic Sanction, he promised to defend Hohenzollern claims to these duchies in return for Frederick William I's concurrence. The latter had accepted the treaty in good faith. But ten years later, when Prussian support was no longer necessary, Charles VI signed another treaty with France and the maritime powers which was equivalent to a repudiation of the Prussian claims. Frederick William's only reply to this Austrian treachery was his remark, pointing to his son, Frederick, "There stands one who will avenge me."

When the gifted and intelligent Frederick II assumed control of Prussian affairs at the age of twenty-eight in May, 1740, he was still immature, vain, arrogant, hasty in his judgments and wanting in experience and foresight. But already in 1740 the basic lineaments of his subsequent statesmanship can be clearly discerned. Notwithstanding the all but universal *étatisme* of the continental monarchies of the old regime, no absolute monarch carried the cult of the state to greater lengths than Frederick II. An irreverent skeptic who scoffed at the very idea of a divine right monarchy, he waxed solemn whenever he mentioned the state.[24] The state, as Frederick conceived it, was the overmastering authority to which not merely the personal interests of the monarch but also the wishes of the people must be rigidly subordinated. The driving force of both foreign and domestic policy was to be the interests of the state. Confronted with a concrete diplomatic situation, Frederick, therefore, never hesitated to violate the moral law if he thought the

24 Even a casual perusal of his *Testamente Politique* of 1752 will indicate this. G. B. Volz, *Die Politischen Testamente Friedrichs des Grossen* (Berlin, 1920).

interests of the state demanded it. This was to accept Machiavelli's conception of politics. Like Machiavelli and Montesquieu, Frederick sought to reduce politics to a mechanistic science, which would limit the scope of chance in the flux of events and chart a course of conduct suggested by calculation and illuminated by the light of reason. Like Montesquieu, whose books he had studied, his ideal was that of a political sociologist. He was not the philosopher on the throne, except in the jest of his enemies, but he studied philosophy and history to clarify his political thought, to examine the peculiar strength and weakness of his own state and discover the energies and limitations of those states among which he had to find his way.

There is scarcely a historian who has not found it startling that this conqueror of Silesia, whose diplomacy soon acquired a reputation for being more than ordinarily deceitful and unreliable even in an age of indifferent political morals, should have published in the year of his succession to the throne his *Anti-Machiavel*. Historians have asked, was not the moral and humanitarian idealism which he expressed in such glowing terms in this essay itself a mask for the perfect Machiavellian, calculated to deceive the European world as to his true sentiments? Yet, surprising as it may seem, this was not the case. As a friend and student of his master, Voltaire, he had become familiar with English humanitarian ideas and constitutional government. As a youth he had read and accepted the Abbé de Saint Pierre's utopian dream of *Eternal Peace*. As a young prince he had absorbed Fénélon's *Télèmaque* and had found there the ideal portrait of a virtuous, just and pacific prince. He had accepted also Voltaire's doctrine that the progress of humanity was the most important theme of history. It is this body of humanitarian and liberal thought that the *Anti-Machiavel* reflects. But was it really possible to realize these new ideals in his militaristic and bureaucratic Prussia? Prussia was not a fully developed national power like France, but a rising, unsatisfied state with impossible frontiers in an exposed position in the heart of Europe. Could this expanding Prussia, too large for an ordinary German electorate and too small for a kingdom, afford to dispense with Machiavellian devices of self-defense and conquest? Frederick's answer to this question was the conquest of Silesia.[25] Yet it should be pointed out that although power politics for the moment completely displaced his humanitarian ideals, the real meaning of his subsequent statesmanship was a heroic, if not very successful, effort to reconcile the claims of humanity with those of power politics.

Frederick was the destroyer of the German Empire. He ignored the constitutional authority of the Hapsburg emperor, whom he treated not as a superior but as an equal. Even when he supported the Bavarian Emperor Charles VII, he used the latter merely as an instrument in the struggle against Hapsburg Austria and as a means of acquiring Prussian military hegemony in Germany.[26] To have suggested to him an appeal to the imperial courts at Wetzlar or Vienna in quarrels with other princes would have provoked only sardonic laughter. In 1750 he ordered that the customary prayer for the emperor in Prussian churches be dropped "as an antiquated and stupid usage." The Empire meant nothing to him and he either magnified or minimized the "Germanic Liberties" of the princes according to his momentary interest. For a time in 1757 he even cherished a plan for breaking away from the Empire entirely.

Frederick's invasion of Silesia was not the execution of a carefully prepared and long-considered plan, as he suggested in his well-known letter to his friend Algarotti. The truth is that nothing was prepared. It was rather a sudden improvisation upon which he decided when he heard the news of the death of the emperor.[27] He was convinced that a state like Prussia could gain only by employing a favorable moment and by speedy action toward a clear and definite objective. This favorable moment had now arrived. He thought it probable that France would employ this occasion to consolidate her influence in Germany. If he attacked Austria now, France must sooner or later seek his alliance. If she failed to do so, which he thought improbable, there was still the possibility of co-operation with England, France's enemy. Such were his thoughts

25 For the best discussion of Frederick's political ethics see F. Meinecke, *Die Idee der Staatsraison in der neueren Geschichte* (Berlin, 1924), 350 ff.; G. Küntzel, "Friedrich der Grosse," in *Meister der Politik*, edited by K. A. von Mueller (Berlin, 1924), Vol. II; Paul-Dubois, *Frédéric le Grand d'après sa correspondance politique* (Paris, 1903), 294; also G. Ritter, *Friedrich der Grosse* (Leipzig, 1936), 81.

26 A. Berney, *Friedrich der Grosse* (Tübingen, 1934), 115.

27 G. B. Volz, "Die Politik Friedrichs des Grossen vor und nach seiner Thronbesteigung," *Historische Zeitschrift*, 151 (1935), 486.

when he marched his armies into Silesia—and, roughly speaking, his calculations proved to be correct. Even so, however, an aggressive policy could succeed only if he were on the ground first, if he surprised all the others, and if he created an accomplished fact. For this reason he sent his armies into Silesia before he even began to negotiate with Vienna. To assert a claim to Silesia before he had done so he thought worse than useless, and in this also his judgment was sound. But it was impossible to flout the principles of law and justice more outrageously. Not certain of the support of any power, embarking on a political gamble, trusting only to the logic of facts and to his armies, he invaded Silesia against the advice of his foreign minister and his generals. They anticipated what actually happened, that his entire subsequent political career would be determined by this first adventurous act of aggression, even if it made Prussia a great power. But this price he was willing to pay.

Present-day historians no longer find it useful to inquire into the justice of the Prussian claims to Silesia. If such claims had once existed, they had been rendered null and void by subsequent treaties. Frederick's real motive derived from the political geography of Prussia. He wanted Silesia to round off his kingdom, and Silesia offered an opportunity for expansion in a direction that would not conflict with the interests of the great western powers. Seventy years later even Metternich recognized the necessity of Silesia for Prussia when Napoleon and Russia offered it and he refused to take it. To retain Silesia Frederick would even have surrendered his Rhenish provinces, which he regarded as a liability. With a good eye for the kind of propaganda which his age understood, he warmed up the superannuated claims. But in his conscience he knew them to be fraudulent. He scarcely hoped to make any impression in Vienna with a formal statement of claims. On seeing the document which his foreign minister Podewils had drawn up he remarked, "Bravo! This is the work of an excellent charlatan."[28] "If there is anything to be gained by honesty, then we shall be honest; if we must dupe, then let us be scoundrels." He never regretted this Silesian venture.

Once in occupation of Silesia, he offered Maria Theresa his alliance, promised to vote for Francis Stephen in the imperial elec-

[28] A. Berney, *Friedrich der Grosse*, 123.

tion, and offered to pay an indemnity of three million gulden for the cession of Silesia. Although her ministers were ready to compromise with Prussia, Maria Theresa refused even to discuss terms with the "robber" of Silesia. She singled out the Prussian monarch as the special object of her detestation, and it did not occur to her that from the point of view of law and justice the conduct of Brühl, Fleury, d'Ormea and even George II was scarcely more defensible than that of Frederick II.

It cannot be said that Frederick was equal to the military crisis which presently arose in Silesia. If a Prussian defeat was averted at Mollwitz (April 10, 1741) and the Austrian army routed, this was due to the firm leadership of General Schwerin and the steady advance of the Prussian infantry. The military consequences of the victory were inconsiderable, but its political importance was decisive. Frederick had escaped disaster. He now ceased to be a madcap adventurer and became a promising ally. All those powers who could discover in their archives any shadow of a claim to Austrian territory suddenly came to the fore: Bavaria, Saxony, Sardinia, and Spain. Charles Albert, the Bavarian elector, who had spent his youth as a prisoner in Austria, had every reason to take the oath of Hannibal against the Hapsburgs, but his claims to Austrian territory were no better than those of Prussia. The Bavarian version of the *Testament of Emperor Ferdinand I*, on which Charles Albert based his claims, was a manifest forgery, as the Austrian ministers amply proved by producing the original codicil of 1547.[29] But Charles Albert wanted to become emperor and an emperor without a more adequate territorial foundation than Bavaria could provide would cut a ridiculous figure. He therefore asserted a claim, apparently in good faith, to all the Hapsburg dominions with the exception of Hungary, though he had neither army nor money to support such exorbitant claims. Saxony, too, always oscillating between Austria and her rivals, came forward in the hope of obtaining as much of Silesia, Bohemia and Moravia as she could get. Philip V and Elizabeth Farnese of Spain sought to recover everything that Spain had lost at Utrecht, especially Parma, the patrimony of Elizabeth Farnese. Spain and Bavaria

29 M. Doeberl, *Entwicklungsgeschichte Bayerns* (Munich, 1912), II, 168; Fritz Wagner, *Kaiser Karl VII und die Grossen Mächte* (Stuttgart, 1938), 22.

had already signed a treaty of mutual assistance at Nymphenburg. One thing is clear, that all these machinations would have been utterly futile had not the Prussian army and France stood behind them. But how came France to unify this European campaign of plunder against the House of Austria?

IV. BELLE ISLE AND THE CONTINENTAL COALITION

Fleury's policy of abstaining from continental commitments in order to concentrate his efforts on a struggle with Great Britain had led him to recognize Maria Theresa and turn a deaf ear to the Spanish request for French support to recover Austrian possessions in Italy. He had refused to accept the legitimacy of Bavarian claims on Austrian territory, though he was willing to support the Bavarian candidacy for the imperial office, if this could be done without a war with Austria. He was suspicious of the adventurous game of Frederick II and refused to listen to the suggestion of a Prussian alliance because the Prussian king might easily be induced to desert his French ally if Austria and England offered him sufficient encouragement.[30]

This line of policy was logical, intelligent, and to the best interests of France. But it was not understood. It was in vain that Fleury explained to a nobility which for the past two centuries had won honor and fame in wars against the House of Austria that this power was no longer a menace to France. When he gave out that he intended to support the Pragmatic Sanction, he was denounced as a pusillanimous and senile dotard. A large part of the ministry and the court were opposed to this sharp breach with the ancient policy of France. Public opinion thought Fleury hesitant and contrasted his conduct with the decisive political action of the Prussian monarch. No one did more toward inflaming this anti-Austrian sentiment than the Comte de Belle Isle, a brilliant grand seigneur, a fascinating talker and an accomplished master in the oily art of backstairs intrigue. Vicomte Fleury has shown in a recent study how this indifferent soldier and mediocre statesman swept Cardinal Fleury into war.[31] With prodigious ambition and indomitable

[30] M. Sautai, *Les préliminaires, etc.,* 271.
[31] Le Vicomte Fleury, *Le sécret du maréchal de Belle-Isle* (Paris, 1934), 7 ff.

courage Belle Isle was determined to blot out the disgrace into which his family had fallen since the days of his grandfather, the Superintendent Fouquet. He applied for and obtained the governorship of Metz, and since the War of the Polish Succession he had acquired a certain notoriety as the nemesis of the House of Hapsburg-Lorraine. Related by marriage to Charles Albert, the elector of Bavaria, he prevailed upon the latter to solicit the imperial office before Louis XV or Fleury had made any decision in the matter. Working now through the French foreign office, then secretly through private influences at the court, writing a continuous stream of memorials and reports, he succeeded in wresting from the king and the cardinal step by step, first the espousal of the cause of the Bavarian client, then a subsidy for Charles Albert, then the acceptance of the unfavorable treaty of alliance with Prussia of June 5, 1741, which imposed upon France far heavier obligations than upon Frederick II, and finally active French military intervention.[32] Fleury's plans for a maritime war with England were forgotten and instead France was now sending two armies into Germany. One cannot but pause to consider the strange singularity of the contrast of this Catholic cardinal, almost a nonagenarian, representing the modern interests of his nation and Belle Isle, the leader of youth, fighting, as he himself was to discover, for an issue long since dead. There were few errors in the history of France more calamitous than this decision to join in the assault upon Maria Theresa.

Now that France had advanced into the central position of this coalition against Austria, the struggle became one of life and death for Maria Theresa. If the coalition were successful, Austria, Tyrol and Bohemia would go to Charles Albert, Moravia to Saxony, Silesia to Prussia, the Netherlands to France and the Italian possessions to Spain. This would have reduced Maria Theresa to a mere queen of Hungary. Indeed, with Prussia already in possession of Silesia and the Franco-Bavarian army invading Austria much depended on the loyalty of Hungary, which was still quivering with the Rákóczy Rebellion. It was a desperate, heroic decision, therefore, for Maria Theresa to throw herself upon the loyalty of her Magyar

[32] These memorials have been published by M. Sautai in the appendix of his study: *Les préliminaires de la guerre de Succession d'Autriche.*

subjects, despite the opinion of her ministers that she might as well entrust her cause to Satan as to Hungary.

There were good reasons for their suspicion, for the Magyars had no enthusiasm for their alien Hapsburg rulers. Since the Treaty of Szátmar in 1711 Hungary had been disarmed and closed off hermetically against the outside world. It was a humiliating affront to the Magyar aristocracy to find themselves excluded from leading offices in the army and the diplomatic service despite their ancient connection with the House of Austria. There had been an open breach between Charles VI and the Hungarian Diet and it had not been called into session since 1728. When it met again at Pressburg in 1741 its temper was sulky, anti-German, and anti-monarchical. Now that the Hapsburg rulers in the male line were extinct and a woman was sitting on the throne, the propitious moment seemed to have come to throw off altogether the yoke of Vienna—this humiliating domination, as one deputy put it, of a proud kingdom by a German duchy. Maria Theresa disarmed the opposition of this sullen and unfriendly diet. She persuaded the Magyars to forget old memories, to abandon their separatist traditions and to cast in their lot with the Hapsburg monarchy. This achievement alone makes Maria Theresa a great historic personage. The Prince de Ligne later remarked that the Magyars would never have done for a man what on this occasion they did for the charm and outraged innocence of the fair Maria Theresa. The high-hearted and courageous queen kindled their pride and chivalry, qualities in which Magyar aristocrats have never been wanting. Hungarian historians refer to this sudden and complete change of temper from downright opposition to a prompt financial and military support as one of the miracles of the House of Austria.[33] It may be true that the moral effect of the decision was greater than its immediate military consequences but it was none the less an event of prime significance. It was the turning point in the history of Hungary, which was to play a role in the Hapsburg monarchy of ever increasing importance.

Yet the price which Maria Theresa had to pay for this loyalty was

[33] Henry Marczali, "Vitam et Sanguinem," *Historische Zeitschrift*, 117 (1917), 412.

exorbitant; she was compelled to make concessions which, when taken together, mark the beginning of the dualism of the Hapsburg monarchy. The queen was obliged to acknowledge Hungary as the most important of all her kingdoms, to exclude all foreigners, to exempt Hungary from her efforts at bureaucratic centralization, and to entertain no legislation that might be construed as hostile to the Magyar nobility. Prussia's rise to the position of a great power by the conquest of Silesia and the independence of Hungary are events which are closely interdependent upon one another. The cession of Silesia and the recognition of the independence of Hungary were the price which Austria had to pay to repel the invasion of the Bourbon powers. Both Prussia and Hungary rose in their struggle against "The Holy Empire" and their victories were usually won together from 1741 down to 1866. Whenever there was a political vacuum in Vienna, both Prussia and Hungary stormed in from both sides and forced a simultaneous extension of their powers.[34]

Meanwhile, the policy which Belle Isle had forced on the reluctant Fleury had one brief moment of success. In the wake of the French armies, which stood in Germany, Austria and Bohemia, Charles Albert was recognized as archduke of Austria by the estates of Upper Austria, then crowned king of Bohemia in Prague and finally, under the combined influence of France and Prussia, unanimously (after the exclusion of the Bohemian vote) elected Emperor Charles VII at Frankfurt on January 24, 1742. Even George II, constantly boggling between his role as elector of Hanover and king of England, had signed a neutrality treaty with France and voted for the Bavarian emperor. France had taken the leadership of an apparently irresistible coalition, had imposed upon the Germanies an emperor of her own choice, and had succeeded in expunging from the election agreement the article which made it an obligation of the emperor to recover Alsace for Germany.[35] All the most powerful princes of the empire seemed to have become the vassals of France.

But this French hegemony was a mirage and the coalition proved

[34] L. von Ranke, *Sämmtliche Werke,* 27, 484; W. Schüssler, *Österreich und das deutsche Schicksal* (1925); Eisenmann, *Le compromis Austro-Hongrois* (1904), 24.
[35] H. Kretschmayr, *Maria Theresia* (Gotha, 1925), 55; F. Wagner, *Kaiser Karl VII und die Grossen Mächte, 1740-1745* (Stuttgart, 1938), 162 ff.

to be a very gimcrack affair. The coalition was held together by no stronger cement than the territorial ambitions of its members. Each ally watched the other with growing suspicion, and instinctively each member adopted a policy of obstruction to common action. If the aim of the war was the destruction of Austria, there was no co-ordination between military strategy and that policy. As a matter of fact, that was not even the policy of France. Why should France conquer all Austria for the Bavarian? Not the erection of a new and powerful Wittelsbach emperor, but the continuation of German disunion, the co-existence of approximately equal German states, was the war aim of Fleury. A coalition war upon Austria required a concentration of effectives and a speedy and decisive march upon Vienna to dictate the terms of the peace. That was Frederick's sound advice to Belle Isle and he was irritated when it was not followed. He wanted a quick decisive campaign, for his own financial resources did not permit an indefinite prolongation of the war. He was further irked by the Saxon-Bavarian treaty, which promised Saxony a portion of his Silesian booty. He soon became convinced that all his allies were playing with cocked dice. Above all, he refused to become a mere instrument of French policy.[36] The result was the secret convention of Kleinschnellendorf with Austria by which Frederick allowed General Neipperg to march against the French in return for the cession of Silesia. This convention, in spite of recent efforts to justify it, is morally and politically indefensible.[37] He gained nothing for himself and he ruined the military prospects of his French ally. It was not necessity, but juvenile impatience and also a desire to cheat the Saxon elector of his portion of the spoils that led Frederick to commit this irreparable error. As it was, he was soon compelled to repudiate the convention, if for no other reason than his own security.

The one upshot of the Kleinschnellendorf affair, besides giving Frederick the reputation of an untrustworthy political ally, was that it convinced Austrian statesmen that in an effort to divide their

[36] K. Uhlirz, *Handbuch der Geschichte Österreichs und seiner Nachbarländer Böhmen und Ungarn* (Vienna, 1927), I; Horn, "Saxony in the War of the Austrian Succession," *English Historical Review* (1928).
[37] That is the judgment even of R. Koser, his most encomiastic modern biographer, *Geschichte Friedrichs des Grossen* (Berlin, 1921), I, 367.

enemies it was possible to arrange a separate peace with Prussia whereas France seemed determined on a complete humiliation. No sooner had Frederick resumed the struggle than he began to bicker with the French over their ineffective prosecution of the war. In his jealous solicitude to maintain the independence of Prussia as against his French ally, he reopened negotiations with Austria. If Maria Theresa was now willing to sign a separate peace with Prussia, it was less because of Frederick's second victory at Chotusitz (May 17, 1742) than in deference to British diplomatic pressure. The English ambassador in Vienna, Lord Hynford, was given full powers to deal with Frederick. Instead, however, of offering Frederick Maria Theresa's minimum concessions, this precipitous diplomatic tyro offered Frederick at once and without so much as a struggle her maximum concessions of the whole of Silesia including Upper Silesia with the coal districts of Oppeln, an indiscretion which stirred up a good deal of resentment in Vienna then and later. Belle Isle, hearing of the negotiations, hurried to Frederick's camp to deter him from signing a separate peace. But the Prussian monarch had only bitter reproaches for the hesitant and incompetent French conduct of the war, the principal burden of which he refused to bear in the face of his financial stringency. In the Peace of Breslau (July 28, 1742) Frederick, after carrying off his booty, for the second time deserted his allies.

With this treaty the War of the Austrian Succession proper was virtually ended. The two most powerful members of the empire were reconciled and Saxony, seeing no further prospects of gain, soon followed. The military consequences of the Prussian withdrawal were decisive. The French, now hopelessly isolated in Prague, were compelled to beat a retreat from Bohemia, a maneuver which did as much honor to the endurance and discipline of the French troops as to the character of their chief. But Belle Isle's great offensive against Austria had ended in ignominious failure. The central block of the Hapsburg dominions, reduced, to be sure, by Silesia, was solidly secure, even though the outlying territories in the Netherlands and in Italy might still be in some danger. The Austrian armies, now disencumbered of their most formidable enemy, were free to overrun Bavaria, which now fell into their hands. The French, who had become thoroughly disgusted with the distant warfare in Germany, withdrew to their frontiers and promptly notified the Bavarian emperor of their withdrawal of further military support.[38]

But the war did not end. On the contrary it was extended on a vaster scale and chiefly for two reasons: Maria Theresa's demand for territorial compensation for the loss of Silesia and the active intervention of Great Britain. For Maria Theresa the loss of Silesia was a bitter pill and she now openly demanded Bavaria as "dédommagement." Bavaria, however, could be acquired only if France, hitherto a mere auxiliary and not a principal in the war, were thoroughly defeated. Indignantly refusing Fleury's peace overtures, Maria Theresa now proceeded to organize a national German war against France with the avowed purpose of recovering the *avulsa imperii*, Alsace and Lorraine. This national war began in dead earnest when Prince Charles of Lorraine led the Austrian army across the Rhine in July, 1744. With the Austrian army before the very walls of Strasbourg and with Alsace still more German in sentiment than after the French Revolution, the military prospects of Austria in the summer of 1744 appeared very bright indeed. This impression was strengthened by the active British intervention in the continental war. The subsequent evolution of this strange but still connected series of wars was so profoundly affected by the overwhelming position which Great Britain now occupied that an analysis of British policy becomes imperative.

V. BRITISH INTERVENTION AND ITS CONSEQUENCES

No historian can escape noting the striking contrast between Great Britain's record of faltering irresolution and military failure in the War of the Austrian Succession and the blaze of her glorious triumph and success in the Seven Years' War. The early failure was, no doubt, due in the first instance to the inability of successive cabinets to produce statesmen of firm grasp and decision, men who could take an accurate measure of the thickening tangle of the continental situation and discover a line of policy best suited to the interests of Great Britain. But there was also a serious division of

[38] Duc de Broglie, *Frédéric II et Louis XV* (Paris, 1885), I, 389.

opinion on the question of strategy against the Bourbon powers. Today all Englishmen are agreed that the incontestable premise of any British foreign policy is determined by the geographical fact that England is an island situated on an exposed flank of Europe where the Channel is but twenty-five miles wide. The main foundations on which any British foreign policy must be based are sea power coupled with resistance to any hegemony on the Continent, or to put it in different terms, the security of the island and the safety of its communications with its overseas empire. In 1740, in the face of the formidable coalition led by France, Englishmen were agreed only on the utter breakdown of Walpole's policy of insular aloofness. Neither the ministry of Walpole, nor the "Broad-Bottom administration" that took its place, nor finally the Pelham administration acted on clear and definite principles of policy or succeeded in co-ordinating political and military action. All of these cabinets were harassed by internal strife and divided by rival parties, some advocating an imperial, others a continental policy. The final result was a conduct of affairs based on conflicting principles, half pursued, involving a vast expenditure of men and treasure to no definite purpose.

The advocates of a purely naval and maritime war criticized the waste of money on a continental army and on subsidies for continental allies. They contended that, being a trading nation, Great Britain should sweep the enemy's commerce from the seas, crush his naval power and capture his colonies, the sources of his wealth. On the other hand, Carteret, Newcastle and Hardwicke, the protagonists of the land war, argued that without active British intervention on the Continent, the powers of the Bourbon alliance would dominate Italy and western Europe so completely that they could close the ports of the Continent to England, thus anticipating by sixty years Napoleon's Continental System; further, that the conquest of French colonies would avail nothing, since they would be reconquered by France in Europe and their temporary loss would not affect the final result. The mistake that both schools of strategy made was in thinking of the army and navy as two disconnected branches of the service and not as two different instruments of the same policy. In fact each branch of the service had precisely the opposite effect to the one expected by their respective defenders. In the end it was Britain's colonial conquests and naval victories that drove the French out of Flanders, and the British army in Flanders that, nothwithstanding its defeat, created the military diversion which assured the continuance of British maritime preponderance. The strategical value of British military intervention on the Continent cannot, therefore, be called in question. It was the degree of concentration on the maritime or the continental war that was the crucial issue. Wisely employed, a British standing army on the Continent was useful for the limited purpose of a diversion, if the main theater of action were elsewhere. Alone, it could never produce a decision, because it was the least scientific military organization in Europe.

To this a fresh perplexity was added by the duality which somewhat unevenly divided the personality of George II as king of Great Britain, and elector of Hanover. In England George II, "the best of the Georges," was an exile who had to bow to the dictation of a ministry. His real home was in Herrenhausen, where he could strut with the uncriticized assurance of a Louis Quatorze. Nationally-minded Englishmen perpetually fretted at the possibility that the men and money voted by parliament might be diverted to Hanoverian interests, while George II was bent on preventing England's foreign policy from jeopardizing his native country. The charge of Hanoverianism was an obvious and cheap weapon of attack and it was indiscriminately used by members of the opposition, however little evidence there may have been for it. Pitt in particular made himself obnoxious to the king with his blustering rodomontade that "this formidable Kingdom is considered only as a province to a despicable Electorate."[39] It frequently happened that measures obviously wise in themselves were regarded with suspicion and opposed because the direction of affairs was felt to be in Hanover rather than in London. All this stifled public sentiment necessary to support a great war.

To Great Britain, engaged in an unsuccessful war with Spain soon to be supported by France, the Austrian War came as a providential relief. There were British statesmen who believed that Great

[39] *Grenville Correspondence* (London, 1852), I, 18.

Britain was unequal to a war against the combined naval forces of France and Spain without a continental diversion. The violent eruption over the succession in Austria now furnished this diversion. But, although Walpole must be ranked among the great master-builders of modern England, he was scarcely fitted to conduct a great war that now involved a triple task: to wage a naval war against Spain, to assist Austria, and to organize a European opposition against the Bourbon ascendancy. Walpole had never shown any particular partiality for the Austrian alliance and if in the end he did promise assistance to Maria Theresa and, as an earnest of good will, proposed a subsidy of three hundred thousand pounds and a force of twelve thousand men, it was less because of obligations under the Treaty of Vienna of 1731 (he had refused to recognize them in 1735) than from apprehension of French continental hegemony.[40] It must be admitted that England and Austria were unsuitable allies. The margin of their common interests was an extremely narrow one. The Pragmatic Sanction was no more inviolable to British statesmen than to the avowed enemies of Austria. Before the war had run its course, Austrian statesmen were ruefully admitting to themselves that every single piece of territory which Austria was called upon to surrender was sacrificed under relentless British pressure to buy off her enemies nearer home, while the Netherlands, which Austria valued least and which concerned Britain most, were returned to her intact after the war. But Austria, financially insolvent, was in no position to pursue an independent policy.

Great expectations accompanied Lord Carteret when, on the fall of Walpole early in 1742, he assumed direction of British foreign affairs. His long diplomatic experience, his brilliant gifts of intellect and oratory, seemed to recommend him for the post. His exceptional proficiency in the German tongue, his wide acquaintance with the German dynasties, which George II regarded as the beginning of wisdom, endeared him to his sovereign. Moreover, he was a Whig by culture and tradition and his foreign policy was based on the Whig doctrine that the maritime interests of Great Britain depended upon the equilibrium of Europe and that the only way to insure that balance was by direct intervention in continental affairs.

[40] K. Pribram, *Österreichische Staatsverträge, England* (Innsbruck, 1907), I, 551.

But in the execution of this policy he transformed it into its exact opposite. Nothing can be less plausible than the statement of Pemberton, his latest biographer, that in setting out to defeat France in Europe, Carteret in some measure anticipated the policy of Pitt.[41] He had none of Pitt's genius, which could see far beyond what the facts of the moment seemed to suggest. Pitt realized that England had only a navy and superior financial strength and he made his military operations on the Continent subservient to his main maritime and colonial effort. Carteret, to be sure, was, like Pitt, an imperialist. In the early days of the Spanish War he had joined in the general cry "Take and Hold."[42] Now, come to power, he proposed to smash the Bourbon ascendancy by continental methods. His supreme ambition was to repeat the performance of William III and form another Grand Alliance that would align Great Britain, Austria, Holland, Hanover and the lesser German states in an irresistible front against French continental hegemony. But the Grand Alliance of William III had now become a sorry anachronism. Austria had other enemies besides France, and if Holland still followed British leading strings, it followed without spirit and without resolution. The Duke of Cumberland, even admitting his modest military capacities, was no Marlborough and he was helpless when confronted with one of the brilliant soldiers of the age, Marshal de Saxe. Above all, Carteret, rushing in to commit Great Britain to a maze of continental entanglements and futile negotiations, did not succeed in justifying his policy to the members of the cabinet, to the parliament and to British public opinion as being an integral part of the struggle for empire with France.[43] To them he seemed to be oblivious to vital British interests overseas. This laid him open to the crushing invectives of Pitt, to the accusations, however unjust, of his colleagues that he was directed solely by the "Hanover rudder," and to the jealousies of the borough-mongering and wire-pulling Pel-

[41] W. B. Pemberton, *Carteret* (London, 1936), 197.

[42] He had over and over again told Walpole, "Look to America, my Lord; Europe will take care of itself. Support Vernon, and you will want no support here." Lord John Hervey, *Some Materials towards Memoirs of the Reign of King George II* (London, 1931), III, 940.

[43] A. W. Ward, *Great Britain and Hanover* (Oxford, 1899), 153; P. Yorke, *Earl of Hardwicke* (Cambridge, 1913), I, 278; C. Grant Robertson, *England under the Hanoverians* (London, 1911), 92.

hams, who controlled both cabinet and parliament and soon compassed his fall.

Yet Carteret created the illusion of being astonishingly successful. He separated Prussia from France by compelling Austria to buy off Frederick with Silesia, which he promptly proceeded to guarantee.[44] He persuaded Hanover to abandon the ill-timed neutrality into which George II had been intimidated. He moved parliament to vote five millions for the war and to increase the subsidy to Austria, and he brought the Pragmatic army in the Netherlands up to thirty thousand men by hiring sixteen thousand Hanoverians and six thousand Hessians. This army won a blundering victory over the French general, Noailles, at Dettingen which completed the destitution of the emperor and led to a complete French withdrawal from Germany. Carteret made a frantic effort to persuade the Dutch to abandon their dilatory tactics and take an active part in the war— and in the end had to content himself with a *promise* of twenty thousand men to join the British forces in Flanders.[45] But soon difficulties began to accumulate. He was now to learn that German politics were not a series of transparencies through which the foreign observer could always see, but a bewildering kaleidoscope that baffled and disgusted the most ingenious diplomats of Europe.

Had Carteret been determined to concentrate all the resources of Great Britain on the colonial struggle with France, he could have done so by forcing Maria Theresa to recognize Emperor Charles VII. This would have enabled him to separate British from Austrian and Hanoverian interests and would have left Great Britain a greater measure of freedom to pursue her maritime career. Instead, he promised Austria compensation for the loss of Silesia and was either unwilling or unable to persuade her to abandon her hold upon Bavaria. This was ominous, for Frederick was adamant in refusing to tolerate the aggrandizement of Austria in Germany. Above all, he would not allow this compensation to be gained at the expense of

44 November 28, 1742. Sir Richard Lodge, *Great Britain and Prussia in the Eighteenth Century* (Oxford, 1923), 41.

45 These negotiations were the occasion for some of Carlyle's ponderous humor, "Pull long, pull strong, pull together—see the heavy Dutch do stir; some four inches of daylight visible below them, bear a hand, oh, bear a hand! The Dutch flop down again as low as ever." T. Carlyle, *Frederick the Great*, Book XIII, Chap. I.

the Bavarian electorate of Emperor Charles VII. Carteret was not equal to the delicate caution which this situation prescribed.

VI. THE ITALIAN WAR

Among all the blunders of Carteret the most monumental was the Treaty of Worms of September, 1743. It caused bitter resentment in Vienna and contributed materially to his personal ruin and that of his system.[46] This treaty dealt with the subordinate Italian front of the war, where Austria and Spain were the principal antagonists, but it reacted upon the entire war with a sinister repercussion. It is true that Spain was already engaged in a maritime war with Great Britain, but Elizabeth Farnese, who ruled her husband Philip V, cared neither for the sea nor, except for the pieces of eight brought by the Spanish silver fleet, for Spanish America. The passionate maternal love of this lady proved nearly as devastating for Spain as the religious dreams of Philip II, for it would not be satisfied with anything less than a throne for each one of her children. A large portion of the reign of Philip V was devoted to throne-hunting expeditions by this solicitous lady. She had been partially successful, for in the Treaty of Vienna of 1738 she had succeeded in advancing her eldest son, Don Carlos, to the kingdom of the two Sicilies. But she had been balked in her effort to regain the Milanese and Tuscany for her second son, Don Philip, who in the meantime had married Marie Louise, the favorite daughter of Louis XV. She felt that henceforth he could confidently reckon on the support of France. To her the peace of 1738 was a mere armistice, and the death of Charles VI supplied a pretext for renewing the contest.

Since the Treaty of 1738 the balance between Bourbon and Hapsburg in Italy was nearly equal, and the ruler who incontestably manipulated this balance was now Charles Emmanuel, the king of Sardinia-Piedmont. The kingdom of Sardinia, astride the opposite slopes of the Alps and touching the Mediterranean at the two ports of Nice and Oneille, commanded the Alpine passes. This simple fact afforded inexhaustible opportunities for a diplomacy of *petite*

[46] Sir Richard Lodge, *Studies in Eighteenth Century Diplomacy* (London, 1930), 30; E. Guglia, *Maria Theresia* (1917), I, 201; W. B. Pemberton, *Carteret*, 230; Alfred V. Arneth, *Maria Theresias erste Regierungsjahre* (Vienna, 1863), II, 279; A. Dove, *Das Zeitalter Friedrichs des Grossen und Josephs II* (Gotha, 1883), 224.

finesse italienne of which the Marquis d'Ormea, the Sardinian foreign minister, was a past master. The side that obtained his support had a decided military advantage over the other. Thrust in between France and Austria, Sardinia, like Prussia, presented the case of geography making conscience impossible. It soon became apparent that Spain could not obtain the coveted duchies for Don Philip unless Sardinia joined the French coalition, and that Austria could not crush the Bourbon aggression unless she came to terms with Charles Emmanuel. No sooner had Spain announced her purpose than there began a spirited bidding between the Bourbon states and Austria for the Sardinian alliance. This placed Charles Emmanuel in the peculiar position illustrated by the story, then current, of the aide-de-camp who, on rousing the king of Sardinia each morning, asked on what side His Majesty intended to fight that day. But between the two bidders there was the important difference that Austria could offer immediate territorial concessions whereas Spain could offer only a post-dated check contingent upon a future victory, which appeared rather more than problematical. Maria Theresa reasoned shrewdly enough that self-interest would in the end compel Sardinia to come to the defense of Lombardy, just as it compelled the maritime powers to defend the Netherlands. She was, therefore, disposed to offer the equally crafty d'Ormea no more than a beggarly minimum. The sudden common danger presented by the landing of two Spanish expeditions in Italy forced them to agree on a provisional convention (February 1, 1742) which enabled them to beat off the Spanish aggressor at Campo Santo.

In this convention no mention was made of territorial compensation, but Charles Emmanuel left no doubt that he meant to be paid for his assistance. He became all the more importunate because Fleury, convinced by the failure of the two Spanish invasions of the indispensability of the Sardinian alliance, now offered him nothing less than the Duchy of Milan, a great deal more than he could possibly get from Maria Theresa. But d'Ormea had no faith in the ability or willingness of the Spanish monarch to honor his drafts in futurity and above all he did not want Don Philip as a neighbor. Still, if Austria refused to meet his terms, he could desert his Hapsburg alliance on giving a month's notice and pass over to the Bourbon powers. What he could not obtain from Austria by direct negotiation he hoped to get through Austria's English ally. Carteret yielded and took the ground that Sardinia must be retained by immediate territorial concessions. Acting as the agent of Sardinia, Carteret forced upon his Austrian ally the Treaty of Worms of September 13, 1743. This treaty, which Austria regarded as a humiliation, involved an accommodation with Sardinia by which Austria surrendered that entire portion of Lombardy which lay on the right bank of the Ticino and to the south of the Po, together with a section of Piacenza; England undertook to subsidize Sardinia and keep a fleet in the Mediterranean; Austria received a Sardinian army of forty-five thousand troops and, in vague terms, a British promise of territorial compensation contingent upon a future victory in Italy.

The Treaty of Worms was an unqualified failure. It was a greater tribute to the power of British guineas than to British diplomatic intelligence. It was an excellent specimen of what Pitt denounced as "Hanoverianism," though it had nothing to do with Hanover, for it led England deeper still into the continental bog. Not one of the ends sought in the treaty was achieved. It provoked France into a renewal of the Family Compact with Spain in the Treaty of Fontainebleau of October 25, 1743, which pledged France to procure an Italian principality for Don Philip and to recover Gibraltar and Minorca for Spain. It provoked a French declaration of war on Great Britain involving not merely Italy and Germany where they were acting as auxiliaries but the entire range of their conflicting interests. The Treaty of Worms drove Genoa, which was to be despoiled of Finale, into the arms of the Bourbon alliance (Treaty of Aranjuez, 1745). And finally it frightened Prussia into a renewal of the war. Carteret's plan for the reduction of the Bourbon powers depended on the success with which he could persuade Prussia to maintain neutrality, for Prussia manipulated the balance of northern Europe as Sardinia did in Italy. But the very wording of the Treaty of Worms (whether intentionally or not we are unable to say), in which the three powers guaranteed the Pragmatic Sanction without mentioning Silesia, aroused Frederick's gravest apprehensions. These fears would have been greater still had he seen Robinson's report from Vienna which referred to "the temporary cessions" of Austria.

The channel through which the news of the treaty was reported to Frederick convinced him that it was an Anglo-Austrian plan to compass the destruction of Prussia, the only undefeated member of the anti-Pragmatic coalition.

With lightning speed Frederick came to the decision that he must tear up the Treaty of Breslau and the convention with England and declare war on Austria.[47] Before he struck, however, he sought to mobilize diplomatically the princes of the Empire on behalf of the Bavarian emperor against Austria. He even contemplated a reorganization of the Empire which included the secularization of ecclesiastical principalities and the appointment of the king of Prussia as the generalissimo of the imperial armies. The project failed, because the loyalty among German princes to the House of Hapsburg was too deep-seated to succumb to so factious a plan. The reorganization of Germany, if it came, had to come from cleaner hands. All that materialized was the paltry Union of Frankfurt, which consisted of Prussia, Bavaria, the Palatinate and Hesse, presently joined by France, now happy to forget her former disappointments with the Prussian monarch. It would be a gross distortion of the truth to call this Union of Frankfurt a coalition to defend a German emperor. Charles VII was no more than a pitiful creature of France and Prussia. It was rather a conspiracy among a handful of princes, financed by a foreign power, supported by Prussia, and employed by both in their war against Austria. It was as "auxiliary" of Emperor Charles VII and on behalf of the "Germanic Liberties" that Frederick marched eighty thousand Prussians into Bohemia in August, 1744.

With his army increased to one hundred and forty thousand men and a full treasury at his disposal Frederick looked into the future with confident assurance. Now that his enemy, Fleury, had died (January 29, 1743) and Louis XV had exhibited a sudden access of energy, he felt certain of a vigorous French military initiative. But all these hopes were brutally dashed to the ground. His adventurous Bohemian campaign of 1744, which led him to the very environs of Vienna, was too bold for a mercenary army dependent upon maga-

[47] G. Roloff, "Friedrich und das Reich während des Ersten und Zweiten Schlesischen Krieges," *Forschungen zur Brandenburgischen und Preussischen Geschichte*, (1913) XXV, 113.

zines for provisions and proved a strategical fiasco that bade fair to become a catastrophe. What saved Frederick was the fact that his intellectual and moral energies increased with the accumulation of misfortunes. A successful Bohemian campaign would have been possible only had the French engaged the main Austrian army under Charles of Lorraine in Alsace. But the sudden illness of Louis XV in Metz paralyzed French military action and Charles of Lorraine was permitted to escape and throw his forces against the king of Prussia in Bohemia. Morally broken, diminished by seventeen thousand deserters, the Prussian army retreated to Silesia.

The danger was increased when presently a political storm gathered that threatened to destroy Frederick. In the Treaty of Warsaw of January, 1745, the maritime powers and Austria succeeded in persuading Saxony, now supported by British subsidies, to declare war on Prussia. It was hoped that Russia would follow with an invading army in the autumn of 1745. Prussia was to be partitioned and Frederick was to be reduced to the electorate of Brandenburg. Meanwhile, Emperor Charles VII died and his son, Maximilian II, having no prospects of reviving his father's pretensions to the imperial crown, made peace with Maria Theresa at Füssen (April 22, 1745), whereby Bavaria was restored to him in return for the promise to vote for Francis Stephen. When, on September 13, 1745, the electoral college elected the latter to be German emperor, the collapse of the Franco-Prussian system was complete. What made matters worse for Frederick was the speedy exhaustion of his financial resources; he had insufficient money to cover the costs of another campaign. Efforts to raise a loan in Holland failed and, for a moment, Frederick seriously contemplated selling the port of Emden to Great Britain. Deprived of the aid of the French, who had their hands tied in Flanders, thrown upon his own resources, Frederick extricated himself from this tight squeeze by his own indomitable courage and the unmistakably superior military skill which for the first time he now revealed. He defeated the Austrians at Hohenfriedberg (June 4, 1745), his first great strategical achievement, but it was his victory at Soor that raised his generalship to the level of European fame and gave him the reputation of invincibility. Another Prussian victory at Kesselsdorf placed

Frederick in control of Saxony. The Prussian occupation of Saxony, coming on the heels of further military disasters on the Italian front, was a heavy blow to Austria. Yet Maria Theresa would scarcely have affixed her signature to the Treaty of Dresden (December 24, 1745), had not France rejected her peace overtures and Great Britain, resolved now as before that Prussia must be eliminated from the anti-Pragmatic coalition, threatened to discontinue subsidy payments if she persisted in holding out. At Dresden Frederick the Great, as his subjects now called him, promised to acknowledge Francis I as emperor in return for Silesia and the county of Glatz. He thereby admitted the complete failure of his German imperial policy and his acceptance of Austrian hegemony in German affairs.[48] Frederick then finally withdrew from the war. If he pleaded necessity for deserting his ally a third time, there was now more justification because of the utter exhaustion of his country.

VII. D'ARGENSON AND THE END OF THE CONTINENTAL WAR

If there is little to admire in the conduct of British foreign affairs, French policy, after the death of Fleury, also went from bad to worse. Louis XV's resolution henceforth to govern himself without a prime minister merely inaugurated that absence of authority above and lack of co-ordination in the wheels of government which was the most conspicuous trait of French history in the middle of the century. Louis was not even honest and straightforward with his ministers. He frequently professed to agree with a minister in private conference only to betray him behind his back, a deceitful habit which in later years led to a whole system of secret diplomacy, commonly called "The King's Secret." What was worse, the fate of France began to be decided in boudoirs, the centers of intrigue and ambition.

Obviously, France had made a bad beginning. The attempt to partition the Austrian dominions had failed a second time. The Bourbon effort to expel the Austrians from Italy had been equally unsuccessful. Frederick II, whose clear eye, unlike d'Argenson's in France, was clouded by no mist of humanitarian phantasmagoria,

---

48 See his "Histoire de mon temps," *Publicationen aus den Preussischen Staatsarchiven* (1879), IV, 431.

had seized the favorable moment and signed a separate peace. Although France in the meantime had burdened herself with a whole series of pledges to Spain, and had openly declared war on both Great Britain and Austria (March 15, 1744), there seemed to be no sufficient reason for prolonging the struggle when, with the death of Emperor Charles VII, the original cause of the war had been removed. The new French foreign minister, the Marquis d'Argenson, was known to desire its early termination. The belligerent Carteret had been dismissed and the Broad-Bottom ministry of Henry Pelham contained a number of pacific members who would be amply satisfied if France evacuated the Netherlands, dropped the cause of the Pretender, and compelled Spain to restore the commercial concessions of the Utrecht settlement. The Dutch were not actual belligerents and the members of the dominant Republican party had reasons of their own for wanting an early peace.

That the war continued on a large scale was due to the quixotic policy of d'Argenson himself, a philosopher and a cosmopolitan idealist who placed his hope, not in an unashamed pursuit of national interest like Great Britain and Prussia, but in the progress of "universal reason."[49] The mind of this "Secretary of Plato's Republic" was filled with plans that were mutually destructive. His knowledge of European affairs was acquired by an assiduous study of books and his practical experience in the realities of diplomacy amounted to nil. With an eye to the eulogy of the French *salons*, he cherished the dream of a France conquering by sheer unselfishness. His plan for the settlement of Italian affairs required the expulsion of Austria and the redistribution of her territories in such a manner that Italy would be divided into a number of nearly equal states which were to form a federation. This, he suggested, would make an end of foreign domination in Italy. But to expel Austria, Sardinia must be won over, and Charles Emmanuel was to be tempted by a sort of hegemony in the federation. In northern Europe the union of the maritime powers was to be broken by detaching the Dutch, which he thought could best be done by abstaining from all expansion, especially in the Netherlands. As for

---

[49] D'Argenson, *Journal et mémoires* (Ed. Rathéry), Paris, 1868, especially Vol. IV. Also Broglie, *Maurice de Saxe et le Marquis d'Argenson*, Paris, 1891, I, 89.

England, d'Argenson proposed the pursuit of a commercial war and the promotion of the cause of the Pretender. It is only fair to say that, with the exception of Italy, d'Argenson very rarely had his own way.

In Italy d'Argenson's ill-conceived intervention did much to ruin the prospects of a Bourbon military victory. The amazingly skillful efforts of the French Marshal Maillebois in his victory of Bassignana (November, 1745) were put to naught, and Elizabeth Farnese, furious over d'Argenson's plan, abandoned even the pretense of co-operation with France. Charles Emmanuel was deaf to the lure of d'Argenson's promises; he had no confidence in the good faith of France, which ten years before had guaranteed Milan first to him and then to Elizabeth Farnese and finally thrown them both over. Moreover, Austria, now at peace with Prussia, was free to throw her resources into Italy and her harmonious co-operation with Sardinia bore its fruit. The Italian war, carried on through six campaigns with varying fortunes, ended in a complete failure of the armies of France and Spain.[50]

But the principal theater of French operations was in the north, on the Rhine and in the Netherlands. As long as Prussia was still in the field there was a sharp debate as to where the main thrust should be made. Frederick demanded that French operations on the Rhine be co-ordinated with those of Prussia in Bohemia, first because a decisive blow at Austria could be struck only in Germany, second, because the conquest of the Netherlands would force Holland, the guardian of the Barrier fortresses, to step out of its role of an auxiliary and become a principal in the war. But both the king and Noailles were opposed to this plan, because the real enemy of France was not Austria but England and the only place at which it was possible to strike an effective blow at England was in Flanders. It was in Flanders, therefore, the familar scene of French military operations, where France concentrated all her military resources. The other theaters of the war, in Italy, in the colonies, at sea were subordinated to this maximum effort to drive the English from the Continent.

The interest which centers on the subsequent conquest of the

[50] S. Wilkinson, *The Defense of Piedmont* (Oxford, 1927), 227, 317.

Austrian Netherlands is inseparable from the brilliant career of Marshal de Saxe, the last general to whom the old French monarchy owed an unbroken series of victories. In the campaigns of 1744 and 1745 he succeeded in breaking down a large section of that wall of Barrier fortresses which had been set up against France. In 1745 he crushed the combined forces of the English and the Dutch at Fontenoy, a victory which dominated the entire war, all the more important since it was not Austria but England with her Dutch and German soldiers that was defeated. What stood out on the day of Fontenoy was the figure of the Saxon marshal, conquering his own illness and physical weakness, dominating by sheer personal ascendancy a weak monarch and a doubting court, rallying a shaken army and wrenching victory from defeat.[51] So well did Saxe exploit his victory that at the end of the year the French stood possessed of practically every town of importance in the Austrian Netherlands excepting only Brussels and Antwerp, to which latter place the British had perforce to retire.

The year 1745 was one of the most critical in the annals of English history because the defeat at Fontenoy was quickly followed by a Jacobite rebellion which aimed at the dethronement of George II and the establishment of a Catholic dynasty on the English throne. An early French plan of 1744 to cover with a fleet from Brest a surprise invasion by Marshal de Saxe had miscarried due to the preponderance of English sea power and to a Channel storm which dispersed the invading fleet. Now, on July 2, 1745, Charles Edward, the attractive and gallant son of the Pretender, encouraged by the victory of Fontenoy and the constant denunciation of the Hanoverianism of King George, secretly slipped out of Nantes in a French privateer and landed safely in Scotland to raise the Stuart banner and to make the last luckless effort to organize the Scottish Highlands as an independent power. From the point of view of

[51] L. H. Thornton, *Campaigners Grave and Gay* (London, 1925); J. Colin, *Les campagnes de Maréchal de Saxe* (Paris, 1900). Liddell Hart's attempt in his *The Ghost of Napoleon* to make out Marshal de Saxe a modern strategist will scarcely bear close examination. It cannot be said that Saxe's strategy transcended the strategy of his day. Even if we remember, as we must, that he never met an opponent above mediocre caliber and that d'Argenson was working at cross purposes with him, he was almost continually engaged in sieges, always sieges, and when he delivered a battle it was to protect a siege. He made no attempt, like Condé or Napoleon, to annihilate the enemy. General Camon, *Maurice de Saxe* (Paris, 1934), 135.

the war at large this romantic exploit of Prince Charlie was devoid of any major significance, except insofar as the Dutch were asked to send the treaty contingent of six thousand men and Cumberland and his army were recalled from the Continent. The British fleet prevented the French government from sending any effective assistance, and Charles' generals refused him the one slender chance he had of rushing on to London. After some early spectacular successes the Jacobite cause foundered on the field of Culloden (April 16, 1746), but its failure was certain from the moment when Prince Charles on his southward march from Carlisle to Derby encountered only a dispiriting indifference among the inhabitants of the countryside. Notwithstanding the splendid gallantry of Charles and his handful of men, Jacobitism as a serious political cause was dead.[52]

Meanwhile Marshal de Saxe, profiting by Cumberland's absence, marched from victory to victory and gained successes that were without parallel in the history of France. He took Brussels and Antwerp, defeated Charles of Lorraine at Raucoux and won another brilliant victory at Lawfeld (July 2, 1747). Belgium, the ancient object of French ambition, lay at the mercy of France. At the same time Lowendal invaded Holland, forced the capitulation of Bergen-op-Zoom and set siege to Maestricht.

The halting support which the United Provinces, certainly the weakest link in the Pragmatic coalition, gave to this war requires a word of explanation.[53] For the refusal of the Dutch to declare open war against either one of the Bourbon powers there were good reasons. Holland was still the great creditor power of Europe, and Amsterdam, with its admirable banking system, was still the center of the European money market. Due to an evident preference of Dutch financiers for foreign securities over investment in domestic enterprises, both England and France were heavily indebted to them. Large scale industry was not familiar to the Dutch. They had no great industrial tradition behind them like the French and English. Their prosperity depended on foreign commerce and on the transport and exchange trade. Unlike the other states of Europe their

52 A. and H. Taylor, *1745 and After*, 1938.
53 P. Geyl, *Willem IV en England tot 1748* (Leyden, 1927); P. Geyl, "Holland and England during the War of the Austrian Succession," *History*, X (1929), 47 ff.; Sir Richard Lodge, *Studies in Eighteenth Century Diplomacy*, 127; A. Beer, "Holland und der österreichische Erbfolgekrieg," *Archiv. für österreichische Geschichte*, 46 (1871), 297.

foreign policy must be subordinated, not to the changing combinations of international politics, but to their commercial and shipping interests. The extreme constitutional decentralization of the republic, which made the state a federation of provinces and each province a federation of towns, enabled the merchant aristocracy to entrench themselves in all the focal centers of power. The great Dutch families, the Cliffords, the de Vry-Temmencks, the Dedals and the Danielsz, who were the backbone of the Republican party which had dominated Dutch politics for nearly half a century, not only held all the important offices in the towns and provinces but controlled also the great banks and merchant corporations.[54] So intimate was this union between business and government that in the course of its evolution the Dutch state had assumed more and more the character of a comprehensive commercial corporation.[55] It was a matter of common knowledge that the town hall of Amsterdam was a mere adjunct of the stock exchange. The studied political opportunism of the Grand Pensionaries Van der Heim and Gilles becomes intelligible only when it is understood that in pursuing their commercial policy, they were bent on holding aloof as much as possible from the continental contests of power. At a time when Dutch shipping was losing steadily to the rising power of Hamburg and the Scandinavian countries, the Dutch could not afford to wage a war that threatened to ruin their commerce.

There was some foundation to d'Argenson's belief that it was possible to detach the Dutch by negotiation. But he was overruled by Louis XV and Marshal de Saxe, who were convinced that peace must be sought on the battlefield. The two vital concerns of the Dutch were to keep Antwerp in its prostrate condition by closing the Scheldt to navigation and to guard the security of the Barrier. Both were now in French hands, and when Lowendal proceeded with the invasion of Dutch Flanders, Gilles and the Republican party found themselves face to face with the same situation that had been fatal to their predecessors in the days of John de Witt. The invasion provoked an Orangist revolution, one of those periodic revolutions which came with unfailing regularity whenever the

[54] E. Baasch, *Holländische Wirtschaftsgeschichte* (Jena, 1927), 352.
[55] Colenbrander, *Patriotentijd* (1924), I, 85.

Republican party was confronted with a serious military crisis. On May 3, 1747, the Prince of Orange, William IV, was elected captain-general and admiral of the Union and became the first member of his House to be chosen stadtholder in all seven provinces. Having overthrown the Republican party, the Orangists must justify their success as William III had done by becoming saviors of the state. But the Orangist victory was neither so complete as it was in 1672 nor was it attended by the same miraculous results. The Republican party as the strongest and most stable element in the state still held all the chief offices both at The Hague and in the provinces. If William IV wished to exercise the same authority as his predecessor, he could achieve his end only by getting the support of the men whose influence in the provinces and municipalities was decisive. In deference to the regents William IV dared not declare war upon France, however absurd the fiction that the republic was a mere auxiliary might now have become. For a moment only was there a surprising show of vigor. The Dutch were prepared to appeal to the patriotism of the people for the grant of a levy of two per cent upon all capital and to join with England in hiring thirty thousand Russians, even if they had to pledge themselves to pay half the cost. They even agreed to put a stop to trading with France. But the United Provinces were financially exhausted. They were unable to raise the necessary money or even to pay the promised contingent. Without a large loan from London, which was then impossible, they could not pay their stipulated proportion of the cost of the Russian troops. This default would throw the entire burden on the British treasury. Never, not even in 1672, had the position of the United Provinces been so desperate. Somehow they had lost the heroic spirit of the seventeenth century. Fortunately for Holland, France was in the same state of financial exhaustion.

VIII. THE WAR ON COMMERCE

Meanwhile, an important controversy of a very different sort was proceeding between Great Britain and her commercial rivals France and Spain. In its essence the war was a commercial one, a struggle of rival merchants and sailors, of navies and privateers, of commercial companies and colonists on the spot. The very intensity of this war on enemy commerce, however, opened the vaster conflict for colonial dominion, fought in geographically diverse regions with concurrent dramas of their own. But it should be stated that for Newcastle and d'Argenson the paramount issue of the war was not the colonial conflict but the balance of power in Europe. The English troops that were thrown into Flanders were not available for colonial campaigns. Until the last year of the war England sent out no military contingent to the colonies. The British navy also, woefully inefficient before its reorganization by Lord Anson, was largely absorbed by the continental conflict in preventing the Bourbon powers from using the Mediterranean for the passage of troops and in defending England against repeated threats of invasion. The British navy in the Mediterranean materially contributed to the victory of the Austro-Sardinian forces in Italy. Only small squadrons, therefore, could be spared for the outer seas.

Among the incidents in this conflict which reacted upon the principal belligerents in Europe two stand out above the others: the conquest of Louisburg by the American colonists and the capture of Madras in India by Dupleix and Labourdonnais. The West Indies, where no conquests were made or attempted, may best be considered in connection with the naval war on commerce.

It is true that neither the French Canadians nor the New England colonists wanted a war in North America. This war was merely the repercussion on American soil of events which had their origin in Europe. Governor Beauharnais, unable to repudiate the policy of his sovereign in France, launched a series of attacks on the frontiers of Nova Scotia and Massachusetts, and, using Louisburg on Cape Breton Island as his base, encouraged privateering operations which threatened the New England fisheries and played havoc with American colonial shipping. Louisburg, more useful as a naval base than as a fortress (which was not yet completed), was admirably placed for raids on the American coastal trade, but its great importance lay in the fact that it stood at the gate of the St. Lawrence, the natural highway into the heart of Canada. No military expedition could pass up that waterway so long as a French fighting squadron was there to block the way. Without such a naval squadron, the fortress of Louisburg was useless, a sentry box without a sentry. Its commercial significance was no less important. It was a revictualing base for the merchant fleets from the French Antilles, for the five hundred French fishing vessels which stopped there annually, and a port of call for the ships of the East India Company.[56] The war in this part of the world hinged on the possession of this base. The only effective defense against it was to capture it. Stirred with indignation over ancient and recent horrors committed by the French and their Indian allies, and also by commercial jealousy, the fire-eating Governor of Massachusetts, William Shirley, and Colonel Pepperell organized an expedition at Boston in 1745 to capture it. The expedition was an American affair, assisted by a British squadron under Commodore Warren, who came up from the West Indies. The port was blockaded and, after a short siege, was taken in June, 1745.[57]

The seizure of Louisburg by British Americans was a threat more deadly to the French colony of Canada than even the Scheldt in French hands was to England, for England had command of the Channel. Governor Shirley besieged Newcastle with his plan which, with a little British help, aimed at nothing less than the conquest of Canada. But, for the moment, the British government was indifferent to Canada. A heroic French effort in 1746 to recover Louisburg with a powerful squadron of twelve ships and five thousand men under the Duc d'Anville ended in disaster. The storm-shattered ships manned by scurvy-stricken men were compelled to return to France, only narrowly escaping complete destruction at the hands of Admiral Anson. The absence of well-organized supplies and an inadequate sea hygiene seriously hampered the French and was the cause of their failure to recover Louisburg. But without additional assistance from England the American colonists were just as incapable of conquering Canada as the Canadians were incapable of doing serious injury to their neighbors without reinforcements from France.

India was only a minor theater of this war, though the ultimate stakes were of immense value. Here the two principal antagonists were the French and English East India Companies, whose position

[56] J. Tramond in Hanotaux-Martineau, *Histoire des colonies françaises* (Paris, 1929), I, 135.
[57] G. M. Wrong, *The Rise and Fall of New France* (New York, 1928), II, 673.

was somewhat ambiguous. While in Europe they were mere private corporations, in India they were political powers.[58] As commercial companies, guided by their directors in Europe, they were far more concerned with their business interests than with their political functions, less anxious to extend their political frontiers than to enrich the stockholders they represented. If, in fact, the conflict between them generated conditions which rendered conquests at once possible and desirable and the war against each other's trade led to a struggle for the possession of India itself, no one perceived this in 1744. The war of 1744-1748 was inspired with no great strategical or even political aim; its object was purely commercial. It was simply a matter of weakening a commercial rival.

The British Company had excellent ports at Bombay and Calcutta and badly defended posts at Madras and Cuddalore on the Coromandel coast. The French Company held Pondichéry, which was well fortified, and lesser posts at Karikal, Mahé and Chandernagor. Thanks to the energy of Labourdonnais Mauritius (Ile de France) became its principal naval base; it was over a thousand miles to the southward, but, though distant, was a factor of first-rate importance as a secure supply base for a campaign on the coast of India.[59] In point of time it was not much farther from the vital area on the Coromandel coast than Bombay, the only docking and repairing station of the British Company.

The first blow in the Indian Ocean was struck when Commodore Barnett seized a number of richly laden French East Indiamen, cut off French trade and made himself master of the eastern seas. Sea power, however, has its limitations. Without troops Barnett could not drive the French out of their settlements. Meanwhile Dupleix, the energetic French governor, planning to counterbalance by successes on land the British superiority on the sea, made secret preparations for an attack on Madras. To that end he appealed to Labourdonnais at Mauritius, who had instructions to co-operate with

[58] H. Dodwell, *Clive and Dupleix* (London, 1920); H. Dodwell in *Cambridge History of the British Empire, British India* (1929), IV, 109; A. Martineau, *Dupleix* (Paris, 1928), V Vols.; A. Martineau's one volume life of *Dupleix* (Paris, 1931); again Martineau in Hanotaux-Martineau, *Histoire des colonies françaises, Inde* (Paris, 1932), V, 131.

[59] P. Crépin, *La Bourdonnais* (Paris, 1922); W. H. Richmond, *National Policy and Naval Strength* (London, 1928), 166; Julien Vinson, *Les Français dans l'Inde, Dupleix et La Bourdonnais* (Paris, 1894).

Dupleix and carry a privateering war into the Indian Ocean. The situation on the Coromandel coast was completely changed when, after two years of warfare, Labourdonnais appeared at Pondichéry with ten ships and over two thousand Europeans, thus wresting the local command of the sea from the British. In spite of the bitter personal quarrel between them, Dupleix and Labourdonnais united their forces and in September, 1746 Madras, inadequately fortified and badly defended, fell into their hands. There is no need to discuss here the quarrel between them that arose over the disposal of Madras. Suffice it to say that Dupleix occupied the city and that, before Labourdonnais sailed (too late as it proved) to escape from the October monsoon, when heavy storms sweep down the harborless Coromandel coast, he left twelve hundred men and four ships with Dupleix.

One of the important results of the expedition was that by this accident Dupleix's garrison at Pondichéry was increased by twelve hundred men. He stood in dire need of them, for now he had to fight for the prize which he had taken from Labourdonnais. The Nawab of Arcot, Anwar-ud-din, supported by the English, had forbidden Dupleix to attack Madras, which he considered to be his dependency. Dupleix refused to evacuate the city and the nawab sent out an army to expel him. Dupleix, however, was master of the situation. Not only did he retain Madras but he routed the nawab's army of ten thousand men with a small force of four hundred and fifty Europeans and some Sepoys. This was the first time for a century that a small body of Europeans had fought a battle against relatively numerous Indian forces and thrown them into confusion. The affair made an enormous impression throughout India. But the sudden appearance of Admiral Boscawen with superior forces reduced Dupleix to the defensive for the remainder of the war, for by this time France was no longer able to send expeditions across the seas. The expedition of Boscawen aimed at the capture of the main seats of French power, Mauritius and Pondichéry. But Mauritius appeared too formidable and Pondichéry actually proved too strong, in spite of the fourteen British men-of-war and four thousand Europeans, the strongest forces ever collected in

India.[60] It was only after the abandonment of the forty-day siege that the news of peace came from Europe.

Significant as these peripheral incidents in Canada and India may appear, they were of secondary importance beside the unspectacular but inexorable economic pressure which sea power exercised on the commerce of the respective belligerents in Europe. To understand the full effect of this commercial war one must keep in mind the difference in the conditions of trade between the eighteenth century and our own day. Unlike the regular flow of oceanic commerce required by modern industrial society, the great volume of the long distance trade in the eighteenth century was carried on in large merchant fleets which sailed at wide intervals. A fleet of East India-men went out one year and came back the next. In the West India sugar trade an outward-bound fleet might comprise as many as two hundred fifty vessels; they came home in two great convoys, one in June and another in September, after the hurricane season. The triangular voyage from Nantes or Bristol to the African Gold Coast for slaves, thence to the West Indies and home again with West India produce occupied some fifteen months. Between the sailings of the larger fleets the trade was carried on by lesser ships sailing independently—"runners" in the West Indian trade, the Spanish *azoges* and register ships. This concentration of merchant fleets offered great opportunities for attack and the effect of a single blow was more disastrous relatively to the total resources of belligerents than today.

Besides the royal navies the chief offensive weapon in this war on commerce was the privateer. The privateer, who played so conspicuous a part in the maritime history of France, was a subordinate figure in Great Britain.[61] The large and well-disciplined British navy rendered the privateer in some sense unnecessary, while in France the very unreliability of the navy called forth a strong privateering movement. From every port of France there issued privateers, financed by those who in the days before the Casino at Monte Carlo wagered on their ability to back the winner. Encouraged by the government, shipowners, chambers of commerce, busi-

60 A. Martineau, *Dupleix* (Paris, 1931), 137.
61 D. Hannay, *Short History of the Royal Navy* (London, 1909), II, 166.

ness houses, corsair captains who had made money, even church dignitaries were found in the list of *armateurs*. Since the *guerre de course* was obviously a highly speculative venture, the equipment of a privateer was a well-organized business enterprise in which one or several companies pooled their resources.[62] They were especially numerous in the West Indies and along the New England and British coasts. In these areas they could never be completely eradicated and their ubiquity and success, even after the destruction of the French battle squadrons, present a remarkable analogy to the German submarine campaign during the Great War. The intensity of their attack on British commerce increased as the war went on and there was little if any diminution of British losses in the last years of the war.[63]

Recent investigation on both sides of the Channel points to the conclusion that the effectiveness of the privateer as the destroyer of enemy commerce has been much exaggerated. In a careful study M. Vignols has shown that, in spite of the enormous profits of a minority of *armateurs* and individual privateers who were either exceptionally able or exceptionally lucky, in the long run the *guerre de course* did not pay in a single port of France.[64] The tradition that St. Malo was built on the fortunes of privateers must be dismissed as a legend. A study of English materials by Mr. Fayle leads to a similar conclusion.[65] An examination of British trade statistics indicates that the British losses during the war were only a small fraction of the total volume of the foreign trade. These losses have been computed at eighteen per cent for the year 1747, at best an approximate guess since there was as yet no compulsory registration of shipping. But whatever the losses, they were fully made good by the prizes which the English took from the enemy. Indeed, the clearances of British shipping at the end of the war indicate a net gain of twenty per cent in tonnage. British trade with northern Europe and America suffered no serious interruption in the course

62 W. B. Johnson, *Wolves of the Channel* (London, 1931), 20.
63 W. H. Richmond, *The Navy in the War of 1739-1748* (1920), III, 115, 273.
64 Léon Vignols, "La course maritime," *Revue d'histoire économique et sociale*, XV (1927), 207.
65 C. E. Fayle, "Economic Pressure in the War of 1739-1748," *Journal of the Royal United Service Institution*, LXIII (1923), 436-437.

of the war. Both the total value of imports from the West Indies and the actual quantities of sugar shipped indicate a sharp decline at the beginning of the war and again when France came in in 1744, but by the end of the war the figures were well above normal again. Imports, which stood at £7,500,000 before the war, averaged £11,500,000 in the last five years before the peace. This steady flow and expansion of trade enabled England not merely to bear her own war expenses but to sustain the armies of her continental allies, Austria, Sardinia, Saxony and finally Russia. In spite of the heavy cost of the war and the great increase in the national debt, the war affected the financial and economic stability of Great Britain very little.

Turning to the question of the effectiveness of the British attack on French commerce, several factors must be considered before a final assessment is attempted. British naval measures did not become really effective until 1747, when trade attack was based on the strategical conception of the Western Squadron which, offensively and defensively, was the key to the subsequent naval successes. Until the last year of the war the British navy was a failure. Before that time French fleets sailed to and from the West Indies without serious difficulty. But the great naval victories of Anson and Hawke in 1747 destroyed French naval escorts and left enemy merchantmen a prey to the supplementary action of British privateers. Again, it is difficult to take an accurate measure of the effectiveness of the British attack on French trade because much of French foreign commerce was in the hands of neutral shippers, particularly of the Dutch who continued to carry French and Spanish goods between those countries and their colonies—at least so long as the naval blockade was not effective. There was also the neutralizing effect of the illegal trade between the American colonists and the French West Indies, which, notwithstanding the embargoes in four New England colonies, seems to have swollen to greater proportions than in time of peace.[66] What further reduced the effectiveness of the British trade war was the practice of British underwriters of maritime insurance to continue to insure those very enemy ships which

[66] F. W. Pitman, *The Development of the British West Indies, 1700-1763* (New Haven, 1917), 285.

the British navy was seeking to destroy.[67] Because French maritime insurance rates were prohibitive, it became a common practice to seek such insurance in London.[68] British insurance brokers found it to their advantage to convey to their French clients such information as would enable them to evade loss by capture. To what extent this practice prevented captures it is impossible to estimate. Until 1747, escaping French fleets were a surprisingly regular occurrence.

Even with these limitations, a balance of the French and British losses points to the conclusion that the French suffered more heavily than the British who, having the larger merchant marine, could absorb these losses without substantial injury to the trade. If we include, as Beatson does, the value of the French prizes taken, there remains a balance of two million pounds sterling in favor of Great Britain.[69] In the West Indies the total French losses must have amounted to a very considerable proportion of all the ships in the trade. What is more, the French shipping that remained was useless, because it could not sail. After the victories of Anson and Hawke no further French convoys put to sea. From this time onward the blockade of the French coast and of the West Indies was measurably effective. A blockade, however, was the one thing that the French sugar islands could not endure. They were always undersupplied with slave labor, the foundation of plantation economy, and the complete stoppage of the French slave trade in 1748 was equivalent to throttling this sugar industry.[70] Moreover, in the absence of domestic provisions, the regular arrival of supplies was a matter of life and death, and the famine became a serious affair, despite the entrance of occasional blockade runners. Had the war lasted longer, they would have been compelled to surrender from sheer lack of food.[71] But by 1748 not only the West Indian but all French and Spanish trade (with the exception of the French Levant trade) seems to have been pretty thoroughly swept from the seas.

Because of the importance of the foreign and colonial trade in the

67 C. Wright and C. E. Fayle, *A History of Lloyds* (London, 1928), 79.
68 P. Charliat, *Trois siècles d'économie maritime française* (Paris, 1931), 53.
69 R. Beatson, *Naval and Military Memoirs of Great Britain from 1727 to 1783* (London, 1804), I.
70 Gaston-Martin, *L'ère des négriers, 1714-1774* (Paris, 1931), 226.
71 J. Tramond in Hanotaux-Martineau, *Les colonies françaises, Les Antilles français*, I, 470.

national economy of France the ultimate military effect of this economic pressure in disposing France favorable to peace can scarcely be denied. Colonial trade contributed to the customs revenue; it provided shipping, secure employment and large freight earnings under the national flag; it was extremely profitable to the merchants. Colonial produce either in the form of re-exports or as raw materials played an important part in France's domestic and European trade. French manufacturers of silk, woolens and linen were hard put to it to get raw materials. The naval defeats, the losses of French shipping and the complete breakdown of the foreign trade in 1748 had its due share in producing the national deficit and the dislocation of French trade and industry. Bankruptcies became ominously frequent. The intendant Tourny reported from Guienne that if free navigation of the sea were not rapidly re-established, his generality would die of hunger.[72] Machault, the minister of finance, said that he saw hell before him if the war lasted. There were, of course, other factors that made for peace: the French military failure in Italy, a powerful cabal of nobles at Versailles who wanted to set bounds to the ascendancy of Marshal de Saxe. But economic conditions were basic; if trade was to be restored, the burden of taxation lightened, the war must end. Continued maritime war would almost inevitably lead to the complete loss of France's western colonies, which were more valuable to her than the mines of Peru were to Spain.

But in Great Britain also the Newcastle administration had reached a state of unmeasured despondency. Even though the English might be victorious at sea, they had suffered military disaster on the Continent. Alarmist statesmen, like the Duke of Bedford, were frightened by the possibility of bankruptcy. With a national debt of seventy-seven millions in 1748 and a land tax of four shillings in the pound, there was slight cause to despair of the solvency of England. Yet it was the specter of bankruptcy that united the members of the government in their determination to bring the war to an end.[73]

[72] M. Marion, *Machault d'Arnouville* (Paris, 1891), 14.
[73] Evan Charteris, *The Duke of Cumberland and the Seven Years' War* (London, 1925), 3.

IX. THE PEACE OF AIX-LA-CHAPELLE

All the important terms of the final treaty were arranged in secret negotiation between France and the maritime powers, and only subsequently accepted by Austria, deserted by Great Britain and provokingly duped by France, after a formal and public protest against the sacrifices imposed on her by her British ally. Though free to settle with Austria, France chose to come to terms with Great Britain, because a peace with Austria could not restore Cape Breton nor put an end to the naval blockade that was strangling her. The shrewd St. Severin and Puyscieulz were bent on breaking up the anti-Bourbon coalition, the only real advantage, they thought, that France could draw from the war, and this they brilliantly accomplished.

With some modifications of decisive import the guiding principle that dominated the settlement was the return to the balance established at Utrecht.[74] This meant a reciprocal restitution of conquests in every continent. France surrendered Madras and the fortifications of Dunkirk to England, and the Netherlands to Austria, agreed to recognize the Hanoverian dynasty and expel the Pretender. England surrendered Louisburg, but received from Spain the confirmation of the *Asiento* and trading rights for four years to compensate her for the years of *non-jouissance*. Austria confirmed the cession of the Ticino frontier to Sardinia, of Parma, Piacenza and Guastalla to Don Philip, and finally of Silesia to Prussia. Francis Stephen was acknowledged emperor and all signatories confirmed the Pragmatic Sanction.

It has often been said that it was Frederick the Great who reaped the greatest advantage from the treaty, though he was not a party to it. The very fact that both Great Britain and France competed at Berlin for the credit of fathering the article which gave a European guarantee for Silesia was an official registration of the new and formidable position which Prussia had won in Europe. In truth, Frederick's acquisition of Silesia was the greatest permanent conquest of territory hitherto made by any power in the history of

---

[74] L. Bittner, *Österreichische Staatsverträge*, I, No. 943; Sir Richard Lodge, *Studies in Eighteenth Century Diplomacy*, 361 ff.

modern western Europe. It became not merely the largest, but, with its rich linen industry and undeveloped iron ores, the wealthiest province of the Prussian monarchy. Without it Prussia could never have become a great power. Its transfer to the Hohenzollern, therefore, marks one of the incisive changes in the history of central Europe. The entire structure of the German Empire had been fatally shaken and the last remnants of imperial authority had shriveled to the vanishing point. Arneth already remarked that with Silesia Joseph II might well have realized his plan of an effective Austrian hegemony in Germany, but from the day when Austria lost Silesia to Prussia and the western half of the Hapsburg monarchy had ceased to be a predominantly German state, such a policy had become impracticable.[75] Henceforward, Austrian statecraft was thrown back upon purely Austrian resources and the independent development of the Hapsburg monarchy was the necessary logical consequence. The Rhine frontier suddenly lost its importance and, withdrawing from the great contests in the west, Austrian policy henceforth centered on the vital area nearer home. But in spite of her heavy losses both in Italy and in Germany Austria remained the most formidable power of central Europe. Further, there is evidence enough to indicate that there was no finality about these Austrian renunciations. Had not St. Severin suggested and Count Kaunitz enthusiastically reported that with the settlement of 1748 the last word had not yet been spoken?[76]

Thus with the patent decadence of Holland, the new power of Prussia and the extension of Bourbon power in Italy, the eight years of warfare had produced profound modifications. The Europe of 1748 was very different from the Europe of 1740.

As between Great Britain and France, however, this "peace without victory" settled none of the vital issues which the war had raised. The war between them had begun over a continental issue with a general breach of paper guarantees; it ended in a gigantic struggle for commerce and empire in which Austria faded into the background. In this contest Great Britain, with all the advantages of sea power on her side, was compelled to yield because the prime

[75] Arneth, *Maria Theresia*, IV, 495.
[76] J. Strieder, *Kritische Forschungen zur österreichischen Politik* (Leipzig, 1906), 3.

object of British policy—a Netherlands in friendly hands—had been defeated by French military power and the financial bankruptcy of Holland. France had literally reconquered Cape Breton and the West Indies in Europe. But all the vital issues had been left in suspense. Great Britain had neither frustrated nor accepted French imperialism; the right of search was passed over in silence; the uncertain frontiers of Acadia had not been defined; Louisburg had been restored, to the disgust of the American colonists, to renew its menace; the expansionist urge of French commerce had been halted neither in the West Indies, nor in Africa, nor in India. But the aggressive and enterprising temper which this war had kindled among the people of England demanded, more than ever before, that Britain's future be sought in her commercial, colonial and maritime destiny. The official diplomacy of England flew in the face of these vital national interests. Newcastle, who had acquired an all but dictatorial control over British foreign policy, was mesmerized by the "old system," which had been consecrated by time and past successes. His entire foreign policy, like that of Carteret, proceeded on the conviction that Great Britain could not face France without the active assistance of her traditional allies, Holland and Austria. Now, due to her own policy, England had lost them both. Austria, humiliated and resentful, found her differences with Great Britain fundamental and insuperable. The one remaining bond between Austria and the maritime powers, the Barrier Treaty, had proved utterly worthless, and during the negotiations of 1748 Austria made no secret of her intention to denounce the galling servitude which this treaty imposed upon her. Holland, financially and morally exhausted, sought refuge in neutrality. The "old system" had failed completely; it was dead, although Newcastle did not know it.

The two statesmen of Europe who did know it, Count Kaunitz and William Pitt, were still without decisive influence upon public affairs. Count Kaunitz, the most sagacious diplomat of the age, drew the upshot of the Austrian experience in this war when he became the author of a vast network of alliances in which Great Britain had no part. In the political life of Great Britain, however, this war had brought to the front the imperial question. With all the dramatic force that the greatest actor of the age and the incarnation of the imperial spirit could impart, William Pitt urged the necessity of a new system, a system which would break the fetters which chained Englishmen to purely continental connections. With his own matchless grasp of the imperial problem in all its bearings, Pitt was to place the British empire in the center of British policy.

Chapter Five

THE AGE OF ENLIGHTENMENT

I. ITS SOCIAL MILIEU

IN THE perpetual oscillation of the civilized world between compulsory co-ordination and freedom, between worldliness and otherworldliness, between the desire of the human mind to see life in the light of scientific intelligence and the nostalgia for religious faith, the decade that followed the Peace of Aix-la-Chapelle marks a decisive turning point. It was at once a culmination and a new beginning. Feudal society was *in extremis*, and modern competitive and industrial society was in the making. Competition had matured the Leviathan State; never had its administrative civil servants been more enlightened or more active. Yet, because it was the instrument of an absolute monarch, a mechanism that stood outside and above the living mass of the nation, it was in imminent and perpetual danger of ossification. Although the point of ossification had not been reached in Austria and Prussia, France, once more the focal center of Europe, was perilously near it. The public clamor for order, discipline and unity that had once accompanied and supported Richelieu's work of co-ordination as the only escape from feudal anarchy, was now superseded by ever more insistent cries for freedom and the removal of government restraint. The Protestant and Catholic churches, appealing to a supernatural authority, had reared the peoples of Europe in a culture dominated by a transcendental outlook. Now all orthodox churches were ruthlessly dissected. Their theology and their social ethic were subjected to a criticism more merciless than any they had undergone before or since. Nearly everywhere fresh currents of thought were wearing away some cliff of institutionalized tradition. The time was ripe for that vigorous renascence of the spirit which has remade the foundations of western civilization in religion and speculation, in science and technology, in political thought and in the social sciences. No area of life, no country, was left untouched by its regenerative influence.

This age, of course, was no more homogeneous than its predecessors. It was rich in varied movements and contrasting personalities. Even if we designate the Enlightenment as the dominant note of the age, it goes without saying that there were movements and men, great men, who were antagonistic to this dominant outlook. It was the age of healthy, manly, upstanding reason, but it was also the age of sensibility and pre-romanticism. Voltaire and Rousseau were intellectual antipodes, but both stood equally removed from Count von Zinzendorf and John Wesley, leaders of a mystical religious revival that placed no faith in the appeal to constructive reason. Again, the far-sighted Italian, Vico, who died in 1744, initiated in his *Scienza Nuova* a modern historical approach to the problems of contemporary thought and made discoveries which his contemporaries ignored; yet this same Vico embodied the spirit of the nineteenth century.[1] There was also David Hume who, though he was a friend of Diderot and frequented the *salon* of Madame Geoffrin, was the author of a skeptical philosophy that struck at the very roots of the confident rationalism of his age.

Still, this Enlightenment was much the strongest originative force of the age, for it dissolved the unity of that intellectual and religious system which had prevailed in western Europe since the days of St. Augustine. Its triumph in the eyes of contemporaries was overwhelming. Its roots were many and its points of departure widely scattered, yet its scope was European and its central ideas, adapted and filtered to suit local circumstances, were more or less identical in all countries. Everywhere from Scandinavia to the Pyrenees, from England to Switzerland, there was the same pervasive appeal to the autonomy of human reason, the belief in perfectibility and progress; everywhere the same tranquil confidence in the capacity of untrammeled reason to discover, by means of the new doctrine of causality, universally valid principles governing nature, man and society; everywhere the same negation, now radical, now timid, of supernatural revelation, the same determined assault on all authority based on this revelation; everywhere the same optimistic

[1] B. Croce, *The Philosophy of Giamattista Vico* (London, 1913), 241.

belief in the cosmopolitan solidarity of all enlightened intellectuals and a virile disgust with nationalism in the realms of thought and institutions.

It cannot be surprising that modern critical judgment on the Enlightenment has fluctuated and still fluctuates.[2] Its very volcanic iconoclasm makes a dispassionate historical estimate difficult. It invaded prescriptive rights with a recklessness that scandalized conservatives then as it does now. Destruction followed the footsteps of the army of "reason" as closely as its shadow. Its best claim to our gratitude was its courageous effort to emancipate mankind from the fetters of authority and tradition. However, the romantics who followed the rationalist philosophers already accused them of having understood neither religion, nor history, nor the principle of evolution.[3] Carl Becker, in a clever little essay, makes sport of their "little infidelities" and amuses himself with the ingenious paradox that the philosophers merely revived in another form the medieval ideal of the Heavenly City of St. Augustine.[4] Whitehead, commenting on the philosophers, declares, like many a romantic before him, that "man cannot live by bread alone, still less can he live on disinfectants."[5] There is obviously something intolerant and amusing about these French *philosophes*. Their own extravagant claims to absolute originality of thought can no longer be sustained. They were frequently guilty of hasty and premature generalization, of proclaiming as the immutable laws of nature opinions based on incomplete analysis, of a nebulous and often confused utopianism, of making open war on metaphysics while indulging in metaphysical argument. But to dismiss the entire movement as being compounded of negations and disinfectants is to mistake its character and the historical circumstances that produced it.

The source of the movement is generally traced to the philosophy and science of seventeenth-century England, notably that of Shaftesbury, Locke and Newton. In Germany it is customary to date the

2 To cite only two recent examples of critical and penetrating but contrasting estimates: George H. Sabine, *A History of Political Theory* (New York, 1937), 543-551, and E. Cassirer, *Die Philosophie der Aufklärung* (Tübingen, 1932).

3 The term "philosopher" is retained here not only because it has become common usage but because the title is no monopoly of the *esprit de système* which they lacked.

4 Carl Becker, *The Heavenly City of the Eighteenth Century Philosophers* (New Haven, 1932).

5 A. Whitehead, *Science and the Modern World* (New York, 1933), 74.

beginning of the *Aufklärung* from Leibnitz, Thomasius, and Christian Wolf, the great popularizer of Leibnitz, who died in 1754, but it was only in the last third of the century that German thought achieved its full maturity with Lessing, Kant, Goethe and Herder. Except for the influence of English deism and of David Hume, British thought in the years covered by this volume was negligible. Intellectual supremacy had passed indisputably to France, where the cross-fertilization of English thought released the genius of some of the ablest intellects and most brilliant writers of the century. Once again the voice of Paris had become the voice of Europe. Looking back over these years, old Joseph de Maistre said, "An opinion launched in Paris was like a battering ram launched by thirty millions of men."[6]

The explanation for this remarkable influence of the French philosophers of the Enlightenment lies on the surface. Toward 1750 the French language, French ideals, French manners and customs had spread like a contagion from one end of Europe to another, creating a cosmopolitan community of culture such as Europe had not seen since the Renaissance. There were numerous reasons for this widespread currency of the French language, but chief among them were the superb quality of French seventeenth-century classical literature and the superior culture which this literature expressed, combining, as it did, sophistication and wit with taste and propriety, logical precision and universality with urbanity and nobility. In a country like Germany it was not altogether alien, for, after two centuries of humanism, here again was a culture saturated with the Latin spirit and a classical prose comparable in every way to that of the golden age of Cicero, Caesar and Augustus. Among scholars French had replaced Latin as the perfect instrument of Cartesian logic, of the mathematical physics and of the positivistic philosophy of d'Alembert and Lagrange.

In the second place the new rationalist literature arose in the restricted and mundane society of the Parisian *salon*, where knowledge was still safe from the ravages of specialism. Here the cultivated society of France and Europe gathered to discuss, applaud or condemn. Here everything that overtaxed the mental muscle of

[6] A. Sorel, *L'Europe et la Revolution Française* (Paris), I, 150.

the average cultured person—the *honnête homme*—was derided as unpardonable pedantry.[7] Rarely has the cult of literary expression been carried to a higher pitch of perfection. These French philosophers were often deficient in depth of vision, but they were invariably keen and alert in the matter of literary statement. The heavy-footed Italian Vico was, no doubt, profounder than Voltaire, but Voltaire could discuss with incomparable verve and clarity the driest and thorniest of subjects—and he was read. The gay free-thinkers who gathered round the dinner table of Baron d'Holbach were not original philosophers, but they were supreme exemplars as propagandists.

There is nothing so instructive as the remarkable correlation between the disintegration of the old intellectual and religious system of Europe and the breakup of the old feudal social system. On the Continent this breakup came first in France. An examination of the social context of the Enlightenment reveals it to be a middle-class movement in its negations as in its affirmations, in the prejudices over which it triumphed as in the new ones which it cultivated. Neither the old nobility, corrupted by court morals or barbarized by the long leisure of rural exile, nor the obscurantist clergy were capable of leading the new society that was in the making. The advance guard of the cultural transformation was the educated sections of the bourgeoisie. Voltaire was the son of a notary, d'Alembert an illegitimate child, Grimm the son of a pastor, Diderot of a cutler, Rousseau of a watchmaker, and d'Holbach, though a German baron, was of obscure birth. They were all, with the single exception of Montesquieu, middle-class men who owed their fame to their talents. It is manifestly absurd to call these men the conscious advocates of a particular social class. They fancied themselves to be laboring on behalf of "humanity," of "man in general." Nevertheless they were defending certain social interests with their metaphysical doctrines of natural rights and freedom of contract.[8]

This is not always apparent. A gulf separates Voltaire from the

---

[7] M. Roustan, *Les philosophes et la société française au XVIII⁰ siècle* (Paris, 1911), 203.

[8] Less illuminating on this point than it might be is the otherwise excellent study by D. Mornet, *Les origines intellectuelles de la Revolution Française* (Paris, 1933); see J. Luc, *Diderot* (Paris, 1938), 13.

literary valets of Louis XIV, but even the humiliating caning which he suffered at the hands of an insolent nobleman did not inspire him with a mortal hatred of the nobility. The feudal edifice was obviously crumbling, yet the class struggle between the bourgeoisie and the dominant aristocracy had not assumed an acute form. The philosophers were convinced of the necessity of reconstruction, but the projects and plans which they produced in endless variety were still vague and utopian, timidly and hesitatingly advanced. When Rousseau proposed a radical change in the structure of the state, he dismissed his own proposal as impracticable. In the systems of political economy which the *philosophes* projected, the declining feudal system and the advancing capitalist system were still mingled and confused. The revolution in the processes of production and exchange was still in its infancy. But underneath the mask of their critical thought and humanitarian idealism which they defended with often quickly blunted weapons, we can perceive the features of the bourgeoisie struggling for freedom from state regulation and the liberty of commerce.[9]

Never had the prospects for such a struggle appeared more propitious than in the years after 1750. Not merely France, but all the principal countries of Europe were carried irresistibly along by a wave of economic prosperity which enriched the middle classes and increased their self-consciousness. The population of France, already the densest in Europe, showed a steady and continuous increase under Louis XV. The growth of industrial production was scarcely less significant than the expansion of colonial commerce, which will be discussed in another connection. The development of rural industry in Flanders, Picardy, Champagne and Upper Normandy had forever destroyed the self-sufficiency of the countryside. From England, after 1750, there came a steady stream of new processes and new inventions—the mechanical loom, the cylindrical calendar, the hot press, the coke smelter, the paper mill, the rolling mill, and later the steam engine. Almost every variety of important industry had come into being—printed cottons, coal mining, metal-

[9] This is the central thesis of Harold J. Laski's *Rise of Liberalism* (New York, 1936), 180-270, where it is expressed with an exclusive emphasis which the non-Marxist will find difficult to accept.

lurgical works, soap factories, and glass works. Almost every type of modern trading association was already known.

In France as in England there was already a close relation between science and industrial technology. Not only did men of science like Mariotte and Coulomb show an active interest in technical problems, but here and there intelligent craftsmen revealed a new interest in the scientific aspect of their work. A few years after the mid-century the Paris Academy began to publish volume after volume containing fully illustrated accounts of matters pertaining to the industrial arts and crafts, and the state itself showed a new concern for technical education.[10] The expanded business operations, the improved standard of living, the increased credit facilities created great fortunes in every large town of the kingdom. All this required better traveling and transport facilities, which were not slow in coming. The French were the first, in modern times, to construct an improved road system. Under the guidance of the great engineers of the *Ponts et chaussées* the highways of France became the best in Europe. The postal system was speeded up and traveling became quicker and cheaper. Peasant purchasing power increased. Commodity prices were rising and transport on river and road became less expensive and more voluminous. Of course, the old mercantilist control mechanisms, the guilds, the government inspectors of commerce and industry, the complicated codes for the regulation of commerce and industry were still there to impede competition and enterprise, but there were so many holes in this system that it could not stop the rising capitalist to whom the future belonged.[11]

This new spirit of competition and eagerness to acquire wealth flew in the face of the medieval scholastic ethics of the French clergy. Bernard Groethuysen, in his brilliant study, has pointed out that the Catholic clergy of the period lamented in their sermons the worldly and secular temper of the epoch, regretted the disappearance of charity and the contempt for the holiness of poverty, denounced the universal greed for money-getting and the un-

10 A. Wolf, *A History of Science, Technology and Philosophy in the Eighteenth Century* (New York, 1939), 498 ff.; F. B. Artz, "L'éducation technique en France au XVIII⁰ siècle," *Extrait de la Revue d'Histoire Moderne* (Paris, 1939).
11 P. Gaxotte, *Louis XV and His Times* (Phila., 1934), 300 ff.

christian ambition to rise above one's station in life.[12] By denouncing interest as usury clerical moralists confronted the new business classes, whose very existence was based on interest, with the alternative of abandoning either their business methods or the ethics of medieval scholasticism. Already there was no doubt as to the nature of their decision, for, so writes a representative of the new age:

There is not a business man, nor a banker, nor a single merchant who does not believe that he knows more about usury than all the Holy Fathers and theologians in the universe. For business men, these understand nothing of affairs; they know only what they can find in their books and these are all useless in business matters.[13]

By refusing to accommodate itself to the business requirements of the middle class the church co-operated in that separation of morals from religion which was one of the special aims of certain representatives of the Enlightenment.

It was in this period that the French middle classes became conscious of their material and moral potentialities. Nothing could be more absurd than to identify the psychological and logical processes by which Rousseau arrived at his opinions with the average thought of the middle classes. They absorbed from the works of the philosophers only what they could use. But, as M. Mornet has shown, they were reading books and by doing so they were democratizing the trade of the writer. By 1750 the reading public, as we know it, had come into existence. In England and France the patron system was fast declining and the modern publishing system had become established, bringing with it the modern newspaper, the modern best seller, and the modern circulating library.[14] This meant that the privileged and feudal intellectualism of the seventeenth century was passing into the democratic intellectualism of the nineteenth century. In England Samuel Johnson, though often in dire poverty, was still able to live by his pen, without achieving popularity or stooping to do work beneath his powers. Johnson's stinging letter to Lord Chesterfield, written on the latter's failure to grant the prom-

[12] B. Groethuysen, *Les origines de l'esprit bourgeois en France* (Paris, 1927), Vol. I.
[13] Quoted from H. J. Laski, *The Rise of Liberalism* (New York, 1936), 190.
[14] A. S. Collins, *Authorship in the Days of Johnson* (London, 1928).

ised support to the *Dictionary*, may be regarded as the epitaph of the patronage system.[15] It is not without significance that Richardson's *Pamela*, in some respects the first modern English novel, was also the first best seller in the modern sense.

In France also the changed position of the writer, his relative independence, gave the average philosopher an economic and moral importance which French writers had never before possessed. Among these philosophic writers the pursuit of literature was no longer an inoffensive diversion but an indispensable means of livelihood. Viewed in this light the unrelenting crusade of Voltaire for "the freedom of the pen" assumes a new significance. The industry of letters enriched Voltaire and the sale of the *Encyclopédie* made a fortune for Le Breton, its publisher, but Diderot had to work fourteen hours a day in an attic for five hundred dollars a year. Because of the excessive severity of censorship and the difficulty of obtaining the privilege of publication, the French publishing industry did not flourish as it did in Holland or across the Channel.[16] It is true that Malherbes, the director of publications, to whom all books must be submitted for examination, was mildly infected with a rationalist outlook, but the permission which he readily granted might be revoked by the *parlement* of Paris or by the Sorbonne, and it was not uncommon for the royal council to intervene at the last moment with a *lettre de cachet*. Under these circumstances provocative books (and what books of this period were not provocative?) were published anonymously or printed abroad in the presses of London, Amsterdam or Geneva, and distributed by an elaborate secret organization. Violent government repressive measures which breathed the bloody spirit of the Counter Reformation— the writing, printing, sale or even possession of an unauthorized book was punishable with death or at least by commitment to the galleys—alternated with short spells of court indulgence or protection.[17] This necessity of outward conformity to the established creed made criticism all the more subtle and deadly in its methods. The

15 R. W. Chapman, "Authors and Publishers," in A. S. Turberville's *Johnson's England* (Oxford, 1933), II, 310 ff.
16 J. M. S. Allison, *Malherbes* (New Haven, 1938), 12.
17 D. Mornet, *Les origines intellectuelles de la Revolution Française* (Paris, 1933), 51.

concluding sentences of the *Apologie* of the Abbé de Prades may serve as a fair sample, "O cruel enemies of Jesus Christ, will you not cease to trouble the peace of the Church? Have you no pity on the state to which you have reduced her?"[18]

The philosophers resented their position. They were never certain from one day to another whether they would be courted or imprisoned. Prison archives reveal that most of the philosophers at one time or another spent short periods in the Bastille or in the prison at Vincennes.[19] While Voltaire enjoyed the security of his Berlin exile and Rousseau fled when the Archbishop of Paris censored his *Émile* and the Paris *parlement* burned it, Marmontel, a second-rate writer, spent eleven days in the Bastille because in his *Belisarius* he had questioned the right to exterminate heresy by the sword. Diderot was never free from government or Jesuit interference during his editorship of the *Encyclopédie*. Books like the materialist La Mettrie's *L'Homme machine* (1747) and Helvetius' *De l'esprit* (1758) provoked a public scandal and led forthwith to the suppression of numerous other philosophic works. But, due to the ineffective and fitful government persecution, the contagion of rationalist thought and the support of the public, the philosophers assumed the airs of an army on the march.

The unity of France was a decisive factor in the steady progress of enlightened ideas. Here no political barriers such as prevailed in Germany prevented men from all parts of the nation from cooperating in the work of research and enlightened propaganda. Scientific periodical publications kept French scholars all over the nation *au courant* with the development of science, natural history or works of scholarship, and did much toward consolidating the critical method. In more than a score of provincial academies the French middle classes, alert to the new reforming spirit, endeavored to apply the Encyclopedist program; they studied the mechanical arts and agricultural and commercial problems, and advocated a reform of criminal law. When Diderot, after 1747, sought collaborators for his *Encyclopédie* he found them not only in Paris but in Flanders, Montpellier, and the Franche-Comté.

[18] Quoted from J. Luc, *Diderot* (Paris, 1938), 27.
[19] I. K. Luppol, *Diderot* (Paris, 1936), 68.

II. ITS INTELLECTUAL SETTING

From the seventeenth century French thought had inherited both the logical rationalism of Descartes and a superb instrument of expression in its classical prose. But it was the impulse that came from natural science that alchemized it into the Enlightenment.[20]

Little by little, during the preceding century, under the stimulus communicated by Galileo and Bacon, investigations based on the experimental method had built up an impressive body of scientific knowledge in physics, mechanics, mathematics, dynamics and astronomy. Before the turn of the century Newton's great scientific synthesis had caused a revolution in the intellectual outlook of mankind. By revealing for the first time the immensity of interstellar space, Newton had torn the veil from the heavens and redrawn the map of the physical universe. Time and space had expanded indefinitely. Instead of the single, simple world there was now an apparently endless number of worlds. By his stupendous discoveries he had reduced the world to quantity, to mathematically computable motions which behaved with perfect mathematical regularity. Although Galileo and Kepler had grasped the full meaning of the permanence and inflexibility of natural law, they were able to apply it only to isolated cases such as falling bodies or the motions of the planets. But Newton, in his theory of gravitation, had discovered a fundamental, cosmic law, susceptible of mathematical proof and applicable to the minutest object as to the universe at large. To the scientist henceforth nature appeared as a gigantic mechanical contrivance, operated by a connected and coherent system of springs and balances, whose functions could be discovered by means of observation, experiment, measurement and calculation. Newton's ideas were slow to penetrate to the Continent, but, thanks to Maupertuis and Voltaire, they became an integral part of the working faith of every educated Frenchman by 1750.[21]

Thereafter the problem which agitated philosophers since the days of Leibnitz, whether or not it was possible to preserve the

---

20 G. Lanson, "L'influence de la philosophie cartésienne sur la littérature française," *Études d'histoire littéraire* (Paris, 1929), 58.

21 Brunet, *Maupertuis* (Paris, 1929), I, 13 ff.

value of personality and maintain the moral sanctions of society in a purely mechanical world order, had become more difficult to solve. It became more difficult still as the various sciences advanced. Now it was especially French science that was proceeding from physics and astronomy to the study of biological problems. The microscope had provided an insight into the intimate structure and functions of different organs and had revealed the existence of vast numbers of lower animals hitherto unsuspected. Medieval beliefs, like that of spontaneous generation, were crumbling under the stress of the experiments of Spallanzani. The investigation of the geological history of the earth and the growing knowledge of animal fossils were firing the imagination of the eloquent Buffon, who ignored the Genesis account of the creation of the world and suggested that the earth must be at least seventy-five thousand years old. Linnaeus (1707-1778), the son of a Swedish clergyman, had already begun to describe and classify plants, animals and the varieties of human species, and the problem of classifying animals according to orders, genera and species was leading him to the further problem of their structural relationships. The study of the physiology of blood circulation, the processes of reproduction, the functions of the brain and the nervous system by Willis, Boerhaave and Haller gave a further impetus to that growing tendency to relate the physiology of the human body to that of animals and living organisms generally.[22] Where physiology ended psychology took up the tale. Years had passed since John Locke had provided a scientific basis for an empirical study of psychology by denying the existence of innate ideas and contending that all knowledge, opinions and behavior were derived from sense experience. Condillac now carried this doctrine to its final conclusion by asserting that even reflection itself was nothing but transformed sensation. Psychological processes, argued Condillac in his *Traité des sensations* (1754), could not be understood until they had been pursued to their original sense impressions.

Thus, beginning with the new astronomical orientation, there was a connected system of demonstrable truth at the disposal of the French philosophers, a series of scientific hypotheses on the geo-

[22] Sir M. Foster, *History of Physiology* (Cambridge. 1904), 204.

logical history of the earth, the origin and relationship of plants and animals, the close kinship between higher animals and human beings, and finally the dependence of all intellectual activity on the senses and the nervous system—all falling within the scope of the same natural laws which made mankind, hitherto an anomaly in the scheme of things, an integral part of the natural world and, as such, subject to its economy. The traditional anthropocentric view of the universe lay in ruins and with it the anthropomorphic conception of God.

Compared with these remarkable advances of natural science, the social sciences remained in a relatively primitive state. They produced no Newton to place them on a solid, uniform and empirical basis. Prevalent theological dogma, whether Protestant or Catholic, was no congenial climate for their development. The religious interpretation of life in the very nature of things extends to totality, and the principle of authority which lay at its base, the conception of man as a spiritual being, the subordination of all social action to an ultimate transcendental aim, the organic unity and universality characteristic of the prevalent ecclesiastic culture— all these were contrary to the postulates on which a solid edifice of social science could be erected. Still, when the first great efforts at a synthesis of the social sciences were made by Montesquieu, Voltaire, the Encyclopedists and the physiocrats, these attempts were possible only because of the progress that had been made in the past. Here, too, the philosophers were not originators; they merely systematized, clarified, and popularized the work that had been done before them.[23]

The social sciences, the numerous disciplines of scholarship and erudition, arose in an atmosphere of religious, political and economic controversy, and they were weapons of conflict before they became objects of research by disinterested scholars. The incessant controversies between Protestants and Catholics, between Jesuits and Jansenists and between the countless Protestant sects had the effect not only of rendering the very notion of a single absolute and exclusive religious truth ridiculous, but of forcing upon the theo-

23 R. Hubert, "Essai sur l'histoire des origines et des progrès de la sociologie en France," *Revue d'histoire de la philosophie et d'histoire générale de la civilisation* (April, 1938), 111 ff.

logians themselves an ever greater refinement of the philological and critical tools of Biblical exegesis. In these discussions of contending religious groups authority lost something of its power and scholarship became more indispensable; it was necessary to produce proof, to interpret correctly Greek and Hebrew texts, even to establish the authenticity of the Biblical text itself. The general assumption of the age of the Reformation that the numerous sacred books of the Bible, written at different times under different historical circumstances, represented a single coherent body of thought and doctrine, a notion that lay at the foundation of the dogma of verbal inspiration, became steadily more difficult to sustain. The demand for an historical Biblical criticism became ever more insistent.[24] The Frenchman Simon and the Jew Spinoza had made faltering efforts at such a criticism, but the first comprehensive plan for a truly modern Biblical criticism came from the prolific pen of the greatest student of Erasmus, Hugo Grotius. Inspired by the belief of his great humanist forbear that the religious creed of the early Christian community could not be recovered until a reliable text of the New Testament writings, free from falsifications and later additions, was established, Grotius in his *Annotationes* suggested criteria of historical source criticism to which the French philosophers found little to add. When Diderot wrote his article on the Bible for the *Encyclopédie* he was able to present a complete outline of all the fundamental problems of Biblical criticism. With this article of Diderot the historical method had advanced into the very center of the theological system and henceforth the principle of the verbal inspiration of the Bible lost its old meaning.

This evolutionary pattern was repeated in the social sciences. The conflict between absolute royal power and the corporate beneficiaries of the feudal system raised the question of the legal rights of monarchy and led inevitably to the study of constitutional and customary law and, once the appeal to ancient usages and the ordinances of the early French kings had been made, to constitutional and legal history. International conflicts and the desire for internal consolidation stimulated the writing of national history. Historical

[24] Aner, *Die Theologie der Lessingzeit* (Halle, 1929), 204; A. Lods, *Jean Astruc et la critique biblique au XVIII*e *siècle* (1924).

study was extended to all epochs and to all phases of historical evolution. The auxiliary sciences of history—archaeology, epigraphy,
paleography, diplomatics and, in a certain sense, geography—had
already reached a relatively high stage of perfection. Early political
economy, shocked into reflection by the contrasting examples of
Spain and Holland, sought the source of national wealth first in
the possession of precious metals, then in the expansion of commerce
and, finally with the physiocrats, in the development of agricultural
production. The coincidence of the conflict of interest and the conflict of ideas in these early economic doctrines is apparent. In the
midst of all these controversies and clashing interests the social
sciences were beginning to yield to evidence, to the critical and historical method; the influence of the master of this method, Pierre
Bayle, was becoming steadily more universal.

Scarcely less powerful was the stimulus that came from another
quarter, from the encroachment of the non-European world upon
the traditional intellectual European horizon. Chinard and particularly Atkinson have pointed out the overwhelming influence
of "exotic" or travel literature, which caused a revolutionary change
in the whole setting and circumstance of European life.[25] The old
medieval conception of a world bounded by the frontiers of Chris-
tendom crumbled before the awe-inspiring spectacle of an infinitely
varied and vaster world, peopled by races and civilizations which
had no common ethnical or cultural origin and certainly owed nothing to the tradition of Judaism or Christianity, hitherto conceived
to be universal. Here were peoples and civilizations at every stage
of development, from the African Hottentots to the highly cultivated Chinese, presenting a picture of the immense variability of
human institutions, religions, laws and customs, far too complex
to be explained in terms of theological tradition or Cartesian doctrine. It is true that travel literature was not new. As far back as
1580 Montaigne had drawn "philosophic" conclusions from the new

25 G. Chinard, *L'Amérique et la rêve éxotique dans la littérature française au XVII*
et au XVIII siècle (Paris, 1913); sounder in scholarship and more useful are the
various works by G. Atkinson, *The Extraordinary Voyage in French Literature before
1700* (New York, 1920); *The Extraordinary Voyage in French Literature from 1700 to
1720* (Paris, 1922); but particularly his *Les rélations de voyages du XVII* siècle et
l'évolution des idées (Paris, 1923), 181-195; see also H. N. Fairchild, *The Noble Savage*
(Columbia University Press, 1928).

anthropological knowledge supplied by such literature. Already in the seventeenth century almost every travel book was an indirect criticism of France. But this literature supported the positivist and experimental mentality of the eighteenth century. The heavy debt which the social sciences of the Enlightenment owed to the reports of missionaries and agents of the great commercial companies is too obvious to require special emphasis. Montesquieu and Voltaire exploited them. They are constantly referred to in all the arguments of the English and French deists and in the works of the early students of comparative religion, such as C. de Brosses and David Hume. Much of this travel literature, it must be admitted, was of little scientific value. The flattering accounts of primitive savages, depicting "unspoilt humanity" as living in a "state of nature" with all the religious and moral sense that was imagined to be inherent in "natural" man, contributed to the upbuilding of the legend of the "noble savage," which played havoc with so much of the political science of this epoch.[26] Although Rousseau and the Encyclopedists succumbed to this legend, it should be remembered that Montesquieu and Voltaire did not.

Briefly, by 1750 the social sciences had emerged from their early immaturity and were prepared to assume the task of measuring institutions, traditions and authority with a new yardstick. They had already become in some sense inductive, historical, anthropological, comparative and critical. They still lacked certain general ideas that could introduce order and unity among them, such as the idea of historical or sociological determinism, the idea of the interdependence of economics, politics, religion and culture in the life of nations, and the notion that there was a continuity and therefore a meaning in the development of human society. It was the function of the Enlightenment to supply these ideas.

III. ITS METHODS

It is often said that the French philosophers were mere popularizers of the thought of their greater seventeenth-century predecessors. This was not their own opinion. When in the middle of the

[26] J. L. Myres, *The Influence of Anthropology on the Course of Political Science* (1914).

century one of their finest spirits, d'Alembert, wrote his *Éléments de philosophie*, he was convinced that he was standing on the threshold of a profound transformation of European civilization. He and his friends felt themselves to be part of a new movement, driven forward by a new and overpowering force that was at work in them and their epoch. The best of them did not surrender themselves blindly to this movement; they endeavored to grasp its whence and whither, its origin and goal, for this goal they wished to determine themselves. They called themselves *philosophes*, but by the term philosophy they did not mean a special province of speculative knowledge distinct and apart from natural science, history and sociology. Philosophy for them was rather the central medium, the animating breath of all these branches of knowledge. Therefore, the Enlightenment, to be properly understood, must be examined not only as to the doctrinal substance of the thought of Voltaire, Montesquieu or Diderot, but as to its intellectual and logical processes. The optimism, the delight and courage which these men exhibited were inspired not merely by the quantitative accumulation of knowledge, but by the conviction that they were in possession of the instrument by which these results had been achieved, an instrument of which the future possibilities appeared boundless. This new instrument they called "reason." Unhappily the words "reason" and "rationalism" have today so many historical connotations that the historian must discard them as too vague to convey any precise meaning.

Certain it is, however, that the *philosophes* did not understand by "reason" what Descartes had meant by it. Their philosophic method was not that of Descartes' *Discours de la méthode* but that of Newton's *Regulae philosophandi*.[27] Newton proceeded, not by way of pure deduction, but by way of analysis. Not abstraction and definition, but observation and experience were his points of departure. Observation was his *datum* and the principle or natural law was his *quaesitum*. Unlike David Hume, Newton saw no contrast between experience and thought, between "matters of fact" on the one hand and the "relations of ideas" on the other. On the contrary, he presupposed order and regularity in the physical world, and this regu-

27 E. Cassirer, *Die Philosophie der Aufklärung* (Tübingen, 1932), 7.

larity he expressed by means of principles or laws stated in mathematical terms. It was this analytical method of Newtonian physics,
applied now to the entire field of thought and knowledge, that
placed its stamp on the thought of the entire Enlightenment. It is
apparent in d'Alembert's famous introduction to the *Encyclopédie*,
in Condillac's *Traité des systèmes*, no less than in Voltaire's *Traité
métaphysique*. These men persistently criticized the seventeenth-
century philosophers because they did not form their concepts on
the basis of observable facts. The order, the regularity, the "reason"
which the eighteenth-century philosophers sought were not the
result of a priori speculation, but were to grow out of an analysis of
the observed facts. The new logic, which the philosophers were convinced would lead to positive and certain results, was, therefore,
neither scholastic nor purely mathematical, but, to use the phrase
of William James, the "logic of irreducible and stubborn facts."

If to Descartes, Leibnitz and Spinoza reason was still equivalent
to those eternal verities which man and God shared in common, the
philosophers used the word in a more restricted sense. Reason was
to them not so much a body of principles and truths as it was a
specific method for acquiring knowledge, an intellectual energy
which could be completely understood only in its exercise. Lessing
put it pithily when he said that the real power of reason lay not
in the possession but in the acquisition of truth. Montesquieu said
substantially the same thing. The defense, consolidation and popularization of this Newtonian analytical procedure was the core of
the Enlightenment, and herein, not merely in their propaganda for
a definite set of ideas, the philosophers recognized their most important task. No more trenchant illustration of this special function
of the Enlightenment can be indicated than the *Encyclopédie* itself,
the arsenal of all this new scientific knowledge, and the most important literary enterprise of the epoch. Diderot, its editor, declared
that its chief purpose was not only to communicate a definite body
of knowledge, but to produce a revolution in the process of thinking—*pour changer la façon commune de penser*.[28] All of them, the
genuine scientists and philosophers among them, no less than the

[28] Ducros, *Les Encyclopédistes* (Paris, 1900), 138; J. Le Gras, *Diderot et L'Encyclopédie* (Amiens, 1928), chap. I.

facile closet speculators, the drawing-room amateurs and the shallow charlatans were convinced that by a general application of the method of analysis they could revolutionize contemporary culture.

It is significant to note that the French philosophers drew no neat distinction, as is done in our own day, between nature and society, between the natural and social sciences. Unlike the later German social science, which was either historical and relativistic or, at its worst, organismic in its thought, French social science from Montesquieu to Auguste Comte was conceived as social physics. Divorced from theology, it became, in Taine's phrase, a prolongation of natural science.[29] Before Comte the French philosophers advocated and employed a positivistic method, and they also exhibited, it may be added, Comte's pontifical air. In other words, the method of pure analysis, mathematical in its essence and hitherto applied only to the realm of quantitative and numerical constants, was now extended to psychological and social processes. Descartes had still drawn a sharp line between physics, the domain of matter and necessity, and metaphysics, the domain of the spirit and liberty. But when Condillac traced perception, memory, idea, imagination, judgment and knowledge to sensations or revived sensations, he had reduced, or thought he had reduced, physical and psychological reality, as it were, to a common denominator.[30] As if each philosopher were bent on outdoing his predecessor, Helvetius in his De l'esprit (1759) carried this doctrine, that all intellectual activity was a mere metamorphosis of sensation, to almost ridiculous lengths. Here the stream of consciousness, ever changing from moment to moment, never to recur in precisely the same way, became a mere mask, a deceptive illusion, and all that remained was a mechanism, measurable and computable like Newton's world machine. The esprit géométrique, limited by Pascal to mathematical natural science, had taken possession of the social sciences. Henceforth the doctrine of historical and sociological determinism, nothing more than the application to the social sciences of the principle of causality borrowed from natural science, was generally accepted.

---

29 H. Taine, The Ancient Regime (London, 1876), 177; R. Hubert, "Essai sur l'histoire des origines et des progrès de la sociologie en France," Revue d'histoire de la philosophie et d'histoire générale de la civilisation (15 Avril, 1938), 139.

30 Condillac, Traité des sensations, ed. by Georges Lyon (Paris, 1921), 32.

Henceforth the state, too, was conceived as a "body" that could be decomposed and resolved into its constituent elements which, in turn, could be analyzed and recomposed by the same method which scientists employed in the physical world.

Many a modern devotee of historicism has derided this juvenile scientific positivism of the philosophers and ridiculed their naïve efforts to measure the incommensurable. Indeed, in its execution this positivistic method often appears preposterous enough. In spite of all their talk of accurate observation, close and exhaustive analysis, the philosophers often repeated the device of Boulanger, who prefaced his history of man with a study of himself, convinced, as he wrote, "that in spite of the difference of centuries and men, there are common sentiments and uniform ideas that reveal themselves universally through the cries of nature, through terrors and panics which have alarmed certain centuries."[31] In the hasty formulas, the facile dogmatism, in which their works abound, they frequently ignored the empirical method which the profoundest among them set forth with incomparable precision and lucidity. Moreover, the atmosphere of the *salon*, which demanded striking and brilliant literary effects, was not conducive to patient research and sober generalization.

But when Condillac and Montesquieu attempted to transform the historical flux of social and political processes into a problem in statics, they were laying the foundations of modern social science. They did not, like the romantics who followed them, seek out those special and personal traits which separate one man from another, but rather those constant and universal characteristics which men possess in common. They were alert to the fact that without an exhaustive sociological analysis of these characteristics any social science was impossible. Although Montesquieu followed the analytical procedure of physics, it should be remembered that he was neither oblivious to the importance and value of history, nor did he attribute to his "principles" or "laws" that universal and absolute character which they still possessed in the metaphysical systems of the seventeenth century. Montesquieu was satisfied with a relative validity; his "principle" was a tentative stopping place in

[31] R. Hubert, *D'Holbach et ses amis* (Paris, 1928), 89.

the endless human search for truth. D'Alembert took the same position. This recognition of the modern notion of the relativity of truth sprang from the healthy conviction that reason in its perpetual progress has no limits which cannot be surpassed and that each apparent solution is merely a point of departure for a renewed effort.[32]

It is not difficult to perceive that there was no sharp breach between the philosophy of the seventeenth century and that of the eighteenth-century Enlightenment. There was no radical change in the forms of thought. The new ideal of knowledge was simply a further development of seventeenth-century science and logic. But there was a plainly perceptible change of emphasis.[33] Compared with Descartes and Leibnitz, the French philosophers placed the emphasis on the particular rather than on the general, on observable facts rather than on principles, on experience rather than on rational speculation. Except for Hume's skepticism, the confidence which they placed in reason was still unshaken.

IV. THE ENLIGHTENMENT AND RELIGION

The eighteenth century was the complete antithesis of the Middle Ages. It was an age of reason based on faith, not an age of faith based on reason. The biting acids of the Enlightenment corroded the orthodox churches, both Protestant and Catholic, and compelled them to adapt themselves to the new intellectual and social environment. The philosophers assailed the principle of supernatural authority, denied divine revelation, assaulted traditional theological dogma, and scoffed at miracles. But the charge that they were rootedly antireligious is a hangover from the period of romantic reaction and is less frequently repeated in our own day. As a matter of fact, the Enlightenment gave birth to a number of modern religious values. It spiritualized the principle of religious authority and humanized the absolute and divine theological systems, and by doing so emancipated the individual from physical coercion to ecclesiastical conformity. It was the Enlightenment, not the Renaissance or the Reformation, that dislodged the ecclesiastical establish-

32 D'Alembert's article on "Éléments de science," in the *Encyclopédie* and his "Éléments de philosophie," *Mélanges de Littérature, d'Histoire et de Philosophie,* IV, 35 ff.
33 Ernst Cassirer, *Die Philosophie der Aufklärung* (Tübingen, 1932), 28.

ments (though scarcely religion in the larger sense) from their central and controlling position in the cultural and intellectual life of Europe, and by emancipating science from the trammels of theological tradition rendered possible the autonomous evolution of modern culture. Together with the Reformation, of course, it was directly responsible for the appalling anarchy in religious values which is the bane of modern society, but it made men alert to the consummate value of dissent, of intellectual heresy and of individual initiative. Broadly speaking, it caused a transformation of the Protestant churches. And did not the Catholic Church itself profit from the storm that now overtook it? If the purified Catholicism of modern times employs moral suasion and abhors physical coercion, relies on the subjective validity of its religious message, accepts religious tolerance and the freedom of religious expression, bases its authority on voluntary consent, this must largely be attributed to the Enlightenment.[34]

In France this literature of negativism and repudiation took the form of an insidious campaign of mockery, irony and derision. Here the philosophers had to do battle with an organized corporation which, because of its close alliance with the state, had special economic privileges, exceptional tribunals, dungeons and chains at its disposal. Church and state, it must be remembered, were an integral part of an ideological system which was still in full operation in France, Spain and Austria. The church proclaimed the religious duty of obedience to a king whose authority had been conferred by the divinity itself, while the king, in his coronation oath, had assumed the solemn obligation to defend the church against its enemies. The church's persistent appeal to the secular authorities for a repressive policy, sometimes bloody and cruel as in the case of the Protestants, sometimes minutely vexatious as in the persecution of such pacific men of letters as Montesquieu and Buffon, but always lynx-eyed, had the natural effect of provoking opposition to a religious system of which rigorous intolerance was so prominent a characteristic. "Impose on me silence on religion and govern-

[34] For a penetrating analysis of the larger religious implications of the Enlightenment see E. Troeltsch, *Protestantismus und Kirche in der Neuzeit* (Berlin, 1922), 600-611; by the same author, "Religionswissenschaft und Theologie des 18. Jahrhunderts," *Preussische Jahrbücher*, Vol. 114 (1903), 32 ff.

ment," said Diderot, "and I have nothing to say."[35] In a century dominated by secular interests and a worldly outlook this lingering political power of a church which, as matters then stood, was a strange union of Byzantine decrepitude and of the energetic ferocity of the Holy Office, was bound to provoke a rising tide of anti-clericalism.[36]

The political influence of the Catholic clergy was all the more pernicious in the eyes of the philosophers, because orthodox Catholic dogma presented not merely a system of religious metaphysics and a code of ethics, but an elaborate cosmology that was equivalent to a complete interpretation of geology, of ethnography, of world history, of the origins of mankind. Bossuet claimed to have discovered a complete system of political philosophy in the sacred books of the Bible. Not merely theologians but physicists and biologists still saw in the Mosaic account of creation an authentic science of nature which, because of the doctrine of verbal inspiration, was immune from scientific criticism. As late as 1726 there had appeared the translation of a volume by the Englishman Derham entitled *Théologie physique*, soon to be followed by a *Théologie astronomique*, a *Théologie de l'eau* by one Fabricius and even a *Théologie des insects* by one Lesser.[37] All this still appeared to churchmen and devout laymen part of a coherent and organic edifice. He who removed one stone imperiled the entire structure. The bond between theology and physics, though weakened, was not yet definitely dissolved. The very territory which the new sciences were bent on conquering was still, as it were, under a theological mandate.

It was this system of theological science that the philosophers of the Enlightenment assailed. In one and the same process of emancipation they endeavored to establish on a firm foundation the autonomy of reason and the freedom of scientific enquiry. The century which d'Alembert called the century of philosophy others called with as much justice and no less pride the century of science. Science had long since ceased to be the exclusive occupation of a few royal academies and learned societies; it was already one of

35 J. Oestreicher, *La pensée politique et économique de Diderot* (Vincennes, 1936), 35.
36 A. Monod, *De Pascal à Chateaubriand, les defenseurs françaises du Christianisme* (Paris, 1916).
37 For an analysis of the contents of this literature, D. Mornet, *Les sciences de la nature en France au XVIIIe siècle* (Paris, 1911), 31 ff.

the vital concerns of all western society. In the nature of the case, natural science occupied the front of the stage. Not only experimental physicists and mathematicians but those very philosophers and historians who were seeking a new orientation for the social sciences were devoting themselves to an assiduous study of the problems of natural science. It will be remembered that Voltaire opened a new epoch, not with his frosty tragedies or his *Henriade* but with his *Éléments de la philosophie de Newton*, that Diderot wrote on physiology, Rousseau on chemistry, and that Montesquieu turned from the study of physics only because of his failing eyesight.

These men ceased to think as Christians because they wished to think as scientists. Whatever their personal attitude toward religion, they sought a science and a theory of human nature free from theological speculation. Voltaire's perverse and frivolous mockery of "Biblical physics" may appear to us as bad taste, but by discrediting this bastard science as the monstrous product of the theological intellect, he sought to expose its root fallacy in method. It was only gradually that a sharp line between the theological and the empirical method was definitely drawn. In Buffon's magnificent work on the *Epochs of Nature* the new method scored one of its first great triumphs. It is true that Buffon later declared his submission to the strictures of the Sorbonne on his departure from Biblical chronology, but his silence on the Mosaic story of creation was more effective than an open declaration of war on the church. Here, for the first time, there appeared an analysis of the geological history of the earth, uninfluenced by theological dogma and based solely on the observed facts, however inadequate it may appear to modern geologists. A clear breach had been made in the traditional system, and Voltaire with his boundless vitality and matchless industry continued the work with weapons which, however antiquated today, were sharp and deadly enough for their purpose. One may regret this work of devastation, but it was the necessary condition of the subsequent progress of modern science. The philosophers succeeded in staking off a definite territory within which ecclesiastical authority and coercion were no longer respected. It was the first great victory of the Enlightenment, all the greater because the church itself finally yielded to this separation of science from theology.

But it is doing Voltaire and history a disservice when Alfred Noyes, his latest biographer, asserts that all Voltaire sought to achieve with his *Écrasez l'infame* was to secure tolerance and to reduce the church "to the condition in which it exists in England."[38] On the contrary, he set himself deliberately to overthrow Catholic theology as well as the ecclesiastical system which was bound up with it. Presently, there appeared a new generation which brushed aside his nice distinctions between faith and superstition, between religion and the church. In the eyes of Diderot, d'Holbach and the French Encyclopedists all religious dogmas were obscure, incomprehensible and absurd. Utterly impervious to theological mystery and insensible to the morality of resignation, obedience, charity and forgetfulness of self which Christianity taught, these men held all religious problems to be pseudo-problems, denounced all religious belief as a tissue of errors and religion itself as priestcraft and an impediment to intellectual progress. The vigorous propagandist d'Holbach who, beginning with his *Le Christianisme dévoilé* in 1756, published one antireligious book after another, persistently repeated his eternal theme that religion, by inspiring fear of an invisible tyrant, had made men slavish and cowardly toward kings and rendered them incapable of managing their own affairs.[39] Diderot, too, after passing through the phase of deism, which he soon came to regard as a shoddy and pusillanimous compromise, demanded the complete renunciation of all religious faith, in whatever historical form it appeared, as the only means of salvation from prejudice and servitude.[40]

These French materialists reduced all physical and intellectual processes, the entire physical and moral order, to matter and motion. What we are and will be, what we think and what we do, are nothing but the necessary effects of the qualities which nature has given us. With them human physiology became the key to a knowledge of the universe. *"Voilà mes philosophes,"* said La Mettrie

---

[38] Alfred Noyes, *Voltaire* (New York, 1939), 492.
[39] See the reprints of significant passages from his numerous books collected by R. Hubert, *D'Holbach et ses amis* (Paris, 1928), 101, 163 ff.
[40] H. Gillot, *Denis Diderot* (Paris, 1937), 54.

of his senses, this physician who had to flee to the court of Frederick the Great for safety after the publication of his *Histoire naturelle de l'âme* in 1745. In its essence this French materialism was neither a scientific doctrine nor a metaphysical dogma but the belief in a thoroughgoing determinism.[41] La Mettrie and d'Holbach were rigorous and consistent determinists. In their materialistic universe there was neither good nor evil, neither guilt nor disorder; all phenomena, whether physical or moral, were equally and irrevocably necessary. It was a stultifying delusion to believe in the freedom of the will. Yet these same men were the most ardent and implacable enemies of the supernaturalism of the Christian religion. The argument that runs through La Mettrie's *L'Homme machine* (1747) is that only by uprooting the ideas of God, freedom and immortality can man order his world rationally. Mankind cannot become happy unless it resolves to become atheist.[42] That, with an argument such as this, these materialists were hoisting themselves by their own petard is obvious enough. If you believe in determinism, it is nonsense to speak of ethical norms. One cannot teach a watch to keep exact time by an appeal to its conscience. With a penetrating eye Voltaire detected the weak point in their argument and accused them of cultivating a fanatical dogmatism of their own after having inscribed on their banner the struggle against the dogmatism and intolerance of the church. He refused to receive the "brief of atheism" (*le brevet d'athée*) from the hands of d'Holbach.

Diderot, too, saw these contradictions, but transformed the vicious circle of freedom and necessity into a superior dialectical play of wit in his novel *Jacques le Fataliste*. He also was a determinist, but he was too jealous a defender of the autonomy of man to fall prey to the crude determinism of d'Holbach and Helvetius. Though enclosed within a whole network of fatalities, man still possesses reason, and Diderot had too profound a faith in the nobility of reason not to believe in its power for good "in proportion as it becomes enlightened." Men become criminals, not because of necessity nor because of original sin, but because of their aboriginal stu-

[41] E. Cassirer, *Die Philosophie der Aufklärung* (Tübingen, 1932), 88-95.
[42] Raymond Boissier, *La Mettrie* (Paris, 1931), 146 ff.

pidity and bad judgment. In his *Fragment inédit* Diderot wrote, "Man is born with a germ of virtue, though he is not born virtuous. He can achieve this sublime state by a study of himself, after having learned to know his duties, after having contracted the habit of fulfilling them."[43]

Diderot was an unashamed pagan in the Dionysiac intoxication with which he enjoyed all the potentialities which life in its fullness offered him. With this paganism he combined a passionate desire for universal knowledge, not merely the science of books but also the living science of nature, which he saw with new enraptured eyes. As a scientist he abandoned the mechanistic and static universe of his philosopher friends and embraced a dynamic and evolutionary outlook. As a philosopher he passed from atheism to pantheism, from materialism to a dynamic pan-psychism.[44] What connected him with the Renaissance was his religion of man, whom he sought to deliver from servitude to an ascetical religion which, he thought, mutilated his nature. He was an authentic descendant of those encyclopaedic geniuses of the Renaissance, who, not content with knowing, demanded that science should serve the process of living, the cause of progress, for he had a firm confidence in the indefinite perfectibility of the human species. Humanistic in his genius, secular in his outlook, modern and scientific in his method, like Bacon, he expected from a popularization of this method the liberation, the rehabilitation and the regeneration of man.

The atheistic sallies of the irreverent Encyclopedist group were scarcely representative of the Enlightenment as a whole. Far more characteristic of its positive religious creed was the deism that came from the free, tolerant and Latitudinarian atmosphere of England.[45] Notwithstanding the great diversity of belief among deists, we may define deism as the worship of a personal or, more frequently, an impersonal deity and the acceptance of a natural religion based on the common ideas of morality engraved on the

43 Quoted from Pierre Hermand, *Les idées morales de Diderot* (Paris, 1923), 189.

44 B. Groethuysen, "La pensée de Diderot," *La Grande Revue*, Vol. 82 (1913), 322 ff.; Jean Thomas, *L'humanisme de Diderot* (Paris, 1933).

45 L. Stephen, *English Thought in the Eighteenth Century* (London, 1927 ed.), 2 vols.; E. Troeltsch, "Der Deismus" in *Gesammelte Schriften* (Tübingen, 1925), IV, 429 ff., 845-846; Mark Pattison, "Tendencies of Religious Thought in England, 1688-1750," *Essays and Reviews* (1861), 254-329; A. W. Benn, *English Rationalism* (1906).

hearts of all men. However questionable the theoretical foundations of deism may appear to modern students of religion, the influence of this widespread if diffuse faith penetrated to most of the countries of Europe. It left a permanent mark on modern German Protestantism. In France it became an historical power. Though merely an episode in England, it was estimated that in 1749 half the educated people were deists of one sort or another, and, thanks to the works of David Hume, of Adam Smith (*Moral Sentiments,* 1759) and the posthumous works (1754) of Lord Bolingbroke, it enjoyed a respectable literary status.[46] The reason for its great influence among the educated may be sought in a natural reaction against the horror and cruelty of the religious wars of the preceding age and against the fruitless logomachies of theological controversy which, instead of creating unity, produced only further dissension. Thoroughly weary of futile theological disputation, men cast about for some formula of reconciliation between the warring Christian sects.

Deism was the logical outgrowth of the new spirit of scientific inquiry, the rationalist faith in the oneness of humanity, and the early beginnings of the modern study of comparative religion. The generation that followed Newton and played with the microscope and telescope began to interpret theological dogmas concerning the nature of God in accordance with new standards. Against the capricious Deity of Calvinist theology there now stood the new conception of God deducible from the rule of law, the harmony and order of his created universe. God, like his universe, was conceived as rational and reliable, not arbitrary, and the sense of relief derived from this optimistic conception was intensified by the conviction that the Creator was not only universal and wise but beneficent. This interpretation of the Divine Nature in terms of scientific concepts led inevitably to the disparagement of the authority of revelation. In the deistic speculations concerning the nature and destiny of humanity, psychology and common-sense morality displaced arguments based on Biblical texts.

But Newtonian physics was but one source of the natural religion of the deists. As interest in religious metaphysics receded into the background its place was occupied by a general comparative study

[46] J. M. Robertson, *A Short History of Freethought* (New York, 1906), II, 166.

of religion, largely intuitionist and only half empirical to be sure, but still a study that proceeded to examine all the great historical religions of the world for their common elements and operated with the general concepts of religion, religious consciousness and the history of religion. This was something radically new, for such general concepts had been utterly alien to the Middle Ages and the older forms of Protestantism.[47] In the eyes of orthodox Catholics and Protestants religion and Christianity, religion and revelation, were identical. They recognized only the one normative Christian revelation, no general human religious consciousness. There was no historical evolution of "religion," there was only the original blissful state of Paradise, the essential depravity of mankind that was the result of the fall from grace, and the restoration of this original state through the instrumentality of the Christian church. The timid efforts of Pico della Mirandola and Erasmus to formulate a general concept of religion during the Renaissance were universally and unequivocally condemned.

Excepting only the lonely figure of Spinoza, the English deists were the first to create general concepts of religion and religious consciousness on the basis of a comparative study of Christianity and of such knowledge of Buddhism and Confucianism, the primitive religions of the Tahitians and the South Sea islanders as this age of colonial expansion supplied. Some of them, like the Dutch humanists of Leyden, sought to bring this new knowledge to bear on an examination of the ancient mythologies of the Greeks and Jews, thus preparing the ground for a study of a general evolutionary history of religion. At this point, however, their rationalism interfered with the full use of their still imperfect historical and anthropological tools. Believing, as they did, in the fundamental identity of human nature at all times, in all countries and latitudes, the deists argued that, once all religions had been stripped of the supernatural and mysterious envelope in which they are wrapped up, their real substance, their *raison d'être*, will be found to consist in the worship of God and a common-sense moral code. Thus, cutting across all religious cosmologies and irrespective of the diversity

---

47 See the careful and scholarly examination by E. Troeltsch, "Aufsätze zur Geistesgeschichte und Religionssoziologie," *Gesammelte Schriften* (Tübingen, 1925), IV, 841-849.

of tongues and ages, there was a universal natural religion, in which all mankind might yet find its essential unity. This natural religion was considered "as old as creation" and such familiar heroes as Socrates, Cicero and Confucius were claimed as its adherents. In view of this essential harmony of all religious creeds, the pretense of a particular revelation, vouchsafed to the primitive Hebrew people and continued in the New Testament, appeared ridiculous and impertinent. In its essence, it is apparent, this deistic natural religion was an attack upon the fundamental premises of revealed religion and a criticism of the Christian churches, which were unable to agree even in the exegesis of their inspired Biblical oracles.

The outcry which the deists provoked in England was less penetrating than in France because Anglican theologians met the onslaught halfway.[48] By their argument that the Christian God was the very God of nature whom the deists preached, they surrendered the fortress. Consciously or unconsciously, they compromised with rationalism and opened the door to the infiltration of the rationalist spirit. It was not orthodox clergymen but none other than David Hume, the radical philosophic skeptic and the most anti-clerical and anti-Christian Scot of his day, who demolished the optimistic creed of deism. The keen edge of Hume's analysis in his *Natural History of Religion*, first published in 1757, cut the very ground from under the "natural religion" of his deist friends.[49]

The existence of a natural religion rests on the basic assumption of the Enlightenment that man is guided by the dictates of reason, that the mind of man is the scene of a uniform play of motive and that the motives of men are quantitatively and qualitatively the same, at all times and in all places. On no other grounds was it possible to imagine a natural religion. But where, asked Hume, do we find such a human nature? Is it an empirical fact or rather an unverifiable assumption, a mere fiction? An empirical study of the nature of man, said Hume, reveals not an identical set of motives but a confusion of impulses; not an orderly cosmos but chaos. Reason

[48] Norman Sykes, *Church and State in England in the XVIIIth Century* (Cambridge, 1934), 346; L. Stephen, *English Thought in the 18th Century*, I, 169.
[49] David Hume, *Natural History of Religion*, Sections I, VI, XIII-XV; B. M. Laing, *David Hume* (London, 1932); John Laird, *Hume's Philosophy of Human Nature* (London, 1932); G. H. Sabine, *A History of Political Theory* (New York, 1937), 597-606.

in itself dictates no way of acting. Primitive man did not begin as a rational philosopher and it is a deceptive illusion to hope that civilized man will end as one. As Hume put it, "reason is and ought only to be the slave of the passions and can never pretend to any other office than to serve and obey them." Here, in the elemental passions, fears and hopes, lies, according to Hume, the root of all religious experience. Superstition, the fear of demons, the desire to make them amenable to the human will, these gave birth to primitive religions, and Hume believed that modern civilized religions were governed by the same psychological forces. In civilized religions superstition assumes a more refined dress, but it does not change its nature. Thus, in the eyes of Hume, the *credo quia absurdum* remains equally true of primitive and of civilized religions. We are not here concerned with the question whether or not Hume's grasp of the elaborate, moralized and dogmatic religions of the civilized world was as perfect as his understanding of the nature worship among savages. In spite of his profession of theism, a definite antireligious bias is admitted even by his most sympathetic modern interpreters.[50] It is apparent, however, that the *Natural History of Religion* opened a new line of scientific anthropological inquiry. It presented a penetrating analysis of the substratum of religious experience and demonstrated that the mainsprings of religion were neither logical nor ethical but anthropological. The upshot of his argument was that religion may have a "natural history," that is to say, a psychological and anthropological explanation, but that there can be no question of its truth. The so-called truths of religion may be valid in the relative sense of being socially convenient and in accord with men's estimate of utility, but, being rooted in sentiment, they lack the practical validity of scientific generalizations. A rational religion, therefore, is a contradiction in terms. With this destructive analysis Hume demolished not only the foundations of "natural religion" but, if we grant the larger premises on which his skeptical philosophy was based, the entire rationalist philosophy of the Enlightenment, its natural rights, its self-evident truths and its universal and immutable laws of morality. Thus it was a philosopher, the most

50 J. Y. T. Greig, *David Hume* (New York, 1931), 83; on Hume's blatant incapacity to understand the working of the religious mind in history, see J. B. Black, *The Art of History* (New York, 1926), 104.

brilliant skeptic of his age, who laid the ghost of natural religion which frightened the orthodox churches of Europe. But Hume's solution was not that of his contemporaries, whose firm confidence in the unity of reason and experience remained undisturbed.

Between the materialism of the Encyclopedists and the skepticism of Hume, Voltaire occupies a middle ground. It is intelligible that his religion should be mainly one of negation, though he did not go so far in the direction of denial as Diderot, nor so far in the direction of compromise as Rousseau's Savoyard Vicar, who was perfectly willing to accept the cultus of Christianity even though he had ceased to believe in its dogma. He did not have Hume's masterly grasp of the spiritual rudiments of primitive people and he was far removed from those modern sociologists who see in religious institutions the original type of all social organization. The one-eyed ruthlessness with which he pursued the iniquitous religious institution that he had to deal with every moment of his life, prevented him from recognizing the deepest drives of Catholicism. There was about him none of that wish to believe and inability to do so that was so characteristic of Matthew Arnold. He never felt himself to be a heartbroken outcast from the snug household of faith, wearying in spiritual wastes of sand and thorn. To say, however, as Lanson does, that he was utterly devoid of any religious sense, is grossly unjust to this luminous genius who spent his life in a passionate propaganda for enlightenment, justice, religious tolerance and intellectual freedom.[51]

Voltairism, if one understands by this term the comic deflation of theological sophisms, existed before Voltaire. But no one either before or after him combined this self-appointed task with his flaming imagination and genius as a writer, with his iridescent personality and versatility of mood, with his impish humor and crackling wit, with the immense erudition which carried him into his-

---

[51] The most persistent modern explorer of Voltaire's religion is Norman L. Torry, *Voltaire and the English Deists* (Yale Univ. Press, 1930), and especially his *The Spirit of Voltaire* (Columbia Univ. Press, 1938), 208-284; A. R. Morehouse, *Voltaire and Jean Meslier* (Yale Univ. Press, 1936), 142 ff.; G. R. Havens, "The Nature Doctrine of Voltaire," *Publications of the Modern Language Association of America*, XL (1925), 852-862; A. O. Lovejoy, "The Parallel between Deism and Classicism," *Modern Philology*, XXIX (1932), 281-299; by no means useless is John Morley, *Voltaire* (London, 1872), 209 ff.; A. Bellesort, *Essai sur Voltaire* (Paris, 1925), 316-352; G. Pellissier, *Voltaire philosophe* (Paris, 1908), 175 ff.

tory, philosophy, science, poetry, drama and imaginative literature, or with his deadly seriousness of purpose. He was, as Georg Brandes calls him, a bundle of nerves, charged with electricity that illuminated his century.[52] It was he who communicated to his generation in a multitude of ways the consciousness of the power and rights of the human intelligence. But he also stood for *bon sens* and the *juste milieu*. No one was more keenly conscious of the limitations of human reason in solving the mysteries of life and death, yet he remained firm in his refusal to accept any authority but reason, a poor instrument, he admitted, but the only faculty that raised man above the animals. He likened metaphysicians and theologians to gladiators who fought blindfolded. Philosophy consists, he said, in stopping when the torch of science fails us. He pursued with withering contempt and venomous satire every manifestation of authoritarian dogmatism whether he encountered it in religion, in science, or among his philosopher friends. The deistic creed of natural religion, which he assimilated from England, was just as much the logical outgrowth of his French classical ideal. Against the Encyclopedists, who called him a bigot, he asserted his steadfast belief in an unknowable Supreme Being, "the eternal geometer," "the first cause" who, having created the universe, left it to its own devices, a God who radiated no warmth, gave him no comfort, showed him no way of deliverance, a God who, it was ironically said, was more his protégé than his protector. He did not doubt that a creation implies a Creator. This simple argument from design sufficed Voltaire, though it no longer sufficed Diderot and Hume. The immanent Deity of modern Protestant thought, the indwelling, creative force of all that is, appeared inconsistent with his mechanistic interpretation of the universe, as did a belief in heaven and hell. But he accepted the principle of the oneness and brotherhood of man and the universal morality which lay at the bottom of the deistic movement, those basic and fundamental principles which God had engraved on the hearts of men. These principles were in perfect agreement with the classical ideal in which his own ideals were so deeply anchored. To square one's conduct with the natural order as revealed by reason, that was Voltaire's

52 G. Brandes, *Voltaire* (Berlin, 1923), I.

Seventy Illustrations
Drawn from Unusual Sources
and Specially Chosen by
the Author

for

COMPETITION

FOR EMPIRE

1740–1763

by

WALTER L. DORN

1. Frederick the Great.
By J. G. Ziesenis, 1763. The only authentic portrait done from life.
Städtische Kunstsammlung in Heidelberg.

François Etienne
Duc de Lorraine et de Bar, Grand Duc de Toscane,
Roy de Jerusalem et c. Co-Regent des Royaumes
et Etats hereditaires de la tres Auguste Maison d'Autriche

2. & 3. The heiress of the Hapsburgs and her husband,
Grand Duke Francis Stephen of Lorraine, in 1745 elected Emperor Francis I.

5. Charles III of Spain.
An engraving after a painting by Raphael Mengs.

4. Louis XV (1763).
By F. H. Drouais.

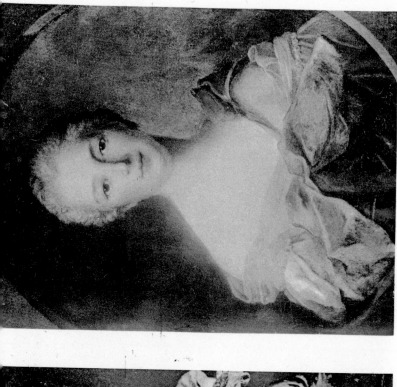

6. Elizabeth Petrovna, Empress of Russia.

7. Madame de Pompadour, "Minister of appointments and dismissals." By Jean Marc Nattier.

8. The Parade Ground at Potsdam.

9. General von Seydlitz in the Battle of Rossbach.

10. The Execution of Admiral Byng.

SCENES OF MILITARY LIFE

11. The Press-Gang.

12. The Torture Chamber, by Alessandro Magnasco.

THE SEAMY SIDE OF LIFE

VIEW of the first part of the Engagement between his Britannick Majesty's Ship the LYON 58 Guns, and the ELIZABETH a French Man of War of 64 Guns, in company with the Dutillet a French Frigat of 20 Guns. On the 9th of July 1745. in the Latitude of 48 00 N°. and 40 Leagues to the Westward of Ushant

A VIEW of the fourth and last part of the Engagement between the LYON and ELIZABETH. The Enemy, who for four hours had the weather-gage of the LYON, at ten at Night becomes the leewardmost Ship, by the Wind shifting, and takes that opportunity of making off, which was not in is power while he was to windward, notwithstanding the LYON was so much shatter'd. As he was shearing off, the LYON rak'd him, but he made no return, and when he was out of Gun shot, the Frigat join'd him, and they made the best of their way directly before ye Wind, but the LYON was not in a condition to pursue em

13. & 14. The engagement on July 9, 1745 between H. M. S. Lion and The Elizabeth,
a French man-of-war conveying Prince Charlie from Belle-Isle to Scotland.
Drawings by Samuel Scott, at Hinchinbrooke.

15. The Election, by William Hogarth.

16. The March to Finchley, after a painting by William Hogarth.

This satirical painting was sent to George II, the last soldier monarch of England, for his approval. The king examined it severely and demanded: "Pray, who is this Hogarth?" "A painter, Your Majesty." "I hate bainting and boetry," replied the enlightened king, "neither the one nor the other ever did any good. Does the fellow mean to laugh at my Guards?" "The painting, an' it please Your Majesty, must undoubtedly be considered a burlesque." "What!" he shouted, "a bainter burlesque a soldier! He deserves to be picketed for his insolence. Take his trumpery out of my sight!" Mortified at this reception of his work, Hogarth erased the inscription to the hero of Dettingen and dedicated the print to Frederick the Great.

17. The Duke of Newcastle.

18. William Pitt.

19. John Carteret, Earl Granville.

20. Marc Pierre, Comte D'Argenson.

21. Etienne Francois, Duc de Choiseul.

22. Count Haugwitz.

23. Count Kaunitz.

CONTINENTAL STATESMEN

24. Maréchal Maurice de Saxe.

25. Marshal Belle-Isle.

26. Daun.

27. Laudon.

FOUR GENERALS OF THE MID-CENTURY

28. The Fort, Trichinopoly.

29. Clive.

30. Dupleix.

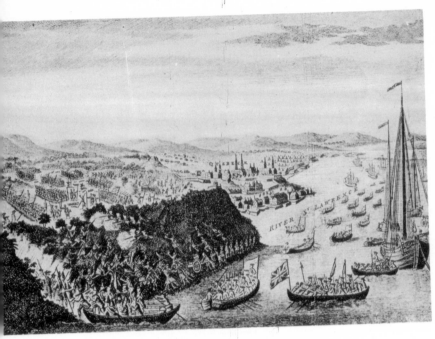

31. Taking of Quebec, September 13, 1759.

32. General Wolfe.

33. Louis Joseph de Montcalm.

34. The launching of a French warship at Rochefort.
Engraving by Ozanne.

35. The port of Rochefort with colonial warehouses.

36. Pondichéry ruined after the siege.

37. The Fort at Calcutta in 1756.

FRENCH AND ENGLISH STATIONS IN INDIA

38. The Death of James Wolfe.
From a contemporary engraving based on the report of an eye witness.

39. Louisburg.

40. Paris: The Place Louis XV (Place de la Concorde) by Jacques-Ange Gabriel.

41. Schönbrunn Palace, by Nikolaus Pacassi.

ARCHITECTURE IN MID-CENTURY

42. Palace of Nymphenburg, near Munich, with formal garden.
Painting by Canaletto.

43. An English park.

Illustrating the change in taste from straight alleys bordered with clipped trees, geometrical ponds, regular cascades and water jets to the informality of English and Chinese gardens.

44. & 45. Sans Souci, the Retreat of Frederick the Great at Potsdam. At the left, the central part of the palace; at the right, the library.

46. Madame D'Epinay.

47. Madame Geoffrin.

48. Madame du Chatelet.
Friend of Voltaire and popularizer of Newton.

LEADERS OF THE FRENCH SALONS

49. Authors being fleeced by their publishers, a satire by D. Chodowiecki.

50. French journalists in a coffeehouse. Etching by Gabriel de St. Aubin.

51. Voltaire.
"The bundle of nerves, charged with electricity, that illuminated the century."
—Brandes.

52. Montesquieu.
A great conservative liberal.

53. Diderot.
Humanist and encyclopedic genius.

54. D'Alembert.
Mathematician and philosopher.

55. Rousseau.
The noble savage.

56. Linnaeus.

57. Comte de Buffon.

58. Maupertuis.

THREE PROMINENT SCIENTISTS

59. David Hume.
English philosopher and historian.

60. Quesnay.
Founder of the Physiocrat School.

61. Julien La Mettrie.
Materialistic philosopher. "A splendid
fellow, if you had not read his books."
—Frederick the Great.

62. Sonnenfels.
Austrian economist.

63. John Wesley.

64. Count von Zinzindorf.

LEADERS OF THE RELIGIOUS REVIVAL

65. Colony of the Moravian Brethren near Frankfurt am Main, 1750.

66. Eros Imprisoned, by Francois Boucher.

67. The Swing, by Jean-Honoré Fragonard.

68. Accordée de Village, by Jean-Baptiste Greuze.

69. La Bénédicité, by J. B. S. Chardin.

70. The Shrimp Girl, by William Hogarth.

way of salvation: "La vertu quand elle est éclairée change en paradis l'enfer de ce monde." One may admit that this was a pure, generous and aristocratic creed, but it was not one from which the mass of society could derive any hope. With characteristic honesty he wrote on the margin of one of his English books, "Natural religion for the magistrates; damn'd stuff for the mob."

Was it from this cold and inanimate creed that Voltaire drew his fire, his firm hand, his joy of battle? It was rather, as Professor Torry suggests, the essential humanism of his outlook that comes nearest to the center of his remarkable personality. He had not the depth of either Hume or Kant, but then, neither Hume or Kant could have done his work. The immense range, the baffling diversity of his interests and writings sprang from this intense humanism. Indeed, he was the greatest humanist of the French Enlightenment. He recognized, it has been aptly said, but one absolute value—the human race. When he wrote history, it was human and spiritual values that enriched his accent. In literature it was the classical and humanistic conception of man that he represented. In philosophy it was chiefly ethics that attracted his attention, and his ethics was a purely human, social and rational science, wholly without religious sanctions. He was in the best sense a cosmopolitan, the most cosmopolitan among French writers who, even in the crisis of the Seven Years' War, placed human above national values when he defended the unhappy Admiral Byng against the vengeance of the Newcastle ministry.

With this we have touched the central nerve ganglia of the Enlightenment as a spiritual movement, its passionate desire to humanize religion. In this matter the Enlightenment was at once a resumption and a further development of the humanistic theology of the Renaissance, of Nicholas of Cues and of Ficino, of Erasmus, Sir Thomas More and the Cambridge Platonists. It announced a religion of the affirmation of life, not one of asceticism and renunciation, a religion which accepted the value of human intelligence, not one which subordinated it to supernatural authority. It is no accident, therefore, that in their arraignment of the traditional system the men of the Enlightenment concentrated their attack on the dogma of the essential depravity of fallen humanity, the basis of ecclesiastical authority. Semler and Reimarus in Germany, Voltaire and Rousseau in France, Hume and the English deists, radically diverse in other ways, were wholly at one in their common opposition to this doctrine of original sin.

Across the path of the philosophers, however, lay the hefty figure of Pascal, who in his *Pensées* had debated this problem of original sin with an intellectual power, precision and clarity such as only one of the keenest analytical intellects which France ever produced could bring to bear on the subject. The significance of Pascal's argument lies not in its content, which had not altered since the days of St. Augustine, but in the fact that, addressing himself to unbelievers, he employed their modern methods of analytical logic, not to exhort, but to *prove* the existence of original sin and the utter incapacity of unaided human reason to solve this problem without accepting the authority of faith. If unbelievers repudiated the doctrine of the fall of man, asked Pascal, how else could they explain his "double nature"? Wherever you encounter man, he lacks harmony and unity, he is a being split and torn by contradictions that cannot be uprooted; he is at once a fallen angel and a beast, great and miserable, powerful and impotent, forever fated to search for the Absolute which he can never attain. This irreducible dichotomy of human nature, argued Pascal, becomes intelligible only through the doctrine of the fall of man.

In Pascal the French philosophers had an adversary who was in every sense their intellectual equal, if not their superior. If they could not destroy his argument and indicate some other source of evil, all their attempts at a "natural" explanation of the world and life were so much wasted effort. Pascal haunted Voltaire all his life. Again and again he tried his critical acumen on this "sublime misanthrope."[53] We cannot here pursue in detail the evolution of his criticism, which began with the *Lettres sur les Anglais* in 1729 and continued in his *Le Mondain, Les Discours sur l'homme, Le Monde comme il va, Vision de Babouc, Le Désastre de Lisbonne* and *Candide*. He somehow felt that mere negation was not enough. His denial of original sin as being contrary to reason and common

[53] J. R. Carré, *Réflexions sur l'anti-Pascal de Voltaire* (Paris, 1935); N. L. Torry, *The Spirit of Voltaire* (1938), 208; E. Cassirer, *Die Philosophie der Aufklärung*, 192.

sense left him face to face with the insoluble problem which even the cruel laughter of the *Candide* could not suppress, the problem of evil in the world. In the upshot, he accepted Pascal's analysis of human nature. Evil exists, only a charlatan would deny it, nor can it be entirely uprooted. But he was just as firm in his refusal to draw Pascal's final theological inference as he was in his refusal to surrender to pessimism. Declining the theological explanation of the origin of evil, his position was that of an agnostic, although by taking this position he became prisoner of Pascal's argument that reason without faith to guide it must end in skepticism: *le pyrrhonisme est le vrai.*[54] But, unlike Pascal, Voltaire was strong enough to live with his doubts and even to be happy with them. The significant thing is that he never returned to theological speculation, but relied solely and alone on the creative energies of man.

More important and more original was Rousseau's solution to Pascal's problem. Rousseau began by conceding all the premises on which Pascal based his argument. Instead of attributing Pascal's gloomy description of human nature to the self-torture of an abnormal mind, like Voltaire, Rousseau took it seriously. In his two discourses on the *Arts and Sciences* and *On the Origin of Inequality* he presented a picture of the corruption and depravity of contemporary society that would have delighted Pascal. Out of step with his contemporaries, Rousseau denounced their culture, their scientific progress, the refinement of their manners as empty sham that could not conceal their utter spiritual poverty. Yet Rousseau, too, rebelled against the doctrine of the total depravity of man. In his opposition to the church he was in full agreement with his former friends, the Encyclopedists. The church was quick to perceive this. When the Archbishop of Paris condemned the *Émile* in 1762, he denounced it on the ground that Rousseau's notion of the natural goodness of man stood in diametrical opposition to everything that the church and Holy Scriptures taught on the subject of the nature of man.

But how was Rousseau to escape from the dilemma in which he had involved himself? If he admitted the fact of "degeneration," how was he to escape Pascal's logical conclusion of the existence of

[54] Pascal, *Pensées*, ed. Havet, XXIV, 1.

"radical evil"? In extricating himself Rousseau once and for all abandoned Pascal's theological and metaphysical argument. He contended, on the contrary, that these contradictions in human nature were due to an empirical and historical development. In attempting to explain the "fall of man," Rousseau placed the responsibility where no one before him had thought of placing it. His originality lies in having discovered a new responsible agent. This agent was neither God nor individual man, but society. Selfishness, vanity, corruption issue from a depraved society. It is society that has made man a tyrant, which has awakened in him needs and passions of which he, in his "natural state," was entirely ignorant. But if society has corrupted man, it is in and through society that he must seek his salvation. How this is to be done, Rousseau showed in his *Social Contract*. Like Voltaire, he contended that man will search in vain for assistance from above. Man must save himself, he must, so runs the argument of *Émile*, become in an ethical sense his own creator. Thus it is in society, in the problem of social justice, that he sought the meaning of human life. This was Rousseau's solution to the religious problem of his day, a solution that was neither theological nor metaphysical, but thoroughly modern.[55]

V. HISTORY

Not least among the extraordinary achievements of the Enlightenment was its conquest of the past. It rescued history from the hands of philologists and antiquaries and popularized it, supplied new and fructifying ideas that enriched the content and extended the scope of history, and in the works of Voltaire, Hume and Gibbon produced some of the most striking monuments of modern historical literature. It would, of course, be absurd to claim for the Enlightenment alone the mastery of the difficult art of thinking in terms of the historical dimension, so indispensable to the modern mind.[56] Although the first stirrings of historical criticism must be traced to the age of humanism and the Catholic Counter Reformation, that art was not completely mastered until the nineteenth century.

55 See in spite of its many faulty conclusions P. M. Masson, *La Religion de Jean-Jacques Rousseau* (Paris, 1916), 3 vols.
56 F. Meinecke, *Die Anfänge des Historismus* (Berlin, 1936), Vol. I.

The documentary and critical foundations for the writing of history had already been laid before the historians of the Enlightenment appeared on the scene. Humanistic philologists had already collected, published, studied, interpreted and commented upon the entire treasure of ancient classical literature. The conflict of confessions had multiplied the source materials of church history. For the first time a large portion of the treasures that lay hidden in the Vatican and other archives and libraries were published and made available for historical study. The end of the seventeenth and the first half of the eighteenth century witnessed the publication of those massive and imposing document collections on medieval history that are still indispensable to modern historians: the Italian Muratori's collection of the historians and antiquities of medieval Italy (1723-1751), Mansi's collection of materials on the general councils of the church (1758), and Duchesne, Baluze and Beaufort's collection of sources on medieval France (1738). Nor were historians entirely helpless in the face of this overwhelming mass of materials, for the Frenchman Du Cange had already published in his *Glossarium* a guide through the jungle of medieval Latin and the Benedictine monk, Jean Mabillon, had developed the critical study of medieval documents into the new and independent science of diplomatics. All this was only raw material, but already there were examples enough of critical and documentary history. There was Paolo Sarpi's penetrating documentary history of the Council of Trent, a work so thorough and honest that it had to be published in another country under an assumed name; there was also the Jansenist Tillemont's *History of the Roman Emperors,* published between 1690 and 1738, the scrupulous accuracy of which elicited the admiration of Gibbon. Much of this work was still formless, diffuse, more collection of materials than actual history, but it was on these works that the eighteenth-century historians based their accounts.[57]

Admirable as the studies of these erudite antiquaries were, their

[57] E. Fueter, *Geschichte der neueren Historiographie* (Berlin, 1911), 245 ff.; K. Ritter, *Die Entwicklung der Geschichtswissenschaft* (Munich, 1919), 207 ff.; P. Smith, *A History of Modern Culture* (New York, 1934), Vol. II, 226 ff.; J. B. Black, *The Art of History* (New York, 1926); W. Dilthey, "Das achtzehnte Jahrhundert und die geschichtliche Welt," *Gesammelte Schriften* (Leipzig, 1927), Vol. III, 210.

historical criticism was amateurish compared with the exacting critical rigorism of Pierre Bayle, the author of the *Dictionnaire critique
et historique* (1697).[58] Bayle was the real founder of modern historical criticism and the intellectual father of the historians of the
Enlightenment. In the eyes of this *minutissimarum rerum minutis-
simus scrutator,* as he called himself, the problem of getting at the
objective truth of history was a mental operation which, in complexity and acumen, was comparable only to the solution of a difficult mathematical problem. Never before, not even by Lorenzo
Valla, had historical tradition been subjected to such a ruthlessly
minute criticism. No flaw in historical logic ever escaped the penetrating eye of this skeptical iconoclast. To get at the reliable and
incontrovertible facts of history was for him not a point of departure but an end in itself. Before Bayle completed any historical
article for his *Dictionnaire,* he had verified every quotation, con-
sulted minutely every source and compared and analyzed with his
keen critical scalpel these sources from every imaginable point of
view.[59] It is no accident that his *Dictionnaire* was a register of historical errors and falsehoods rather than a repository of positive
information. It was he who transmitted to the rationalist historians
the dictum that history was, after all is said, nothing more than a
record of the crimes and misfortunes of mankind.[60] It is to Bayle
also, rather than to Voltaire, that rationalist historians owed the
emancipation of history from the shackles of theological interpretation. By demonstrating that historical truth must emerge from a
critical and objective examination of human records and indicating
that in his quality of historian he could find no evidence of the intervention of divine Providence in human affairs, Bayle did for Biblical, ecclesiastical and secular history what Galileo had done for the
natural sciences.

But all this still produced no intelligible conspectus of human
history as a whole. It was only the leading ideas of the Enlightenment, the notion of empirical causation, the belief in the essential
solidarity of the human race in spite of the continuous warfare
among peoples, and the idea of progress that made a conceptual

58 Delvolvé, *Religion, critique et philosophie chez Pierre Bayle* (Paris, 1906), 226 ff.
59 Lacoste, *Bayle, Nouvelliste et critique littéraire* (Paris, 1929), 27 ff.
60 Bayle, *Dictionnaire,* article on "Manichéens," Remarque, D.

mastery of the chaotic and meaningless facts of history possible. It is saying very little when it is so often repeated that Voltaire and Hume interpreted the past in the light of their own ideas and in ways acceptable to the self-complacent age of reason. They sought not merely to establish a chain of causation between the events of history but just as much to assess its value, to weigh the past in the balance of the present, to separate what was worth cherishing from what they considered superannuated, thus making their history as much a part of the living present as any contemporary novel or drama. Into the serene and arid world of Tillemont and Muratori they introduced the "philosophy" of the Enlightenment, defacing the past and vitalizing it at one and the same time. What was new and significant in the constructive part of their work was their application of the whole culture of their age to the whole past which they knew and understood. Voltaire and his school created the concept, if not the word, of civilization and they proposed to introduce into their histories all the successive transformations through which mankind had passed in religion, politics, government, economics, science, literature and the arts, and to trace the line of progress from primitive barbarism to the great culture of the Enlightenment. What attracted them to the study of history was less the "unique event" of Ranke and his school, considered for its own sake, than a reasoned account of the evolution of man in general, less the individual and the accidental than the "spirit of the times" and the "spirit of nations."

At the base of Voltaire's conception of civilization lay the great monarchies of Europe with their military, legal and administrative institutions such as they have been described in the second and third chapters of this book, all seeking to intensify their political power but also to promote agriculture, industry and commerce, the foundations of cultural progress. Verifiable proof for his belief in the essential solidarity of the peoples of Europe in spite of the incessant strife of the competitive state system, Voltaire found in Newtonian science and in "sound philosophy," the joint results of the co-operative labors of Italians, Frenchmen, Englishmen, Dutchmen and Germans, and in the academies of science which the governments of Europe had established to avail themselves of the intellectual energies released by the new science. These academies, from St. Petersburg and Stockholm to Madrid, from London to Vienna, promoted everywhere the same spirit of positive, exact and mathematical inquiry and co-operated in rearing a growing edifice of universally valid truth and in applying this knowledge to all phases of human existence. "The academies," he wrote in his *Siècle de Louis XIV*, "have created this republic (of scholars). Modern scientists in every branch of knowledge have forged the bond of the great society of enlightened spirits which can be found everywhere and is everywhere independent. This bond continues and it is one of the consolations in the face of the evil which ambition and politics spread over the face of the world." From the center of this "great society" he saw the belief in the autonomy of reason and in the independence of scientific inquiry, religious tolerance and respect for the freedom of personality, refinement of taste in manners, literature and the arts advancing to captivate jurists, public officials and ever wider circles of the educated public. Though conscious of the causal interrelationship of other motor factors of social evolution, he was convinced that intellectual history was the controlling force, and that the political, economic or religious structure of civilization in any given epoch was the result of conscious ideas. Thus Voltaire became the enthusiastic prophet of progress and into this mold he cast his *Siècle de Louis XIV* (1751) and the incomparably more important *Essai sur les moeurs*, a history of European civilization from Charlemagne to Louis XIII (1753). This program was new, grandiose and overpowering.

But how did Voltaire reconcile this belief in progress with his other conviction that human nature is always and everywhere the same? If human nature has always been the same, then the human intellect has no history; it is beyond history, and the appearance of change and progress vanishes as soon as you look underneath the glittering surface of historical events to the basic principles which at all times are identical. It is commonly asserted, and Carl Becker has once more emphasized the point, that Voltaire's artificial distinction between human nature and human customs is no real answer to the problem.[61] All this is very true, but a careful reading of the *Essai* suggests a more intelligent solution of the problem. Voltaire did, indeed, contend that mankind cannot alter its essential nature, but the central idea of the *Essai* was to show that the nature of man revealed itself only in the course of historical evolution. "Reason" as the basic human energy was present from the earliest times and it remains fundamentally the same in all epochs, but it is only in the course of history that reason acquired a mastery over the mass of customs, superstitions and habits under which it lay buried. Progress, therefore, as Voltaire conceived it, is to be looked for neither in reason nor in humanity but in the gradual assertion of reason. To Voltaire reason itself was something time-less and eternal, but the function of the historian was to show how this eternal force manifested itself in the history of mankind.

It has often been pointed out that in the execution both of the *Siècle* and the *Essai* Voltaire fell short of his remarkably modern program, which required a sympathetic discussion of all civilizations, all epochs and all peoples. It is obvious that he did not do this. Indeed, not a single chapter of either book will bear up under the close scrutiny of modern historical criticism, not even those superb chapters of the *Siècle* dealing with literature and the arts.[62] But the defects of Voltaire's history are less those of his system than of his fiery temperament, and it is absurd to accuse him and the entire Enlightenment of wanting in the historic sense because of these shortcomings. The philosopher in Voltaire constantly interrupted and overpowered the historian. In spite of his matchless erudition and wide reading he lacked the patience for quiet, reflective and adequate analysis. When he turned to history it was less for the sake of the past than for the didactic purpose of enlightenment in the present. His *Siècle*, French critics have pointed out, is as much a criticism of France under Louis XV as it is a history of the age of Louis XIV. Impatient of the long road, he was forever pointing out how infinitely far the Middle Ages were removed from the superior insight and knowledge of his age of reason. Consequently,

[61] See the chapter on "History" in Carl Becker, *The Heavenly City of the Eighteenth Century Philosophers* (New Haven, 1932).
[62] R. Lowenstein, "Voltaire as an Historian of Seventeenth Century French Drama," *Johns Hopkins Studies in Romance Literatures and Languages*, Vol. XXV (1935), 180.

he frequently lapsed into that same naïve teleology which he criticized in Bossuet's *Histoire universelle* and which he elsewhere
condemned, the only difference being that he employed his rationalistic instead of Bossuet's theological yardstick. In some respects
these defects were the faults of his virtues, for the *Siècle* is the first
modern specimen of history as a great work of art. Though devoid
of the studied and sparkling verbalisms of a Guedalla or the constant witticisms of a Montesquieu, his terse and compact history
is never dull, and in spite of its evident erudition it is singularly free
from the dead freight of learned antiquarianism.

Yet, despite the progress in the development of an historical outlook made by Voltaire, by d'Alembert in his introduction to the
Encyclopédie, which contains an excellent study of the historical
evolution of natural science, by Lagrange in his *Mécanique ana-
lytique*, a masterful study of the history of science, by Delandes in
his *Histoire critique de la philosophie* (1756), the analytical temper
of the period, which emphasized fixity and permanence rather than
historical change or evolution dominated most of the writers of this
epoch. If there was any exception to this rule, it was David Hume,
whose *History of England* (1754-1762) marks the culmination of
his work as a philosopher and man of letters.[63] It is true that as a
work of scholarship Hume's *History* cannot be taken very seriously.
He undertook the task lightly, and performed it in the same spirit,
writing the book, it was said, with his feet on the couch. He was
careless and uncritical about his facts and he did not trouble to go
to the sources. Still, just as his incisive intellect led him beyond the
Enlightenment in his theory of knowledge and in his religious
philosophy, so his conception of history was no longer quite that
of the Enlightenment. This may seem surprising, since Hume the
historian lays himself open to the same criticisms as Voltaire: he
began with the same axiom of the uniformity of man "in all races
and at all stages in the world's history," he exhibited the same incapacity to grasp the irrational factors of history, and he, too, conceived history as a study in ideology. But with Hume this static view,
though it is still present in his *History*, began almost imperceptibly

63 For a somewhat different estimate of Hume as historian, J. B. Black, *The Art of
History* (New York, 1926), 77 ff.

to dissolve. Unlike Voltaire, he believed neither in "reason" nor in progress, and he was more profoundly preoccupied with the historical process and with change as such. He placed facts above theories, and the individual and unique aspects of history advanced more into the foreground. His emphasis on the facts of history filled him with horror of those sweeping generalizations in which Voltaire still indulged. He was unable to discover a deep seated plan in human history. He was skeptical even of its utility and declared it simply "the fairest and noblest occupation of the mind." "What spectacle can be imagined so magnificent, so various, so interesting? What amusement, either of the senses or the imagination, can be compared with it?"[64] Comparing him with Voltaire, Hume gives the impression of a great renunciation, but he also marks the beginning of a new orientation the full scope of which he did not realize himself.

VI. SOCIAL SCIENCE AND POLITICAL THOUGHT

It is one of the salient traits of the Enlightenment that the philosophers looked upon their criticism of state and society not as an act of destruction or negation but as one of restoration. Even the boldest innovators among them were convinced that they were collaborating in the recovery of the lost "title-deeds" of humanity, which antedated all existing governments and societies. To moderns the curious mixture of idea and interest that lay embedded in the natural rights theory is obvious. The philosophers did not discover this theory of the inalienable rights of man, but they made it the foundation of an ethical and social gospel, introduced it into practical politics and gave it the dynamic force which revealed its explosive energy in the French Revolution. All of them, even the empiricists, believed in the theory that universally valid and immutable norms, a priori natural rights, exist and must exist. Even Montesquieu contended that "to say that there is nothing either just or unjust except what positive laws command or forbid, is to say that before describing a circle all the radii are not equal." But it is significant that their argument on behalf of the natural rights theory moved steadily farther away from metaphysics in the direction of empiricism, away

[64] David Hume, "Of the Study of History," Essays Moral, Political and Literary (London, 1898), II, 388.

from reason toward pure experience. In their eyes the rights to liberty of person, security of property, freedom of discussion were rooted less in the dictates of abstract reason than in a commonsense view of fundamental human needs, impulses and inclinations. This utilitarian tendency supplied a drastic stimulus to the development of social science. But the social science of the Enlightenment was by no means free from value judgments. Indeed, the supreme purpose of social science, as Condorcet later contended in his *Tableau,* was to secure and guarantee the free exercise of fundamental rights.[65]

Taine's famous contention that the philosophers were visionaries who spent their time in building up an abstract, utopian City of God, irrespective of political and historical realities, can no longer be supported.[66] In spite of the utopianism of Rousseau, who separated himself from them with éclat, their sense of reality cannot be denied. They were, of course, unanimous in their insistence on the primacy of reason in any effort at political and social renovation, but the voice of reason, as they conceived it, was neither insurrectionary nor bloodthirsty. It is not abstract intellectualism that most aptly characterizes their political and social thought. On the contrary, they were convinced that it was only in society that man could realize his full potentialities and they were profoundly imbued with a sense of the social function of all knowledge. Their social science aimed at a genuine insight into the causes of the evils of contemporary society, dealt with real problems and sought realistic remedies for abuses in justice, administration and taxation. Rousseau apart, none of the philosophers of the first generation agitated for a radical and complete transformation of state and society. With few exceptions, they were, like Voltaire, defenders of an enlightened despotism. With all the authority which his wide culture and European reputation gave him, he pleaded for the freedom of person, the press, religious thought, for the abolition of slavery and serfdom and the reform of criminal law. But political utopias excited his sardonic laughter.

65 Condorcet, "Tableau des progrès de l'esprit humaine, 9° époque," *Oeuvres* (1804), Vol. VIII, 223.
66 D. Mornet, *Les origines intellectuelles de la Revolution Française* (Paris, 1933), 469 ff.

Nous tromper dans nos entreprises,
C'est à quoi nous sommes sujets,
Le matin je fais des projets,
Et le long jour des sottises.[67]

Diderot, it is true, advanced to democratic political ideals, but it cannot be said that he was a consistent political philosopher.[68] The Encyclopedist group were political opportunists and d'Holbach, the most consistent religious and metaphysical radical among them, was no exception. Like d'Alembert, who represented their best ideals, they recommended against the evils of their day, not a revolution, but a *"guerre de chicane."*[69]

When in 1748 Montesquieu published his *Esprit des lois* few of his philosophic contemporaries were surprised by his violent hatred of despotism, clericalism and slavery. Montesquieu was an aristocrat and a monarchist. As a member of the *petite noblesse* he labored for a monarchy tempered by *"corps intermédiaires"* and fundamental laws, in other words, for what his former colleagues, the magistrates, called the restitution of the ancient constitution of France. The tremendous influence that issued from this ingenious book, therefore, runs in curiously bifurcated channels. Both the aristocratic reactionaries who desired to revitalize the feudal estates and the French *parlements* as the only safeguard against the crown, and the honest liberals who made his idealized pattern of the English constitution with its principle of the separation of powers the basis of modern liberal constitution-making drew their inspiration from this book.[70]

Despite all its glaring imperfections and logical inconsistencies Montesquieu's *Esprit des lois* opened a new epoch in realistic political discussion. Casting aside the customary procedure of seventeenth-century philosophers, of deducing from eternal reason and

[67] G. Lanson, "La reforme voltairienne," *Voltaire*, Paris, Hachette, 180; H. R. G. Greaves in *Economica*, Vol. X, 40.

[68] This must be said in spite of Jean Oestreicher's *La pensée politique et économique de Diderot* (Vincennes, 1936).

[69] D'Alembert, "Jugement d'Émile," *Oeuvres*, Didier (Paris, 1853), 295 ff.; W. H. Wickwar, *Baron D'Holbach* (London, 1935), 182.

[70] These two aspects of his influence have been studied by E. Carcassonne, *Montesquieu et le problème de la constitution française au XVIII siècle* (Paris, Presses Universitaires, n. d.); and by J. Dedieu, *Montesquieu* (Paris, 1913); see also G. Bonne, *La constitution britannique devant l'opinion française de Montesquieu à Bonaparte* (Paris, 1913); K. Martin, *French Liberal Thought in the Eighteenth Century* (Boston, 1929), 147 ff.; H. Sée. *L'évolution de la pensée politique en France au XVIIIe siècle* (Paris, 1925), 55.

the nature of man certain consequences as to the most desirable political order, Montesquieu revealed himself in this book to be the closest eighteenth-century observer of empirical and social variations and suggested a sociological relativism that was to be of supreme importance for the future development of social science and history. The *Esprit des lois* is the first modern study in ideal sociological patterns. It was Montesquieu's purpose to prove that the constitutional types which pass by the name of republic, aristocracy, monarchy and despotism, possess a definite and necessary internal structure in which the motor factors of social evolution such as climatic and environmental conditions, soil, trade, the techniques of production, political constitutions and legal systems, customs and habits that have become ingrained in national character, stand in a correlative position to one another and to the whole. No mere observation of political and social phenomena will reveal this internal structure, for, since the peculiar combination of these factors is endlessly variable, constitutional and legal systems must vary also. But this appearance of variability vanishes as soon as we proceed from facts to principles, from the endless variety of empirical forms to driving forces. By examining in this way a great variety of historical and contemporary republics and comparing them it is possible to discover *the* republic, to arrive at a universally valid notion of what a republic is and of what inner law governs all historical republics. Thus, when he describes the essence of a republic as being the principle of virtue, he does not confuse this principle with any specific historical republic, but merely indicates what it should be to be, properly speaking, a republic.[71] He then proceeds to describe the network of interacting forces on whose particular interrelationship the structure as a whole depends. In some cases he pursues this interrelationship in detail, examining the kind of education, the administration of justice, the special nature of marriage and the family, even the general character of domestic and foreign policy. All these, he is at pains to prove, depend on the specific structure of the state in a very special manner. None of these factors can be altered without affecting the equilibrium of forces in the state as a whole.

71 *L'esprit des lois*, XVI, 11.

Whatever objections one may raise to Montesquieu's superficial and oversimplifying procedure, it should be emphasized that with his typology of constitutional patterns he introduced a new method into political science, a method that has become an integral part of twentieth-century sociology. The scholarly and historical apparatus on which he based his system is sadly antiquated today in view of our profounder sociological grasp and wider historical horizon. On this score even his contemporaries criticized his work mercilessly.[72] Because of its essentially static character even his doctrine of constitutional types is no longer adequate. But if the idea of the historical evolution of constitutional forms was entirely foreign to his thought, this was a defect which he shared with most of his contemporaries. Once we disentangle his method from the concrete book that lies before us, however, it becomes evident that this method requires a careful comparative and inductive study of empirical and historical detail as well as an exhaustive conceptual analysis. With all his obvious limitations, Montesquieu was a master at both.

The dynamic outlook in history and politics which Montesquieu lacked acquired a greater importance in the work of the Encyclopedists, whose bulky volumes began to appear in rapid succession after 1751. From the countless articles of the *Dictionnaire raisonné* M. Hubert has reconstructed in his admirable studies their general doctrine of the origins, the structure and the evolution of human societies.[73] The greater largeness of view which the *Encyclopédie* possessed, when compared with the work of Voltaire and Montesquieu, it owed chiefly to the fact that it aimed to bring together all human knowledge; indeed, it was to be the *"livre où seraient tous les livres."* The Encyclopedists used, generally objectively, all the older works of erudition, accounts of voyages, juridical treatises, histories of literature and philosophy, as well as the nascent political economy of the physiocrats. To be sure they, too, believed in the existence of metaphysical norms to which human societies should conform; hence their acceptance of natural religion, natural morality,

[72] For a catalogue of his errors and inconsistencies see the brief but penetrating criticism of George H. Sabine, *A History of Political Theory* (New York, 1937), 550-560.
[73] René Hubert, *L'esprit des sciences sociales dans l'Encyclopédie* (Paris, 1923); and "Essai sur l'histoire des origines et des progrès de la sociologie en France," *Revue d'histoire de la philosophie et d'histoire générale de la civilisation*, Fasc. XXII (1938), 149.

natural rights and a natural economy. But they also employed Condillac's explanation of the origin of ideas and accepted the doctrine of historical and sociological causation which they conceived, as indicated before, in terms of a mechanistic physics and biology. Ideas and social institutions depend on the biological constitution of human nature, but also on climatic, geographic, demographic, economic and historical conditions which vary with time and place. It is only by examining all these factors that social phenomena can be studied in all their complexity. Again, the Encyclopedists did much to develop and popularize the idea of progress, although their theory of progress had neither the precision nor clarity of that of Turgot or Condorcet. By using Leibnitz's idea of continuity they sought to relate to one another all the great epochs of human civilization and thus present an account of the progress of the human intellect such as we find neither in Voltaire nor in Montesquieu.

Far more significant for the development of social science was the new political economy of the physiocrats. The founder of this French school of economists was the talented and versatile François Quesnay, who began his brilliant career as a biologist, then became the physician of Madame de Pompadour and later of Louis XV and, as a man of sixty, published his first economic studies in the *Encyclopédie* in 1756, followed in 1758 by his *Tableau économique*, the sacred text of the new faith.[74] Although from 1759 onward Quesnay was the famous head of a school of enthusiastic disciples, physiocratic doctrine did not issue in finished form from his mind. Quesnay had the same experience with his followers which Karl Marx had with the Marxists; orthodox physiocrats became more physiocratic than their leader. Lacking a disciplined unity of thought, they developed the doctrine by means of their own commentaries on the *Tableau*. It was especially the elder Mirabeau who became the devoted apostle of the new faith. In his *Philosophie rurale* (1763) he

74 G. Weulersse, *Le mouvement physiocratique en France de 1756-1770* (Paris, 1910), Vol. I; G. Weulersse. *Les physiocrates* (Paris, 1930), 3 ff.; J. Schumpeter, "Epochen der Dogmen- und Methodengeschichte," *Grundriss der Sozialökonomik* (Tübingen, 1924), Vol. I, 19-124; W. Hasbach, "Die philosophischen Grundlagen der von Quesnay und Smith begründeten politischen Ökonomie," *Staats und socialwissenschaftliche Forschungen*, Vol. 10 (1890), 58 ff.; A. Oncken, *Geschichte der Nationalökonomie* (Leipzig, 1920), Vol. 1, 314 ff.; for the latest discussion, together with recent literature, R. Gonnard, *Histoire des doctrines économiques* (Paris, 1930), 199.

presented the first full exposition of the two essential ideas of the system, the primacy of agriculture and the existence of natural economic laws.

The physiocrats translated the current philosophy of the Enlightenment into the language of economics, but they were also the heirs of the older tradition of Boisguilbert and the French agrarians. They called themselves *philosophes économistes* and they shared with the philosophers a rationalist, hedonist and utilitarian outlook. They accepted the doctrine of natural rights, but they demanded these rights as the necessary presupposition of economic prosperity. In other words, with Quesnay the *droit naturel,* freedom of person and security of property, became essentially economic. They, too, were reformers and, like the philosophers, they sought to ameliorate the conditions of human life by means of science. The object of their interest was the source of wealth, their practical goal the participation of the greatest number in the wealth they produced. Like the philosophers, they believed in international solidarity and were opposed to the rivalries and jealousies encouraged by mercantilism. The wealth of one nation, they said, depends on that of another. With the philosophers they shared also the positivist conception of social science. To Quesnay economics was an exact science which he defined as a system of laws "susceptible of a demonstration as severe and incontestable as those of geometry and algebra."[75] That with such a belief Quesnay had little use for the historical method in the study of economics cannot be surprising. History was to him an accumulated mass of errors and its study encouraged an "absurd fatalism." But to infer from this, as is still too often done, that the physiocrats were utterly devoid of an historic sense, would be unjust. Indeed, they considered economic history of pre-eminent importance. Karl Marx was not so far wrong when he pronounced them the precursors of the economic interpretation of history. For they reduced all social science to economics even at the expense of its spiritual aspects.

Physiocracy was the only systematic synthesis which the Enlightenment produced and in this respect it marks a return to the *esprit de*

[75] Quoted from A. Oncken, *Geschichte der Nationalökonomie* (Leipzig, 1920), Vol. I, 343.

système of the seventeenth century. That it was shot through with a priori ideas and operated with a deductive method, building up a system on the basis of certain axioms, is obvious enough. But what was a point of departure for the later orthodox physiocrats was for Quesnay himself the result of an inductive analysis. He began with the facts of observation and made a careful study, free from apriorist phantasy, of the agricultural situation of France in his day and he always retained his practical, utilitarian and reformist outlook.

Whatever the intrinsic merits of its distinctive doctrines, physiocracy was first and foremost an agricultural system. Quesnay was the champion of the landowners of France, still an overwhelmingly agricultural country, in their revolt against the restrictive mercantilist legislation which favored industry and commerce at their expense. Convinced that agriculture alone was really productive of economic abundance, the physiocrats deplored the growing urbanization of the country. In place of the mercantilist protectionism which gave a privileged position to the "sterile" classes of merchants and manufacturers, they proposed, as it were, to set up a protectionist system for the agricultural third estate. They were most certainly proponents of an economic liberalism, but their defense of agrarian interests came first and their liberalism second. In their effort to free the landowner from the burden of government regulation, they made the absolute security of private property the central principle of their economic doctrine. All the various liberties which they advocated are in reality corollaries of the right of private property. Thus, free trade was primarily conceived as the freedom of the agriculturist to produce whatever he pleased and to dispose of his products without restrictions, although the merchant, too, was to share in this freedom. The entire system aimed at an individualistic economy in which the individual was free to pursue his private interest. Quesnay argued that self-interest imposes on each individual the obligation to strive for the greatest possible improvement of his lot and that the resultant free competition is at once the best guarantee of economic prosperity and the best defense of society against the individual. To the degree in which it is realized—and it is the duty of the sovereign to see that it is realized—each individual becomes the instrument of the happiness of others.

Quesnay was an optimist, but he was far removed from believing in a pre-established harmony between the natural laws that govern the physical universe and the equally binding natural laws that govern human society. While the physical universe moves on in its eternal course, the harmony between the positive laws of human society and the laws of nature can be established only through the faculties of reason. Reason must first ascertain and proclaim these natural laws before they can be put into practice. It is just this discovery of the natural laws of society, which statesmen may evade only at their peril, that made Quesnay, in the eyes of physiocrats, the founder of a scientific political economy.

It was quite natural for physiocrats to think of the principles of government as determined by economics. They rejected both the constitutional monarchy of Montesquieu with its checks and balances and the authoritarian democracy of Rousseau, but they had no desire to surrender the state to the arbitrary despotism of the sovereign. They preferred, it is true, to see all power united in the hands of a single, enlightened despot, but this sovereign was to be a "legal despot," that is to say, he was to recognize the imperative duty of making the code of the laws of nature the invariable rule for all positive legislation. Thus, the actual despot was to be the law of nature itself. Admitting Quesnay's good intentions, it must be said that, compared with the realistic political system of Montesquieu, this vague and utopian constitutionalism marks a decided regression.

Into this society of Parisian philosophers there came in 1742 a penniless vagabond of thirty, the strange, original and superior citizen of Geneva, Jean-Jacques Rousseau. He was cordially received, he formed close friendships with Diderot and Condillac, frequented the *salons*, wrote for the *Encyclopédie*, and became, externally at least, a philosopher. But there was a deep contradiction in this association. Already his first publications foreshadowed the later rupture which, when it came after 1756, was to prove irreparable. Between this visionary Don Quixote and the high priests of the Enlightenment there was an impassable gulf. They revolted against church and state in the name of a philosophy which had a fixed and definite outline; he shared their opposition to the former, but he also revolted against the entire philosophy and ethics of the Enlightenment. Voltaire saw only certain remediable flaws in the organization of contemporary society, but Rousseau proclaimed in the flaming words of an Old Testament prophet the fundamental guilt of society itself. They were satisfied with progressive, partial improvements which would naturally follow as the result of intellectual illumination, but Rousseau condemned all partial solutions and rejected every compromise with existing society. Among them he was the only radical. He spoke as a man of the common people, as one who had suffered intolerable injustice, with a democratic passion that was the secret of his immense influence. He demanded a moral reformation of his generation, a revivification of its religion and a purification of its manners. He passionately asserted the moral and legal equality of all men, the sovereignty of the people and the supreme authority of the general will. Voltaire and Montesquieu based their program of reform on a careful assessment of past and present. For Rousseau, whose eyes were unerringly fixed on the future moral regeneration of humanity, the past counted for nothing. Their sole hope was in the progress of knowledge and science. Rousseau cast both aside, surrendered himself to his primal emotions and built a philosophy on them. He opposed the dynamism of his emotions to the static outlook of his contemporaries and dressed his volcanic outbursts of sentiment in a magnetic literary style that roused his readers to the same pitch of fervor as himself. To his former friends he was an incomprehensible maniac who attacked everything that they considered sacrosanct, and he denounced them as the enemies of society who corrupted morals, undermined faith and reverence. Turning away from Paris in April, 1756, he sought refuge and solitude in the Hermitage, a country house on the edge of the forest of Montmorency near Paris, which Mme. d'Épinay turned over to him. There, during the next six years, he wrote his greatest works, the *Nouvelle Héloïse*, the *Émile* and the *Social Contract*. How could this man legitimately complain of persecution on the part of the philosophers? He was the negation of all their sense of intellectual security and of their profound confidence in reason and science. He struck at their intellectual roots, and, historically speaking, their resistance was necessary and justified. What he called a "conspiracy" to ruin him was on the part of his opponents nothing more than an effort to preserve their intellectual integrity.

Whether we admire or condemn Rousseau, we cannot, even today, ignore him. He is still a force among the living, and the problems which he tapped, such as the relation between freedom and authority in the modern state, are still our problems. Yet, despite the vast and scholarly literature that has appeared on the Genevan philosopher, especially during the past decade, full agreement as to the final meaning of Rousseau's thought has scarcely been achieved. One need only recall some of the most recent studies by Schinz, Hubert, Masson and Cobban to perceive that a wide divergence of interpretation still persists.[76] To some Rousseau is still the protagonist of modern individualism, who stood for the unlimited freedom of the "rights of the heart" without ethical restraint, while to others he is the founder of a disciplined state socialism which forces the individual into the straight jacket of the community where he enjoys neither freedom of action nor freedom of opinion. Growing fewer are those who regard his works as nothing but a tissue of contradictions.

Two things emerge from these exhaustive and critical studies of Rousseau. The first is that it is useless to search his works for a fully developed and systematic body of doctrine. He was the originator of a new movement and as such he was more concerned with its primary impulse than with its ultimate goal. The second is that his thought cannot be understood apart from his character and personal experience. He wrote as one who seeks to objectify the conflicts of his own unhappy personality and the misery that resulted from his impact on a society in which he was an alien. He entered the sophisticated society of Paris burdened with a Puritanical conscience and a brooding sense of sin, handicapped by boorish and uncouth

[76] Recent biographies: C. E. Vulliamy, *Rousseau* (London, 1931); M. Josephson, *Jean-Jacques Rousseau* (New York, 1931). Special studies: A. Schinz, *La Pensée de J.-J. Rousseau* (Smith College Anniversary Series, 1929); E. H. Wright, *The Meaning of Rousseau* (New York, 1929); P. M. Masson, *La religion de J.-J. Rousseau* (Paris, 1916), 3 vols.; A. Cobban, *Rousseau and The Modern State* (London, 1934); H. Hoeffding, *J.-J. Rousseau's Philosophy*, Eng. tr. (New York, 1933). The writer finds himself in closest agreement with the following studies: Ch. W. Hendel, *Jean-Jacques Rousseau, Moralist* (New York, 1934), 2 vols.; R. Hubert, *Rousseau et l'Encyclopédie* (Paris, 1928); Ernst Cassirer, "Das Problem Jean-Jacques Rousseau," *Archiv für Geschichte der Philosophie*, vol. 41 (1932), 176-213; 479-513; and "Discussion" in *Bulletin de la Société de Philosophie*, 32 année, no. 2 (Avril-Juin, 1932).

manners that made him socially impossible, yet convinced of the "natural goodness" of his character, in a word, as the "noble savage" whom he later idealized in his works. This society of flatterers, *railleurs,* detractors of probity frustrated, humiliated and demoralized him. It placed him into situations calling for more virtue than he had in him. His life was irregular and quixotic, he contracted a liaison with a servant girl, sent his children to the *Enfants Trouvées,* and generally engaged in practices he had to condemn. Thus, civilization appeared to him to have the inevitable effect of causing the moral disintegration of men. He sought wholehearted personal affection among his philosopher friends, but found only the polite and polished manners which struck him as false and artificial. Poverty forced him to work out his destiny in Paris, which he detested as the scene af his demoralization; and here he saw and felt how profoundly social inequalities made and unmade the very lives of men. This bondage of the social order stirred in him a nostalgia for real "freedom," henceforth the besetting thought of his life.

Like a stream of molten lava his suppressed indignation against everything which his philosopher friends venerated burst forth in his *Discourse on the Arts and Sciences* of 1750 which he wrote as a prize essay to the question of the Academy of Dijon, *Has the Restoration of the Arts and Sciences Had a Purifying Effect on Morals?* The answer, he said, must be emphatically, No! Men in present society exhibit revolting habits of vice, hypocrisy, insincerity, injustice and dishonesty. They are both bad citizens and bad men. He pleaded for a return to nature, to the purity and honesty of that imaginary golden age when science and letters were unknown, when men lived in primeval simplicity and ignorance. He made this appeal not on the basis of any historical or scientific insight. Rousseau was neither historian nor anthropologist and he was not the first to make this appeal. Although interest in exotic peoples was then at its height, these studies of primitive societies scarcely influenced him. They did not concern him. Nothing is more characteristic of him than his remark, "Let us begin by ignoring the facts, as they do not affect the question." Again, when he spoke of a "state of nature," he employed it as a hypothetical logical device and was thoroughly aware that no such state had ever existed. No historical or anthropological information, he held, can give us any real knowledge of man. The only source for such knowledge is self-knowledge and self-consciousness, the sole source from which Rousseau drew all his arguments and proofs. To distinguish between the happy and innocent *homme naturel* and the depraved *homme artificiel* one does not need to examine either history or anthropological studies of the Hurons, for every man carries this pattern about with him. This is the discovery on which Rousseau prided himself. Briefly, he advanced his own experience and intuitions against the entire scientific and sociological knowledge of the age of reason. Now this is individualism, and Rousseau's first and second *Discourses*, in which he repeated his denunciation of civilization, appear to be a clear commitment to an unlimited personal individualism.

But this is only one phase of his thought. This apparently extreme individualist became the author of the *Social Contract* (1762). For the society which he had cast aside as the cause of all the corruption and misery of humanity he now wrote a code. In view of the position he had taken in the two *Discourses*, one should expect him to set definite limits to the powers and functions of society, lest it infringe the sacrosanct rights of the individual. He did nothing of the kind, for the *Social Contract* proclaims and glorifies the unlimited absolutism of the state. It signified a complete departure from the state of independence and an entrance into a commonwealth where all that a man claims as his own and as his right is subject to the law of the whole, the general will. Indeed, Taine's characterization of Rousseau's state as a prison and a monastery does not appear too severe. For this reason the older students of his thought, like Morley, Faguet, Vaughan, contended that the state absolutism of the *Social Contract* marks a sharp breach with the individualism of the two *Discourses*.

Rousseau himself always protested the unity of his thought, and in general his opinion was correct. In his *Rousseau Juge de Jean-Jacques* he wanted it understood that he was an enemy neither of the human race nor of civilization, that he had no intention to throw men back into barbarism and chaos, that he merely wished to rectify contemporary overestimation of the arts and sciences and that his **real** purpose was to point out that men became evil to the same degree to which they had departed from the simple and honest virtues of primitive society. In order to check the pace of this decline he had chosen to write on morals and politics. It would be to no purpose to destroy the institutions of existing society, for their destruction would leave all social vices intact. But if this is the case, how then was it possible to set up an acceptable social order and at the same time avoid the corruption and perversion of contemporary society? This is the central problem of the *Social Contract*.

Rousseau told his contemporaries that while a return to the state of nature was impossible, the road to freedom lay open to them. In spite of the varied interpretations of Rousseau's concept of freedom, he has defined the term with a precision which excludes caprice: freedom is obedience to an irrefragable law which the individual has imposed on himself. The essence of Rousseau's concept of freedom is not a revolt against law but voluntary consent to a law which he recognizes as necessary. He was no more an extreme individualist than he was a consistent collectivist. Here lies the key to Rousseau's political thought. Nothing was further from his mind than to emancipate the individual from all law and order. His problem was "to find a form of association which will defend and protect with the whole common force the person and goods of each associate, in which each, while uniting himself with all, may still obey only himself and remain as free as before."[77] The establishment of such a state signifies the substitution of rational justice for instinct in the conduct of men. Only by entering such a state do men become moral and autonomous personalities. It has rightly been said that the basic moral category of Rousseau is not man but the citizen. Although in the subsequent period he generally passed for the champion of the independent primitive man, he always placed this moral concept of personality far above the instinctive animalism of the state of nature. By entering his state men gained in the enlargement of their perceptions and capacities and in the general elevation of the quality of their minds. They became for the first time intelligent beings. In short, Rousseau reversed the position which he had taken in the second *Discourse*, in which he said that "the man who thinks is a depraved animal."

77 *Contrat Social*, livre I, ch. 6.

If Rousseau now declared himself in favor of intelligence and science, it was because he was first and foremost a moralist. He had disagreed with the philosophers so violently because they sought salvation in knowledge and science alone. The position he now took was that knowledge and science constitute no danger to man if he accepts the primacy of the moral order. In other words, political and intellectual freedom are useless and dangerous to man so long as he does not possess moral freedom and obey an imperative moral law. Practically, of course, freedom is destroyed the very moment when subjection to the will and command of another is demanded. A law that is not equally effective for all is a contradiction in terms. Therefore, the establishment of legal and moral equality among all citizens is the prime function of Rousseau's republican polity. Physical and intellectual inequality and the inequality of property, he admitted, are beyond human remedy and, therefore, not to be regretted. He thought the state free to interfere with property only insofar as difference in wealth jeopardized the legal and moral equality of men as citizens. Beyond that he did not go. There is no explicit communism in the *Social Contract*. It was not against poverty as such that Rousseau revolted, although he was forever living in straitened circumstances. What roused his indignation, what he denounced with all the impassioned eloquence at his command was the degrading dependence of certain classes on the will of others, the political and moral disfranchisement that was the inevitable result of the organization of contemporary society. On this point the *Social Contract* and the educational program of the *Émile* proclaim the same message. If youth is to be educated to independence of will and character, so runs the central thought of the *Émile*, it should be protected against the violent imposition of an alien will. The external compulsion of things the young were to learn at the earliest possible moment, but they must be carefully guarded against the tyranny of men. With this thought in mind the whole tendency of Rousseau's political and social thought becomes intelligible. He was seeking a society in which the bond of union and law were equal for all, so that no one could gain any private superiority over the others. This law, the general will, all citizens must learn to obey as they do a law of nature, not as though it were an alien command, but because they recognize the necessity of doing so. It is perfectly plain that this is possible only in a society which itself makes the laws which it obeys, and this, in turn, presupposes a radical revolution in the entire political and social structure of existing society.

In the past it was not moral conviction or intellectual insight but brutal physical necessity that drove men out of a state of nature into civilized society and kept them there. Now, however, the spell was to be broken. The old state, that was the product of an emergency, was to become a rational state. So long as men blindly obeyed their impulses and physical necessity the state was a playground for the conflicts of private ambition and self-love. It thus became the scourge of humanity. Now Rousseau demanded man's mastery over state and society in the same sense that Bacon demanded man's mastery over nature. This time man was not again to fall prey to his impulses, he was to choose and judge, take the helm into his own hands and determine the course. Now this is a thoroughly rational demand, but it is a moral rationalism that takes precedence over mere knowledge and science. Thus, although Rousseau was at loggerheads with his age, he was still a child of the Enlightenment. Notwithstanding his gospel of sentiment, the *Social Contract* rests on a moral conviction. It is, therefore, not mere sensibility but a new moral purpose which triumphs in Rousseau's sentimentalism. As no other philosopher of the Enlightenment he prepared the way for Kant, who in turn placed him beside Newton.

VII. THE EMOTIONAL REVIVAL

When in 1750 Rousseau published his violent diatribe on the arts and sciences, the dominant classical culture of France betrayed certain unmistakable symptoms of weakness and lassitude. Reason and the classical spirit were still sovereign in French literature, but this sovereignty was no longer exclusive. The classical drama had become artificial, barren and formalistic. Its heroic impulse had lost its power and its pathos had degenerated into rhetoric. In Voltaire's dramas tragedy had become mere analysis and dialectics. French lyrical poetry had never been lighter or more mobile, but it had lost its poetic content. Its vital springs had dried up, it became, in Lanson's phrase, a "poésie sans poésie," a didactic vehicle for philosophic or moral truths.[78] In French painting artifice had triumphed. The grand style and noble taste, the cult of the simple and natural as taught by Boileau and Le Brun, had yielded to the taste for the brilliant and pretty in the work of Boucher and Fragonard. Their work did not exclude nature, but it was nature heightened by the beauty spot and rouge that moved them most. The witty smiles, the intelligent grace, that play about the eyes and lips of the portraits of Latour and Perroneau still arrest our attention. Artifice had triumphed also in the social decorum of the colorful aristocratic society that gathered in the Parisian *salons*, in its elegant gallantry and polite sociability, in its taste for delicate refinements and subtle nuances, in its exquisite art of conversation which, combining the subtle play of ideas with quickness of wit, it called *"esprit."*

A restless impatience with this hypercivilized society and its classical ideal of order and symmetry directed by intellect had already manifested itself in many quarters. Sentiment asserted its claims, and there was a vague aspiration for a life, a literature and an art more natural and less complicated by artifice. It can be seen in the popular enthusiasm for the virgin beauties of the new world and for the simple purity of the noble savage; in a growing taste for the countryside and the popularity of the natural charms of English and Chinese parks which supplanted the formal French gardens with their geometric patterns; in the simplification of feminine fashions which liberated women from the stiff armor in which they had been imprisoned; in the preference of Latour for oval faces without complicated headdress and of Greuze for the "négligé" of young girls. It asserted itself in the tearful sentimentality of the bourgeois novels of the pre-romantic Abbé Prévost. Marivaux in his *Marianne* revealed an interest in simple peasant folk "who attract by the simple freedom and sincerity of their sentiments," and described the men of the *salon* as the "living-dead" whose emotions had been sterilized by excessive analysis.[79] These men were reacting

[78] G. Lanson, *Histoire de la littérature française* (Paris, 1912), 5 partie, ch. II.
[79] P. Trahard, *Les maitres de la sensibilité française au XVIIIᵉ siècle* (Paris, 1931), Vol. I, 57 ff.; D. Mornet, *Le romantisme en France au XVIIIᵉ siècle* (Paris, 1912), 17; A. Monglond, *Histoire intérieure de préromantisme français, de l'Abbé Prévost à Joubert* (Grenoble, 1929); A. Reichwein, *China and Europe, Intellectual and Artistic Contacts in the Eighteenth Century* (New York, 1925), 116 ff.

against the discipline of the drawing room, against the tyranny of intellect over emotion, of culture over personality. They cultivated simplicity, tenderness and the elemental passions. Sensibility was in the air and we are not surprised to find even a man like Diderot sobbing at the slightest provocation.

This urge towards tenderness and passion, towards warmth and color, towards a richer interior life, far from being confined to France, was European in the broadest sense. Everywhere the human spirit was set on fire with a new enthusiasm. We can see something of the new temper in those two great spiritual awakenings, German Pietism and English Methodism, which constitute a second and non-violent Protestant Reformation that revitalized not only religion but contributed its share to the new incandescence that lit up German and English life and letters in the second half of the century. Significantly enough, both movements issued from the middle classes and appealed to the broad masses of the nation. In England Methodist preachers were the first organizers, orators and creators of mass opinion and mass emotionalism. In Germany the Pietist movement, sweeping across the frontiers of countless principalities and ignoring social classes, had a nationalizing influence.[80] At a time when the only native German speech that was heard at many a German court was the Sunday sermon, Pietist leaders taught the cultivated and upper classes to abandon their French culture and to speak, pray, sing and confess in their mother tongue. They thus worked in the same direction as Lessing and Winckelmann, who sought to emancipate German literature from French classical influence.

The most energetic apostle of Pietism in the middle decades of the century was the gentle Count von Zinzendorf, doubtless the most inspired religious leader of northern Europe before Kierkegaard and the only German between Leibnitz and Winckelmann to exercise any influence outside of Germany. This cultivated nobleman, who discarded his noble title in Philadelphia, introduced a stimulating atmosphere into the stuffy and overheated Pietism of Spener and

80 See the excellent study by K. Pinson, *Pietism as a Factor in the Rise of German Nationalism* (Col. Univ. Press, 1934), 111.

Francke. He and his followers, the Moravian Brethren of Herrnhut, it is true, denounced the rationalist deism of the Enlightenment, but they also revolted against the abstruse logical machine of Lutheran and Calvinistic dogmatic theology. Creeds which imprisoned God in a revelation regarded as final and complete and claimed as the exclusive possession of this or that church, were abhorrent to them. They were genuinely tolerant on religious grounds and welcomed into their conventicles Lutherans and Calvinists, Catholics and Arminians. Indifferent to dogma, they sought to kindle the fire of a vital personal religious experience, a "religion of the heart." They believed that the spirit of Christ had not manifested itself to the church at a single stroke; its basic principles had to be reinterpreted again and again to adapt them to circumstance, time and the individual. According full respect to each individual as the special creature of God with a religious life peculiar to himself alone, Zinzendorf carried the principle of religious individualism to its logical conclusion. Though in depth these German Pietists can scarcely be compared with the Spanish mystics of the sixteenth century, they employed, like these older mystics, an erotic religious terminology and emphasized the importance of self-observation and self-analysis, discipline, conversion, awakenings, and a personal struggle for salvation. The similarity between their spiritual technique and that of the *Spiritual Exercises* of St. Ignatius of Loyola is apparent. Their belief in the paramount importance of an interior emotional life produced among their adherents a sizable crop of religious correspondences, spiritual diaries, illuminations, dreams, personal inspirations, and, it must be added, frequent instances of emotional hysteria and shameless religious exhibitionism. But the very religious psychology for which the rationalistic deists were searching we find among these followers of Zinzendorf. Despite his hostility to the Enlightenment, Zinzendorf at bottom agreed with Lessing in the belief that the essence of religion is sentiment and practical morality. Lessing's gospel of love and tolerance as reflected in his *Nathan der Weise* was also that of Zinzendorf. When he died in 1760, Zinzendorf's sentimental religious movement had entered the broad stream of German culture and literature. Together with

Rousseau he must be regarded as one of the originators of the German romantic movement.[81]

Closely related to German Pietism and largely influenced by it but internationally and socially of incomparably greater importance was the Methodism of John Wesley. Pietism founded no independent church, but Methodism, spreading from the academic society of Oxford to the vast unlettered populations of towns and villages throughout the British Isles and beyond the ocean, established a new Protestant denomination that soon mounted into millions. Pietism was swept up and absorbed by the more powerful drive of the *Aufklärung*, but the two English evangelical revivals, led respectively by John Wesley and George Whitefield, although differing sharply and deeply on theological points, broke the force of the dominant rationalistic and Latitudinarian tradition in the Established Church and produced a fundamentalist religious reaction. This retrograde intellectual influence, its denunciation of science as leading to atheism, its depreciation of scholarly study and criticism of the Bible, stronger in Whitefield who altogether lacked the education and culture of Wesley, is the least satisfactory aspect of this remarkable movement.

Not without good reason has John Wesley been called St. Francis in breeches. The movement which he originated in 1739, a year after his conversion, was Franciscan in accent and organization. Theologically Methodism had nothing new to contribute; its roots reached back to Luther and St. Paul and to the religious sensibility of the Moravian Pietists. Although a high churchman who had no quarrel with the official church either in doctrine or discipline, Wesley was a stinging rebuke to the prevailing temper of Anglicanism. He carried the irradiating warmth of his mysticism and his devotional intensity into the market place and the fields to the low and lowest of the populace, to the miners of Wales and the workers of Newcastle and London, to those brutalized and gin-sodden wretches whose life Hogarth depicted with savage honesty in his

---

[81] O. Uttendorfer, *Zinzendorfs Weltbetrachtung* (Berlin, 1929); O. Pfister, *Die Frömmigkeit des Grafen von Zinzendorf* (Berlin, 1925); E. Troeltsch, *Protestantisches Christentum und Kirche in der Neuzeit* (Berlin, 1922), 661 ff.; A. Eloesser, *Die Deutsche Litteratur vom Barock bis zu Goethes Tod* (Berlin, 1930), Vol. I, 86 ff.; A. W. Nagler, *Pietism and Methodism* (Nashville, 1918).

jolly *Beer Street* and his repellent *Gin Lane*. To these ignorant and depraved classes, neglected by the official church and by an indifferent aristocracy, he brought the almost incredible message of the supreme value of the individual soul, the doctrines of faith and Christian perfection, the assurance, joy and elation of a personal salvation. The masses flocked to the sermons of the Methodist preachers and when the local parsons, irritated by their rivals' eccentric style and extravagant enthusiasm, denied them the use of their pulpits, they resorted to open field meetings, attracting audiences of five, ten, fifty and even eighty thousand listeners. They revolutionized pulpit eloquence. Instead of the cold, polished and fastidious homilies on the *dieu fainéant* by rationalist parsons, they improvised their impassioned appeals, stirred up the emotions of their audiences, evoked in their hearers a sense of the horror of sin and the desire for instantaneous conversion. There is no need to dwell on the contagious emotionalism, the tears, groanings, the hysterical paroxysms of the early Methodist revival; they were the inevitable accompaniments of all such revivals. Compared with the passionate oratory of Whitefield, who was often unable to proceed for his tears while half the audience was convulsed with sobs, Wesley himself was calm and argumentative. His great psychological effect was due to the fact that he sought to produce in his hearers an experience similar to his own conversion.

Gifted with a genius for organization, Wesley gathered around him his hierarchy of preachers, local preachers, stewards, class leaders and members of the society, and impressed on them his own moral earnestness and religious discipline. His journeys on horseback throughout the three kingdoms averaged eight thousand miles annually for many a long year, during each of which he rarely preached less than three times on week days and five times on Sundays. No single eighteenth-century figure influenced so many minds. He built not only chapels, but set up printing presses from which poured an endless stream of cheap tracts, hymn books, abridgements of classical works, along with biographies and magazines. Congregational singing, which he learned from the Moravians, appealed to the people with all the attractiveness of a great novelty. The hymns of Charles Wesley rank high as productions of creative imagination; they are interesting records of introspection and owe their suggestive power to the fact that they are transcripts from the stirring experience of the two brothers. In this way Wesley saved vast areas of English life from brutality and barbarism. Gin-drinking revels became religious revivals. What the theaters, literature, picture galleries and operas were to the upper classes, who remained hostile to the movement, the fellowship of the Methodist chapel and congregational singing were to the lower classes of English society.[82] If we accept the conclusion of the distinguished French historian, M. Halévy, the stability of modern England in spite of the economic iniquities of the Industrial Revolution, which might well have produced the counterpart of the French Revolution in England, was due largely to the Methodist revival.[83]

Methodism contributed its own strength to the early stirrings of the romantic impulse. To the prevailing sentiment, much of which Babbitt rightly denounced as unreal "emotional sophistry," the Methodists added the stronger and deeper emotions of a sincere religious experience.[84] John Wesley filtered the emotions of his followers and directed them not only into devotional and spiritual but into lyrical channels.

But this emotional lyricism was no longer a monopoly of the Methodist. It had already invaded English literature which, relinquishing its insularity and becoming for the first time European, radiated a powerful influence and helped to form taste in France and Germany. Even though in England official authority was still on the side of classical rationalism and Samuel Johnson, the central figure of English criticism, was an enemy of sentimentalism, the silent transformation was already proceeding apace. It appeared among the funereal or elegiac poets, Thomson, Young, Collins and

82 C. E. Vulliamy, *John Wesley* (London, 1931); W. B. Brash, *Methodism* (London, 1928); G. Eayrs, *John Wesley, Christian Philosopher and Church Founder* (London, 1926); S. G. Dimond, *The Psychology of the Methodist Revival* (London, 1926); F. B. Harvey, "Methodism and the Romantic Movement," *London Quarterly and Holborn Review* (July, 1934); A. W. Harrison, "Romanticism in the Religious Revivals," *Hibbert Journal* (July, 1933); J. H. Overton, *The Evangelical Revival in the Eighteenth Century* (London, 1939); F. C. Gill, *The Romantic Movement and Methodism* (London, 1937). Still useful is the admirable chapter on early Methodism by W. E. H. Lecky, *History of England in the Eighteenth Century* (New York, 1883), Vol. II, 567 ff.; E. Halévy, "La naissance du Méthodisme," *La Revue de Paris* (August, 1906), 519, 841.

83 E. Halévy, *The Influence of the Evangelical Movement on the History of Modern England*, Lecture in Leeds University (Oct. 22, 1925).

84 I. Babbitt, *Rousseau and Romanticism* (New York, 1919), 355.

Gray, who by 1750 had provoked a distaste for the mechanical brilliance of classical convention and a desire for tender emotions, for a subjective appreciation of the beauties of nature, for half lights, mists and that brand of egoist melancholy which was the invariable accompaniment of nascent romanticism. We find it in the ecstasy of worship awakened by the picturesqueness of the landscape in the *Seasons* (1744) of James Thomson, in the *Night Thoughts* (1745) of Edward Young and *The Pleasures of Melancholy* (1747) of Thomas Warton, where the new cult of feeling reached the stage of psychological inversion in which the poet extracts a mournful kind of joy from human suffering. The same note of sentimental melancholy was echoed in the *Odes* (1746) of William Collins and by Thomas Gray, whose *Elegy* (1750) is the essence of sensibility. Among some of these pioneers romantic sentiment was associated with the revival of moral and religious preoccupations, among others it was attended by an imaginative escape from existing civilization to the ruins and monuments of a remote and foggy past. A new and sympathetic enthusiasm for things medieval, for Gothic churches, old castles, ruined abbeys and medieval ballads asserted itself. When James Macpherson published his *Fingal* in 1761 and palmed it off as an epic poem translated from the Gaelic of Ossian, he was an impostor, but he was original enough to touch and thrill the whole of Europe. Ossianism became the rage of incipient romanticism.[85]

The greatest triumph of the age of Johnson, however, was the creation of the modern English novel by Richardson, Fielding, Smollett and Sterne. No doubt Henry Fielding's *Tom Jones* (1749), Tobias Smollett's *Roderick Random* (1748) and *Peregrine Pickle* (1751), Laurence Sterne's *Tristram Shandy* (1760) are all superior to Samuel Richardson's *Pamela* (1740), *Clarissa Harlowe* (1751) and *Sir Charles Grandison* (1754) in literary distinction and originality, correctness, elegance and wit, and they are much less tedious and banal. As a pure man of letters Richardson was not the equal

[85] E. Gosse, *History of Eighteenth Century Literature* (London, 1889); "The Age of Johnson," *Cambridge History of English Literature* (New York, 1933), Vol. X, Chapters V, VI, VII, X; E. Gosse, *Gray* (1889); W. L. Phelps, *The Beginners of the English Romantic Movement* (New York, 1893); Millar, *The Mid-Eighteenth Century* (1902).

of his rivals and he was certainly not as representative of English life as was Fielding. Yet if we take into account the intellectual history of the period and the larger field of European literature, Richardson's work was of incomparably greater significance. This unpretentious London printer was the prophet of the sentimentalism which was soon to conquer the whole of Europe. The irresistible fascination which he exercised over the English and European public was due to his realistic study of the movements of the human heart set in the frame of contemporary bourgeois manners, to the careful psychological analysis which sounded out every emotion with the clear-sightedness of a Puritan moralist, and to the fact that at the very moment when the middle classes were growing in social consciousness, his novels expressed their grievances, prejudices and criticisms of the corruption and privileges of the aristocracy. Richardson was as important in the development of the German as he was in the growth of the English novel. The German and French literary markets were inundated with imitations and sequels. Gellert, Wieland and Klopstock joined in the chorus of encomiastic praise. In France, Voltaire was enthusiastic and Diderot was carried away to the statement that he could sacrifice all modern literature with the single exception of Richardson's novels. But it was above all in their influence on Rousseau that Richardson's psychological and sentimental novels became significant.[86]

It was with Rousseau that the new sentimentality first crystallized into a definite program. He set out to emancipate his generation from the tyranny of intellectualism and confront the analytical reason, which was the foundation of the culture of his day, with the elemental power of passion. He gave to the cult of sensibility a moral dignity and an artistic value which it did not possess before him. Though not himself a poet, he was the rediscoverer of lyrical poetry. It is this rediscovery of an all but forgotten world that explains the sinister power with which his *La Nouvelle Héloïse* (1761) took hold of his contemporaries. They saw in this novel,

86 L. Cazamian on Richardson in "The Age of Johnson," *The Cambridge History of English Literature* (New York, 1933), Vol. X, ch. I; A. Dobson, *Richardson* (London, 1902); E. Schmidt, *Richardson, Rousseau und Goethe* (Berlin, 1895); H. S. Canby, "Pamela Abroad," *Modern Language Notes, Vol. XVIII* (1903); J. Texte, *Rousseau et les origines du cosmopolitanisme européen* (Paris, 1895).

which leaves us singularly cold today, not a mere work of creative imagination but the revelation of a veritable *vita nuova*. What irked his philosopher friends, what they could not comprehend, was the fact that he not merely described the force of sentiment as a disinterested spectator but that he embodied it and lived by it as no one had embodied and lived by it before him. Yet the *Nouvelle Héloïse* is anything but the apotheosis of sentiment.[87] The entire conception of the book is based on the primacy of conscience and moral judgment which serve as checks on expansive emotion. He writes, *"Ôtez l'idée de la perfection, vous ôtez l'enthusiasme; ôtez l'estime, et l'amour n'est plus rien."*[88] It is just this duality of Rousseau's sensibility, based as it is on a new sentimental as well as a new moral pathos, that accounts for his tremendous influence on his contemporaries.

VIII. ART

In the domain of art as in that of thought French leadership in the middle decades of the century was undisputed. Something very like dry rot began to infect English architecture when the generation of architects that succeeded Wren began to die out in the middle of the century. In Germany Balthasar Neumann had no successor, and with the completion of the princely residences of Schönbrunn, Würzburg, Munich, and Sans-Souci at Potsdam the greatest century of German architecture had come to a close. Only France still produced a Jacques Gabriel, whose plan of 1754 for the Place de la Concorde, with its magnificent structures on the north side, reveals a profound grasp of ancient classical form and constitutes one of the glories of Paris and the world. In painting Spain and Holland were exhausted and England, except for Hogarth, may be safely ignored. Italy remained the fatherland for all artists, but, except for Tiepolo, Guardi and Canaletto, its creative force was spent. Until the mighty eloquence and clear logic of Winckelmann's *History of*

---

[87] Much nonsense has been written on Rousseau's sentimentality, notably by E. Seillière, *Rousseau* (Paris, 1912), and in America by Irving Babbitt, *Rousseau and Romanticism* (New York, 1919), 157 ff.

[88] *Nouvelle Héloïse*, p. I, Lettre XXIV; see also C. W. Hendel, *Jean-Jacques Rousseau, Moralist* (New York, 1934), II, 39 ff.; E. Cassirer, "Das Problem Jean-Jacques Rousseau," *Archiv für Geschichte der Philosophie*, Vol. XLI, 486; P. Trahard, *Les maîtres de la sensibilité française au XVIIIᵉ siècle* (Paris, 1932), Vol. III, 1 ff.

Art Among the Ancients presented the first serious challenge, Germany was under the spell of French art.[89]

In Boucher, Chardin, Fragonard, Greuze, Vernet, to mention only some of the most prominent, France produced an abundance of original artists whose creative vitality and variety of inspiration excited the admiration of Europe and recalled the brilliant days of the Italian Renaissance. While Italian and German artists worked in isolation, these masters of the French school were grouped around the Academy, where they encouraged, stimulated and rivaled one another. Moreover, since 1737 there were annual, after 1751 biennial exhibitions, the *salons*, which had the effect of extending patronage from king and court, from the aristocracy of birth and finance to the wider circle of interested middle classes. Almost simultaneously France, already sovereign in artistic production, became the home of modern art criticism. In response to the solicitation of his friend Grimm, Diderot in 1759 began to write from year to year those appraisals of contemporary painting which opened a new epoch in the history of art criticism. The essential purpose of art criticism, as Diderot saw it, is to clarify the penumbra of *impression* and *taste* and to draw both into the light of conscious knowledge. Whatever art historians may say of the unhappy immediate effects of this combination of critical aesthetics with painting, it remains one of the imperishable achievements of the Enlightenment to have combined artistic criticism with artistic production and to have helped to point the way for the transformation of one into the other. Diderot was followed by a host of other critics whose booklets and pamphlets excited public curiosity and helped to form taste.[90]

The age of the Enlightenment, which challenged all authorities, and the dissolute court of Louis XV, which abandoned itself to reckless, pagan enjoyment of life, were mirrored in the splendor,

[89] Max Osborn, "Die Kunst des Rococo" in the *Propyläen-Kunstgeschichte* (Berlin, 1929), Vol. XIII; C. Justi, *Winckelmann und seine Zeitgenossen* (Leipzig, 1898), Vol. I; Jean Pommier, "Les salons de Diderot," *Revue des cours et conferences* (30 mai, 1936); A. Fontaine, *Les doctrines de l'art en France de Poussin à Diderot* (Paris, 1909); H. Gillot, *Denis Diderot* (Paris, 1937), 101 ff.; R. Blomfield, *A Short History of Renaissance Architecture in England* (London, 1897), 2 vols.; S. Rocheblave, *L'âge classique de l'art français* (Paris, 1932); René Schneider, *L'art français au XVIIIᵉ siècle* (Paris, 1926); Louis Gillet, *La peinture aux XVIIᵉ et XVIIIᵉ siècles* (Paris, 1913); E. and J. de Goncourt, *L'art du XVIIIᵉ siécle* (Paris, 1906), 3 vols.

[90] Jean-Gabriel Lemoine, "Les vraies idées de Diderot sur l'art," *L'Art Vivant* (Sept., 1929).

grace, easy familiarity and piquant charms of contemporary art. Biblical subjects and religious themes receded into the background. Strength, sublimity and stateliness disappeared. The great aristocratic lords and princes were no longer depicted as unapproachable deities but as the elegant and sociable men of the drawing room. Inevitably, portraiture occupied a prominent place, and in the hands of Latour, Vanloo, Nattier, though linked with the past by a thousand ties, it was carried to a remarkably high state of perfection. The peculiar service which art was expected to render to this refined society, corrupted in morals, frozen in aristocratic prejudices and fashionable conventions, subject to all the vices of a decadent civilization, is curiously illustrated by the story told by the Goncourt brothers.[91] When Madame de Pompadour made up her mind to pander to the jaded appetites of the king, she had a famous female model of the day introduced into a painting of the Holy Family which was destined for the private chapel of the queen. The portrait served its purpose, it roused the curiosity of the king who promptly invited the model to the Parc-aux-Cerfs.

Boucher has rightly been regarded as the representative artist of this brilliant society, the personification of the "gallant taste" and the "style of Louis XV." He reflected its taste in his elegant and graceful pastorals and in the mythologies, which transmuted the Olympus of Virgil and Homer into the Olympus of Ovid, in the suave and sinuous curves of his denuded goddesses and shepherdesses; who flaunt their lovely bodies frankly provoking an erotic response. Venuses flowed steadily from his brush in great number. This single-minded devotion to Venus brought him abundant reward, for his paintings of delicate and elusive femininity made him the most popular idol of his day and earned him an income of fifty thousand livres a year. Returning to Paris from Rome he was reported as saying, "Raphael is a woman, Michelangelo is a monster; one is paradise and the other is hell; they are painters of another world; it is a dead language that nobody speaks in our day. We others are the painters of our own age; we have no common sense, but we are charming."

This statement is not untrue, for he was cheerful, sportive, full

91 E. et J. Goncourt, *L'art du XVIII⁰ siècle*, I, 213.

of fancy and intensely sociable. If he lacked Chardin's profounder feeling for character, he became the supreme decorator of this age of brilliant luxury, of its carriages and ceilings, its panels and friezes, which he covered with chubby children and women in piquant poses. Yet he was the purveyor of pretty trifles. He was very nearly surpassed in picturesque and decorative grace by his student Fragonard, in whom this witty and coquettish civilization found another superior prophet.

Though a generous critic and capable of appreciating the virtuosity with which Boucher triumphed over technical difficulties, Diderot, like Delacroix later, regarded him as a decadent artist. All the greater was his enthusiasm for Oudry's animals and Vernet's marine pictures, above all for Greuze, the creator of a new type of moralizing pictorial melodrama which served to rehabilitate the art of an age too long devoted to debauchery and vice. Egged on by Diderot, who insisted on making art a matter of ethics, and obviously touched by the rising tide of moral sentimentalism, Greuze sought to instruct, to correct, to move his spectators to transports of tender sympathy and emotion. He chose his subjects from the realm of the domestic, the *honnête*, the homely pathos of middle-class people. No painting of the eighteenth century was greeted with greater popular enthusiasm than Greuze's *Accordée de Village*, which was exhibited in 1761, the year of the *Nouvelle Héloïse*. But Greuze's return to nature was still suffused with the perfume of an older epoch and his moralism was hypocritical. The only artist who found his way back to nature without wallowing in sentimental mud was Chardin, an honest craftsman of the lower middle class, who became the greatest painter of his age. Beside the crowd of dancing puppet painters, as Goethe called his contemporaries, Chardin, out of touch with the world of fashion, was an artist of unaffected simplicity. An infinite artistic seriousness and sincerity characterized all his work, hence his indifference to subject. His greatness lay not in his subjects, which were not so different from those of the Dutch painters of the seventeenth century from whom he drew his inspiration, but in his conception, in the fact that he painted every object with the combined reflection of all other objects, in the delight with which he attempted to solve, usually successfully, purely pictorial problems, especially the problem of light. When Chardin painted, his brain was in his eyes. A warm inner flame animates many of his pictures, most arresting and touching perhaps in his *Le Bénédicité*, which was exhibited in 1740 and was purchased by Louis XV. Frederick the Great was equally enthusiastic over his work, and purchased many of his pictures. Here was a simple bourgeois artist who spoke a warm and independent language in his kitchen scenes, symbolizing the matured capacity of the middle class for cultural leadership.

There was only one other great artist of these years who refused to sacrifice his art to the pretty indecencies of Boucher or the sobbing sentimentalism of Greuze, and this was William Hogarth, the foremost and the most English of the British painters. He was a typical representative of the English middle class and a revolutionary artist. He revolted against tradition, against the French, against the connoisseurs who duped Englishmen into purchasing faked and inferior Italian masters, and he was the first painter to discover the advantage of large-scale production. Refusing to sink to the level of a portrait manufacturer, like his English contemporaries, with the prospect of dependence on the patronage of the wealthy upper classes, he was confronted with the necessity of devising means for reaching a less lucrative but more extensive market. He made his paintings the originals on which he based numerous engravings and sold these engravings by the hundred and thousand for a few shillings apiece.[92] This new and different method of production and distribution required also a modification of subject matter. He became the pictorial chronicler of the life and manners he saw about him, a satirist and a humorist. He turned to such moral homilies as the *Idle Apprentice*, *The Rake's Progress,* and *Mariage à la Mode,* to realistic descriptions as they were already embodied in the fiction and drama of the period. He announced that he "wished to compose pictures on canvas similar to representations on the stage," a dumb show. It must be said that he followed this aim far too literally, his compositions too often taking on the restricted limits and conventional poses of the actual stage. He felt that he had discovered a new

[92] Austin Dobson, *William Hogarth* (London, 1907), 33 ff.; H. Read, *Art and Society* (New York, 1937), 177.

province of painting. Yet he added nothing to the formal perfection and technical craftsmanship which painting had already developed when he began to practice the art. Much as we may admire Hogarth for the intensity and power of his genius, it can scarcely be on the basis of design and execution, although the best of his work, *The March to Finchley* and the *Shrimp Girl*, exhibits an executive mastery of his subject which the peculiar character of his training would scarcely lead one to anticipate. But his satire is too much lacking in wit and subtlety, it is too commonplace, though it is always uncompassionate and powerful, and sometimes terrible.

Chapter Six

COMMERCE AND EMPIRE

IN THE process of the expansion of Europe over the world, predatory or otherwise, the old mercantilist imperialism had already passed its meridian. The mercantilist creed and the old colonial system which it called into existence were, as will be pointed out presently, decadent, although the forces which dissolved the one and disrupted the other some years later had not yet begun to appear. In the meantime the old colonial powers had yielded leadership to others. Spain, Portugal and to some extent Holland had failed to meet the double task of successful colonial powers, which required not merely the development and defense of their colonies but the creation at home of a vigorous and expansive industrial organism to serve as the foundation for effective commercial and naval influence in the transmarine world. It had become equally apparent that only such powers could permanently assert the supremacy of the white race as were actually great powers in Europe. Only Great Britain and France could satisfy these conditions.

Since 1748 peace was the legal situation between the French and British governments. But with all colonial controversies between them remaining unsettled and no determined effort on either side of the Channel to settle them, this peace could not be otherwise than precarious. What intensified the danger of a renewal of war was the circumstance that they faced each other in four different parts of the world: North America, the West Indies, Africa and India, and fought for the control of four different commodities: negroes, sugar, tobacco and indigo. The peace scarcely extended to the realm of commercial competition, let alone to the rival colonists. In the past sixty years the wars of England and France in Europe had found ever louder echoes in their overseas territories, and the gap between their interests in Europe and their interests elsewhere had narrowed down as their contacts throughout the world became

251

more numerous and more intimate. The settled tradition that overseas fighting between rival agents of private companies did not involve their home governments was becoming steadily more difficult to uphold. When private interests in London or the French seaports appealed to their governments to come to their aid, these governments were now more disposed than before to respond, even though giving that aid involved heavy expenses or the danger of war.

I. COLONIES AND NATIONAL ECONOMY

By the middle of the eighteenth century the age of colonial chimeras was over and the colonies had become an important and integral part of the national economy of Great Britain and France. It would be an error to attribute the wave of industrial and commercial prosperity that swept over France after 1750 solely to colonial commerce. The phenomenon was in a certain sense pan-European and had multiple origins. Yet its close and unmistakable relation to the colonies already struck the observant Voltaire.[1] In France it was most conspicuous in the rapid growth of the great Atlantic seaports: Nantes, the principal seat of the slave trade; Bordeaux and La Rochelle, places of international importance and centers for the storage and distribution of the chief West Indian products.[2] The shippers, merchants and mariners of Le Havre and Marseilles had an important share in both the African and West Indian trade, while the ports of the north supplied the largest contingent of Newfoundland fishermen. Lorient had become the chief entrepôt of the French East India Company at the time of its greatest financial prosperity.[3] The French merchant marine was rapidly recovering from the losses of the last war. Colonial commerce enriched the maritime provinces and animated the internal trade routes throughout the nation. Every region of France felt the effect of the magnificent progress of St. Domingue, Guadeloupe, Martinique and Cayenne, either by way of supplying these colonies with manufactured commodities, provisions and building materials or by the

1 See his *Fragments sur l'Inde.*
2 Gaston-Martin, *Nantes au XVIIIe siècle* (Paris, 1928); E. Garnault, *Histoire du commerce rochelais au XVIIIe siècle* (Paris, 1891), Vol. III; Th. Malvezin, *Histoire du commerce de Bordeaux,* Vol. III.
3 W. H. Dalgliesh, *The Perpetual Company of the Indies in the Days of Dupleix* (Philadelphia, 1933), 25-32.

consumption of colonial products.[4] West Indian sugar was no longer classed as a luxury but had become an article of common consumption among rich and poor alike. Sugar refining had become one of the major industries of France.[5]

The overseas colonies furnished important accessories to the French textile industries—dyestuffs, of which indigo was the most common—not only to the infant manufacture of cotton but also of linen and wool. We have some difficulty today in grasping the very large position which the colonies occupied in the entire volume of French foreign commerce, but the fact remains that the relative value of French colonial trade was greater in the eighteenth than in the nineteenth century. Thanks to the re-exportation of West Indian sugar and, to a lesser extent, of cacao and coffee, France dominated the markets of the Levant and southern Europe. The entire French trade with the Baltic area, still carried on, it should be pointed out, through Dutch and British intermediaries, depended on the West India colonies. Indeed, two-thirds of all her colonial products were re-exported to the countries of the Continent,[6] and the time was not far off when trade in colonial products constituted one-third of the entire volume of French foreign commerce.[7] Well might the merchants of Nantes contend, as they did with some exaggeration in 1756, that colonial trade was the cornerstone of the entire foreign commerce of the kingdom. This increased movement of merchants, artisans, sailors and goods between France and her colonies served to extend business interest in the colonies to ever larger elements of society. Countless families of the nobility, both military and official, and of the middle classes had younger sons in St. Domingue or Martinique discharging public functions or, like the Rohans and Choiseuls, exploiting vast sugar plantations.

It was already apparent to most contemporaries that foreign and colonial commerce held proportionately a much larger place in

[4] L. P. May, *Histoire économique de Martinique* (Paris, 1930), 290.

[5] P. M. Bondois, "Les centres sucriers français au XVIIIe siècle," *Revue d'histoire économique et sociale*, XIX (1931), 27-77.

[6] L. P. May, "La France, Puissance des Antilles," *Revue d'histoire économique et sociale*, XVIII (1930), 469; also A. M. Wilson's chapter on the commercial expansion of France in *French Foreign Policy During the Administration of Cardinal Fleury* (Cambridge, 1936), 290-317.

[7] A. Girault, *Principes de colonisation et de legislation coloniale* (Paris, 1927), 5th ed., I, 201.

British national economy than was the case in France. If there was any doubt, the great difference between a population of some twenty-three million Frenchmen and six and one half million Englishmen and Welshmen might carry the point home to them. There can be no question that before 1780 France was at least the manufacturing equal of England. It is also true that in 1750 England, like France, was still a grain-exporting country; and one should not forget that Arthur Young still considered the landed interest of England ten times more important than all other interests.[8] Technical and economic forces were conspiring to give impetus to the consolidation of the agricultural land of England, and unreserved political approval was being given to land enclosure, a movement that was to bring about a wholesale elimination of small landowners. These great agrarian changes, facilitated by a systematic improvement in methods of cultivation and stockbreeding, were soon to produce revolutionary results.[9]

It is undeniable, however, that in 1750 overseas expansion was already conditioning the entire life and character of the English people, even of the landowning aristocracy which, while affecting to despise trade, participated in it and married it. The great estates of eighteenth-century England, the magnificent houses in town and country were built up in large part from resources accumulated overseas.[10] England already passed for the wealthiest country in Europe, and most continentals, like Voltaire, attributed this happy situation to her merchants and traders. In truth, before the Industrial Revolution brought fortunes from mining, they could be gained only by foreign and colonial trade or by ownership of property in London, which was the creature of foreign trade. How colonial trade produced fortunes may be seen from the career of a Lancashire pinmaker who became a Manchester cotton manufacturer and trader; his son, Samuel Touchett, became an important figure in cotton, the slave trade, insurance, billbroking and

8 D. G. Barnes, *History of the English Corn Laws, 1660-1846* (New York, 1930), 29; H. Sée, *Modern Capitalism* (London, 1928), 84.

9 T. H. Marshall, "Jethro Tull and the New Husbandry," *Economic History Review,* II, 44-60.

10 J. B. Botsford, *English Society in the Eighteenth Century as Influenced from Oversea* (New York, 1924); C. R. Fay, *Great Britain from Adam Smith to the Present Day* (London, 1932), 132.

moneylending. In the Seven Years' War he fitted out a fleet of five ships to help capture Senegal from the French.[11]

Some three thousand ships were required to carry the trade of the British colonies alone. Between 1698 and 1774 the colonial trade of England increased fivefold; at the former date it comprised 15 per cent of the overseas trade, at the latter no less than 33 per cent.[12] London was already the heart of the financial, industrial and commercial life of the empire. Two-thirds of England's foreign and colonial trade was concentrated there. With its docks, warehouses and ship canals it had become an emporium of world trade.[13] The rapid growth of Bristol, Liverpool and Glasgow, too, was inseparable from the sugar, slave, coffee and tobacco trade of the plantation colonies.

As even a casual glance at her social and business structure will indicate, England was better prepared to pursue the career of an imperialist power, as the eighteenth century conceived it, than any other country in Europe. The complete absence of serfdom made her inhabitants free to move as, perhaps, no other people. The companies of foreign trade had ceased to be monopolies and there was no limit imposed, as in Spain, on the amounts that might be bought and sold. With the exception of the Hudson Bay and Levant Companies, transatlantic trade was open and offered great rewards to men of enterprise and capital. The skillful cultivation of foreign markets by regulated companies, and to a lesser extent by joint stock companies, had given the English merchant trading connections all over the world from Russia to Mexico and Brazil.

In this world struggling for room to expand—which meant then, as now, markets that would absorb a rapidly growing industry— the England of William Pitt had become frankly acquisitive and definitely capitalistic. Since the Revolution of 1688, as Lipson has so emphatically pointed out, England was moving steadily in the direction of *laissez faire*, and the capitalist classes did not hesitate to challenge the right of parliament to dictate to them the conditions

---

[11] See Miss Sutherland's *A London Merchant, 1695-1774* (Oxford, 1930).
[12] H. Heaton, *Economic History of Europe* (New York, 1936), 326; G. L. Gipson, *The British Empire before the American Revolution* (Caldwell, Idaho, 1936), I, 33.
[13] D. George, *London in the Eighteenth Century* (London, 1925).

on which they should employ their labor.[14] These classes, permeated by a growing economic individualism, resisted or ignored the occasional attempts to fetter their freedom of action.

Industrial processes, geared up by the agencies which had taken charge of selling, had slowly been modified in the preceding years, and the succeeding decades were to witness a still more profound change in productive technology. Large-scale production had already become a recognized feature of certain industries, particularly of the textile manufactures and the metal trades, and if production on a small scale still predominated, entrepreneurs were multiplying from year to year. With a growing class of entrepreneurs, who were accustomed to seek out new markets both for the supply of raw materials and the disposal of finished products and who were accustomed to handle large labor forces, English industry revealed a capacity to meet the requirements of distant and and varied markets.[15] The Bank of England set the pace of monetary economy. By contrast with the Bank of Amsterdam, which was established to create an international bank money in place of the disturbing variety of coins which circulated in western Europe, the outlook of this British institution was definitely national. In the meantime the extension of commercial credit and the development of commercial banking in England left France with her primitive banking system trailing far behind. In 1750 trading on credit had become customary in practically all important branches of the trade and industry of England. While commercial credit was not new, bank credit was and its systematic employment had a stimulating effect on industry and trade.[16] All these factors contributed to impart to the business life of England an uncommonly expansive vitality. Convincing proof that England was capable of supplying her colonies with the things they desired may be drawn from the fact that three fourths of her total exports to the latter were goods of British manufacture, only one fourth having their origin in other countries.

[14] E. Lipson, *Economic History of England, The Age of Mercantilism* (London, 1931), III, 265.
[15] E. Lipson, "England in the Age of Mercantilism," *Journal of Economic and Business History*, IV (1932), 695.
[16] E. A. J. Johnson, *Some Origins of the Modern Economic World* (New York, 1936), 57.

There was no English statesman in these years who did not believe that colonial and foreign commerce was the foundation of English prosperity. Adam Smith rightly contended later that colonial trade had been overdeveloped to the detriment of foreign, but this view marked a revolution in economic theory for which England was not yet prepared. Not even Newcastle fancied that it was possible for England to isolate entirely what she was doing in the colonies from what she did in Europe.[17]

II. THE FRENCH AND BRITISH IMPERIAL SYSTEMS

At first glance there was a remarkable similarity between the French and British colonial empires both in their economic structure and in their geographical distribution. Yet it would be difficult to imagine a sharper contrast. The expansion of England was, as it has been aptly described, the expansion of English society, which emigrated to escape from the pressure of the state.[18] The establishment and development of free institutions in her overseas empire constitute a notable achievement in the sphere of politics. French imperialism, on the other hand, originally was and became ever more exclusively an affair of the state, a trait accentuated by its mercantilist character. The British empire of 1750 was, roughly speaking, a congeries of all but completely self-governing units, each colony reproducing within its limits the liberal political institutions and laws of England. The entire imperial edifice was placed under the scrutiny of the board of trade, which accumulated a wealth of experience and expert knowledge on colonial affairs that made it an invaluable liaison body between the central government and the colonies. Within this framework a policy of "salutary neglect" facilitated the growth of prosperous and industrious communities whose high standard of living impressed every foreign observer, but it also contributed to that intense localism which, expressed in the incessant conflicts between provincial governors and their legislatures, made any effective co-ordination for imperial purposes extremely difficult, if not impossible.

In the French empire, quite in keeping with the passion for

[17] Lillian Penson, *The Colonial Background of British Foreign Policy* (London, 1930).
[18] See G. Unwin's criticism of Seeley, *Studies in Economic History* (London, 1927), 341.

assimilation and centralization characteristic of the monarchy, there were neither local liberties nor anything resembling colonial autonomy. While in France itself the monarchy generously tolerated certain provincial diversities as venerable and harmless relics of the past, in the colonial domain it introduced its own special institutions, which harmonized with the obsession of Versailles to rule everything. Everywhere it placed beside an administrator (the intendant) a military lieutenant-governor and reduced both officials to the centralized, uniform and minute direction and control of the ministry of the marine. This simple circumstance, that the ministry of the marine administered the colonies, placed its indelible stamp on the entire French colonial system. It would seem that an industrious, pioneering colonial population has nothing in common with a line-of-battle ship, yet the French colonies were governed as if they were war vessels permanently at anchor. "The general rules that prevail in the colonies," said Entrecasteaux, a prominent colonial governor, "should be the same as in the navy."[19] All ships at sea are subject to the same perils—therefore there must be absolute uniformity. But this rule, applied to the colonies, could only create confusion and paralyze initiative. Nowhere can this strange parallelism between the rules and administrative procedures of the navy and colonial administration be studied to better advantage than in the regulations on colonial provisions and markets. Everything was foreseen, fixed and regulated from a common center; all local needs were thought to be accurately known and every new problem was solved bureaucratically on the basis of its precedents. Little wonder that de Tocqueville thought he had found in Canada the deformity of the old French administrative system, as through a microscope.[20]

Whether it was a result of this identification of colonial enterprise with state action or a mere coincidence, the fact remains that the majority of the French people were indifferent to the colonies. For the great peasant masses these distant possessions were hidden in a fog of legend. Except for the speculative mania under John Law, it had never been otherwise. The Law *Krach*, however, permanently frightened away the French bourgeois, who sedulously

---

[19] Chr. Schefer, *La France moderne et la problème coloniale* (Paris, 1907), 46.
[20] *L'ancien régime et la Revolution*, 373, note XXIV.

avoided the colonies and invested his money nearer home in lands, offices and mortgages.[21] Immediate concern with the colonies was confined to vested interests, to colonists, traders and speculators in the seaports and to an occasional theorist who studied the problem only to reduce it to a formula. Recently the attempt has been made to lay this popular indifference or hostility to colonies at the door of the enlightened philosophers. Gaxotte speaks of a veritable anti-colonial campaign and stigmatizes Montesquieu, Voltaire and the authors of the *Encyclopédie* as the worst offenders.[22] Much of this anti-colonial literature may be dismissed as issuing from a defeatist psychology of war-weary intellectuals during and immediately after the Seven Years' War. But to speak of these enlightened thinkers as having failed completely to recognize colonial expansion as a dominant factor of the age or as having opposed and hampered it with all means at their disposal is inaccurate and mistakes the real motives of their criticism. The truth is that, except for the followers of Quesnay, the philosophers represented no coherent or special body of opinion in this matter. They were for the most part rootedly orthodox mercantilists, and they shared this creed with the rest of the nation.

Everywhere the mercantilists thought of colonies as the dependencies of national commerce, as the local branches of a central business firm, or as farms which supplied the parent country with commodities which its soil could not produce and which in turn offered secure markets for home manufactures. It was this double role of colonies that interested the mercantilist—and he took good care to specify that there should be no other. There is no thought of the expansion of national culture, still less of mere conquest of overseas territory. Colonies were to be commercially profitable. If they were not, they were not only useless, but dangerous. Because only tropical and subtropical exploitation colonies met these specifications, the French preference for the West Indies persisted, whereas the colonies of temperate climates, which tended to become mere replicas of the mother country, producing the same crops and providing in part for their own manufacturing needs, were thought to be rela-

[21] J. Tramond, *Manuel de l'histoire maritime de la France* (Paris, 1916), 140.
[22] P. Gaxotte, *Louis XV and His Times* (Phila., 1934), 180; C. L. Lokke, *France and the Colonial Question* (New York, 1932), is guilty of the same error.

tively worthless. The French philosophers did not dissent from this creed. Montesquieu's view was typical. He, too, believed that the prime function of colonies was to extend the commerce of the mother country;[23] among all the French colonies he, too, found the Antilles alone wholly "admirable," "because they produce what we cannot grow," although he denounced the institution of slavery.[24]

In 1753 the French government, faithful to its mercantilist principles, recalled Dupleix from India, because he, the representative of a commercial company which was to serve no other purpose than to produce dividends, had embarked on a policy of conquest which aimed at French territorial supremacy in India. By a curious coincidence the volume of the *Encyclopédie* containing the article on colonies appeared in the same year, and this article lays it down that colonies of commerce *"dérogeraient à leur institution si elles devenaient conquerantes."*[25] Again, when Voltaire wished "Canada at the bottom of the Arctic Sea together with the reverend Jesuit fathers," or referred to Canada contemptuously as a waste of wilderness and snow, these were not absurd witticisms but faithful and brilliant summaries of the general disdain of French mercantilists for Canada, which in their eyes was a serious financial liability.[26] The Duke of Choiseul did not disagree with them when, in the Treaty of Paris, he vaunted himself on having trapped the English into returning the Antilles by ceding to them Canada, which he did not exhaust all efforts to retain. On the other hand, Voltaire grew rhapsodic when he spoke of Louisiana, "the most beautiful climate in the world, where one can grow tobacco, silk and indigo" and other subtropical produce. Ideas such as these, far from being a monopoly of the philosophers, were all but universal in France. Ministers shared them and, though they did not logically deduce their conduct from rigorously controlled premises, carried these premises in their minds nevertheless.[27]

A close examination of the European concept of empire, whether we call it the French *"exclusif"* or *"pacte colonial"* or "the old colo-

23 *De l'esprit des lois,* liv. XXI, chap. XVI.
24 R. P. Jameson, *Montesquieu et l'esclavage, étude sur les origines de l'opinion anti-esclavagiste en France au XVIII⁰ siècle* (Paris, 1911).
25 *Encyclopédie,* article on "colonie," Vol. V.
26 *Oeuvres complètes de Voltaire* (Paris, 1877-1885), XXXIX, 440.
27 A. Duchêne, *La politique coloniale de la France* (Paris, 1928), 93.

nial system" of Britain expressed in terms of the Acts of Trade and
Navigation, will indicate that the general presumption was still
largely in favor of tropical and subtropical colonies. Since at all
times and in all places the success of any colonial enterprise depends
on the question of labor and the sole solution of the labor problem
in these areas was slave labor, negro slavery became one of the basic
institutions of the old colonial system. The West Indies had become
enormous plantations where legions of blacks slaved to supply
Europeans with tropical produce. Since the life of the average negro
on a plantation was but seven years and negro slaves, for whatever
reason, did not multiply, incessant reinforcements were necessary.
Both the French and British empires were erected on the foundation of slave labor and vital imperial interests were at stake in the
competition of their nationals for the control of the African slave
trade. This trade had become one of the nerve centers of the old
imperialism, because it involved not merely the West Indies but
the trade of the two rival East India Companies and in some measure
that of the North American colonies.

In France the slave trade was a privileged industry and the
French government granted, on the basis of an ordinance of 1672,
a premium on the head of every negro transported to the new
world, a system that continued down to the end of the old regime.
In a letter which is as interesting for its psychology as for its argument the chamber of commerce of the city of Nantes contended that
colonial commerce was the principal source of the wealth of France,

. . . and the commerce of Guinea is so much the base of it, that if
French traders abandoned this branch of commerce, our colonies would
necessarily be provided with negroes by foreigners and by infallible
consequence with all the European goods which they consume; not only
would (France) be deprived of all the advantage of exportation, but
also of those colonial commodities which are necessary for our own consumption; in a word, the abandonment of the Guinea trade would
necessarily cause the loss of (all) colonial commerce. It follows that we
have no commerce so precious to the State as the Guinea trade which it
cannot do too much to protect.[28]

[28] Gaston-Martin, *L'ère des négriers* (Paris, 1931), 10; Dubuc, *Lettres critiques à M. Raynal*, 54.

That British traders held similar views may be seen from a letter of a West India merchant who claimed that,

> . . . British trade to the plantations . . . increases or diminishes in proportion to the numbers of negroes imported there, who produce the commodities with which our ships are usually loaded and enable the planters to live well and purchase great quantities of British commodities.[29]

For the prosperity of the British empire the African slave trade was even more important than for the French, who had only their sugar islands and the Isles of Bourbon to supply. African slaves were indispensable not only for the British sugar plantations, but for the production of rice and indigo in the Carolinas and of tobacco in Virginia and Maryland. This slave labor on subtropical plantations which produced but a single crop stimulated the vast provision trade of Ireland, Pennsylvania and New York and also the fisheries of Massachusetts Bay.[30] The African slave trade sustained the rum industry of New England and offered the greatest market for the coarse fabrics of the East India Company. Mercantilists considered it a valuable trade, for no cash was needed for the *carrera de Indias*. The rum made from the sugar cane of the islands was sent to produce drunkenness in Africa and Africa paid for it with kidnaped labor which was to grow more sugar cane to be worked into more rum to buy more slaves. The bills on Liverpool for sugar represented the profit. When the great Chatham thundered his eloquent defense of the cause of the "shugger islands" (for so he pronounced it) right or wrong, this was what he meant: the manufacture of delirium tremens with which to purchase cheap labor which could rapidly be used up at hand-worked sugar mills to produce more sugar to be sent through the same round.[31] Any attack on slavery or directly or indirectly on the slave trade would disorganize the entire plantation system. Therefore Montesquieu's denunciation of slavery and similar attacks of the Encyclopedists, while they created some public excitement, had no practical results. In England economists were still defending the slave trade as the

29 Quoted from C. M. MacInnes, *England and Slavery* (Bristol, 1934), 31; see also C. R. Fay *Imperial Economy* (Oxford, 1934), 10.
30 L. H. Gipson, *The British Empire before the American Revolution*, II, 315.
31 D. Hannay, *The Sea Trader*, 318.

most important branch of British commerce and the time had not yet come when a majority of Englishmen would declare that this evil must cease.

Next to slavery the salient trait of the empires of the old regime was their mercantilist character. Formally, these economic empires of the eighteenth century were not empires, but only expressions of economic imperialism. What is commonly called "the old colonial system" was not an end in itself, but merely a phase of a much wider scheme for the advantageous conduct of foreign trade.[32] The central problem of foreign trade, as the mercantilist saw it, was how to foster those trades that were favorable while eliminating those that were unfavorable. So long as the balance of trade was a fetish, it was only reasonable to develop trade with the colonies, where the balance could be regulated so as to be especially favorable to the motherland. Since in all countries colonial commerce held a favored place, the attempt to solve this focal problem gave a definite shape to colonial policy. Everywhere these attempts had produced elaborate and complicated legislative codes for regulating colonial commerce. In France they were embodied in the letters patent of 1717 and 1727 defining the *"exclusif,"* and in Great Britain in the Acts of Trade and Navigation, familiar to every student of colonial history. Both codes were calculated to achieve the same results. They combined encouragement with restraint and protection with prohibition; they sought to foster national interests, to keep profits among the members of the imperial family, to strike at enemies and add to the economic welfare and the political strength of both colonies and the mother country. If these codes, as Adam Smith later pointed out, were not the easiest way of increasing wealth, they at least indicated one way of securing national power and wealth at the same time. Unfortunately the system aimed at in these codes was never simple and its increasing elaboration and complexity prevented speedy revision and annually increased the

[32] C. R. Fay, *Imperial Economy* (Oxford, 1934); J. F. Rees, "The Phases of British Commercial Policy in the Eighteenth Century," *Economica*, V (1925), 130; and the brilliant and profound chapter by the same author, "Mercantilism and the Colonies," *Cambridge History of the British Empire* (Cambridge, 1929), I, 561 ff.; C. M. MacInnes, *An Introduction to the Economic History of the British Empire* (London, 1935), 139 ff.; for France see especially J. Tramond, *Le régime commercial des Antilles au XVIIIe siècle* (Paris, 1904).

strength of the vested interests. There was much confusion, contradiction and obsolescence everywhere and, what was worse, the system was already at variance with the realities of colonial economic life.

The basic principles underlying these mercantilist codes may be quickly summarized. If, as the mercantilist contended, the colonies were so many farms whose chief function was to supply the parent country with commodities which otherwise it would have to purchase from foreigners, their trade was merely a local branch of the trade of the parent country. Their existence apart from the mother country was inconceivable, and any tendency toward a separate economic life, which might in time develop into serious rivalry, merited stern and effectual discouragement. "It is a law founded on the very nature of colonies" said Postlethwayte in these years, "that they ought to have no other culture or arts wherein to rival the arts and culture of the parent country."[33] The system aimed at making the parent country at once the entrepôt for all important colonial staples, the bottleneck upon which colonial commerce converged, and the imperial workshop, whose manufactures enjoyed a monopoly in the colonial market. Imports and exports were to be a monopoly of the merchant marine. This last monopoly of the carrying trade was designed not only to support the shipping interests of the parent country, but to prevent the fraudulent introduction into the colonies of foreign merchandise and the exportation of colonial commodities to other countries. The whole scheme of a self-sufficing economic empire, which this system envisaged, had the supreme object of procuring that favorable balance of trade for the mother country which was the final objective of all colonial powers.

This combination of restrictions imposed and favors granted passed in France under the name of *pacte colonial*, as though there had been a kind of contract between the colony and the mother country. Theoretically, its terms appeared very seductive. It seemed to promote the prosperity of the colonies while it gave satisfaction to varied interests in the mother country. It promised to satisfy everyone, the colonists who were assured of selling their crops in the exclusive home market, the shippers who were assured of the

[33] M. Postlethwayte, *Britain's Commercial Interest Explained and Improved*, I, 153.

transport service, the home consumers and the industrialists, who had access to exotic commodities and a privileged market for their manufactured products, and even the national treasury, which was assured a certain revenue. Yet the entire scheme rested on a mistaken premise. It took for granted that colonial production and home consumption on the one hand and home productive capacity and colonial needs on the other would remain perfectly or nearly perfectly proportionate. But if the mother country could not produce or expedite to the colonies such articles as were indispensable, or if, being able to do so, she could supply them only at a much higher price than other countries could offer them, the system could not be made to function. The obligation to purchase very dearly in France what they could purchase very cheaply from their English or Dutch neighbors not only irritated the French colonists but stimulated their appetite for the great profits of illicit trade, the perpetual bogey of the mother country. Paradoxically enough, the system could be made to function only in the absurd hypothetical case where it became useless: if there were only one mother country with one set of colonies. The mere existence of other countries with colonies of their own was sufficient to throw the entire system out of balance, for competition, which no legislation could prevent, had its inevitable results.

The system did not work, notwithstanding the stubborn belief of French and British statesmen in its basic excellence. It defied realities. Many of its features were unenforcible and were not executed. Almost the only enforcible part of the Navigation Laws of Great Britain was that relating to the nationality of ships used in the colonial trade, but even that part might break down. The whole scheme suffered from superannuation and its great defect was that it could not be adjusted to the new situation without being scrapped or ignored. When the first Navigation Laws were passed in the third quarter of the seventeenth century it was still possible to think of the colonies as farms which produced raw materials for the English household. By 1750, however, the situation was entirely altered. The mercantilist had always been the mouthpiece of the merchant. But now the British merchant was becoming an industrial capitalist with an interest in the colonies that may be described as a manufacturers' imperialism. Whatever the Navigation Laws said to the contrary, manufacturing was developing also in the colonies.[34] Through no fault of their own the American colonies were not responding to the board of trade's policy of imperial self-sufficiency. In spite of their rapid development, their trade with the mother country remained relatively small, because they could not produce in quantity those "enumerated" commodities which the Navigation Laws earmarked for exportation to Great Britain.

It was inevitable that certain compromises, relaxations and exemptions should be made. The draconic severity of the French letters patent of 1727, prohibiting all colonial trade with foreign countries, was relaxed in favor of Irish and Danish salt beef; French traders were permitted to carry sugars to Spanish ports, and the wide tolerance of local colonial administrators went further still.[35] In the British system it was not the intention to center all imperial oceanic trade in England, nor did all the westbound trade have to pass through that country. Colonial fish was never on the "enumerated" list; rice could be sent to southern Europe after 1730, and the same privilege was extended to sugar after 1739. But these modifications did not touch the crucial problem. If French and English colonists found it more advantageous to purchase directly from another country and if the avoidance of their respective metropolitan ports lowered the shipping charges, they could and did resort to wholesale smuggling. The modern rumrunner has shown us how difficult it is to protect an extended coast line. In the eighteenth century, when coasts were inadequately patrolled and customs officers were few and ill-paid, when colonists either sympathized with or were directly interested in this "free trade," the system of the Navigation Acts worked only insofar as public opinion in the colonies thought it should work. It was the golden age of smugglers everywhere and, though it is difficult to estimate the extent of their activity, it was sufficient to raise serious doubts in the minds of many historians whether the system caused any real friction in the colonies at all.[36]

34 G. L. Beer, *British Colonial Policy, 1754-1765* (New York, 1907), 110; C. R. Fay, *Imperial Economy*, 8.

35 L. C. Wroth and G. L. Annan, *Acts of French Royal Administration Concerning Canada, Guiana, the West Indies and Louisiana, Prior to 1791* (New York, 1930), 1160, 1215, 1228.

36 J. F. Rees, *Cambridge History of the British Empire*, I, 592.

The late Professor Egerton summed up the situation as follows, "A state of things under which it appears to have cost between £7000 and £8000 to collect a revenue from £1000 to £2000 can scarcely be justified by the results."[37]

Any attempt to pronounce a final estimate on the balance of advantage and disadvantage of the system as it affected both colonies and mother countries will reveal the value of suspended judgment. Its effect was not everywhere the same. Nowhere were the interests of the colonists completely disregarded and no historian today will hazard the older view that it constituted an economy of oppression. The gains which the English continental colonists drew from shipping and bounties were a great compensation for the losses occasioned by the restriction on certain manufactures. In the French empire the system had the effect of making planters dependent on the merchants who, representing the mother country and defending the official doctrine, usually commanded the sympathy and support of the government. Furthermore, the French system did less to extend and develop French foreign commerce than to displace it. As for Great Britain there is, as Mr. Rees points out, no basis for making any precise generalization.[38] It was widely known that the Acts of Trade were extensively evaded both in the colonies and in Europe. But whatever the defects and difficulties of enforcement, contemporaries both in France and Great Britain were satisfied that the colonial system had attained its purpose of promoting prosperity and enhancing national power. The merchants of the French and British seaports were content. The seafaring population had abundant employment. All contended that statistics proved that the total volume of foreign trade had greatly increased and that colonial trade accounted for the largest portion of this increase. The modern economic historian may doubt whether the mercantilist legislation was responsible for this. Even if the Acts of Trade had been actually observed, it does not follow that trade would not have taken the same course even without their positive enactment. In fact the growing investment of private capital in colonial enterprise and the extension

[37] Quoted from C. M. MacInnes, *An Introduction to the Economic History of the British Empire* (London, 1935), 143.
[38] J. F. Rees, *Cambridge History of the British Empire*, I, 593.

of the new credit facilities may well have been a far more potent stimulus than the doubtful authority of the Acts of Trade.

III. THE WEST INDIES

In the ubiquitous commercial competition between Great Britain and France, the West Indies occupied a pivotal position. They were not merely the greatest centers of production for the muscovado and sugar markets of Europe, but the focal point of the entire commercial competition of the two nations. The sugar islands were exploitation colonies pure and simple and almost every necessity of civilized life, including slave labor, had to be taken out to them. The provision and the slave trade had become inseparable features of plantation economy. The French government had been no more successful than the English in its effort to force the islands to grow their own supplies of food. In time of war this dependence produced a dangerous situation, for a blockade which cut off either the supply of slaves or of provisions made surrender inevitable.

Notwithstanding their precarious strategic situation the French sugar islands were more productive and prosperous than the British. With St. Domingue, Martinique and Guadeloupe at the head of the list, the French islands with their fresher soils constituted one of the most profitable of all colonial possessions.[39] The sugar production of St. Domingue alone surpassed the total production of all the British West Indies. It has already been pointed out that the French had effectively crowded British sugars out of the continental market. But in the eyes of the British merchant the situation became serious when he learned that the French were increasing their African trade, were drawing provisions and lumber from Ireland and the North American colonies, and, with their tropical products, were actually, though indirectly, invading the British market itself.[40]

However much the French might idealize their West Indian possessions, the mercantilist scheme worked no better in the sugar islands than it did elsewhere. Metropolitan monopoly of colonial

39 J. Tramond in Hanotaux-Martineau, *Les colonies française* (Paris, 1929), I, 443; L. Vignols, *Les Antilles françaises sous l'ancien régime* (Paris, 1928); M. Satineau, *Histoire économique et sociale de Guadeloupe* (Paris, 1928); A. Martineau, *Trois siècles d'histoire antillaise* (Paris, 1935).

40 F. Pitman, *The Development of the British West Indies*, 282; C. M. Andrews, "Anglo-French Commercial Rivalry," *Am. Hist. Rev.*, XX (1915), 552.

trade was not oppressive to the English planter and the factor was often no more than his agent. But in the French empire the merchant and planter were enemies, engaged in a perpetual warfare of prices, and in this contest the French merchant had the greater bargaining power. The French colonists paid a higher price for imperial self-sufficiency. French slave traders could not or did not supply more than one half of the number of slaves which their islands absorbed, and the higher French shipping rates raised the cost of planter provisions to a price level that was from one-fourth to one-third above that of the British and Dutch shippers.[41] Since the French colonists were unwilling to immolate themselves for the concept of a self-contained empire, which possessed little reality to them, it was inevitable that they should seek to balance accounts by a wholesale illicit traffic with the North American colonies of Great Britain.

These British continental colonies and the entire group of West Indian islands were made for mutual trade and intercourse. Each depended on the other from a very early date in the history of the colonies. Nowhere in the western world was the population increasing so rapidly as in the northern colonies and, as the farmers and lumbermen of Pennsylvania and New York extended their production, their merchants began to frequent the French West Indian markets to sell there the surplus which the British islands could not consume. In exchange they sought not merely the by-products of sugar, rum and molasses, the disposal of which the French government allowed, but French sugar and cotton which they needed for their own consumption but might, on occasion, transship to London as English produce. In addition the slavers of old and New England were perpetually haunting the coasts of the French islands to sell their cheaper slaves. It was only natural that this trade, however necessary to the prosperity of the French plantations, should arouse violent complaints from the interested parties in both France and Great Britain. The slavers of Nantes, the French East India Company, the linen and milling interests, all objected to seeing their colonial monopoly diluted. Again and again they appealed to the French authorities to enforce the penalties against smuggling. But all efforts to stop the trade were unavailing and American colonial

41 P. de Vaissière, *Saint-Domingue* (Paris, 1909), 33.

vessels continued to put into the French island ports, alleging the necessity of illusory repairs whose costs could be defrayed only by selling the cargo.

In England also nearly everyone still considered the West Indian islands to be the most important and valuable part of the British empire. The North American colonies had long hugged their wealth. Commercially they were less dependent on England and their export trade was firmly rooted in foreign markets. The British West Indies, on the other hand, had yielded and were still yielding great fortunes, in many cases to absentee proprietors who had become the great vested West India interest in London. In the preceding decades this West India interest had become a dominant factor in the control of British colonial policy. Yet a shift in the center of gravity of the British empire was already becoming dimly visible. In spite of the vast profits of the sugar and the still greater profits of the slave trade, the continental colonies after 1750 were already a far more important market for British manufactures than the West Indies. While the population in the northern colonies was increasing, in the West Indies it seemed to be arrested. The production of the English islands was not increasing as fast as the demand in the home market. Indeed, in Barbados and the Leeward Islands production was actually declining. The smaller British islands were so fully cultivated that they could hardly yield more. Jamaica alone, only one third of whose rich soil was under cultivation, had room for more plantations and seems to have increased its crop steadily through war and peace.[42] Experience had shown that only large *latifundia* had a capacity for survival, while many of the small white cultivators were driven out of business or were compelled to emigrate to Dutch and Danish islands. It was evident that the British islands had ceased to attract new capital investment. Seven-eighths of the plantations were burdened with old debts and could be retained by their owners only under favorable conditions.[43] Though this was neither unique (it was also true of the French islands) nor serious, in time of war old creditors became anxious about the security of their debts and often

42 W. J. Gardner, *History of Jamaica* (London, 1873), 156.
43 F. Pitman, "The Settlement and Financing of British West India Plantations," *Essays in Colonial History by Students of Charles McLean Andrews*, 252.

refused to make new advances. The prosperity of the planter class had become visibly unstable.

This situation may serve to explain the frantic efforts of the planter's association and of the London West India interest to keep up the price of sugar and recover their lost monopoly in the British imperial market. In the first they were reasonably successful. The prices of West India produce improved steadily after the thirties, and the planters could afford to buy more, although the size of their crops remained nearly the same.[44] The latter problem however, remained intractable. The great gap between North American production and British West Indian consumption grew wider from year to year. So long as the New England, New York and Philadelphia traders could buy French sugar at prices from twenty-five to thirty per cent cheaper than those of Barbados and the Leeward Islands and French molasses for what they were willing to pay, their provision trade with the French islands was bound to increase in peace or war. The Molasses Act of 1733 was not executed and customs officials winked at its systematic infraction. Nor could the West Indian planters make much use of the privilege of exporting sugar to southern Europe, granted by the Act of 1739, first because the law was clogged with numerous restrictions, second because the French and Portuguese could undersell them in Mediterranean markets. All their efforts to make capital out of the unpatriotic character of the "flag of truce" trade between the continental colonists and the French islands in the last war were doomed to failure. A last attempt was made by the West India interest after 1749 to transform the Molasses Act into a statute which aimed at absolute prohibition of all American commercial intercourse with the French islands. But neither the board of trade nor parliament seriously entertained legislation so drastic and so obviously prejudicial to the American colonies. The West India interest was plainly losing its former dominant influence. Between 1750 and 1756 the blustering planters had to confine themselves to passing in their island legislatures a series of laws prohibiting trade with the French. It had become obvious that for the British West Indies the path of patriotism was iden-

[44] R. Pares, *War and Trade in the West Indies*, 475.

tical with their own interests. For the continental colonies it had already become impossible to cease trading with the French islands in peace or war since their very livelihood depended upon it. The quarrel, therefore, did not end here. It was, in fact, only the prelude to those disputes which arose in time of war over the propriety of trading with the enemy.

The Anglo-French rivalry in the West Indies was purely commercial, although any provocative incident might stir up a naval conflict between the two powers. Such an incident was provided by the French occupation of some of the neutral islands, a group of smaller islands (St. Lucia, St. Vincent, Dominica, Tobago) in the chain that lines the Caribbean Sea to windward. In view of the weakness of the French navy, this policy of territorial expansion was no less imprudent than the French occupation of the Ohio valley. The French settlers on these islands outnumbered the English and very little stood in the way of making them officially French possessions. What made an international issue of them was the fact that they were a capital base for English smugglers and the fear of British planters that they might be used to harbor French privateers in a renewal of the war which all expected. An Anglo-French agreement to evacuate them until the Delimitation Commission had examined their respective claims proved to be a sham on both sides. For a time the French entertained a plan of offering them to Frederick the Great of Prussia, but he, having no navy, refused to accept them. When finally the governor of Martinique seized St. Lucia in retaliation against Boscawen's capture of the *Alcide* and *Lys*, he gave the signal for the opening of the war in the West Indies.

More successful were the British in retaining their supremacy in the African slave trade. With more than a hundred and fifty ships engaged in the trade the British slavers averaged some twelve thousand slaves annually while the French average did not rise much above seven thousand. The British possessed fourteen forts on the Gold Coast and were setting to work to crowd their French rivals off the entire littoral. Although it was a recognized principle that the sovereignty of the Africans was unimpaired by these forts, the British contended that in the regions of their stations they had the right to exclude all foreign ships.[45] In certain areas, particularly at Anamaboe, which supplied more slaves than all the other coasts together, the British succeeded in excluding the French entirely. In the bloody encounters between the rival slavers, which became a matter of common occurrence, the merchants of both countries called upon their respective governments for intervention. The governments, however, instead of negotiating from court to court, resorted to naval demonstrations. Since the reorganization of the Royal African Company by the Act of 1750, which threw the trade open to independent merchants, parliament appropriated considerable sums annually for the maintenance of British forts and factories. Compared with this generous support which the British traders obtained from parliament and the navy, the occasional dispatch of a French man-of-war was relatively ineffective. When France sent out two ships, Britain sent three. But the enterprising slavers of Nantes refused to accept this situation with resignation. Expelled from Anamaboe, they sought out the Wydah and Angola coasts and traded with remarkable success. They armed certain tribes against their pro-British neighbors and paid regular tributes to certain African chiefs with a view to obtaining concessions which were not unlike those obtained by Dupleix in India, except that they were on a more modest scale. Never before did the French have so many ships in the trade and never were their cargoes more numerous. In spite of all the obstacles which the British placed in their path, the volume of the French slave trade surpassed all previous records.

IV. INDIA

India, it need scarcely be pointed out, was not an integral part of the French and British imperial systems. India was a foreign country and for Frenchmen and Englishmen alike the Indian and far eastern trade were merely local branches of their foreign commerce in the keeping of privileged companies. It should be remembered that down to the end of the century European mercantilists rated the West Indian far above the East Indian trade. In the mid-century Britain's Indian and far eastern trade amounted to scarcely

[45] W. H. Wyndham, *The Atlantic and Slavery* (Oxford, 1935), 5; Eliz. Donnan, *Documents Illustrative of the History of the Slave Trade to America*, II, 109-113.

one half that of the West Indies, and India was never more than a minor contributor to the wealth of France. The brilliant exploits of Dupleix and Bussy left most Frenchmen indifferent. The fact, however, that this Indian trade had become closely interlocked with the African and West Indian trades gave it an especial importance. From the West Indies came, besides tropical produce, a great quantity of bullion and specie mostly of Spanish origin. Much of the latter was re-exported to India, where it was exchanged for cottons and calicoes. These, in turn, were shipped from England to the African coasts to be exchanged for slaves or directly to the West Indies to clothe negroes on the plantations. Although this heavy export of bullion coincident with the Indian trade still aroused serious misgivings among English mercantilists, the argument of the company that its trade finally brought more bullion into the country than it shipped out was generally accepted.

Whether or not this export of bullion was harmful, the steady progress of the English East India Company enabled it to pay a dividend of eight per cent, where it remained down to 1755.[46] The less fortunate French company could meet its dividend payments only because of its tobacco monopoly, which bore no relation to the vicissitudes of oriental commerce. It owed its advantageous situation to state protection and its shareholders not unnaturally regarded themselves as *rentiers* to whom the royal treasury owed a fixed revenue. Although its capital was extensive and its revenues considerable, state tutelage discouraged initiative among the directors of the company.[47]

It goes without saying that we are here concerned less with Indian affairs than with the position of Europeans in India in the mid-century. This position varied in independence as one proceeded from northern to southern India. In the north, in Bengal, European factories were strictly supervised and neither the French nor the British were permitted to strengthen or enlarge their fortifications. On the Orissa coast the local nawabs, who had usually purchased

46 H. H. Dodwell, "British India," in *Cambridge History of the British Empire* (Cambridge, 1929), IV, 109.

47 W. H. Dalgliesh, *The Perpetual Company of the Indies in the Days of Dupleix* (Philadelphia, 1933), 58; A. Martineau, *Dupleix et l'Inde française* (Paris, 1920), I, 38; Virginia Thompson, *Dupleix and His Letters* (New York, 1934), 70.

their offices from the subahdar of the Deccan, often sought to in-
demnify themselves by imposing heavy duties on Europeans. Only
in the south, on the Coromandel coast, did Europeans hold fortified and garrisoned cities like Madras and Pondichéry. This relatively independent position of the French in the south was the
starting point of Dupleix's political experiments. In the last war the
two rival companies had defended their commercial privileges; they
had not fought for political predominance in southern India. But
their relations were radically altered by Dupleix's policy which, at
least so far as India was concerned, was new.

Since the publication of the searching treatises of Cultru, Dodwell
and Martineau, it need scarcely be pointed out that Dupleix's policy
of political intervention and territorial dominion in India was not
derived from any theoretical speculation on colonization, but was
the empirical result of temporary expedients provoked by the position of affairs in the neighborhood of Pondichéry after the Succession War.[48] It is well known that Dupleix did not formulate his
views into a coherent doctrine until the circumstances which led to
his recall forced him to justify his conduct to the directors in Paris in
his famous *mémoire* of October 16, 1753.

The point of departure of Dupleix's policy was the maladjustment
between the Parisian control of the company's finances and its Indian
branches, which could make purchases only with such funds as were
remitted to them from France. Experience had shown that the vessels sent out by the company often arrived either too late or not at all,
with the result that at critical moments funds were lacking. So long
as both companies found it necessary to maintain diminutive mercenary armies to defend their trading stations, this chronic lack of
funds might prove disastrous. To prevent soldiers from deserting
Dupleix had frequently spent his own money and even pledged his
own credit. In the competitive system that prevailed among Europeans in India, he was convinced, the company could not support
itself by the profits of trade alone; what was needed was the control
of a territory large enough to guarantee "a fixed and constant income," rents, taxes, monopolies, and tributes paid by Indian poten-

[48] P. Cultru, *Dupleix, ses plans politiques, sa disgrace* (Paris, 1901), 288; H. H. Dodwell, *Dupleix and Clive* (London, 1920); A. Martineau, *Dupleix et l'Inde française*
(Paris, 1928), IV, 205.

tates. Up to this time the two rival companies had relied upon purely commercial methods for the extension of their trade. Now Dupleix became alive to the possibility of exploiting political methods also. He aimed at the exercise of a protectorate over local Indian rulers, at assigning to their courts French agents who would advise them and a military force to give authority to their advice. The commercial and financial advantages to be derived from such a system were obvious. The central point of his doctrine, as explained in the *mémoire* of October 16, 1753, was to collect a "fixed and constant revenue" from the native states of India. That Dupleix was an imperialist, that his objective was political and territorial dominion is beyond dispute. It is quite another matter to ask whether political dominion was his prime inspiration. Since his foremost concern was after all the extension of commerce, this appears to be very unlikely.

As this policy gradually unfolded itself, Dupleix was at great pains to reassure the Paris directors that its execution required no additional company funds. To procure funds it would only be necessary to wage war in India; it would be quite enough if the company sent out soldiers, who would fall to the charge of native Indian princes. It has already been pointed out that the Paris directors and the king considered it dangerous and imprudent to interfere in the affairs of the native Indian princes with the thought of profiting from their quarrels. They did not conceal their indignation when they learned that Dupleix had embarked on a double war in the Carnatic and in the Deccan. This war represented a complete reversal of the policy of the company. Dupleix, it must be admitted, had no illusions about the difficulty of obtaining their approval for his projects. Until 1753 he did not reveal to them the full scope of his program; he exaggerated his successes, minimized his reverses and announced repeatedly that a lasting peace was close at hand. Experience in the Succession War had taught him that, if he were successful, he might be rewarded for acts which the directors would never have permitted had they been on the ground. Convinced that success justifies audacity, he proceeded on his own responsibility. He therefore played a desperate game when, without the consent of his company and even against its will, he embarked on an enterprise which aimed at a vast French empire in the equatorial triangle of India. To the execution of this grandiose project he brought brilliant qualities of mind and character, a genuine heroism and tenacity of purpose, a magnificent resourcefulness and ability. But he lacked the sense of measure of a true statesman in gauging the difficulties that obstructed his path. The war-ridden provinces which he controlled did not produce the revenues he expected and his army was too inadequate for the consolidation of his conquests. If he failed in the end, he at least revealed to the British the secrets of empire and the British have never failed to do homage to his genius.

The immediate opportunity for putting his policy to the test presented itself to Dupleix in 1749 when a double succession quarrel arose in two native Indian states, in the Carnatic in the southeast and in the Deccan to the north. Two rival claimants, one desirous of seizing the Carnatic, the other the Deccan, appealed to Dupleix for assistance. The fact that the subahdars of the Deccan in theory possessed the authority to appoint the nawabs of the Carnatic, which they regarded as a dependency, made the situation all the more tempting. Dupleix promptly placed some officers and troops at their disposal, on condition that they pay all the expenses and grant him such favors as he might think he had a right to expect. Both French candidates were, for the moment, successful. They rewarded their French benefactors with certain territorial and financial grants. But these territorial concessions, coupled with the prospects of a French protégé dominating the Carnatic, alarmed the English. Fearing that their commerce, if not completely ruined, would be at the mercy of France, the English company became the champion of those princes whom the French had either dispossessed or threatened. The English thus entered into the same sort of agreement with the ruler of Tanjore and Muhammed Ali, the dispossessed pretender to the Carnatic, as Dupleix had made with the successful nawab of the Carnatic. Knowing that peace treaties in Europe forbade open hostilities in India, the two rival companies engaged themselves as the auxiliaries of their respective clients in India. They fought against each other not as principals, but indirectly, thus following the precedent established in Europe during the Austrian Succession War. All the early opposition of the directors at home failed to prevent their Indian branches from becoming so deeply involved that the issue between

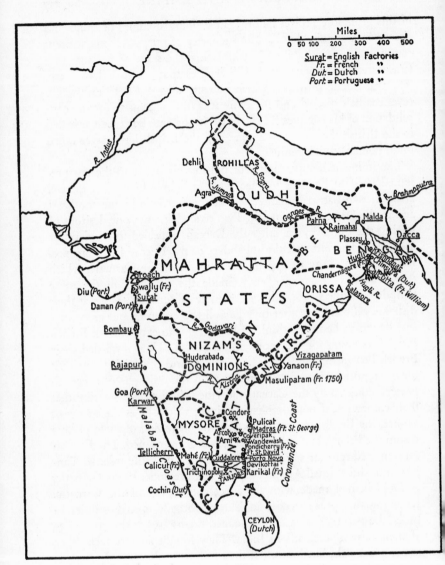

INDIA

them presently became one for the domination of India itself. As was inevitable in India, military strategy was at the mercy of finance and Dupleix, finding himself with a deficit of several million livres, was soon compelled to raise loans and throw his personal resources into the scales. Thanks to the brilliant statesmanship of his lieutenant, Bussy, he was successful in the Deccan. But his war with the English and Muhammed Ali over the Carnatic led him ever deeper into the bog at Trichinopoly.

In the Carnatic the English had a decided military advantage over the French, not because they had more or better troops but because in Stringer Lawrence and Robert Clive they had two officers of initiative and audacity. Dupleix never succeeded in counterbalancing this British superiority of command, at least not until he discovered the energetic Mainville, but then it was already too late. The entire success of the campaign depended on the reduction of Trichinopoly in the south. But Dupleix's best officer, Bussy, was immobilized in the Deccan, where, though victorious, he could contribute nothing to a final triumph. It was before the walls of Trichinopoly and not in Hyderabad where Dupleix's fate was ultimately decided.

This division of his forces, a major strategical error, gave the English time and opportunity for making that breach in the French position which finally caused the entire structure to collapse. In the north Bussy soon proved himself to be a statesman of consummate capacity and wisdom, a great personality who remains one of the brilliant figures of French colonial history. For seven years he retained his mastery over the Deccan. He carried out his purpose without brutality and showed how a European could manage a native ruler less by force than by the gentler methods of diplomacy. Clive later did not disdain to profit from Bussy's wise example. Yet it remains doubtful whether the control of the Deccan was worth all the trouble which Dupleix expended upon it. Bussy's expedition, in spite of all the concessions he obtained, was never more than self-sufficing. Compared with the vast resources which the English later drew from Bengal, the sun-scorched plains of the Deccan were, as Dodwell suggests, not worth having.[49] The truth is that, once hav-

[49] H. Dodwell, *Dupleix and Clive*, 99; A. Martineau, *Bussy et l'Inde française* (Paris, 1935).

ing occupied the Deccan, Dupleix could not abandon it, lest the English fill the vacuum created by the French withdrawal. Thus while Bussy was marching his troops from Hyderabad to Poona or Nagpur, Dupleix exhausted his remaining forces in an utterly useless siege of Trichinopoly. There he lost what he had gained in the Deccan.

The policy of Dupleix failed less because of the systematic and blind opposition of the company than because of the mistaken calculations of its governor, who promised more than he could perform. No doubt it is true that when Clive compelled the French forces to capitulate on the island of Srirangam (June, 1752), the French cause in the Carnatic was still far from hopeless. Dupleix, at his best in such desperate circumstances, redoubled his activity; he succeeded in sowing dissension between the English and their native allies and, having at last found in Mainville an officer whom he could trust, he resumed the offensive in almost every quarter. But it was too late. The news of the disaster of Srirangam, reaching Paris as it did by way of London, precipitated the board's decision to recall Dupleix. In the ensuing controversy between Dupleix and the company, the latter had the better argument. To be sure, by their tacit acceptance of Dupleix's conquests, the directors had, in a certain sense, committed themselves to his policy. Implicitly they had contracted financial obligations which it was wrong later to repudiate. Yet for three years they had advised him to come to terms as soon as possible and to conform to the commercial character of the company. Above all, the French company was not willing to stake its trade on the issue of a serious war with its English rival. Dupleix's calculations had missed fire; he had counted on a short limited war, and now, thanks to English opposition, the struggle appeared to drag on endlessly. With his forces badly divided he had attempted too much. The board had at its disposal hostile sources of information from India which denounced his plans as a house of cards. His own denatured reports, never quite describing the situation as it actually was, awakened their worst suspicions. There seemed to be no way of enforcing their instructions short of his recall. Machault, the secretary of state for the navy, thinking that this latent conflict with Great Britain might at any time lead to an open war which the king wanted to avoid, favored it. He feared that France might lose everything, if she risked her fortune in Europe, Canada and India at the same time. The defense of Canada, which was an actual possession, was a national obligation, but France as yet had no really vital interest in India. In view of the determined English opposition the future of Dupleix's colonial empire appeared still too problematical.[50]

It is quite possible that the recall of Dupleix sealed the fate of the French empire in India, but it is by no means certain. Godeheu, who was sent out to India to replace Dupleix, was not altogether that stupid imbecile for which he has been sometimes held. He came, of course, to liquidate the policy of Dupleix and to restore peace by making the most humiliating concessions. Had his peace treaty with the English company been carried out, France would have lost almost everything. But this treaty was not executed. Whatever our judgment of Godeheu, he did not in fact abandon any of the actual conquests which Dupleix and Bussy had made. When he left India the French still held half of the Carnatic, the entire Orissa coast, the four circars, and Bussy was still in control of the Deccan. But political and economic motives had now become so thoroughly interwoven that it had become impossible for the French and English to live side by side without serious quarrels. The wrangling soon began again, even before the news of the outbreak of the war in Europe was known in India.

V. NORTH AMERICA AND THE OUTBREAK OF THE WAR

Local and desultory clashes between French and British traders in the four quarters of the globe had become the normal accompaniment of the purely commercial rivalry of two expanding nations. But they were not sufficiently provocative to force their home governments into an armed conflict. Although the French had outstripped their competitors in many important branches of industry and although commercial rivalry tended in some areas to become one for territorial dominion, there was ample room for both in the West Indies, in India and on the African coasts. North America, in spite of its limitless expanses of unsettled woodland and plain, was another matter. It was the conflict over their undefined and over-

[50] A. Martineau, *Dupleix, sa vie et son oeuvre* (Paris, 1931), 275.

lapping claims to this unmeasured and uncharted American hinterland, a military and not in the first instance a commercial issue, that was the determining cause of the Seven Years' War.

Nowhere did the violent contrast between the two competing imperial units leap so sharply to the eye as on the North American continent. The thirteen English colonies were effective settlements with seaports and commercial communities that rivaled those of England and with an expanding agricultural population that pressed ever farther inland. But they were conspicuously devoid of military organization and adequate leadership. The French occupation of the waterways of the St. Lawrence, the Great Lakes and the Mississippi betrayed the military and absolutistic tradition of France at every step. In Canada every *habitant* from fifteen to sixty years of age was subject to military service and the militia was as vital an institution as the standing army was in France. In the event of another war with Great Britain this military superiority might be maintained, at least for successful defense, if the French navy could dispute the British control of the sea long enough to transport reinforcements to the scene of conflict. But once the reduced peace establishment of the British navy was placed on a war footing and the mastery of the seas passed, as was probable, to the English, the French military superiority was of doubtful value. In the meantime many a member of the English board of trade might envy the coordination and unity of administration and command, the superior technical precision with which the French monarchy managed its imperial affairs. Beside this impressive front the great sprawling mass of the independent and recalcitrant British colonies, with their divergent interests and particularist traditions, appeared weak and defenseless.

Yet this front lacked a substantial background. The effective French settlement, extending in a narrow corridor along the St. Lawrence from Montreal to Quebec, contained at most a population of sixty-five thousand. Beyond this there was nothing but a network of forts, roaming *voyageurs*, hunters and trappers. It has already been pointed out that in France Canada was generally regarded as a bastard colony, a colony of an inferior type. By all the standards of mercantilist principles Canada was a liability, even if its defense was necessary as a matter of national prestige. It did not yield sufficient revenues to meet the needs of local government. Its imports always exceeded its exports, with the result that the colony became a burdensome charge on the mother country. But for the financial resources regularly sent out by the royal treasury for the payment of officials and public works, the colony could scarcely have survived. Canadian commerce was never considerable. The fifteen ships that went out from France to Quebec in good years were a small average.[51] Its sole important export, the fur trade, was, to be sure, of enormous value, but the profits of the fur trade were so fantastically variable that it was impossible to base the economic existence of the colony upon it.[52] In Montreal and Quebec the exorbitant pretensions of the priests and monks of the Catholic Church, which guarded with jealousy its right to exclude religious dissenters, hampered the development of the colony. They alone held more than two million *arpents* of arable land, while the laity held less than six million. At the beginning of the century almost one half of all the *habitants* were concentrated on ecclesiastical *seigneuries*. Indeed, French Canada narrowly escaped being a second Paraguay. Above all, New France did not possess the expansive energy that was the most striking trait of the English colonies. The fur trade absorbed the enterprising elements of the rural population. Due to the seigneurial regime, which involved a rigid and paternalistic system of economic control, Canadian agriculture was primitive and the methods of cultivation were extremely careless. The colony, instead of thrusting vigorously outward, tended rather to fold in upon itself. Because of the seigneurial laws of inheritance the holdings of the Canadian peasant, extending along both banks of the St. Lawrence, became steadily narrower as each concession was parceled out in lots of diminishing area.[53] Thus, even if France succeeded in dispatching a large army to the new world, it was more than doubtful that Canadian agriculture could support it.

[51] J. Tramond, in Hanotaux-Martineau, *Histoire des colonies françaises* (Paris, 1928), I, 121.

[52] L. Vignols, "La mise en valeur du Canada à l'époque française," *Revue l'histoire économique et sociale* (1928), XVI, 773; H. A. Innes, *The Fur Trade in Canada* (New Haven, 1929); J. W. Jewdwine, *Studies in Empire and Trade* (London, 1923), 326.

[53] J. E. Lunn, "Agriculture and War in Canada, 1740-1763," *Canadian Historical Review* (1935), XVI, 125.

Opposed to the French Canadians, who accepted without difficulty the feudal and monarchical institutions of their mother country, were the Puritans of New England, who were inspired by an insane jealousy of aristocracy and monarchy in any form, and by an undying hatred of the Catholic Church. In religion they represented the "dissidence of dissent"; politically they were rooted in the Cromwellian tradition; in every aspect of social life they sought to subordinate the claims of society to the advantage of the individual. While the French *habitant* cherished loyalty and respect for his mother country, the English settlers met every interference in American colonial affairs with jealousy and resentment. New France accepted only Frenchmen as settlers and, such as they were, the *habitants* were lamentably wanting in initiative and a vivid sense of individual responsibility. The thriving English colonies, on the contrary, exercised a potent attraction on people of different nationalities and varied religious persuasion, and these independent and assertive spirits were naturally inclined to push forward from the coast into the great possibilities of the beyond. Everywhere the English colonists were pressing westward, and everywhere French soldiers were preparing to drive them back. People from New England and New York were moving toward Canada on the St. Lawrence and Lake Ontario; Pennsylvania was marking out new counties ever farther westward; farther south settlers, traders and land speculators from Virginia were advancing into the Ohio country, which France claimed as her exclusive possession. When the final test of strength with France came, the English colonists, numbering perhaps a million and a half, constituted the wealthiest and most vigorous white settlements to be found anywhere, while New France, though entrenched at every strategical point on the North American continent, could throw into the balance besides her fifteen thousand militiamen only a paltry two thousand colonial regulars. It is not likely that the advancing tide of English settlers would permit a handful of Frenchmen to cut in behind them with the avowed intention of excluding them from the entire interior of the continent. It was already too late for France to attain the objective for which she was striving. The disparity between the two contending colonial units was already too overwhelming.

It must be said that neither the French government at Versailles nor its Canadian governors shared this view of comparative fighting effectives. In both of the focal areas under dispute, in Acadia and in the Ohio valley, they embarked on a vigorous defensive. Claiming that the Treaty of Utrecht had not ceded to Great Britain the northern portion of modern Nova Scotia, the French governors promptly began to establish two new posts, Fort Beausejour opposite the English Fort Lawrence and Fort Gaspareau on Baie Verte, and redoubled their efforts to spread discontent among the French Acadians of Nova Scotia. But the conflict soon became localized in the contested zone of the Ohio valley, which the French claimed on the double ground of discovery and actual possession. Governor La Galissonnière, the originator of the grandiose scheme for occupying the land between the Appalachians and the Mississippi, had been convinced by one reputed to be an expert in these matters, that to allow the English to strike root in the Ohio valley would expose the entire area as far as the Mississippi, would endanger the line of communication between Canada and Louisiana, would deprive the French of their influence over the Indians in these regions, and would endanger the very existence of Canada itself.[54] The ministers at Versailles firmly supported him and issued definite instructions to his immediate successors, de la Jonquière and Duquesne, to expel all English traders and settlers from these regions. All these French governors were soldiers rather than diplomats and they regarded the situation confronting France in America as one might expect a soldier to view a purely military problem. Underestimating the potential forces which lay dormant and in disorder among the mutually jealous English colonies, they began to pour troops into the country and erect a line of forts from Fort Presentation on the St. Lawrence to Crèvecoeur in the Illinois country. By 1753 there were as many as fifteen hundred troops in the Ohio valley. Duquesne completed the work when in 1754, after expelling the Virginians, he built Fort Duquesne, the last link in the chain of forts, at the junction of the Allegheny and Monongahela rivers, making it the center of French power on the Ohio.[55]

[54] J. Tramond in HanotauxMartineau, *Histoire des colonies françaises* (Paris, 1928), I, 146.

[55] R. Waddington, *Le renversement des alliances*, 20.

The cumulative effect of these claims and the measures taken to enforce them made an intercolonial war in America inevitable, whatever might be the ultimate bargain between the powers in Europe. It was especially the Virginians who were aroused. The traders who had been expelled belonged for the most part to the influential Ohio Company, which had been formed in 1749 with capital coming partly from the great Virginian estate-owners, the Lees, Fairfaxes and Washingtons, and partly from London merchants. The formation of this company was the most conspicuous, if not the first, effort on the part of land speculators and potential settlers to take possession of this region. The raising of the French flag in the disputed country was quickly answered by Governor Dinwiddie of Virginia, who sent the young George Washington to the French forts in the Alleghenies to warn the invaders that they were on territory "notoriously known to be the property of the Crown of Great Britain."[56] Here two rival and equally irreconcilable claims confronted each other. The French refused categorically to withdraw and the reinforcements they sent to Fort Duquesne gave them an overwhelming local superiority. Washington, who was sent to expel them, became involved in a typical border incident in which a French officer, Jumonville, was killed. He was presently forced to surrender at Fort Necessity and retreat across the Alleghenies. The merely local opposition of the Virginian empire builders had failed and the French forward movement was for the moment triumphant. But these incidents produced a great jolt in the English colonies and from this time forward the French and English were actually though not professedly at war. Governor Dinwiddie saw that if the danger of an invasion of Virginia was to be averted and the future development of the English colonies safeguarded, direct assistance from England was imperative. The question thus arose, would the home governments acquiesce, negotiate or fight.

Important as was the place of the American colonies in the old British empire, it is well known that in England they were not cherished. Even the narrowest mercantilist admitted their value as a market for English manufacturers, but this fact apparently did not

[56] Osgood, *The American Colonies in the XVIIIth Century*, IV, 290.

weigh sufficiently with the imperial authorities to balance their insolent independence and their persistent violation of mercantile restrictive enactments. It is not too much to say that, but for the perpetual French menace, many Englishmen would gladly have abandoned the New England colonies. But whatever their economic shortcomings, in a conflict with France their strategical importance might prove decisive. For this reason alone they had to be protected and maintained. But this is not the same thing as saying that an open collision between the colonists had made the Seven Years' War between Great Britain and France unavoidable. This war became inevitable only at the moment when the two governments, neglecting to explore the possibilities of a pacific solution, declared their unreserved solidarity with their clashing colonists.

Notwithstanding its indubitably provocative measures in the new world, a general war with Great Britain was not part of the design of the French government. For the sake of peace it had sacrificed Dupleix in India, and, as the sequel amply proved, it was prepared to suffer the most humiliating indignities to avoid a general war. In England also the Duke of Newcastle, the very antithesis of a wild imperialist, thought it reckless to risk a war with France. When the colonial danger signals flashed, his eyes were fixed on Europe, where British diplomacy was engaged in the futile effort to revive the defunct "old system." An act of aggression, he thought, would snap the slender ties which still bound Holland to England. Moreover, Sir Benjamin Keene, the British ambassador in Madrid, had reported that he was hopeful of detaching Spain from France only so long as England avoided the appearance of aggression.[57] This bugbear of an eventual alliance between France and Spain and the consequent pooling of their financial and naval resources frightened Newcastle into extreme diplomatic caution. He wanted, above all, to avoid the repetition of Britain's unhappy experience in the last war, in which France defeated on the Continent Britain's victories on the seas. He was, therefore, in favor of temporizing on the colonial issue until his continental schemes had matured.

Such a policy, far from being ridiculous, was difficult to pursue

[57] Sir Richard Lodge, *The Private Correspondence of Sir Benjamin Keene* (London, 1935); by the same author, "Sir Benjamin Keene," *Royal Historical Society Transactions*, Fourth Series, XV (1932), 26.

in the midst of an angry and outraged people. Its obvious weakness lay in the fact that Newcastle made no honest effort to sift the real intentions of the French government or to specify a formula to meet the difficulties of the situation. Mirepoix, the French ambassador in London, who had been instructed to come to some amicable agreement with Newcastle, was also notoriously ignorant of colonial affairs. Thus, neither from England nor from France was any deliberate policy on the colonial issue forthcoming. Having no settled convictions on colonial affairs, Newcastle fell an easy prey to the relentless pressure of the war party in England.[58] The Duke of Cumberland and Henry Fox, supported by William Pitt, who wished to embarrass Newcastle and render himself necessary, employed every means calculated to precipitate England into a general war with France. Cumberland, who passed for the leader of the war party, had made up his mind, erroneously as we know, that France intended war and that the time had come to assert British rights by military means even without waiting for a formal declaration of war.[59] With more hesitation Lord Anson, at the head of the admiralty, shared this view.[60] Step by step Newcastle was compelled to yield ground to the war party until England was so deeply committed in America that war followed as a matter of course.

The first step was taken when in October, 1754, the British cabinet agreed to dispatch an expeditionary force of two thousand men to North America under General Braddock, who was to proceed on the basis of a fourfold offensive plan drawn up by Cumberland. The purpose was to drive the French out of the new positions they had taken. Newcastle and Hardwicke had intended to send this force off secretly so as not to provoke France to reprisals. But Fox, now secretary-at-war, announced it with much parade in the *Gazette*, with the apparent object of hurrying on a war.[61] Once it was informed of the contents of Braddock's instructions, the French government, in spite of its pacific intentions, could hardly do less than

58 T. W. Riker, *Henry Fox* (Oxford, 1911), I, 263; Lord Ilchester, *Henry Fox* (London, 1920), I, 221.

59 E. Charteris, *The Duke of Cumberland and the Seven Years' War* (London, 1925), 122; Coxe, *Lord Walpole*, II, 368.

60 E. H. Lecky, *History of England in the Eighteenth Century* (London, 1883), II, 486.

61 P. Yorke, *The Earl of Hardwicke* (Oxford, 1913), II, 256.

send a counter-expedition. Orders were sent to Brest at once to prepare three thousand men,[62] who, however, did not sail until May 3, 1755. Meanwhile, as soon as the French decision to reinforce the Canadian garrison was reported in London, the British cabinet boldly resolved that "these reinforcements must never reach their destination." Accordingly, orders were given to Vice-Admiral Boscawen as early as April 27, 1755, to proceed to Halifax and, after combining with the American squadron under Keppel, seek to prevent the French from landing any troops even at the cost of destroying the French fleet. This was no longer a defensive measure, but an order to commit an open act of aggression. Once the orders to Boscawen had been given, it was making mockery of diplomacy to continue the pacific discussions with Mirepoix. Yet this is precisely what the British ministers did. While Granville and Fox were dining amicably with Mirepoix, reassuring him that in sending Boscawen no hostile act was intended, the American continent became a battlefield where Great Britain was officially present.

It is well known that both British commanders fell foul of their main purpose. Boscawen succeeded only in capturing two French war vessels, the *Alcide* and *Lys*, while the rest of the fleet, under the competent leadership of the French admiral, passed on to disembark at Louisburg and Quebec. The results of Braddock's mission were no less negative. Of the four objectives of Cumberland's widespread strategical plan only one was moderately successful. On the Nova Scotia frontier Colonel Monckton with two thousand New Englanders drove the French from Fort Beausejour and from their settlements on St. John's River. Johnson failed at Crown Point and Shirley at Fort Niagara. The English ministers expected to hear of Braddock's success and of his eventual advance on Quebec; they heard instead the news that he was cut to pieces on his way to Fort Duquesne. The French were now actually in a stronger position than before.

From sheer want of vigorous direction both countries had drifted through a succession of small conflicts into an undeclared war in 1755. It would seem that the curious mixture of diplomatic pettifogging and intermittent violence characteristic of the feeble con-

[62] A. Lichtenberger, *Montcalm et la tragédie canadienne* (Paris, 1934), 35.

duct of affairs in both countries must now come to an end. But Boscawen's attack on the French fleet merely provoked Mirepoix's recall from London. When Newcastle learned the news of his departure on July 24, he remarked, *"Voilà, la danse commencée,"* but the dance which he affected to lead produced so little sound and fury that popular enthusiasm or even public interest were scarcely stirred. Newcastle followed neither the advice of Cumberland's war party to prosecute the war with vigor and consistency, nor, while any chance of peace yet remained, did he make any determined effort to come to some understanding with France. Vague half measures, timid and hesitant expedients, uncertainty as to the immediate object to be attained were the inevitable results. While there was still time to strike an effective blow at French commerce before the large East and West India trade fleets had entered home waters, the English ministers haggled over the question whether the instructions to be given to Admiral Hawke should order the seizure of French commercial or war ships. When the order was finally given in September, 1755, to the commanders of all British naval stations "to seize and take by all means in your power all French ships, men-of-war as well as merchantmen," the great French merchant fleets had already passed safely into French ports.[63] The seizure of three hundred French commercial vessels by the end of the year was an unstrategic meddling with trade or what Granville called "vexing your neighbor for a little muck."

While England drifted, military initiative and advantage passed to France. But at Versailles unity of leadership and vigor were also wanting. France resolved to put England clearly in the wrong. Obviously not yet ready, she refused to play England's game and declare war, even after the seizure of French ships and sailors. She denounced these acts of British piracy and waited to see if England would disavow them. She demanded, as a condition for resuming discussions on America, the restitution of all merchant and war vessels including their crews and cargoes and indicated that an unsatisfactory answer would be regarded as a declaration of war.

But what could France do in a war? British naval superiority made it imprudent to take the offensive in the new world or at sea.

63 E. Charteris, *Cumberland,* 174.

French diplomatic errors had made an attack on Hanover and Flanders impossible. A direct blow at the heart of England was all that was left. Belle Isle's plan of an invasion was thoroughly modern in its conception. By means of a sudden blow at London it aimed at destroying England's credit system and morale and at preventing the government from sending further aid to America. Strategically sound also was its combination with elaborate diversions against Halifax in Nova Scotia and against Minorca in the Mediterranean, both designed to force upon England a dispersion of her naval forces and to create uncertainty as to the real strategical objective of the French. The descent upon England failed because of the strong position of the British western squadron. But La Galissonnière's victory over Admiral Byng in the Mediterranean enabled the French Toulon fleet to take possession of undergarrisoned Minorca.

By their impotent offensives, their piecemeal and spasmodic measures the British ministers had succeeded at last in stirring France to vigorous military action. The display of military forces on the French coast and the concentration of transport barges at Channel ports remained a serious threat. In their panic the English ministers kept an undue proportion of the fleet in the vicinity of home waters, thus weakening the squadron of the unhappy Byng. Under the stress of the same fear they now finally, on May 18, 1756, declared war after having fought it unofficially already for two years.

Under the feeble direction of Newcastle England had suffered an unbroken succession of reverses on both land and sea. To retrieve these required the stronger intelligence and more solid will of William Pitt.

Chapter Seven

THE DIPLOMATIC REVOLUTION

THE sudden and dramatic regrouping of partners in the European alliance system in 1756 was the prelude to the bloody convulsion of the Seven Years' War. Its importance, among other things, lies in the noticeable decline of French political influence abroad and the intrusion of Russia as a formidable military factor among the rivalries of western Europe. It was precipitated by a succession of miscalculations and blunders on the part of panic-stricken diplomats and by the almost unbelievably clear-sighted and persevering cunning of Count Kaunitz, the master diplomat of them all. Although it was not generally intended, it corresponded to deep-seated shiftings and changes which time and statesmanship had wrought. Its history has often been obscured by legend and national partialities. To be sure, the old legend of the three spiteful women, Maria Theresa of Austria, Madame de Pompadour, the mistress of Louis XV, and Elizabeth of Russia, leagued together and sacrificing the interests of their states to wreak their feminine vengeance on the poison-tongued Frederick the Great, has now been happily laid to rest. But its place has been taken by a scholars' quarrel, now some fifty years old, on the question whether on the part of Frederick this was an offensive or a defensive war, the upshot of which has not always been clearly or even fairly stated.[1] To do it full justice requires a historian whose sympathy is not quenched by his laughter and whose large European outlook is not smothered by national preference.

I. THE BRITISH INITIATIVE

At the moment when Great Britain and France went to war over the command of the sea on May 18, 1756, neither government desired

[1] This is true of Sir Richard Lodge, *Great Britain and Prussia in the Eighteenth Century* (Oxford, 1923), 93; of Dr. E. Daniels in *The Cambridge Modern History* (London, 1934), VI, 251; and especially of Max Lehmann, *Friedrich der Grosse und der Ursprung des Siebenjährigen Krieges* (Leipzig, 1894).

a continental war. None the less the imperial issue went to the heart of their European connections, for each of the great maritime rivals of the west had its *liaison* with one of the rival German land powers of the east, Austria and Prussia. France was still allied with Prussia, and Denmark, Sweden and the Ottoman empire were attached to this alliance. In opposition to them was the historic connection of Great Britain, Holland, and Austria. Still more venerable was the enmity between France and Austria, which had survived the last war and appeared even to Kaunitz to be one of the permanent factors of continental politics. Outside these powers, Russia in the north had broken with both France and Prussia. Common opposition to the Ottoman Porte and to Prussia cemented the alliance between Austria and Russia. Because of their steady co-operation in the west and their close commercial relations Great Britain and Russia were on friendly terms. On the surface the old orientation of the powers remained unaltered after 1748. In reality everything was in a state of flux. The first visible change occurred on the periphery. In Spain the disgrace of Ensenada, the warmest partisan of the French alliance, had produced an agreement with Austria and Sardinia (the Treaty of Aranjuez) which guaranteed the *status quo* in Italy. But it was the basic incompatibility between Great Britain and Austria that gave the first impulse to the impending reshuffling of political partnerships which is known as the diplomatic revolution.

There is no need to add to the blaze of derision with which the reputation of the Duke of Newcastle, the principal English foreign minister, has been handed down from generation to generation. He was a weak and faltering statesman, and his utter lack of imagination, his fussy ways and morbid fears, causing him at one moment to apprehend disaster and the next to be intolerably dictatorial, made him an unsuitable foreign minister.[2] Although he held office for nearly half a century with a continuity which has rarely been approached, his outlook remained wholly insular and his ignorance of continental affairs was extraordinary. He actually believed that if

[2] The most damning estimate of him is that of L. B. Namier, *England in the Age of the American Revolution* (London, 1930), 76; a more satisfactory appraisal is that of Evan Charteris, *Cumberland and the Seven Years' War* (London, 1925), 142.

England paid a high enough price everything and everybody could be bought, including the Tsarina of Russia. He regarded a subsidy treaty as a legitimate commercial operation, and agreed with his colleague, Holdnerness, who said, "As we pay the piper, it is not unreasonable for us to have the tune we like."[3] But to do him justice, it should be said that, if his faulty diplomacy did some damage, he avoided the worst pitfalls. He prudently sought to keep all doors open until the last moment, and actually succeeded in doing so. Above all he kept the diplomatic initiative in his hands while France remained criminally inactive.

From the moment when a war with France became the accepted postulate of every political discussion in England, the intractable problem of defending the Austrian Netherlands and Hanover against France and Prussia advanced into the foreground of British diplomacy. If France should decide to march her troops into Hanover, she could repeat the strategy of the last war and render British conquests overseas useless. Newcastle did not have acumen enough to see that the security of Hanover contained a profound strategic solution of the British imperial problem. But whatever the danger of continental complications and commitments, the security of Hanover dominated Newcastle's policy. In his effort to find a protector for Hanover, he first tried to strengthen the all but broken Austrian alliance. But, Austria, convinced that the Netherlands were indefensible in any case, flatly refused to send any additional troops to Flanders. In their views on this province the two powers had arrived at the parting of the ways. Maria Theresa persisted in looking upon herself as an independent sovereign of the Austrian Netherlands, while Newcastle regarded "the Low Countries as a kind of common country in which we, the Dutch and the empress-queen are all interested."[4] As for defending Hanover, Kaunitz was quite willing to offer protection, but only on condition that England committed herself to the Austro-Russian offensive plan for the destruction of Prussia—a condition which the English cabinet dismissed as preposterous and absurd. Within a few weeks the Anglo-

[3] D. B. Horn, *Sir Charles Hanbury Williams and European Diplomacy, 1747-1758* (London, 1930), 227.

[4] William Coxe, *History of the House of Austria* (London, 1877), III, 351.

Austrian alliance degenerated into a paper war of mutual recrimina-
tion. The clear divergence of the vital interests of both states was
now apparent. It was the revolt of the now financially independent
Austria, to use the phrase of Frederick II, against her British
banker. Austria, the cornerstone of the "old system," had fallen
away. This Austrian indifference reacted upon Holland. Standing
between the two fires because of the Franco-Prussian alliance and
alarmed by the dilapidated condition of the Barrier, Dutch politicians openly threatened to desert to France unless England took
effective measures with Austria for the defense of the Netherlands.

Deserted by both Austria and Holland, Newcastle in dire perplexity turned to Russia. "We can do nothing," he said, "without
the Dutch, the Dutch can do nothing without the Austrians, nor
the Austrians without the Russians." A connection between England
and Russia seemed perfectly natural. Russia was dependent on England for colonial goods, while England drew from Russia the bulk
of her indispensable naval stores.[5] Both were on the worst possible
footing with Prussia, which, as a French ally, threatened Hanover.
Russia was as dangerous to East Prussia as Prussia was to Hanover.
Frederick the Great would be certain not to commit himself to a
western war unless he were secure from a Russian attack in the east.
The English ambassador, Hanbury Williams, succeeded in arrang-
ing a subsidy treaty with Russia on September 30, 1755, which contained in a secret clause a prohibition of separate negotiations with
"the common enemy," a vague phrase which was to cause considerable trouble when the question arose who that common enemy
was. In return for the subsidy Russia agreed to maintain fifty-five
thousand men on the border of Livonia. Nothing was farther from
Newcastle's mind than a change of system. He still lived in a fool's
paradise, supposing that it was possible to revive the Austrian alliance. He knew that British public opinion was resolutely opposed to
a continental war and, armed with the Russian subsidy treaty, he
flattered himself that he had banished such a contingency. The
effect of the treaty, however, was to set the entire continent in
motion.

[5] R. G. Albion, *Forests and Sea Power* (Cambridge, Mass., 1926); D. Gerhard, *England und der Aufstieg Russlands* (Berlin, 1934), 15.

II. COUNT KAUNITZ'S GRAND DESIGN

If we are to grasp the full import of the reversal of alliances, we must endeavor to understand the mentality and the objectives of its real author, Count Kaunitz of Austria.[6] When Count Kaunitz took charge of the Austrian chancellery in 1753 he was a mature personality with a rich and varied diplomatic experience in Italy, France and the Netherlands behind him. He was one of the notable figures of Austrian history, broader in outlook than Prince Eugene and more empirical and less doctrinaire than Metternich. In his special province of foreign affairs he will always pass as a rare type, the model diplomat of the century of the Enlightenment. Next to Frederick the Great no other European statesman in these years was more completely saturated with the ideas of this movement on its purely scientific side than was Kaunitz. Sharing the mechanistic conception of the social sciences with the men of his century, he believed himself to be in possession of a "political algebra," as he called it, that enabled him to calculate with unerring certainty. With his rationalistic and fanatically systematic procedure he was confident of having achieved a mastery of international affairs so complete that surprise would be eliminated and risk reduced to a negligible quantity. All his great memorials betray this systematic bent and syllogistic reasoning.[7] At every critical juncture of Austrian diplomacy he posed the question whether the existing political system should be retained or abandoned. Step for step, with a passionless serenity and with infinite patience, he examined every angle, all the *pros* and *cons* of political action. The purpose of his memorials was to leave the reader *sans réplique*, to draw him into that magic circle of dialectics from which escape was impossible. In his instructions to Austrian ambassadors abroad this systematic pedantry led him to a curious species of diplomatic casuistry which provided a solution for every imaginable contingency, a characteristic remi-

6 A. Ritter von Arneth, "Fürst Kaunitz," *Archiv fur österreichische Geschichte*, Vol. 48; by the same author, *Maria Theresia*, IV, 365-387; G. Küntzel, *Fürst Kaunitz-Rittberg als Staatsmann* (Frankfort, 1923).

7 A fair example of his technique is his address to the Austrian State Conference on August 21, 1755, "Preussische und österreichische Acten zur Vorgeschichte des Siebenjährigen Krieges," *Publicationen aus den K. Preussischen Staatsarchiven* (Leipzig, 1899), 74, 145.

niscent of the exhaustive casuistry of eighteenth-century legal codes. He emerged from this process of reasoning with an assurance so complete, that when, for example, he placed his plan for the destruction of Prussia before the Austrian ministry in 1755, he argued that every contingency had been met and failure was impossible. On paper at least Frederick the Great was annihilated before a single shot was fired. If it was all a delusion and a snare, it was because Kaunitz's crude mechanistic conception of politics left no room for imponderables or for the moral energies of his opponent. Kaunitz, however, towered over all of Frederick's enemies in intellectual stature, in the clarity of his aims, in his dry wit, in energy and superior diplomatic skill. Here at last Frederick, with his sudden flashes of insight, his rapid fire decisions, his impulsive and often precipitous leaps, had found his equal if not his superior in diplomacy. What a canny and even contemptuous game it was that this adept in all diplomatic tricks played with the once proud monarchy of France, the hereditary foe of Austria, inveigling her against her vital interest into a war with Prussia and offering her a beggarly pittance for her pains! Scarcely less surprising was the profound devotion of the Jesuit-ridden Maria Theresa to this infidel, who abhorred the *infame* as heartily as Voltaire himself. But Kaunitz was irreplaceable, and it was he who taught the pious empress-queen that in international affairs a *bissel Falschheit* (a bit of mendacity) was a tragic necessity.

Kaunitz regretted the days of Prince Eugene, the golden age of Austria, when the overwhelming majority of German princes, even the Prussian, enthusiastically followed the leadership of their Austrian emperors. But now, he contended, the loss of Silesia had deprived Austria of European influence and nailed Austrian foreign policy down in the direction of Prussia. A resumption of the historic Austrian advance against the Ottoman Porte and against France would be impossible so long as Prussia continued as a great power. Prussia had become the strongest disintegrating force in the Empire and the Franco-Prussian alliance had become the spearhead of French influence in Germany. If Austrian foreign policy was ever to regain the freedom and splendor of the days of Prince Eugene, if French influence was to be driven from Germany and if Austria was ever to recover Lorraine from France, then Prussia must first be completely destroyed. It would be a most brilliant triumph of Austrian diplomacy if Russia and France could be won for such a plan. If Russia, in return for active assistance, demanded East Prussia, Germany would not lose, for East Prussia lay outside the frontiers of the Empire. Sweden might be compensated with Pomerania, Saxony with Magdeburg, and Denmark with Holstein, whose ruler, the Grand Duke Peter of Russia, might be transferred to Oldenburg. If France could be persuaded to give her tacit consent to the destruction of Prussia or, perhaps, even to offer some financial assistance to set the Russian armies on the march, it would be no great sacrifice to surrender the Netherlands, which in any case could not be defended. Kaunitz did not believe in the possibility or even the desirability of a permanent alliance with France. Co-operation was to continue only while he was occupied with the task of drawing the poison fangs of his Prussian enemy.

Such was Kaunitz's great plan, which received the formal approval of the Austrian ministry on August 21, 1755.[8] But the necessary preliminary condition for the success of such an enterprise was the disruption of the Franco-Prussian alliance, no easy task, since by Kaunitz's own admission the two powers were natural allies. A strong Prussia was a French necessity if only for the purpose of restraining Austria. Yet Kaunitz could offer France substantial concessions; he could promise Austrian neutrality in the war with England and allow France to occupy Ostend and Nieuport for the duration of the war; he could promise to support the candidacy of the French Prince Conti for the Polish throne; he could arrange to have the Infante Don Philip exchange his little Italian duchies for a more satisfactory establishment in the Netherlands which, like Lorraine, might one day revert to France. In return he might appear to ask for very little; he would not demand an active French participation in his projected war with Prussia; at most would he ask for some financial assistance, but he would insist on the French denunciation of the Prussian alliance. The most important condition of his proposal, French acquiescence in the dismemberment of

8 See the text of the plan in *Publicationen aus den K. Preussischen Staatsarchiven*, 74, 145; J. Strieder, "Maria Theresa, Kaunitz und die österreichische Politik von 1748-1755," *Historische Vierteljahrschrift*, 13 (1910), 494.

Prussia, he concealed in the form of a favor which he proposed to confer upon France. Frederick, he hinted, was a treacherous and disloyal ally, was even now dealing with France's enemy, Great Britain.

Knowing that the entire French cabinet, with the exception of Machault, was composed of pro-Prussians, Kaunitz instructed Starhemberg, the Austrian envoy to Paris, to convey his proposal to the king through some secret channel, preferably through Prince Conti or Madame de Pompadour, and to treat the whole affair as one of confidence between sovereigns. On August 30, 1755, Starhemberg delivered into the hands of Madame de Pompadour the confidential letter from Maria Theresa. Madame forthwith passed it on to the king.[9] To Louis XV these promising overtures were not unwelcome. He had a warm admiration for the Austrian empress and he heartily disliked the active, soldierly, free-thinking Protestant Frederick. The Prussian alliance, so far as he was concerned, existed for reasons of state only; he was shocked by Frederick's critical tone in dealing with France and irritated by the latter's scurrilous strictures on his private life, which the pleasantries of Potsdam had made the subject of laughter throughout Europe. He committed the discussions with Starhemberg to the Abbé de Bernis, a favorite of the Marquise and, perhaps, the best informed of all his ambassadors. It was not until the discussions were well under way that other ministers were taken into the king's confidence.

The effect of the French reply was to turn Kaunitz's secret proposals topsy-turvy. France demanded the proofs of Frederick's disloyalty, which Kaunitz could not supply. Nor was France yet so forgetful of her interests as to tolerate, much less to participate in, an attempt to destroy Prussia. The only thing that Kaunitz achieved was to convince Bernis of the sincerity of Austria's intention not to serve as "the land soldier" of England. Although the discussions

[9] It is difficult to see at what point the feminine passions of the Marquise played a decisive part in the negotiations which led to the Austrian alliance. It is true, she was sympathetic to it and more than one important document passed through her hands. But it was Louis XV, not the Marquise, who was the chief actor in this affair. It was the treacherous Abbé de Bernis who in his mendacious *Mémoires* gave Madame de Pompadour an undeserved reputation by attributing to her childish immaturity the failures of French policy. Leon Cahen, "Les Mémoires du Cardinal de Bernis et les débuts de la guerre de sept ans," *Revue d'histoire moderne et contemporaine* (1909), XII, 73; P. de Nolhac, *Madame de Pompadour et la politique* (Paris, 1928), 153.

were continued, no further progress was made until Paris learned of the Convention of Westminster.

III. PRUSSIA AND THE CONVENTION OF WESTMINSTER

For an explanation of this treaty we must turn to the position in which Frederick the Great found Prussia after the Peace of 1748. Although the acquisition of Silesia had increased the population of Prussia by roughly one half and its public revenues by one third, Prussian resources by conventional standards were still ridiculously inadequate to support the position of a great power. Its population of four million in 1756 was not a third that of Austria, not one fifth that of France and not quite one half that of the British Isles. To use the familiar expression of Voltaire, Frederick was still a *"roi des lisières."* There was still no geographical cohesion among the various provinces of the monarchy; East Prussia was entirely isolated, the Saxon border was only seven miles from Berlin, and Silesia was connected with Mark Brandenburg by a narrow corridor only seven miles wide. In any serious war with a western power the Rhenish-Westphalian and East Frisian provinces were wholly indefensible. Among these provinces there was no consciousness of common statehood. On the eve of the Seven Years' War a Berlin preacher spoke from his pulpit "of all these provinces which we must regard as our fatherland."[10] It was the experience of the Seven Years' War which first made the name Prussia common coinage.

The cramped circumstances of the Prussian monarchy, coupled with his personal conviction that in the European state system every monarch must seek to expand or perish, led Frederick to consider further possible acquisitions. Most useful of all would be Saxony, then West Prussia and Swedish Pomerania. In his political testament of 1752 he commended the conquest of these regions to his successor.[11] But sober political judgment convinced him that such expansion would be possible only under exceptionally favorable circumstances. He therefore called them mere "reveries" and "chimeras." For the moment, at least, another problem demanded

---

[10] H. Delbrück, "Der Ursprung des Siebenjährigen Krieges," *Preussische Jahrbücher* (1895), 79.

[11] G. B. Volz, *Die Politischen Testamente Friedrichs des Grossen* (Berlin, 1920), 59-65.

his attention. France and Austria had been centuries building up their power. Yet here was Prussia, recently almost unthought of, suddenly leaping from third to first class. Europe stood bewildered and aghast. All of Prussia's neighbors without exception were distrustful, suspicious and apprehensive. Frederick himself said, "In Vienna they take me for an irreconcilable enemy of the House of Austria; in London they think me more restless, more ambitious and richer than I am; Bestuzhev believes that I am plotting mischief and in Versailles they say that I am falling asleep over my interests. They are all mistaken, but unhappily these apprehensions have consequences."

The pressure of these consequences began to weigh heavily upon him, particularly now since, in addition to Austria, he had to include Russia among his determined enemies. Under the influence of English and Austrian ambassadors and especially of the Grand Chancellor, Bestuzhev, Empress Elizabeth of Russia had conceived a violent aversion to the Prussian king. This animosity can scarcely be attributed to Frederick's literary blasphemies, because in his published writings Frederick observed a remarkable restraint when he mentioned Elizabeth.[12] Whether he practiced the same restraint when speaking of the "Little Mother" at his lively supper parties in Sans-Souci may be doubtful. But in this matter Elizabeth had similar complaints to make of the French also.[13] The truth is that Russia had good national reasons for opposing the rise of a new power in northern Europe. In Poland and Sweden Frederick's policy ran counter to the growing influence of Russia. It may be argued that in view of the Austro-Russian alliance and the close co-operation of both powers with Saxony-Poland, Frederick's opposition was defensive. Yet even defense can take an aggressive turn. In 1752 he seriously recommended the support of Sweden's ambition to recover Livonia. Now Livonia, which together with Finland still belonged to Sweden, encircled the environs of St. Petersburg. In effect Prussia was proposing to throw Russia back from the Baltic to the position she had in the time of Tsar Feodor.[14] The Russo-Austrian defensive

---

[12] Even the aggressive passage in his "Palladion" is rather harmless. *Oeuvres de Frédéric le Grand* (Berlin, 1846), XI, 242.

[13] K. Waliszewski, *La dernière des Romanov, Elizabeth Ière* (1902), I, 388.

[14] E. Daniels, "Friedrich der Grosse und Maria Theresia," *Preussische Jahrbücher* (1900), 100, 30.

alliance of 1746 was unobjectionable enough, although it contained
a secret article to the effect that if Frederick should attack Austria
he was to lose Silesia.[15] Since that time, however, both Elizabeth
and her chancellor were prepared to assume the offensive against
Prussia. In 1749 it was only the firm and decisive support of France
that enabled Frederick to prevent a Swedish succession war. But
from this time forward Frederick was compelled to face the possibility of a war on two fronts. While such a war against Austria and
Russia must always remain a hazardous adventure, his confidence
in the technical superiority of the Prussian army led him to believe
that he was equal to it, though he doubted whether East Prussia
could be defended. But if one or the other of the western powers
joined the Austro-Russian alliance he believed himself to be irre-
trievably lost.

Since he had no navy of his own, Frederick had nothing to fear
from Great Britain. For obvious reasons France was the more useful
ally and could be the more dangerous enemy. Without French
assistance he could not have won the First Silesian War and now
Prussia's precarious situation required the retention of the French
alliance at almost any price. In fact, Prussia's new position as a great
power depended upon it. He himself expressed the necessity of the
French alliance in the following terms:

Alsace-Lorraine and Silesia are two sisters of whom France has married one and Prussia the other. This connection forces them to pursue
a common policy. Prussia cannot suffer France to be deprived of Alsace
or Lorraine and Prussia is in a position to defend France by penetrating
at once into the heart of the Austrian dominions. For the same reason
France cannot suffer Prussia to be deprived of Silesia. That would weaken
excessively a French ally who is useful in the north and in the Empire
and who can protect Alsace or Lorraine by means of a diversion.

A permanent antagonism between Austria and France appeared
to him to lie in the nature of things, and a necessary corollary of
this antagonism was France's imperative need of the Prussian
alliance. The historic trend of French expansion toward the Rhine,
which Frederick once called the natural frontier of France, must

---

15 Borkowsky, *Die Englische Friedensvermittlung im Jahre 1745* (Berlin, 1884), 99;
E. Guglia, *Maria Theresa,* I, 283.

provoke the equally natural and determined Austrian opposition. That was the dictate of reason and the teaching of past centuries. So assured was he of the soundness of this analysis that he made no especial effort to cultivate French friendship. To French inquiries concerning the renewal of the alliance, which was to expire in 1756, he made only vague replies. It seemed more prudent to keep a free hand as long as possible and not to commit himself prematurely and without necessity on the Franco-British imperial controversy. Even without a formal treaty he believed himself certain of French support. Yet, to understand his subsequent behavior, we must know that he rated this support very low. He made no effort to conceal his extreme impatience with the indecision and feeble conduct of French foreign affairs.[16] He accused Rouillé of drifting aimlessly, without system and without a clear purpose. He thought the long-suffering moderation of France in the face of repeated English insults without parallel in history. He had urged vigorous and immediate preparation, and saw only dallying and sloth. Again and again he called upon his French ally to act, and when at last even the piratical English raids on French commerce, doing damage that mounted into millions, failed to stir the French to action, he began to suspect that someone in Versailles, presumably Madame de Pompadour, had been corrupted with English money.[17] This conspicuous feebleness of France compelled him to provide for his own security.

Thanks to his efficient system of espionage, the king had received intelligence of the secret clauses of the Russo-Austrian defensive alliance of 1746, which he thought passed beyond the bounds of a purely defensive pact and were directly aimed at him.[18] Other reports confirmed his belief that Austria, with the connivance of Russia and Saxony, was merely waiting for a suitable moment to make war upon him. He at once began to increase his armaments. He felt that Prussia would not really be prepared for a war until he had a mobile army of one hundred and eighty thousand men and

[16] In its emphasis on this point, but not in its main contention the study by F. Luck-waldt has had a clarifying effect. F. Luckwaldt, "Die Westminsterkonvention," *Preussische Jahrbücher* (1895), 80, 261.
[17] He spoke freely of thirty or forty millions which the Marquise had deposited in English banks. P. de Nolhac, *Madame de Pompadour et la politique* (1928), 115.
[18] *Politische Correspondenz Friedrichs des Grossen*, IX, 84, 328.

a war chest of twenty million thalers, enough to cover the cost of four campaigns. In 1756 he actually had one hundred and fifty thousand men and had accumulated a little more than thirteen millions in his war chest.[19] If the Franco-British conflict spread to the Continent, he would be confronted with a choice of evils. If he supported his French ally, then Russian, Austrian and Saxon troops, subsidized by Great Britain, would attack him. In that case he would be fighting on behalf of an ally as a mere auxiliary in a quarrel which was no concern of his, in which he might be ruined and from which he could gain nothing. He held no high opinion of French military power and he was alarmed lest France, having involved him with an Anglo-Austrian coalition, would abandon him to his fate as he contended she had done in the Second Silesian War.[20] The other alternative—to refuse to assist if France were attacked on the Continent and to stand by—was still worse. That would deprive him of his only ally and encourage Austria and Russia to carry out their offensive designs against him. Whichever way he turned ruin stared him in the face. He was anxious, therefore, to produce a situation in which he would not be forced to chose between these dire alternatives.

Newcastle's persistent efforts to arrange subsidy treaties with the lesser German states led him to suspect that England was bent on a continental war. If that was true, then it would obviously be to France's advantage to anticipate an English attack and invade Hanover at once. He therefore urgently pressed the occupation of Hanover upon his French ally. He calculated, somewhat brutally perhaps, that in this way he could avoid the *casus foederis* of his French alliance.[21] When Rouillé, however, suggested that Prussia was in a better situation to execute an invasion of Hanover, Frederick indignantly refused, commenting ironically that he was no *condottiere* in French pay. A little later he called upon France to invade Flanders, which could be taken in a single campaign—"*quelle belle perspective pour la France.*" In this case again he could avoid the *casus foederis* and would not be bound by any existing treaty to guarantee

19 Albert Naudé, *Beiträge zur Entstehungsgeschichte des Siebenjährigen Krieges* (Leipzig, 1896), II, 25.
20 *Politische Correspondenz*, XI, 144, 232.
21 Frederick to Knyphausen, May 6, 1755, *Politische Correspondenz*, XI, 145.

the Austrian Netherlands.[22] Since in both instances France had clearly refused, he correctly assumed that it had become the settled policy of France to avoid a continental war entirely. In the meantime he had also learned that Austria had refused to support Great Britain in the defense of Hanover. But if France desired no continental war, why should not Prussia do what it could to localize the conflict and reassure Great Britain on the matter of Hanover?

This thought crystallized into a resolution the moment Frederick learned of the Anglo-Russian subsidy treaty of September 30, 1755. So far as Britain's policy toward Prussia is concerned this subsidy treaty was a stroke of genius. If Newcastle had intended to blackmail Frederick into a treaty with England, he could not have done it more effectively. In Frederick's mind the Russian menace would not become really acute until one of the two western powers agreed to subsidize the Russian army. This had now happened; his sense of security had vanished; and the only avenue of escape was an understanding with England. Although for England an arrangement with Prussia would be a *pis aller* for a more satisfactory alliance with Austria, Prussia would be an even more valuable ally than Russia. As the neighbor of Hanover, Prussia was at once more dangerous and more useful, and less expensive than Russia. The Russian troops in Livonia were a long way off, while Frederick's more formidable army was on the ground. It was with the feelings of a drowning man clutching an unexpected life buoy that England welcomed the Prussian alliance. Without a moment's hesitation Frederick signed the convention of Westminster with England on January 16, 1756. The two powers now had a common interest, the preservation of peace in Germany, and they agreed to oppose the entrance into or passage through that country of any foreign troops—which as matters then stood could only mean French or Russian troops. This convention gave Frederick a certain measure of security. He had pledged himself to defend Hanover against the French, who had just assured him that they had no intention to at-

[22] The best study on the preliminaries of Westminster is by G. Küntzel, "Die Westminsterkonvention," *Forschungen zur Brandenburgischen und Preussischen Geschichte*, IX (1897), 186; somewhat less useful is the study by F. Wagner, *Friedrichs des Grossen Beziehungen zu Frankreich und der Beginn des Siebenjährigen Krieges* (Hamburg, 1896), 25 ff.

tack it, and he flattered himself that together with England he had
also neutralized Russia, for it was a cardinal point of his analysis
of Russian affairs that Russia could risk no offensive war without
English subsidies. He even fancied that he had thwarted the aggressive designs of Maria Theresa, whose offensive was contingent upon
Russian participation. He intended no breach with France; he
merely wanted to show the French that he was a much courted
person, to raise in French eyes the value of the Prussian alliance. He
even provided for the contingency that the French might wish to
reverse their policy and embark on a continental war, for he specifically excepted the Austrian Netherlands from his treaty of guarantee with England.[23]

IV. THE REVERSAL OF ALLIANCES

The convention of Westminster was designed to pacify the Continent, but its effect was to shake Europe to its very foundations.
First, Maria Theresa, as she informed the English ambassador on
learning the news, was shaken as if by a stroke of paralysis. She
was scandalized to learn that her English ally had signed a treaty
with "the mortal and constant enemy of my person and family."
The versatile Kaunitz rejoiced and at once began to scatter rumors
throughout Europe that there were secret clauses which concealed
offensive intentions. In Versailles it provoked a general indignation
that was to have sinister consequences. Frederick's unpardonable
crime was to present France with a *fait accompli*. It must always
remain surprising that the secretive Frederick, who could not be
desirous of throwing down the gauntlet to France, should have
ventured to keep her in the dark until it was too late. The key to
French resentment is to be sought less in objection to the substance
of the treaty than in Frederick's failure to consult his ally before-
hand. If he had been quite open and frank with France before
signing, it is not improbable that he might have obtained a French
blessing to the neutralization of Germany.[24] As Frederick failed

23 The Duc de Broglie's argument in his *Alliance autrichienne* (Paris, 1895), 12, that
Frederick intended a complete *volte face* cannot be substantiated.
24 This is the opinion of R. Waddington, *Le renversement des alliances* (Paris, 1896),
271; of Sir Richard Lodge, *Great Britain and Prussia in the Eighteenth Century*, 85;
and of R. Koser, *Geschichte Friedrichs des Grossen*, 7th ed. (Berlin, 1925), II, 349; also
D. B. Horn, *Hanbury Williams and European Diplomacy*, 215-220.

to explain this secrecy and French indignation increased, it became not so much a question whether it was desirable or undesirable to attack Hanover, but whether it was tolerable that Prussia should presume to dictate what France should or should not be allowed to do. In spite of all of Frederick's protestations of loyalty to France, the convention of Westminster was generally regarded in Versailles as the treacherous desertion of her one important ally. The Prussian alliance was not renewed. Frederick's action stung Louis XV into walking directly into the trap that Kaunitz had so shrewdly set for him. In the discussions which led to the first Treaty of Versailles Kaunitz had all the advantage of the diplomatic initiative, which Frederick had found so conspicuously wanting in the indolent Louis XV, who together with Madame de Pompadour desired peace at any price.

Nothing can be more firmly established today than the fact that France on the eve of the Seven Years' War was not compelled to choose between Austria and Prussia.[25] A firm, clear-sighted direction of French foreign affairs could have obtained Austrian neutrality without completely breaking with Berlin. As late as January, 1756, Kaunitz had offered Austrian neutrality without demanding the dissolution of the Franco-Prussian alliance. While it is true that France had every reason to resent the treachery of Frederick the Great, it was sheer folly to base a foreign policy on that resentment. In view of the incompetence and discomfiture of the British ministry, distracted by personal jealousies and constant changes, it was a mistake to jeopardize French prospects of a maritime victory over Great Britain by embarking on a defensive alliance with the Austrian sovereign whose consuming passion was vengeance on Prussia. It was already in the first Treaty of Versailles, approved unanimously by the council and signed on May 1, 1756, that France strayed from the narrow line of national interest. It was a one-sided treaty.[26] By its terms France closed the door on an invasion of Flanders and did not even demand that Austria break with England, but was content

[25] This is also the opinion of R. Pinon, in his very brief but intelligent "Histoire diplomatique, 1515-1928," in Hanotaux' *Histoire de la nation française*, IX (1929), 317; the contrasting opinion by Duc de Broglie, *Alliance autrichienne*, 375, 414, is no longer tenable since the publication of the Austrian documents.

[26] R. Waddington, *Le renversement etc.*, 335.

with neutrality. Not a word was said about the cession of the Netherlands. On the other hand, France promised to come to the assistance of Austria with twenty-four thousand men, if the latter were attacked. It was, to be sure, a purely defensive treaty, but none the less, as Broglie puts it, it smelled of powder, for with it France assumed all the liabilities of Austrian foreign policy whose director, Kaunitz, was determined to incite Frederick into a declaration of war and still keep up the appearance of defense.[27] The treaty was a blank check in the hands of the Austrian chancellor.[28] France was henceforth drawn into the Austrian orbit and this eventually involved the abandonment of the historic federative system of French foreign policy, which had grouped around her the client states of Germany, Poland, Sweden and the Ottoman Porte. It is true that the rise of the two great military powers, Prussia and Russia, necessarily signified a reduction of the traditional French influence in central and eastern Europe, but French diplomacy here abetted the process. The treaty with Austria implied an alliance with Russia and ultimately the surrender of Turkey.

No less sensational was the effect of the convention of Westminster in Russia. By refusing to inform Russia in advance of the complete reversal of her policy Great Britain committed the same tactical error that had cost Frederick his alliance with France. The result also was the same, though the breach between Great Britain and Russia never became quite complete. The news of the convention arrived at St. Petersburg at the awkward moment just after the ratifications of the Anglo-Russian subsidy treaty had been exchanged. The glaring contradiction between the two treaties leaped to the eyes of the directors of Russian policy at once. Elizabeth felt herself insulted by this sudden and complete change in British policy, which made her appear in the humiliating light of one who was bought, a mere mercenary who could be used in any way that British interest seemed to suggest. The first treaty clearly aimed at introducing Russian troops into Germany, the second no less specifically at excluding them. Although from a British point of view

27 For evidence that such thoughts were constantly in the minds of Austrian statesmen see Starhemberg to Kaunitz, May 13, 1756, *Publicationen aus den Preussischen Staatsarchiven*, 74, 350.
28 Duc de Broglie, *Le secret du roi*, I, 147.

they were part of the same policy of pacifying the Continent, this
was not the Russian standpoint. Elizabeth had signed the subsidy
treaty only because Bestuzhev had persuaded her that Great Britain
would use it in the spirit of the common maxim of all the directors
of Russian policy: *delenda est Borussia*. For ten years Great Britain
had stirred up Russian hostility against Prussia, and now she had
pledged herself to that same "common enemy" to thwart any attempt at an invasion of Germany by Russian troops. Kaunitz
promptly took advantage of this inconsistency to point out the
treachery of England. England and Russia were moving toward a
rupture. Russia, to be sure, did not formally repudiate the subsidy
treaty, but informed the English minister of her decision not to
accept English subsidies until there was a full agreement on the
"most secret declaration," which stipulated that Russian troops could
be used only against Prussia and in concert with Austria.[29] This
marks the decisive turn in Russian policy.

The English ambassador, Williams, however, scored one last
minor triumph when he persuaded that grand rogue, Bestuzhev,
who had only recently inspired Russian envoys abroad to send in
false reports of the aggressive designs of Frederick, henceforward
to work for a reconciliation between Russia and Prussia. This time
Bestuzhev's change of front was due less to his English pension
than to the imminent possibility of a change of rulers in Russia.
The complete breakdown of the health of the dissipated empress,
who had just passed her forty-seventh year, gave no promise of a
long reign. All the parties at the Russian court calculated on the
eventuality of a sudden change. The Grand Duke Peter was known
to be an idolatrous admirer of Frederick the Great, and the Grand
Duchess Catherine, upon being informed that Austria was intri-
guing to exclude her from the throne, became a warm partisan of
England. Bestuzhev, his nose always turned to the wind, cultivated
them both. He succeeded at least in preventing an open breach with
England. But his prestige was irreparably shaken. Elizabeth observed his capers with open eyes and denounced him as a traitor
who was sold to Great Britain.[30] It was only her inability to find a

[29] D. B. Horn, *Hanbury Williams and European Diplomacy* (London, 1930), 221 ff.
[30] L. v. Ranke, *Sämmtliche Werke*, 30, 162-163; R. Koser, "Russland und Preussen,"
Preussische Jahrbücher, 47, 490; K. Waliszewski, *La dernière des Romanov*, 110-129.

suitable successor that kept him in power. He was opposed at every turn by the ruling party of the Shuvalovs, who contrived to manage Elizabeth through the young Ivan Shuvalov, her *favorite en titre*. One thing was certain, so long as Elizabeth lived the efforts of Williams and Bestuzhev toward a reconciliation between Russia and Prussia had little chance of success.[31] On the contrary, in the spring months of 1756 Elizabeth was burning with impatience to precipitate an offensive war on Prussia. In March and April the Russian council decided to proceed without England, to encourage Maria Theresa to attack Prussia and to promise the assistance of a Russian army of eighty thousand men. If Austria were willing, the war was to open in the summer of 1756 and Austria was to be offered a formal offensive alliance against Prussia in which Sweden and Saxony were to participate.[32]

It is evident that Kaunitz's task in Russia was not to blow on the flames of war, but to hold the Russian empress in leash until he had made his final arrangements with France, lest by some premature and precipitous action Elizabeth betray his whole offensive design before it was completed. He felt himself so certain of Russia that he ignored the Russian proposal for an offensive alliance. He was convinced that no Russian army could be mobilized without a foreign subsidy, and this subsidy of two million florins, which Austria was obliged to pay according to the treaty of 1746, he proposed to obtain from France. Resolved not to commit England's fatal error, he took Elizabeth into his confidence on his dealings with France and obtained not only her full approval but her promise to join in the agreement. He saw, however, that the backward state of Austrian military preparations would necessitate postponing the assault on Prussia until the spring of 1757.[33] He had some difficulty in persuading Maria Theresa, who was impatient to strike in 1756, of the wisdom and necessity of this delay.[34] Elizabeth, too, after some indignant opposition, yielded to his arguments. Both Russian chan-

---

[31] D. B. Horn, *Hanbury Williams*, 250; R. Waddington, *Le Reenversement etc.*, 508.
[32] Esterhasy to Maria Theresa, April 22, 1756, *Publicationen a. d. Preuss. Staatsarchiven*, 74, 321.
[33] A. Naudé, *Beiträge zur Entstehungsgeschichte des siebenjährigen Krieges* (Leipzig, 1895), I, 74.
[34] H. Kretschmayr, *Maria Theresia* (Gotha, 1925), 124.

cellors also accepted his plan without reservation. So far as Russia was concerned Kaunitz's fondest hopes were more than fulfilled.

Kaunitz was playing a game of high political intrigue, misrepresenting Russian policy to France and French policy to Russia in order to whip together his offensive alliance against Prussia. He wanted no triple alliance, but two separate treaties, one with France, the other with Russia, which would enable him to keep all the threads of the enterprise in his own hands. With amazing tenacity and dexterity he was slowly drawing his offensive net about the king of Prussia, but he was still some distance from his goal. The Franco-Austrian defensive alliance of May 1, 1756 had still to be converted into one with an offensive edge, and that in the teeth of the opposition of several ministers who were determined Prussophiles. Such men as d'Argenson and Rouillé condemned French connivance in the Austro-Russian plan to annihilate Prussia as a monumental political stupidity that would leave Germany at the mercy of Austria and drive out French influence from the Empire. However, France was still drifting without unity of policy, and if the ministry pursued one line, Louis XV and Bernis, who was still in charge of the discussions with Austria, pursued quite another. It appears that Frederick's military preparations in June and his closer relations with England caused a marked change of sentiment at the French court. All the evidence points to the fact that Louis XV and Bernis were favorable to Kaunitz's enterprise. At all events, on August 20, 1756 Starhemberg jubilantly reported to Kaunitz that at last France had yielded on all crucial points; that, though she still refused to participate, she would support an army of German mercenaries; that she agreed to pay the subsidies for Russia; that she empowered Austria to make agreements with Sweden and other states which, in effect, implied a partition of Prussia.[35] Yet there were still differences between them on all points and there was still a wide gap between what France demanded and what Austria was willing to offer in the Netherlands.

[35] Starhemberg to Kaunitz, Aug. 20, 1756. *Public. a. d. P. Staatsarchivan*, 74, 512-531; Bernis, *Mémoires*, I, 285, contended that these concessions were made contingent upon a previous Prussian attack. It is clear that Starhemberg was aware of no such condition. On the untrustworthiness of Bernis' *Mémoires* see, besides the article by L. Cahen mentioned above, G. Küntzel, "Die Memoiren des Cardinals Bernis," *Forschungen zur Brandenburgischen und Preussischen Geschichte*, 15 (1902), 117.

Thus matters stood when on August 29, 1756 Frederick the Great plunged Europe into the Seven Years' War by invading Saxony. In the babel of contradictory contentions which characterize the literature on the origin of this war a few points are indisputably certain. At the moment of Frederick's invasion of Saxony the offensive coalition which Kaunitz was planning against Prussia was not yet complete. There existed not a single formal offensive alliance against Prussia. It is equally certain, however, that Austria and Russia intended to attack Frederick in the spring of 1757, and it must remain problematical whether Bestuzhev, whom Elizabeth was excluding from the discussions with Austria, could have prevented it. France had not yet entered into a formal engagement with Austria either to participate in the enterprise or to push the attack on Prussia to the point of annihilation, although, if we are to believe Starhemberg, Bernis had committed her in principle to both. Whether Bernis had made these commitments of August 20, 1756 with the consent of the royal council must remain doubtful and is, perhaps, considering Louis XV's manner of conducting foreign affairs, unimportant. In any case, a French participation, while it was extremely desirable to Kaunitz, was not a *conditio sine qua non* of the Austro-Russian offensive.[36] What would have happened had Frederick not, by one of those quick and impulsive decisions which were characteristic of his policy, invaded Saxony, it is impossible to know and useless to conjecture. What is certain is that Frederick solidified the coalition which his invasion of Saxony was designed to disrupt.

Now France, hitherto hesitant, pressed for an offensive alliance, while Kaunitz was content to demand fulfillment of the defensive Treaty of Versailles. Eventually Kaunitz was forced to yield, and in the second Treaty of Versailles of May 1, 1757, France committed herself to the *destruction totale de la Prusse*, and pledged herself to pay a heavy subsidy of twelve million livres, to send an army of one hundred and five thousand men into the field and subsidize ten thousand German mercenaries; not until Austria recovered Silesia was France to receive four Belgian cities and the Infante

[36] A. Naudé, *Beiträge zur Entstehungsgeschichte etc.* (Leipzig, 1895), I, 71; a point which H. Delbrück, who accepts the idea of a Prussian offensive, concedes *Preussische Jahrbücher*, 86 (1896), 416.

Don Philip to be transferred to Belgium with full sovereign rights. The magnitude of Kaunitz's triumph becomes apparent when we compare these terms with what he offered France in 1755. What more did France receive than Austrian neutrality in the Franco-British conflict? If the destruction of Prussia failed, France would come off empty-handed. But the supreme irony of Kaunitz's policy lay in the success with which he had jockeyed France into trying to restore Austria literally to that position in Germany from which all French statesmen since Richelieu had been attempting to expel her. Incapable of continuing Louis XIV's policy of continental hegemony, France had lapsed into the position of a vassal state of Austria. In Russia Kaunitz's triumph was, if possible, greater still. What Austria offered Russia in the offensive alliance of May 19, 1757 was almost nothing. Austria promised to pay subsidies which were really paid by France. In return Russia joined the defensive Treaty of Versailles of May 1, 1756 and placed her entire army at the disposal of Austria—without any prospect of territorial compensation.

V. FREDERICK THE GREAT AND THE ORIGIN OF THE WAR

The inexorable sequence of cause and effect that produced the Seven Years' War seems, so far as historical investigation can ascertain it at present, fairly well established. It was the Anglo-Russian subsidy treaty that frightened Frederick into the convention of Westminster, which was the immediate cause of the Diplomatic Revolution. Again, it was the anti-Prussian resolutions of the Russian council of ministers of March and April, the consequent Russian military preparations of June and those of Austria in July, and finally the report that the Austro-Russian attack would be postponed until the spring of 1757, that led to the outbreak of the war, for they were the main factors which determined Frederick to anticipate the attack and assume the odium of aggression.

For months after the convention of Westminster the Prussian monarch persisted in his illusion that, with the power of British finance behind him, Russia had been immobilized and French resentment made innocuous. That France could ever be desirous or capable of financing a major continental war on Prussia in addition to her costly maritime war with Great Britain appeared to him incredible. When, however, in June his agents and spies in various quarters, especially in Dresden, gave him authentic, if incomplete reports of Kaunitz's offensive coalition, he began gradually to realize that in signing the convention with England he had committed an irreparable blunder. Then Great Britain also, after months of disingenuous deception and optimism, at last frankly admitted to him the seriousness of the Russian menace.[37] His worst suspicions of Russia were confirmed when he learned of the unconcealed Russian military preparations in June. In a desperate attempt to dispel the danger from this quarter he resorted to counter-preparations which had been effective once before in 1749. But on this occasion this favorite expedient of militarists failed. Although he discontinued his armaments when the Russians, in deference to a request from Kaunitz, ceased with theirs, he had succeeded only in provoking similar preparations in Austria. After weeks of uncertainty as to the intentions of Austria, he received (July 21), through the agency of a neutral diplomat at The Hague, the report of the Austro-Russian agreement to postpone their common attack until the spring of 1757. It was this news that forced on him the conviction that the only escape from the dilemma was to anticipate the attack of his enemies. "If Austria," he said, "is pregnant with war, I shall offer the service of the midwife." But before he mobilized his armies, he twice requested Maria Theresa, the second time more specifically than the first, whether she could give him the assurance, in clear and unequivocal language, that she would attack him neither in 1756 nor in 1757. In the deliberations of the Austrian cabinet over the answer to be given to this question, one minister at least rose to demand that the Prussian monarch be given a frank and satisfactory reply. But Kaunitz sternly opposed this. Was he, who had labored so long to maneuver Frederick into just this position, now to surrender his great advantage?[38] How could he give up his agreements with Russia and France and allow his entire system to collapse? The pious Maria Theresa had learned her lesson of the necessity of "trifling mendacities" too well to dissent from the answer that was finally given. Kaunitz's reply, that Austria had

37 H. Tuttle, *History of Prussia under Frederick the Great* (Boston, 1888), II, 279-281.
38 E. Guglia, *Maria Theresia*, II, 147.

signed no offensive alliance against Prussia, though technically correct, ignored the substance of Frederick's request and was therefore provocative. Since this reply was no more satisfactory than the first, Frederick marched (August 29) his troops across the borders of Saxony, which he erroneously regarded as the center of the European plot to ruin him.

In the public opinion of Europe Frederick had thus become the aggressor and his invasion of Saxony set the mechanism of the hostile alliances in motion. His foreign minister Podewils had warned him that this would almost inevitably happen. Rouillé had twice warned him that France would fulfill her treaty obligations if Austria were attacked.[39] The English ministers also had warned him, though they made no resolute effort to prevent his aggression. His own brother, Prince Henry, had admonished him that to try conclusions with such an overwhelming coalition was to tempt the Almighty. Even his private secretary, Eichel, thought him reckless. He, therefore, had every reason to know what he was doing and what he was bound to expect. Why then did he embark on this desperate adventure? Historians have asked, why did he not bide his time to see if Kaunitz could find an adequate ground for war and draw the still wavering France completely into the Austrian coalition? Were there not reasonable grounds to hope that the moody and changeable Elizabeth, whose constitutional indolence and tendency to procrastinate were well known, might still yield to the pressure of the optimistic Williams and of Bestuzhev, who were both attempting to thwart Russian co-operation with Austria? Was it politically wise, even admitting the strategical wisdom of immediate military action, to anticipate a danger that was still remote and contingent?

In their effort to explain Frederick's conduct in this crisis both camps of opposing historians have committed the fatal error of thinking invariably in terms of a rigid and unalterable principle which, like some fixed idea, is reputed to have guided the foreign policy of Frederick the Great. Either, like Lehmann and Daniels, they have contended that Frederick's conduct in August, 1756 becomes intelligible only if it is assumed that he deliberately precipi-

[39] *Politische Correspondenz*, XIII, 128-130.

tated the Seven Years' War for the purpose of conquering Saxony, or, like Naudé and, to some extent, Koser, that he was simply and solely preoccupied with keeping the peace. It would seem that neither group has fully grasped the peculiar psychology of the Prussian monarch. The controlling principle of Frederick's foreign policy was neither an inordinate ambition for expansion nor the pacifist's ideal of peace for its own sake. In his statecraft war and peace were determined by what he called *raison d'état*, and it was the interest of Prussia alone, as it passed through the alembic of his personality, that directed his foreign policy.

Later and more discriminating historical survey of the facts has dispelled the view of Lehmann that Frederick began this war with the deliberate intention of conquering Saxony. The whole tenor of his correspondence, public and private, points to the opposite conclusion. Not only was the situation of 1756 too unfavorable for such a war, but it was Frederick's settled conviction that a war of conquest could be successful only if supported by a French rather than a British alliance.[40] On the other hand, it is certainly true that, after his unhappy experience with Saxony in the Second Silesian War, he was convinced of the necessity of annexing Saxony to Prussia. It is equally true that for economic and strategical reasons he had planned the instant occupation of Saxony in case of another war with Austria long before the situation of 1756 arose. Yet, a strategical offensive is one thing and a political offensive quite another. No doubt after the war was well under way the two offensives merged into one and the same enterprise. But his war was not for that very reason a planned and premeditated undertaking. Confronted with the fearful threat of Kaunitz's coalition, which was greater than he knew, he felt that he must strike or perish. If he struck quickly, his prospects were not utterly hopeless. He was ready, his enemies were not. He seems actually to have believed that France would risk no continental war.[41] And if France did join his enemies, it was all the more important not to await the consummation of their plans. If his enemies were firmly resolved on war—and his confidence in the value of audacity led him to believe that he

40 G. B. Volz, *Die Politischen Testamente Friedrichs des Grossen*, 63.
41 *Politische Correspondenz*, XIII, 341.

might be successful—then he meant to be compensated not only with Saxony but with West Prussia also. But preposterous as it may appear, his occupation of Saxony was, in the beginning at least, something in the nature of a peace demonstration, and there is no good reason to doubt the sincerity of his promise of August 25 to Maria Theresa that he would withdraw his troops the moment she gave him the desired assurance of security. No one can reproach Maria Theresa because she did not, perhaps could not, give him this assurance. It was too late for compromise; in reality the choice which confronted her was either to accept the king of Prussia as an equal—perhaps even as a superior—or to render him forever harmless. No historian can grudge her decision in favor of the latter, although when she loudly protested to a bewildered Europe that she had been outrageously attacked, she must be denied the reputation of an honest woman.

Chapter Eight

THE SEVEN YEARS' WAR

I. THE STRATEGY OF DIVERSION

IN THE Seven Years' War the powers of Europe, now indubitably stronger and more highly nerved, for the second time within sixteen years passed through the paroxysm of a double collision. The disputes arising from the conflicting imperialisms of France and Great Britain came to a crisis at the very moment when the tempest, precipitated by Frederick's invasion of Saxony, burst upon Prussia. Separate and distinct in their origin, the Anglo-French contest for supremacy in three continents and on the seas, and the continental crusade for the destruction of Prussia became fatefully involved with one another. This connection had a decisive effect on the final result of both wars.

No sooner had Frederick invested the Saxon fortress at Pirna and drawn the first Austrian blood in the indecisive battle of Lobositz than Kaunitz invoked his defensive treaties, thus rendering the intrusion of French and Russian armies into central Europe inevitable. Frederick promptly appealed to Britain for assistance on the ground that his loyalty to Britain had provoked the hostile coalition. To France this new situation presented a not unpromising opportunity. Outnumbered and outfought by the British navy in the last war, she had contrived to reconquer her colonies in the Netherlands. Allied with Austria that road was now closed to her. In the meantime she had not radically altered the comparative ratio of her naval strength, and her maritime prospects remained dismal. Yet France might still hope to repeat the strategy of the last war by a conquest of Hanover. The convention of Westminster, designed to protect that electorate, had become thoroughly obsolete. At war with a coalition of the three foremost military powers of Europe, Frederick could offer Hanover no effective assistance.

Great Britain was once more confronted with the dilemma inherent in her insular position. Should she, as an influential section of opinion in the City demanded, adopt a policy of non-intervention in Germany and abandon Hanover and Prussia to their own devices? That was the somber advice of William Pitt, who roundly condemned Newcastle's subsidy treaties with Hanover and other North German states, including the treaty with Prussia. Had the British government acted on this counsel of despair, there would have been slender chance of a Prussian survival; Hanover and all Germany would have fallen before the headlong onslaught of the two Catholic powers, Austria and France, leagued with Orthodox Russia. France, at the head of this panoplied and triumphant coalition, could have seized the ports of Emden and Bremen, closed them together with a large part of the Continent to British commerce, and retained them as counters for the peace conference. Above all she could then have devoted her undivided energies to the maritime war against Great Britain, which would then have been completely isolated.[1]

A more auspicious alternative for Britain was to retain Newcastle's system of continental alliances and, while acting on Pitt's doctrine that Britain's principal effectives must be employed on the sea and in the colonies, to use Hanover as a base of operations for a military diversion on a large scale, aimed at drawing French military and financial resources away from the maritime war into the false direction of a continental campaign. This is what Pitt later, with characteristic exaggeration, called "conquering America in Germany"—with German soldiers and German generals, one should add.[2] It was obvious enough that England could not successfully try conclusions with France on land, where the latter was superior; but she could employ her financial superiority to subsidize the armies of Hanover, Brunswick and Hesse and she could conclude a military alliance with Prussia, the only independent military power that could supply such an allied army, operating in Westphalia, with adequate leadership and material support.

But the timidity of George II and the early blunders of Pitt intervened to prevent an immediate adoption of this strategy, which

[1] A. Schaefer, *Geschichte des Siebenjährigen Krieges* (Berlin, 1867), I, 354.
[2] It should be remembered that he employed this phrase at the end of the war when a new king and a new ministry made shift to abandon the continental war altogether.

ultimately proved so effective. The main French army, one hundred thousand strong, was already advancing on Hanover. Unable to secure neutrality for his electorate or send adequate reinforcements for its defense, George II ordered the Duke of Cumberland and his forty-five thousand Hanoverians to remain on the defensive and to avoid any appearance of confounding the cause of Hanover with that of Prussia. Cumberland beat a hasty retreat to Stade on the North Sea, where on September 8, 1757, he signed with the Duke of Richelieu the disastrous convention of Kloster-Zeven. This convention left the electoral dominions entirely at the mercy of the French, promised the dispersion of a large part of Cumberland's army, exposed the central provinces of Prussia to a French invasion, and failed to secure any of the advantages which the British king hoped to gain by his desertion. The convention was not an armistice, it was a capitulation.[3]

Pitt cannot be exculpated from a certain responsibility in this affair. He was no friend of Cumberland and regarded the latter's fate with singular indifference. He wanted to support Frederick as "the last bulwark of the liberties of Europe," but, in his desire to keep clear of Hanoverian interests, he tried all methods of gaining his end other than the correct one of strengthening Cumberland's army. Truly, his diatribes against Hanover, which had once served their purpose, had now come home to roost. If the convention of Kloster-Zeven were carried out, the ruin of Prussia was inevitable. Only by slow stages did Pitt realize that the collapse of the allied army in western Germany must be made good and that similar collapse in the future must be averted by coming to a full understanding with Prussia.[4]

It was the military genius of Frederick that finally helped to dispel the fog that had settled over British foreign policy. His own campaign of 1757 had opened with a ghastly failure and for a time disaster after disaster broke upon Prussia. Unsuccessful in his effort to destroy Browne at Prague and badly beaten by Daun at Kolin, Frederick was compelled to abandon Bohemia in a retreat which

3 E. Charteris, *Cumberland and the Seven Years' War* (London, 1925), 254; R. Waddington, *La guerre de sept ans* (Paris, 1899), I, 501; A. v. Ruville, *William Pitt, Earl of Chatham* (London, 1907), II, 140.
4 R. Lodge, *Great Britain and Prussia in the Eighteenth Century* (Oxford, 1923), 100.

fell just short of being a rout. The spell cast by victorious Prussia
was broken and the crop which Kaunitz had sown was fast ripen-
ing. The Russians under Apraxin defeated Marshal Lehwaldt at
Gross-Jaegersdorf (August 30, 1757) and the loss of East Prussia
seemed imminent. Seventeen thousand Swedes broke into Pomerania
and soon the entire northern frontier of Prussia was on fire. The

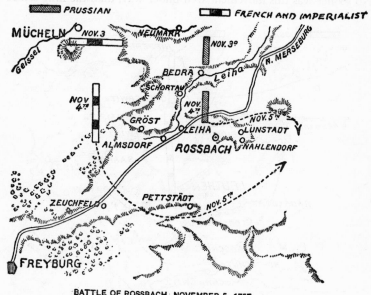

BATTLE OF ROSSBACH, NOVEMBER 5, 1757.

Rhenish provinces, East Frisia and Hanover lay at the mercy of
the French, while the convention of Kloster-Zeven set Richelieu free
to carry the war into the heart of Prussia. Two of Frederick's best
generals, Schwerin and Winterfeldt, had fallen in battle. With so
many provinces under enemy occupation, the king's financial
resources were fast ebbing away. In the southwest a second Franco-
German army of fifty-five thousand men, under the joint command
of the Prince of Hildburghausen and Soubise, was threatening
Leipzig.

Determined to maintain his hold on Saxony, Frederick marched
rapidly westward to meet the advancing enemy. He encountered

the allied army strongly entrenched on some rising ground over-
looking Rossbach, but, outnumbered two to one, he could not hope
to dislodge them by a frontal attack. He made a feint of withdrawing, but Soubise, thinking only that he could delay no longer without
permitting his adversary to escape, hit upon the ill-fated plan of
enveloping Frederick's left wing and cutting his communications.
No sooner was this movement well under way, than the king seized

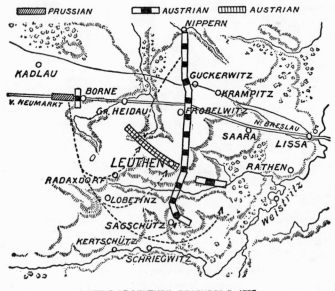

BATTLE OF LEUTHEN, DECEMBER 5, 1757.

his opportunity, turned his men about and assailed his deluded
enemy in front and flank. The enveloping allied army was itself
enveloped and in a few hours cut to pieces in what proved to be the
most popular of Frederick's victories. But the more difficult task
of reconquering Silesia, which in the meantime had fallen into
Austrian hands, still lay before him. One month after Rossbach to
the very day Frederick achieved a still more brilliant triumph over
the Austrians at Leuthen (December 5, 1757). Daun brought back
to Bohemia only thirty thousand men out of the eighty thousand

he once had. Frederick reconquered the lost ground, and his iron grip held Silesia, never again to be loosened.

By the end of the year the fortune of war had completely changed. The moral effect of these dazzling victories stupefied Europe. Frederick had fought against three powers, had fought four battles, and had won three of them. His defeat at Kolin, now repaired, raised rather than lowered his military fame. The French philosophers openly applauded his victories, claimed him as one of their own, hailed him as the champion of free thought against the religious obscurantism they found at home. They ridiculed French generals in satirical songs.

> *Soubise dit, la lanterne à la main,*
> *"J'ai beau chercher! Où diable est mon armée?*
> *Elle était là pourtant hier matin.*
> *Me l'a-t-on prise, ou l'aurais-je égarée?*
> *Prodige heureux! La voilà, la voilà!*
>
> *O ciel! que mon âme est ravie!*
> *Mais non, qu'est-ce donc que cela?*
> *Ma foi, c'est l'armée ennemie."*

Voltaire, though he had not forgotten his quarrel with Frederick, covered the brow of his Potsdam friend and enemy with laurels. Cardinal Bernis, once the full scope of the Austrian defeat was brought home to him, hysterically advocated immediate peace before further victories should make Frederick the master of Germany and the despot of Europe. Only the adamant refusal of Maria Theresa kept him in line.[5]

Nowhere was the impression created stronger than in London. Rossbach was welcomed as an English victory. It had shattered the myth of the invincibility of the French army. On the night of Frederick's birthday the streets of London were ablaze with illuminations. Enthusiasm ran strong among religious people, especially among the Methodists, who saw in the infidel Frederick the Gideon of the Reformed Faith, the new "Protestant hero." Old George II breathed more freely, and Pitt now accomplished the most conspicuous *volte face* of his career. He, who for twenty years

[5] R. Koser, *Geschichte Friedrichs des Grossen* (Berlin, 1925), II, 565.

had denounced German entanglements, prevailed upon the king on November 28, 1757, three weeks after Rossbach, to repudiate the convention of Kloster-Zeven, thus removing the last vestige of a separate and fatal Hanoverian policy. The army of observation at Stade was not disbanded. On the contrary, strengthened by both English and Prussian contingents, it was placed under the command of Prince Ferdinand of Brunswick, one of the ablest generals in the Prussian service. Parliament, which had reluctantly voted £164,000 for this army in 1757, made a grant of no less than £1,200,000 for its support in 1758. Pitt saw that he had been wrong in opposing an alliance with Frederick, and frankly admitted it. To prevent Prussia being crushed by the gigantic confederacy of five powers was a necessity of Pitt's new policy.

A complete understanding with Prussia, to be sure, was not easy, for Great Britain and Prussia, like France and Austria, looked at the war from different angles. Britain's enemy was France, which Frederick tried, though unsuccessfully, to conciliate. What Frederick most ardently wanted was not a British subsidy, which at first he haughtily refused, but a British fleet in the Baltic to operate against the Swedes and the Russians. That, however, Pitt could not grant him, for until the end of the war the British navy could not dispense with the naval stores coming mainly from the Baltic and Russia.[6] But Frederick was no longer in a position to decline Pitt's offer of a subsidy of £670,000, the largest that Britain had ever accorded a continental state. In April, 1758 he signed the subsidy treaty, which contained the significant clause that neither party should carry on separate peace negotiations. So long as Pitt was in office the Anglo-Prussian alliance functioned satisfactorily.

These events laid the foundations for a strategy which dominated the Seven Years' War. Ferdinand of Brunswick succeeded in halting French armies of ever-increasing size. His campaigns in Westphalia performed the double function of creating a continental diversion for Great Britain and of protecting Frederick's western flank against what should have been, by all past reputation, his most formidable foe. Henceforth the war in Europe became a duel between Prussia and Austria-Russia in which the two seconds, the

---

[6] R. G. Albion, *Forests and Sea Power* (Cambridge, 1926), ch. VI.

French and the Anglo-Hanoverians, neutralized each other in the west. France had thus been maneuvered into playing a subordinate role on the Continent, absorbed in unstrategical operations which soon exhausted her. There is no good reason for suspecting, as does Colonel Reboul, a secret understanding between France and Prussia; it was patent enough that France had no compelling interest in disturbing the new balance in Germany resulting from the rise of Prussia, and therefore none in intervening actively in the *querelle allemande* between Austria and Prussia.[7]

II. PRUSSIA'S STRUGGLE FOR EXISTENCE

The prey which Frederick II had seized with a greedy hand in the First Silesian War and had prudently secured in the second, he now had to defend in the most rigorous and exhausting war of his life. Limitations of space and a desire for intelligibility forbid our accompanying this central figure of the continental war on the *via dolorosa* of all his seven campaigns, until he emerged from the bloody ordeal a hero covered with glory but a bent old cynic at fifty. It is more useful and, perhaps, more interesting for the modern student to attempt an answer to the crucial question which was ventilated in all the journals, chancelleries and armies of Europe after the fog of war had lifted: what was it that saved Frederick II from the ruin which the overpowering coalition had prepared for him? Was it, as Napoleon fifty years later contended, the personality of Frederick, his military genius and strategy, the disciplined and orderly strength of Prussia and the moral stamina of the army; or was it the inherent weakness of the coalition and the military blunders of its generals; was it the chance event of the death of the Tsarina Elizabeth on January 5, 1762, which dissolved the coalition before the war had run its course; or was it a combination of all these? In their search for an answer, contemporaries pointed to such incidents as the mysterious halt in the French offensive after Kloster-Zeven; the treasonable retreat of the Russian general Apraxin, after his victory at Gross-Jaegersdorf; Charles of Lorraine's brainless crossing of the river Lohe, near Breslau, before

[7] Col. F. Reboul in Hanotaux, *Histoire de la nation française, Histoire militaire* (Paris, 1925), VII, 527.

the battle of Leuthen; the accidental victory of Frederick at Liegnitz, and so on. These allied mistakes, however, were counterbal-
anced by equally serious errors of judgment on the part of Frederick,
who lost no less than eight battles out of a total of sixteen. Far more
important than such individual episodes were certain larger factors
which persistently reasserted themselves in almost every campaign.
Kaunitz's masterpiece, the great coalition, so irresistible on paper,
suffered from all the defects of most eighteenth-century combinations. It was inspired by no common ideology, no deep-seated community of sentiment. Even Frederick, who was a master at political
propaganda, was skeptical of his ability to make capital out of the
defunct religious issue between the Catholicism of France and
Austria and the Protestantism of Prussia and Great Britain.[8] The
coalition was a union of courts and as such was subject to the influence of cabals, to the corruption of ministers and generals, to
a chance change of rulers, above all to the limited financial resources
and the divergent interests and war aims of its members. The impressment of Sweden by France and Russia added little to its
strength. Subsidized by France and operating ineffectively in
Pomerania, the Swedes could at best compel Frederick to divide his
forces. The same thing may be said of the ill-disciplined and inferior troops of the thirty odd princes of the Empire whom Emperor
Francis mobilized against Prussia in January, 1757.

To some extent these defects of the coalition were of Kaunitz's
own making. Had the Austrian chancellor been less close-fisted
with his allies and less exclusively preoccupied with purely Austrian interests, had he abandoned in time his stubborn refusal to
make commitments regarding the division of the spoils, he would
in all probability have received more cordial co-operation from
France and Russia. It was a mistake to offer France so paltry a reward for the disproportionately heavy burden she had contracted
to assume. If France was to make her supreme effort on the Continent, it was an error not to cede the Austrian Netherlands to her
outright. It should be admitted that the favorites of Madame de
Pompadour—Soubise, Contades, Richelieu and Clermont—were no
great generals, although they were not much worse than the rest.

8 O. Klopp, *Friedrich der Grosse* (Gotha, 1868).

What France lacked was not soldiers of talent and character, as Chevert, Broglie and Saint-Germain brilliantly demonstrated, but initiative, and that Kaunitz, had he been less timorous, might well have stimulated and encouraged by holding out the prospect of the acquisition of all Belgium. As it was, the purposeless carnage in Westphalia was in the highest degree unpopular in France. Frenchmen fought for no more definite objective than the temporary occupation of Hanover, and fought, on the whole, with such a conspicuous lack of enthusiasm and energy that they were soon regarded in Vienna as Austria's worst enemies.

Kaunitz's hope for the recovery of Silesia, therefore, depended upon harmonious political and military co-operation with Russia. But this hope also proved a disappointment. Unwilling to permit herself to be exploited in order that Austria might recover Silesia, Russia demanded the annexation of East Prussia and a portion of Poland. Kaunitz balked at this and did not improve matters by keeping the issue in suspense. The prospect of Russia dominating both the Baltic and Poland was vastly more terrifying to both France and Austria than the new power of Prussia.[9] Meanwhile immediate military decisions had to be taken in common against a monarch who enjoyed all the advantages of unity of command and of operations on interior lines. From the very beginning of the war the movements of the Austrian and Rusian armies were so imperfectly co-ordinated and often determined only after such interminable and embittered discussions, that a profound mutual suspicion soon poisoned the military partnership. On two critical occasions the Russians had good reason to complain of Austrian desertion: once in 1758, when the fatal tendency of the Austrians to linger in the Bohemian mountains prevented effective support of the Russian advance before the battle of Zorndorf; and again in 1759, after the two Russian victories at Kay and Kunersdorf, when the Austrians refused to join them in a thrust that might have administered the *coup de grace* to Frederick and made an end of the war. These disappointments in military comradeship must not be overlooked in the final Russian desertion under Peter III.

[9] Flassan, *Histoire générale et raisonnée de la diplomatie française* (Paris, 1809), VI, 207.

Apart from the repeated breakdown of the Russian supply system, the failure of these Russian offensives must be laid at the door of the Austrian commander-in-chief, Marshal Daun. Daun was a capital specimen of those bloodless generals of the old regime who regarded war not as a volcanic and violent conflict of physical and moral forces, but as an artful game of maneuvering. There was a palpable contradiction between the offensive purpose of the coalition and his obviously defensive tactics. In approved eighteenth-century manner Daun "maneuvered" and fought for position, aimed at smaller successes like seizing enemy magazines and cutting communications in the hope of inducing hunger and desertion in his opponent's army, but, except when the Prussians exposed themselves unduly as at Kolin, Hochkirch and Maxen, he sought consistently to avoid a major battle. The Austrian war council urged him on to strike vigorous offensive blows but, obsessed with the fear of the superiority of the Prussian cavalry and the greater mobility of their infantry, Daun persisted in avoiding the open plain. The only offensive battle he ever planned was forced on him by Maria Theresa and ended in Frederick's victory at Liegnitz. It may seem astonishing that this great temporizer was retained as commander-in-chief, yet his methods were generally accepted as accomplished military art.[10]

Compared with Daun's feeble and anaemic strategy, Frederick's conduct of the war was a marvel of audacity, elasticity, dauntless courage and swift judgment. He was flexible enough to vary his strategy to fit the changing political and military situation of Prussia during the war. There were times when he vied with and even outdid Daun in position warfare. Yet a brief glance at the map of Prussia is sufficient to show that it was impossible for Frederick to confine himself to a war of position on several fronts without courting certain disaster. East Prussia and the Rhenish provinces were untenable outposts and were soon abandoned. But even in the central mass of Prussia—Brandenburg, Pomerania, Halberstadt, Magdeburg—connected with Silesia by only a narrow strip of land

10 Gen. Curt Jany, *Geschichte der Königlich-Preussischen Armee* (Berlin, 1928), II, 252: by the same author, "Der Siebenjährige Krieg, Ein Schlusswort zum Generalstabswerk," *Forschungen zur Brandenburgischen und Preussischen Geschichte*, Vol. 35 (1932), 165.

at Krossen, there was not a single defensible frontier. The Elbe and the Oder offered no obstacle to an advancing enemy and the city of Berlin remained unfortified. "How am I to fight a defensive war," the king wrote after the Battle of Kunersdorf; "and still cover Berlin, which is open on all sides?"[11] Elementary geographical necessities, limited resources in money and man power, forced Frederick into offensive warfare. Engaged in a war on three fronts, with two or three hostile groups of forces converging upon him, he was compelled to maneuver in such a way as to crush each adversary in turn. Separately he was a match for any one of them, though he soon found that no troops in the world were more difficult to overcome than the long-service regulars of the old Russian imperial army. His crucial problem was always to prevent the Austrians and Russians from effecting a junction, if need be by forcing a battle on one or the other. At the height of his career he performed miracles of speedy, decisive action. He sought a decision by battle as a matter of principle whenever there was the slightest chance of success. The very necessity of shuttling back and forth between several fronts and the need of finishing off one enemy before he attacked the next, compelled him to deal smashing, decisive blows. It is in this, says Reinhold Koser, his principal biographer, that he transcended the atrophied system of contemporary warfare and approximated the strategy of Napoleon.[12] Nothing, however, could be less plausible. Indeed, the strategy of Frederick becomes fully intelligible only when the difference between him and Napoleon is clearly recognized.

Napoleonic strategy implied a sharp breach with the entire system of eighteenth-century warfare. Napoleon threw into the discard the traditional practice of weakening his main army by sending out detachments and observation corps to engage in petty fencing over fortresses, magazines, roads or provinces. Resolutely concentrating the gigantic masses under his command, he sought the complete annihilation of the enemy army as his supreme objective. His chief concern was always to have superior numbers of troops on hand, to

[11] *Politische Correspondenz Friedrichs des Grossen,* Vol. XVIII, 11357.
[12] R. Koser, "Die preussische Kriegführung im Siebenjährigen Kriege," *Historische Zeitschrift,* Vol. 92 (1904), 242; R. Koser, *Geschichte Friedrichs des Grossen* (Berlin, 1925), II, 308.

march them directly against the enemy's main army, to surprise his opponent by deceptive cavalry feints and, if possible, to envelop him by forced marches and cut off his retreat; on the day of battle to concentrate the attack on a decisive point of the enemy front, to prepare the advance by a massed artillery barrage, to attack in echeloned columns which supplied ever fresh reserves and, after the decision had fallen, to pursue the enemy to the "last breath of horse and man." With the large national armies of the revolutionary epoch Napoleon could place an entire country under effective military occupation, disarm it, and dictate the peace.

For a strategy such as this Frederick's resources were pitifully inadequate. A strategy of annihilation is possible only with a decisive physical and moral superiority. But Frederick's army was perpetually outnumbered. To prevent excessive losses in his mercenary army he concerned himself constantly with the fortresses in the rear of the enemy, with the security of his base of operations, his magazines and his supply system. He had to weaken, fatigue and exhaust his enemy by frequent and vigorous blows not in themselves decisive, to cut off his adversary's commerce and revenues, until the sum total of these partial blows, battles and maneuvers was sufficient to force the enemy to yield. Frederick's individual victories, even that of Leuthen (admittedly one of the most brilliant in modern military history), were singularly indecisive. There is no good retort to Delbrück's remark that many of his battles were no more than a glorified kind of maneuvering. No mere dramatic recital of his great battles after the manner of the conventional historian, therefore, will make Frederick's conduct of the Seven Years' War intelligible to the modern student. Battles were not his pivotal and exclusive means of winning the war, for the simple reason that he did not, indeed could not, like Napoleon, carry his victories to the point of the complete disarmament of his adversary. In the first two campaigns he was able to set the pace; thereafter he had to fight the war on the enemy's terms. In the last years, to avert complete disaster, he had perforce to drag his army, rapidly deteriorating and declining in man power, through the campaign by means of such familiar artifices as deceptive maneuvers, night marches and lesser lightning thrusts. Thus in the end necessity drove him into doing what Daun did by preference. It was by means of such a strategy, which Delbrück aptly calls a strategy of exhaustion (*Ermattungsstrategie*) that Frederick fought the Seven Years' War.[13] Indeed, no other manner of successful warfare was possible for him. Daring campaigns in the style of Charles XII of Sweden would have been fatal; the cautious maneuvering advocated by his brother, Prince Henry, no less so.

A graphic illustration of the constricted strategical limits within which Frederick was forced to operate is his Bohemian campaign of 1757, which was, in a certain sense, the high point of the war. If Frederick did not, as one might expect of an enterprising general possessed of a momentary numerical superiority, carry his offensive directly into the heart of the Austrian dominions, it was because of the diplomatic uncertainties of the moment. But his deliberate delay in opening hostilities until the autumn of 1756 and his somewhat leisurely occupation of Saxony, gave the Austrians ample time to concentrate troops in Bohemia and Moravia. It is astonishing that during the winter months he entertained no plan for a spring offensive, preferring rather to await developments in the hostile camp. It was not until the political atmosphere had clarified in March, 1757 that he eagerly accepted the fiery Winterfeldt's bold suggestion of a concentric invasion of Bohemia with the purpose of surprising the Austrians in their winter quarters, seizing their magazines, and occupying northern and eastern Bohemia before the French and the Russians could move or before Daun could arrive on the scene.

This plan surpassed in audacity and scale anything which his contemporaries had hitherto attempted. The surprise was successful. Through four defiles in the mountains the Prussian army of one hundred sixteen thousand men came pouring into Bohemia, seized the Austrian stores, swept up the scattered Austrian contingents and threw them back upon Prague. At Prague lay Marshal Browne, presently superseded by the less competent Prince Charles of Lorraine, with one great army. Daun was advancing with another. In

[13] H. Delbrück, *Friedrich, Napoleon, Moltke* (Berlin, 1892); H. Delbrück, *Geschichte der Kriegskunst* (Berlin, 1920), IV, 415; O. Hintze, "Delbrück, Clausewitz und die Strategie Friedrichs des Grossen," *Forschungen zur Brandenburgischen und Preussischen Geschichte*, Vol. 33 (1921), 131-177; General Bonnal, *De Rossbach à Ulm* (Paris, 1903); Lieut. Col. Rousset, *Les maîtres de la guerre, Frédéric, Napoleon, Moltke* (Paris, 1899).

the midst of the successful execution of his plan Frederick now
recklessly resolved to hazard his forces in a supreme effort to
annihilate the entire army of Prince Charles. This was a fatal
strategical error, for with his imperfect military instrument the king
was unable to destroy the army of Prince Charles in the short
space at his disposal before the arrival of Daun's forces. The battle
of Prague was a Prussian victory, but the forty-four thousand Austrians who threw themselves into the fortress of Prague made in-

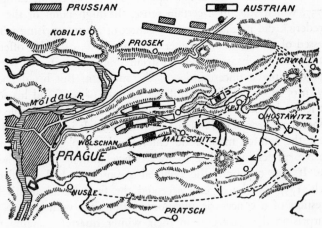

BATTLE OF PRAGUE, MAY 6, 1757.

evitable a wearisome siege for which the Prussians were not prepared.

But even had Frederick succeeded in demolishing the army of
Prince Charles and won the battle of Kolin, which he lost to Daun,
it was not his intention to march on Vienna, after the manner of
Napoleon, to dictate the peace. It is true, he later contended, that had
he won the battle of Kolin, he could have dictated peace and that
the French and Russians would not have dared to move.[14] But the
actual military situation did not justify such extreme optimism.
In the battle of Kolin he attacked Daun, who not only enjoyed a
great superiority in numbers but occupied a position that was all

[14] See his *Testament politique* of 1768. G. B. Volz, *Die politischen Testamente Friedrichs des Grossen* (Berlin, 1920), 161.

but impregnable. For this very reason it is more than probable that, even had he won this battle, Frederick's losses would have been greater than those of Daun. The latter would simply have retreated to the south, and Frederick could not have followed him, because with his mercenary army he was eternally fettered to Prussian magazines. Moreover, the Prussian army of eighty thousand men, already reduced by one fourth, was too insignificant a force to occupy so vast a country as Austria and still maintain its communications with Saxony.[15] Even a Prussian victory at Kolin, therefore, would not have disarmed Austria, let alone a coalition of

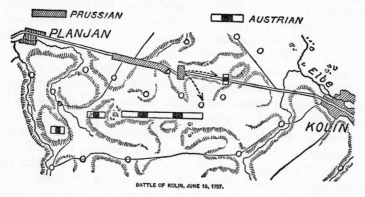

BATTLE OF KOLIN, JUNE 18, 1757.

three powers. Frederick did not, assuredly, lack Napoleon's dash and enterprise, but a Napoleonic strategy was far beyond his meager resources. The entire Bohemian campaign was sheer waste. The siege of Prague had to be abandoned and the Prussians evacuated Bohemia in disgrace. Had Frederick, instead of making this wild *pointe* to Prague, consistently held to the defensive strategy which enabled him to win such magnificent triumphs as Rossbach and Leuthen, the war would have been less costly and difficult than it was.

Thenceforth Frederick's conduct of the war assumed the character of a series of offensive blows or sorties within the scope of a defensive strategy. Such were his frustrated attack on Olmütz in

[15] See the penetrating analysis by K. Lehmann, "Ermattungsstrategie oder Nicht," *Historische Zeitschrift*, Vol. 151 (1934), 48.

Moravia and his victorious assault on the Russians at Zorndorf in 1758. Unhappily, in order to hold his own he was condemned to the necessity of being victor in perpetuity. The slightest reverse laid bare his capital and imposed upon him a calamitous retreat. In each succeeding campaign he had to begin the whole business over again. In spite of his doctrine that all Prussian wars must be "lively and short," he was irrevocably involved in a war of endurance. He no longer had troops enough to take the offensive and his forces were being used up more quickly than those of his powerful rivals. His central task of keeping the Austrians and Russians at a distance from one another was becoming more difficult from year to year. Indeed, in the summer of 1759 Laudon, with the flower of the Austrian army, succeeded in cutting his way through to the forty thousand Russians under Soltykov and together they planned a concluding drive on the heart of Prussia.

Overwhelming necessity made Frederick give battle to his combined enemies at Kunersdorf on August 12, 1759. The disparity in numbers between the seventy thousand Austrians and Russians and his own army of fifty-three thousand was not in itself alarming. Invariably outnumbered in the battles of the war, Frederick had perfected the tactical device of the oblique battle order, which enabled him to cope with a numerically superior enemy.[16] Briefly stated, this stratagem consisted of a flank attack by one wing of his army while "refusing" or holding in reserve the other wing, which was thrown into the front in echeloned columns as it was needed or was used to cover the retreat in the eventuality of a reverse. He concentrated cavalry and heavy artillery on the attacking wing to prepare the advance of the infantry and further strengthened it by an advance guard of shock troops, the grenadier battalions, called the *attaque*. By thus discarding the conventional parallel battle order with frontal attack and employing, instead, his oblique battle order, he could hurl his small but highly mobile army upon the flank of the enemy where he had a local superiority and overwhelm the corresponding wing of his antagonist before the larger but unwieldy masses of the latter had time to alter their front. By rolling up the

16 *Oeuvres de Frédéric le Grand* (Berlin, 1846), XXVIII, 74, 88, 110; Gen. Jany, "Die Feldschlacht in den Kriegen Friedrichs des Grossen," *Hohenzollern-Jahrbuch* (1911), 50-75.

one wing of his adversary he normally swept along the remainder of the latter's front in the same devastating movement. If the movement was carried out with swiftness and precision half of the enemy army never came into play. At Prague, Leuthen, Zorndorf, and later at Torgau, Frederick employed this adroit tactical device

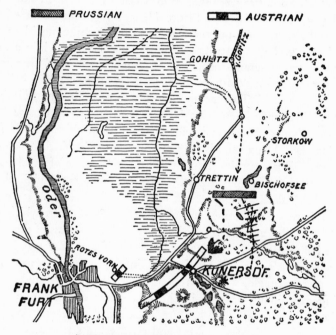

BATTLE OF KUNERSDORF, AUGUST 12, 1759.

with brilliant success and threw superior enemy forces into confusion.

But at Kunersdorf this favorite device failed him. He did, it is true, succeed in rolling up the enemy's left wing as far as the center with his own reinforced right, but the difficult terrain and the knolls, behind which the Russians and Austrians had taken up strong positions, brought the Prussian attack to a halt. Impatient and desperate, Frederick sent his left wing, which he had kept in reserve to cover an eventual retreat, into action. But the fatigued

Prussian troops, who had gone two nights without sleep and lacked both food and drink, were completely demoralized by the murderous charge of Laudon's Austrian cavalry as they clambered up the Spitzberg under the broiling heat of the August sun. General Seydlitz, the hero of Rossbach, was carried wounded from the field. Two horses were shot from beneath the king. In vain did Frederick grasp the flag of Prince Henry's regiment in an effort to stop the rout. "Will not some accursed bullet strike me!" he was heard saying. This shattering defeat at Kunersdorf cost him a loss of twenty-five thousand men. "I have no more resources," he wrote to his minister Finckenstein, "and, to tell you the truth, I believe everything is lost." The enemy had only to give him the finishing stroke. We already know why this was not done. Soltykov had lost nineteen thousand men and had no desire to sacrifice himself for the Austrians. Daun had his eye fixed on Silesia. Frederick's enemies separated. What the king himself called the "miracle of the House of Brandenburg" came to pass. The victors did not exploit their triumph. Frederick was given an opportunity to recover.

In this recovery the mechanism of the Prussian state, which revealed a sudden and unsuspected vitality under the stress of the war, offered him material assistance. The Seven Years' War was in no sense a people's war, but for the first time the common experience of a great struggle, with its repeated enemy invasions and plundering expeditions, aroused in the inhabitants of the kingdom a lively sense of cohesion. What Frederick called the *esprit de corps et de nation* of his army officers and civil servants (the latter went without salaries during the war) now swelled into a genuinely popular Prussian patriotism, kindled by the heroic conduct of the monarch. Fourteen- and fifteen-year-old junker boys hurried to enlist, while the peasants of Pomerania and Brandenburg flocked to the colors to form the dependable core of the Prussian army. Recruits came even from the mountain districts of Silesia and from the occupied villages of the lower Rhine, which were exempt from the obligatory service of the Prussian canton system. The victory at Rossbach, hailed throughout Germany as a national triumph over the French, excited the first timid pulse beats of German nationalism.[17] In spite of himself and of his undisguised preference for French culture, Frederick became a national symbol, and national sentiment was an important factor in the last years of the war when he was forced to turn everywhere to recruit his depleted resources.

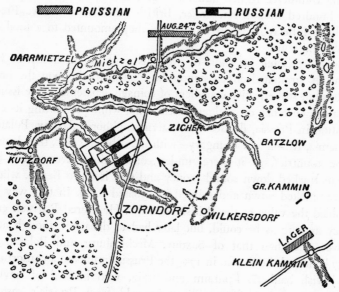

BATTLE OF ZORNDORF, AUGUST 25, 1758.

Most baffling of all was Frederick's financial solvency during the war. The scarcity of capital and the absence of an organized money market in Prussia made it impossible for him to finance the war by means of loans or to accumulate a national debt, as was done in France and Austria.[18] After the first campaign his war chest was exhausted and enemy occupation and periodic plundering expeditions caused the revenues of Prussia to drop sharply. To continue the war on such paltry resources was impossible. If he wished to survive, Frederick was compelled to make his enemies pay for the costs of the war. This he did by levying pitiless exactions on Saxony,

[17] F. Meinecke, *Weltbürgertum und Nationalstaat* (Berlin, 1928), 35.
[18] H. Mauer, *Die private Kapitalanlage in Preussen im 18. Jahrhundert* (Berlin, 1921).

Mecklenburg and other hostile territories that had the misfortune to be occupied by Prussian troops. From Saxony he drew five million *reichstaler* in each of the first four years of the war, twelve millions in 1760, seven in 1761, and eight in 1762. It may be mentioned in this connection that the war cost Saxony, with its flourishing commerce ruined and its wealth destroyed, something like one hundred million *reichstaler*. British subsidies also gave Frederick no little relief. Paid four times, they amounted to a total of sixteen millions.

But all this fell far short of even his most urgent needs. In his painfully straitened circumstances he finally struck upon the dangerous but still effective expedient of coinage debasement. He issued devalued currency on a gigantic scale and, while prohibiting its circulation in Prussia, flooded his eastern neighbors—Saxony, Poland, Bohemia, Russia and Hungary—with the debased coins, thus laying these countries, as it were, under contribution. Everywhere his agents tracked down sound money and sent it on to Berlin, where it was melted down and minted in debased form. In this way he doubled the value of the British subsidies. He spared Prussian currency as long as he could, but later had to debase it, though at a slower rate than that of Saxony, Mecklenburg and Poland. In 1757 he leased the Saxon, in 1759 the Prussian mints to a consortium of Jewish bankers, Ephraim and Itzig, who boasted of having drawn more than fifty millions in gold from Prussia's eastern neighbors. From that time forward he had plenty of money, though his diabolical employment of Jews as the special agents of his crime stirred up a perfervid wave of Prussian anti-semitism. In this way Frederick covered from one-fourth to one-third of the entire costs of the war, which have been estimated at one hundred forty millions.[19] It goes without saying that this practice was disastrous to commerce and trade. Its destructive consequences were felt in Prussia for many years after the war. As a war measure, however, it was brilliantly successful. Frederick never suffered from lack of

19 A. O. Loehr, "Die Finanzierung des Siebenjährigen Krieges," *Numismatische Zeitschrift*, Vol. 58 (1925), 95-110; R. Koser, "Preussische Finanzen im Siebenjährigen Kriege," *Forschungen zur Brandenburgischen und Preussischen Geschichte*, Vol. 13 (1900), 153; O. Hintze, *Die Hohenzollern und Ihr Werk* (Berlin, 1916), 377.

money and actually emerged from the war with more, though hopelessly debased, money than when he entered it.

All these factors, contributory to the defeat of the aggressive designs of the coalition, would have been of little importance had it not been for the superb endurance and the indomitable will of the Prussian monarch himself. Napoleon contended that it was not the Prussian army but Frederick who frustrated the coalition, and more than a century of historical scholarship has been unable to upset this judgment. It has often been remarked that Frederick was a matured personality in 1756. Yet it was only the terrible physical and spiritual rigors of this war that transformed the dainty royal epicure into a hardened stoic, converted the rationalist *bel-esprit* into an ascetic of the army camp, a haggard little man with his face unwashed and clothes untidy and soiled by grease and Spanish snuff, bowed down and chastened in his arrogance by humiliation and defeat but doggedly pursuing his one inflexible purpose, the survival of Prussia. As a sensitive, imaginative and intelligent youth he had once fancied that his deepest impulses were those of a philosopher, a literary critic, a musician. His father's keen delight in administration had been foreign to him. Horrified at the sight of the wounded and the shrieks of the dying, he frequently expressed his disgust at having to ply the bloody trade of war. Even yet in the lull of the fighting, at night in his headquarters, he was often heard declaiming Racine with an emotion that moved him to tears, playing his own compositions on the flute, reading French authors or writing a sheaf of bad French verse. Nonetheless he now administered and waged war with that last and final ounce of energy which accrued to him from his all but superhuman self-discipline. The tyranny of the state which he imposed on his people held him, too, in its relentless grip.

Although Frederick shared all hardships and privations with his men and rode into the battle with them, he was isolated in the midst of his officers, who did not share his culture. There were moments of intimacy with the common soldiers, who called him "Papa" or "Old Fritz," but the longer the war lasted and the more inferior his soldier material became, the more did he thunder against the *coujons, canailles* and *marodeurs,* until there came the moment when he feared his army more than the enemy. There was a good deal of criticism of his methods among the officers, and his brother, the crabbed Prince Henry, a talented representative of the old school of maneuvering, contended that all the king knew of the art of war was to give battle. They scarcely understood him.

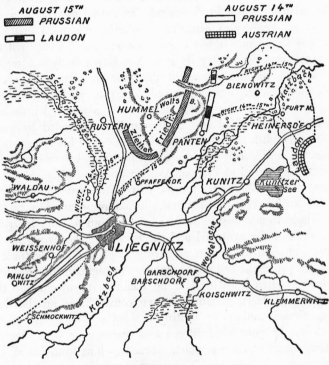

BATTLE OF LIEGNITZ, AUGUST 15, 1760.

How was it that Frederick escaped complete destruction after his ruinous defeats at Kolin, Breslau, Hochkirch, Kunersdorf and Maxen? Was it only because of the phenomenal stupidity, or, as Frederick put it, the *"divine ânerie"* of the allied generals? Surely this was less important than the extraordinary resilience of the king himself. His many defeats, his telling blows, his amazing display of endurance, his lightning recovery from desperate situations inspired his opponents with a wholesale respect for his prowess.[20] Only a few days after his smashing defeat at Kunersdorf, quickly followed by the loss of General Finck's entire army at Maxen, he had gathered troops enough to block Daun's march on Berlin. Morally intact, he contended that "the last bundle of straw and

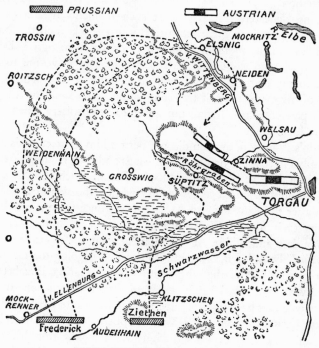

BATTLE OF TORGAU, NOVEMBER 3, 1760.

the last loaf of bread will determine which of us will remain in Saxony."

By exertions which astonished his enemies Frederick had gathered sufficient forces to take the field in 1760. His resources were obviously dwindling and it seemed that the Prussian Tiger was trapped. He compared himself with a person afflicted with the dropsy who "from day to day marks the progress of his disease,

[20] See the penetrating and charming study of Frederick in the critical moments of the war by H. Rothfels, *Ostraum, Preussentum und Reichsgedanke* (Leipzig, 1935), 15.

feels the cold messenger of death in his limbs and calculates in advance the moment when his heart, too, will die." But Liegnitz and Torgau proved to the Austrians that his heroic will was unbroken. In 1761 with more than one hundred thousand troops he once again succeeded in keeping his enemies at bay, although his situation was, if possible, more hopeless still. Pitt and his friend, d'Argens, delicately hinted that at such moments trifling concessions might conjure great storms. But Frederick replied, "Never will I survive the moment in which I am forced to sign a dishonorable peace; no eloquence, no inducement can drive me to subscribe to my own disgrace. I will either bury myself beneath the ruins of my country, or, if this consolation is too sweet for the fate which persecutes me, I shall put an end to my misery when I can endure it no longer."

Daun's strategy of evasion did not permit him to execute his audacious plan of striking first at the Russians and then risking his entire army in a decisive battle with Austria. But so much is certain, that in the contest of moral forces victory was on the side of Frederick. Even after the Russians and Austrians had once more succeeded in uniting their forces in full view of his camp at Bunzelwitz, they did not dare attack him. At this moment, chance, *"sa sacrée majesté le hazard"* he called it, brought him relief. It is going too far to say, as is generally said, that the death of the Tsarina Elizabeth on January 5, 1762, saved Frederick from certain destruction. It is of course true that he could not have resisted indefinitely the combined forces of Russia, Austria and Sweden. But then, by all the rules of contemporary warfare his situation was hopeless from the start. If his own powers were nearly exhausted, his enemies also had fought it to the stumps. France could no longer pay her subsidies and Maria Theresa was forced to reduce her army by twenty thousand men. The antagonists were alike worn out, but the elimination of Russia, soon followed by Sweden, gave Frederick an actual military superiority over Austria.

III. THE DICTATORSHIP OF WILLIAM PITT

While Frederick II stood his ground precariously against the continental coalition, his British ally conquered a vast empire. The

groundwork for the achievement of this mighty result was prepared by the diplomatic adjustments already described. By utilizing
her financial resources and her continental connections to support
a military diversion against France, Great Britain remained free
to devote her main effort to the sea and to the colonies. But Great
Britain and France, besides being engaged in their own maritime
and colonial war, were both deeply involved in the continental war
as subsidy-paying powers. The success of the one and the failure
of the other must, therefore, in large measure be explained in terms
of finance and credit. The partial reconstruction of the British
navy, both ships and officers, by Lord Anson, the silent man in the
admiralty, now produced magnificent results, particularly since
the army and navy co-operated consistently in making and securing
conquests in all parts of the globe. The British navy crippled its
French antagonist in Europe, prevented the capture of overseas
posts and successfully maintained uninterrupted trade communications. During the war the volume of British commerce actually
increased, in spite of the heavy damage done to smaller vessels by
French privateers. This expanding trade supported British credit.
Money was freely obtainable all through the war until the administration of Lord Bute, whereas French commerce and credit were
effectively destroyed. Gaston Martin's studies show that the slave
trade of Nantes was quite annihilated. Malvezin's statistics for Bordeaux prove likewise that the Seven Years' War was much more
disastrous for France than the Succession War.[21] The value of
French trade with the colonies, which had risen well above thirty
million in 1755, dropped below four in 1760. All these British successes on the periphery would have been impossible, however, without the drastic change in the government which concentrated in
the vigorous hands of William Pitt the political and strategical
conduct of the great war which is immortally linked with his name.

Pitt rose to power in defiance of the iron rule of caste which
closed important offices to commoners without family connections
or great fortune. He had to climb on hands and knees to a subordinate post, the paymaster's office, and the shifty Duke of Newcastle, who may have desired him as a colleague but feared him as

[21] Malvezin, *Histoire du commerce de Bordeaux*, III, 306.

a rival, was there to see that he should not pass that fixed line. Pitt was bursting with desire to be secretary of state and to lead the House of Commons, a position which he thought was commensurate to his importance. Balked in this ambition, an intense indignation gathered strength in him and soon developed into an indomitable and superhuman force.[22] He haughtily refused the role of Newcastle's hireling to defend government measures in parliament and, almost friendless and penniless, struck out on an independent course of his own. Dismissed from his paymaster's office in November, 1755, he thundered at the feeble and distracted Newcastle with all his matchless powers of oratorical invective, overawing the house of commons, expounding England's true policy and teaching the country, as Fox put it, how to wage war. Hated by the king and the Whig aristocracy and disbarred from power, he appealed to the country at large and, though without the slightest leaning toward social reform, succeeded in winning popular support. For this very reason one must not scan his early career too closely for moral scruple or intellectual consistency. He played the game of politics on the lines of a showman announcing his circus, posing now as the incorruptible Roman senator, then as the suffering patriot who drove over all England to display his martyred person to the people. Yet it cannot be denied that the love of country, which was cant to some of his associates, was a religion to him. Until 1756 he was a swashbuckler; thereafter he became the very incarnation of modern England, of its shippers and sailors, of its merchants and bankers, above all of the commercial and territorial imperialism of Great Britain.

The unbroken succession of Engish disasters with which the war had opened played into Pitt's hands. In North America the French had been everywhere successful; their forts dominated every access to Canada and the Mississippi. Braddock and Boscawen had failed, Montcalm had taken Oswego, the ruler of Bengal had stormed Calcutta and, worst of all, Minorca, which was still rated above Gibraltar, had been disgracefully lost. Public opinion was seething with

---

22 Lord Roseberry, *Chatham, His Early Life and Connections* (London, 1910), 234; A. von Ruville, *William Pitt, Earl of Chatham* (London, 1907), II, 45; B. Williams, *The Life of William Pitt* (London, 1914), I, 251; the competent article in the *Dictionary of National Biography*.

indignation at these disasters, which in fact were all primarily due to ministerial blundering and inaction. Everywhere rose the cry for the punishment of Admiral Byng, the commanding officer of the Mediterranean fleet. Members of parliament received petitions to call the ministers to account for sending him out too late. The naval court-martial, deliberating under the pressure of rising public resentment, condemned the unhappy Byng to death—literally, as Voltaire ironically put it, to encourage the other admirals. As a matter of fact, Byng had done nothing to justify the verdict. Of the crime of which he was declared guilty—neglect of duty in battle—he was entirely innocent. For the offenses of which he was guilty—the desertion of Minorca and disobedience to admiralty instructions—there was no legal penalty. The court somehow felt that the death penalty was excessive and recommended him to His Majesty's clemency. But that was denied him, for all around there stood the fallen ministers with their bribes and their boroughs, ready to crush any one who suggested that Byng was not the sole author of the loss of Minorca. There is, perhaps, no more conclusive example of the extent and diversity of Whig patronage than the tale of the gates of mercy being shut against Byng.[23]

Meanwhile Newcastle and his ministry had resigned. The withdrawal of Fox and the categorical refusal of Pitt to enter the cabinet with him, had left him no other alternative. Pitt had become inevitable. The combined pressure of the Tory agrarians and the city merchants forced him upon the reluctant king. But Pitt's first ministry also failed, because he found it impossible to govern without the Whig magnificoes, above all without Newcastle's parliamentary majority. His opponents did not actively conspire against him; they simply refrained from supporting him. The real blow came from the court, where Cumberland made Pitt's dismissal the condition of his acceptance of the command of the Hanoverian army.[24] Pitt's friends in the ministry resigned at once and for eleven weeks England was without a government. During this interregnum the public excitement was intense. London voted Pitt its freedom and

[23] Brian Tunstall, *Admiral Byng, the Loss of Minorca* (London, 1928), 240.
[24] E. Charteris, *Cumberland and the Seven Years' War* (London, 1925); W. E. H. Lecky, *History of England in the Eighteenth Century* (London, 1883), II, 503; P. Yorke, *Earl of Hardwicke* (Cambridge, 1913), III, ch. XXVII.

the other chief towns soon followed suit. The king sought vainly to form a government without Pitt by calling in turn on Newcastle, Fox and Grenville, but these Whig leaders had now reached the conclusion that a government in which Pitt was not the actual leader was impossible. Pitt still refused to share his power with Newcastle and Fox, though experience had taught him that he could not stand alone. But by giving up his opposition to entering the same ministry with Newcastle he secured the latter's parliamentary majority, while by accepting Fox he obtained at least the benevolent neutrality of the Whig magnates. By shuffling places Pitt gained everything he desired. Thus was formed on June 29, 1757 the new coalition ministry which, combining Pitt's following in the country with Newcastle's parliamentary placemen, in the next three years proved to be the most successful government in English history. Since all groups and factions were represented in the cabinet, the king could no longer play Pitt's rivals against him and Newcastle could no longer exploit his parliamentary majority. Pitt himself became secretary of state, leader of the house of commons, and unchallenged first minister.

The concentration of political and executive authority and the enlistment of all parties and groups, including now the Scots and the colonists, in an energetic prosecution of the war were, without doubt, Pitt's greatest achievement. He had sole control. In his hands all the strands of government were now gathered. The clumsy constitutional machinery of Britain became an effective instrument of organized action. In the secret committee of the council, where large questions of policy and strategy were settled, Pitt was and for the next few years remained a dictator. The Duke of Newcastle, though still the nominal head of the administration, was degraded to a mere dispenser of patronage, with which Pitt disdained all connection. Should the duke venture to oppose Pitt even in his special domain, the treasury, the great war minister threatened him with public accusation or immediate resignation. The terrified duke was soon writing to his friend, Hardwicke, that he had good reasons to believe that Pitt was satisfied with him.

Apart from finance, the main business of government was in the hands of the two secretaries of state for the northern and southern departments. Pitt, as secretary of state for the southern department, reduced his colleague, Holderness, to an absolute cipher. They, that is to say Pitt, controlled every act of war, every detail of diplomacy and domestic administration. They alone had authority to give orders in the name of the sovereign. However obsequious Pitt, whom the nation had thrust upon the king, may have been in the presence of the monarch (he bowed so deeply that, it was said, you could see his nose between his legs), in essential matters he brooked no royal contradiction as long as he was in office. Though a parliamentary minister in a constitutional monarchy, he was no less tyrannical and dictatorial than Frederick the Great. He shunned no labor, no fatigue, no expense. He communicated his own fiery energy to every department of the government. He suspended the rule of seniority as the ground for promotion in the army and navy, appointed and cashiered commanders as he saw fit, wrote their instructions and dealt directly with the officers of combined expeditions in which co-ordinate action between army and navy was involved. Having once appointed his agents, he trusted them with full powers and, after the fate of Byng, military responsibility was a terrible reality. Never before had the scattered energies of Englishmen, Scots and colonists been so firmly united, never had they appeared so strong to themselves or to the outside world. It is true that the landowning classes, upon whom the heavy burden of taxation fell, and those who had not invested in the national debt and were alarmed by its rapid growth were less enthusiastic. But for the moment the methods and achievements of Pitt appeared equally remarkable to contemporaries. As Frederick the Great wrote, *"c'était la meilleure tête de l'Angleterre."*

Pitt's chief source of power was his popularity, and he neglected no occasion to court and increase it. He was ready to listen to seamen, officers, planters, colonial agents, if they had anything to say. But his special clientele, his real constituency, were the merchants of the city of London.[25] The bond that united Pitt and the traders was one of mutual self-interest. He asked them to make heavy sacrifices, subscribe to his loans, feed his unrivaled information of

[25] Kate Hotblack, *Chatham's Colonial Policy* (London, 1917), 11-27; Q. S. Leadam, *Political History of England* (London, 1909), IX, 458-459.

commercial and colonial affairs and, incidentally, to keep him in office. In return he held before them the glowing vision of the growth and prosperity of the British empire as a trading concern. Many of his expeditions were planned with the aid and advice which he received from the merchants. His friend, William Beckford, a Jamaica planter and parliamentary member for the city of London, needed only to give the hint and a naval expedition was sent to the French West Indies, which were inconvenient rivals of his own estates.

Pitt proved himself equal to all the military, diplomatic and financial difficulties which confronted an administrator of a worldwide war. His first task was to provide the means to wage this ubiquitous struggle. For this purpose an obsequious and silent parliament voted ten and a half million pounds and almost two millions for subsidies in 1758, raised one hundred thousand land troops and sixty thousand sailors for a total of four hundred twelve British ships of all classes. Pitt sent eight thousand troops and an immense fleet under Boscawen to America, strong reinforcements to the West Indies and an expedition to Africa. He seconded the efforts of the company in India. Undeniably there was a reckless profusion in his methods. This was notably true of those peddling little raids which he inspired against the French coast at Rochefort, Saint-Malo, Cherbourg, and Saint-Cast. They did only a small amount of local damage and, except insofar as they raised the spirit of Englishmen, were relatively useless.[26] His other measures, however, were better suited to the purpose of the war. To cut off French reinforcements to the colonies Admiral Hawke's blockade with seven ships made the English masters of the French coast from Brest to Rochefort. To protect the American colonial fish trade another fleet of fifteen ships under Admiral Osborn cruised along the Spanish coast and in the Mediterranean. It should not be forgotten that it was through their trade with Mediterranean ports that the American colonists gained the specie which enabled them to make their returns to Great Britain, the two million pounds a year which afterwards Pitt declared had carried Great Britain triumphantly through the war.

[26] J. Tramond, *Manuel d'histoire maritime de la France* (Paris, 1927), 404.

While Pitt was thus engaged in rousing the spirit of the nation and marshaling its forces to crush the naval power and the colonial settlements of France and plant on their ruins a still vaster British empire, he had to be careful not to increase the number of Britain's enemies. Russia, which had no serious quarrel with England, presented no difficulties. But throughout the war England and France never ceased to struggle for the control of Spanish policy. Spain refused Pitt's bribe of Gibraltar for an alliance, but she also rejected the French offer of Minorca. Thanks to the Spanish Queen Barbara and the pro-British foreign minister, General Wall, it was possible to prolong Spanish neutrality at least until the death of Ferdinand VI in 1759. No less serious was the menacing attitude of the neutral sea powers, Holland, Denmark and Sweden. A single false step in the assertion of British belligerent rights might easily have crystallized these states into a dangerously hostile maritime union or have forced them to pool their fleets with those of France.[27]

It was no secret that neutral shippers were covering French European and colonial trade. Unable to provide French merchants with adequate naval protection, the French ministry of marine relaxed its exclusive navigation laws by the wholesale issuing of licenses and passports to neutral shippers. The strategic position of St. Eustatius enabled the Dutch to appropriate a greater share of the French West Indian trade. The Dutch, moreover, were the chief providers to the French of naval stores and contraband of war.[28] The war being one against French trade, Pitt could not allow this traffic to go on without a challenge. His main anxiety was to put an end to this contraband trade without driving the neutral sea powers into open warfare. He refused to recognize the Dutch principle of "free ships, free goods," and ruthlessly enforced the British "Rule of the War of 1756" to the effect that during a war neutrals could not, without running the risk of seizure and condemnation in a British prize court, engage in a trade with the colonies of a belligerent which was denied in time of peace.[29] To

[27] J. Corbett, *England in the Seven Years' War* (London, 1907), II, 5 ff.
[28] R. Waddington, *Histoire de la guerre de sept ans*, III, 422 ff.
[29] A. P. Higgins, "Maritime Rights and Colonial Titles," *Cambridge History of the British Empire* (Cambridge, 1929), I, 551.

enforce this rule and at the same time prevent an open rupture was no easy task. By means of the blockade of the French West Indies in 1758 Pitt succeeded in paralyzing the trade of St. Eustatius, though he could not suppress it entirely. But the rough, piratical tactics of British cruisers and privateers, who used little discrimination as to what ships they seized, caused him endless difficulties. Dutch ships were taken and condemned in English prize courts without mercy and often without justice; sometimes they were seized again on their emerging from port after the prize courts had set them free. Such practices aroused universal resentment throughout Europe, for Danes, Swedes and Spaniards fared no better than the Dutch.[30] The only redress against a privateer were the prize courts, and Pitt was reluctant to interfere with them. Yet he did what he could to palliate the legitimate grievances of the Dutch. What caused most of the difficulty outside of the "Rule of 1756" was the activity of small privateers, a class of vessel which Pitt's new Prize Bill of 1759 excluded from receiving letters of marque to prey on enemy trade. They were drawn into the navy and in future their work could be carried on only by large ships financed by wealthy merchants or corporations who could be held responsible for illegal acts. By such a policy of moderation and concession Pitt succeeded in preventing an open rupture with neutral maritime powers.

IV. THE DUKE OF CHOISEUL

It is difficult to conceive of a sharper contrast than that between the whole British nation, united in support of the implacable Pitt, and monarchist France, lacking all unity and coherent direction. He who would get at the roots of the French defeats at Rossbach, Quebec and Quiberon Bay must not lose sight of the internal affairs of the kingdom itself. Though still the foremost power of Europe in population and military resources, France entered this gigantic war amid a welter of domestic controversies that weakened authority and prevented the crystallization of a determined national will. Discipline, obedience, devotion to duty, which had once constituted the greatness of the monarchy, were manifestly in decay. Violent

---

[30] P. Yorke, *Earl of Hardwicke* (Cambridge, 1913), III, 135.

disagreements and revolts divided the court, the *parlements*, the provincial estates, the enlightened *salons*, the very men in the street. The intolerant clergy persecuted the Jansenists and the enlightened philosophers, who in turn released their critical shafts against church and state alike. Every one argued and criticized, but few obeyed. Badly supported by the upper classes and at loggerheads with his *parlements*, Louis XV had to wage war in the face of an irritated public opinion.[31]

The most pressing need was to provide money for the war. Unfortunately the clergy had brought to naught Machault's efforts at tax reform in 1751 and by doing so had put the government at the mercy of the *parlements*. There was plenty of wealth in France, but the antiquated system of taxation did not tap it, and without the backing of the magistrates public loans had little chance of success. The king had levied a previous *vingtième*, a property tax which did not touch labor, but the rebates and exemptions granted to large numbers of nobles made it only feebly remunerative. Refusing to strike his flag to England, Louis XV courageously added a second *vingtième*, on July 5, 1756, thus doubling the burden of taxation. In justice to Louis it should be said that by levying this new tax he demanded that the rich and powerful must bear an equitable share of the burden of war. But that, in the eyes of the magistrates, was its great offense, and it was only with the utmost difficulty that the government succeeded in executing the measure. At once the *parlements* of Paris, Toulouse, Besançon, Bordeaux and Montauban issued protesting remonstrances, opposing the tax and denouncing tax inspectors as unprincipled ruffians whose aim it was to alleviate the burdens of the peasantry by casting them on the shoulders of the aristocracy. The deluded masses, whom the *vingtième* was designed to relieve, supported the upper classes and applauded the obstructing *parlements*.

At the very moment when the popular agitation and rioting was most intense, on January 5, 1757, Damiens, an isolated fanatic, made an unsuccessful attempt upon the life of the king. Louis was not seriously wounded, but for some weeks the entire kingdom was thrown into panic. When questioned, Damiens confessed that he

[31] A. Dussauge, *Le ministère de Belle-Isle* (Paris, 1914), 11 ff.

had been incited by the inflammatory speeches of the members of *parlement*. "If I had never entered a court of justice and had stayed on in the service of army people," he said, "I should never have got here."[32] The *parlements* were compromised and yielded—for the moment. Louis, anxious to establish concord among his subjects and unite them against the enemy, sacrificed his two ablest ministers, Machault and d'Argenson. It was rumored that they were dismissed because they had advised Madame de Pompadour to leave Versailles and retire to the country. It is more probable that Machault, the enemy of the privileges of the clergy, the magistrates and the estates, had to go because Louis was convinced there could be no permanent peace with the *parlements* so long as he remained in office. The vacant places were filled by mediocrities who changed so rapidly that the Duchess of Orleans, sending her congratulations to a new secretary of state, remarked, "At least you will learn if he is still in office." Bernis was the leading figure in the council and he was not the man to replace the useful heads whom the king had dismissed.

France was not wholly unprepared for the war. The navy had not been entirely neglected. Rouillé and Machault had pushed the ship-building program and in 1756 France had sixty-three, possibly seventy-two, ships-of-the-line. Efforts had also been made to revive the professional spirit among the naval officers, dulled by years of dawdling about the dockyards, by establishing the *Académie de la Marine*. But the lack of experienced commanders and the traditional French naval tactics of cutting and running whenever a British fleet was encountered excluded the possibility of major triumphs at sea. Yet in spite of British naval superiority French fleets sailed freely to and from the colonies in the first three years of the war.

The colonies were far from being abandoned. In 1756 Montcalm landed in Canada with two thousand men. In the next three years he received funds amounting to one hundred nine millions. In 1758 d'Aché was sent out to India with a squadron and four hundred men who, together with the one thousand six hundred men carried out by Godeheu, gave Lally-Tollendal three times as many

32 P. Gaxotte, *Louis XV and His Times* (Philadelphia, 1934), 235.

soldiers as Dupleix had had at his disposal. So highly did the French government value the preservation of the West Indian islands that it sent out no less than four great expeditions during the war. The capture of Minorca rendered Mediterranean operations unimportant and the Toulon fleet was free to sail for Martinique in 1757 and in 1759. To defend its sugar islands the French government did not hesitate to send out in 1758 detachments from the Atlantic fleet itself.

But the faint-hearted Bernis saw no more brilliant prospects on the sea than he did on land against Frederick. His epistolary jeremiads to Choiseul betray a defeatist attitude. Already in the summer of 1758 he wrote,

No trade left, consequently no money or circulation. No navy, consequently no strength to resist England. The navy has no more sailors, and having no money cannot hope to procure them. What must be the result of this state of affairs? The loss of all our colonies forever; our land forces cannot protect our coasts. . . . Even if we save Louisbourg, what help can we send to our colonies without ships or money? . . . I tell you, my dear Count, that even if the King of Prussia were crushed, we should be ruined nonetheless. England carries on all the trade there is, and we shall never reduce her to reasonable conditions unless we can interrupt it.[33]

So hopeless did he believe the situation to be that in his opinion only immediate peace with England could avert irreparable ruin. But the Duke of Choiseul, who replaced him in December, 1758, was made of sterner stuff.[34] Brilliant and versatile, blessed with superabundant Gallic wit and resourcefulness, Choiseul introduced a fresh spirit into the French conduct of the war. While yet the young, vivacious son of the grand chamberlain of the Duke of Lorraine, he was known for his audacity and gallantries at Versailles, where he earned the gratitude of Madame de Pompadour by re-

[33] Bernis to Choiseul, Aug. 20, 1758, *Mémoires et Lettres du Cardinal de Bernis* (Paris, 1903), II, 259.

[34] A modern critical study of Choiseul still remains to be written. Besides *Mémoires du duc de Choiseul* on which one should consult P. Muret's articles in the *Revue d'histoire moderne et contemporaine*, Vol. VI (1905), 229-248 and 377-399; Ch. Filon, *L'ambassade de Choiseul à Vienne en 1757-1758* (Paris, 1872); Soulange-Bodin, *La diplomatie de Louis XV et le pacte de famille* (Paris, 1894); A. Bourget, *Études sur la politique étrangère du duc de Choiseul* (Paris, 1907); now also Louis Blart, *Les rapports de la France et de l'Espagne après le pacte de famille* (Paris, 1915), ch. I.

vealing to the powerful favorite an intrigue between Louis XV and his cousin, Mme. de Choiseul-Romanet. From that moment all barriers were down. He was sent as ambassador to Rome in 1754 and to Vienna in 1757. His calculated advocacy of the Austrian alliance won for him the favor of Maria Theresa, and by his shrewd critical sense he gained an increasing influence in determining the policy of his home government. Supplanting Bernis at the foreign office, he dominated Louis XV through the Marquise and soon acquired a pre-eminent rank and influence in the royal council. He breathed confidence and optimism, and his penetrating grasp of political realities made him a not unworthy successor of Fleury. By gradually gaining control of foreign affairs, army and navy, he secured the unique position of a dictator, not unlike his great opponent across the Channel.

Convinced of the necessity of a change of policy, Choiseul promptly set to work to bring the French system of alliances more into harmony with the vital interests of France. Hitherto military and financial resources had been lavished upon the subordinate German war, while the really important conflict, the maritime war with England, had been allowed to suffer. In the third Treaty of Versailles of March, 1759 Choiseul reduced French subsidies to Vienna by one half and limited the Austrian alliance to operations in western Germany. He refused to guarantee the return of Silesia, but he also renounced Belgium on behalf of Don Philip. Yet he kept open the possibility of a separate peace with England.[35] To fluster the English he encouraged a maritime union of Russia, Sweden and Denmark for the protection of neutral rights in the Baltic. It was impossible to establish a balance of maritime forces against England without the active support of the Spanish navy. But Choiseul's furious efforts to persuade Spanish statesmen that the beleaguered French colonies were the last bulwark of the Spanish Indies against English aggression remained for the moment without success. There was no escape from the distressing conclusion that France had to fight her war alone.

It was plainly impossible for the French navy to overwhelm the British fleets in every one of the numerous areas of colonial con-

---

[35] A. Schaefer, *Geschichte des Siebenjährigen Krieges* (Berlin, 1870), II, 234.

flict. At best the colonies could be expected to hold their own while a decision was forced elsewhere. But that was possible only if the decision came quickly. Choiseul accepted the doctrine of the Count of Broglie, the director of the King's Secret, that the war could still be, if not won, at least balanced by triumphs in Europe. With a logical consistency that commands admiration he resolved to stake his entire fortune on a single, desperate military card, a descent upon England. To save the French colonies, to assist Austria against Prussia, to cause the collapse of the army of Prince Ferdinand of Brunswick, he was determined to strike at the financial heart of the enemy by making a direct attack on the British islands, the fountainhead of the colonial offensive and the source of the subsidies that nourished the German war. There was no flaw in this reasoning, but a crack-brained plan was drawn up by Belle Isle without the slightest reference to the British naval forces. There was to be a double invasion of England and Scotland. Troops were collected in Belgium, Normandy and at Vannes in the Morbihan, on the southern side of Brittany. A squadron at Dunkirk under Thurot, a dashing privateer, was to sail north and draw off the English fleet by menacing the coasts of Scotland and Ireland. Meanwhile La Clue with the Toulon fleet was to pass through the Straits and join the main French fleet under Admiral Conflans at Brest. Together they were to cover the passage of the army, which was to come out from Vannes in flat-bottomed transports and land on the coast of Suffolk. Even admitting that the plan was feasible, secrecy and speed were indispensable to its success. But the delay in constructing the transports caused a postponement in the execution of the plan until the autumn of 1759. The English were informed and given ample time to take counter-measures.

Not for an instant did Pitt permit himself to be deflected from his efforts to sweep the French from North America, the West Indies and the eastern seas. There was no hint of the panic of 1755 in the England of 1759. Fresh squadrons under Moore and Hopson sailed for the West Indies and under Saunders and Wolfe for Quebec. Not a single soldier did Pitt withdraw from the Continent. It was only after these preparations had been completed that he occupied himself with Choiseul's plan of invasion. Every French port from Dunkirk to Toulon was blockaded. Hawke with the grand fleet blockaded Brest, while the duty of preventing the junction of La Clue and Conflans was entrusted to Boscawen and Broderick, who held the Strait of Gibraltar. Rodney watched the flotilla preparing at Le Havre and Boys kept a vigilant eye on Thurot at Dunkirk; Sir Percy Brett hung back in the Downs. Choiseul's scheme could succeed only if La Clue evaded first Boscawen and then Hawke; if Boscawen, finding that he had been evaded, did not at once join Hawke; and if the two were not united before the necessarily slow operation of embarking the soldiers at the Morbihan and bringing the swarm of flatboats to the British shores was completed. But even supposing that the French concentration could have been effected, it would have been met by a concentration of superior British forces, for, having the advantage of shorter distances, the reserve squadron in the Downs could have joined Hawke at once. La Clue did, indeed, manage to escape Boscawen at Gibraltar, but the latter dispersed and destroyed his fleet off Lagos on August 19, 1759. After this failure, a combined operation was no longer possible. Choiseul, rather than allow himself to be criticized for doing nothing, then endeavored to do with a part of the navy what would have been perilous even if tried by the whole concentrated fleet. At the moment when bad weather compelled Hawke to retire from the dangerous coast, Choiseul ordered Conflans to slip out of Brest, pick up the transports at Vannes and convoy them to the British coast. But Hawke, duly warned, followed in hot pursuit and destroyed the French fleet in the inspiring November battle of Quiberon Bay, one of the "most heroic achievements in the long history of the Royal Navy."[36]

Choiseul saw his hopes fade. Everything had been lost for want of a navy commensurate to its task. The polite irony of Maurepas on the necessity of having a navy to make successful war on a maritime power had at last struck home. It was too late to repair the neglect of years when in 1761 Choiseul became minister of marine. Lagos and Quiberon Bay remained the pivotal naval bat-

[36] A. T. Mahan, *The Influence of Sea Power upon History* (Boston, 1896), 301 ff.; J. Corbett, *England in the Seven Years' War* (London, 1907), II, 41-70; D. Hannay, *Short History of the British Navy* (London, 1909), II, 183; R. Jouan, *Histoire de la marine française* (Paris, 1932), I, 239.

tles of the war in European waters. French commerce was driven
from the seas, though at the end of the war it revived somewhat.
When the curtain fell on the drama of the war there were one
thousand two hundred English naval prisoners in France and
twenty-five thousand French prisoners in England.[37] Henceforth
the principal duty of the British navy was to co-operate with the
army in conquering French colonial possessions.

V. THE COLONIAL WAR

1. *Canada*

For Pitt this war was pre-eminently a war over North America,
where the French had hitherto more than held their own. He never
lost sight of the central principle of his colonial policy, that France
was "chiefly to be dreaded as a maritime and commercial power."
Indubitably his war aims grew with his success, but what he valued
in Canada was above all the Newfoundland and St. Lawrence
fisheries and the fur trade which, like the African gum and slaves,
were to have their allotted place in his commercial empire.

The strategical problem of the American continent was simple
enough. The contested region of the Ohio valley and the entire
west must fall into British hands at the moment when French
Canada ceased to sustain them. The conquest of French Canada
must, therefore, be the prime objective. So long as the fortress at
Louisburg was supported by a French fleet, the approach by sea
was closed. Louisburg had once more to be captured.

British measures for the control of the sea routes, both on the
French coast and in America, to prevent reinforcements from being
sent from France, have already been referred to. Pitt now proceeded
to collect on the American continent an overwhelming force of
twenty thousand English regulars and more than twenty-two thousand colonial volunteers, numbers such as had never before been
thrown into the balance of colonial conflicts. He sent out three great
expeditions against the French positions: the first under Amherst, a
general of commanding ability, supported by Admiral Boscawen,
was directed against Louisburg; the second under Abercrombie and

[37] R. Castex, *Les idées militaires de la marine du XVIII siècle* (Paris, 1911).

Howe was to attack Canada from the south; the third under Forbes was sent over the Alleghenies against the French forts in the Ohio valley. Pitt had seized the vital point; Canada was to be attacked from all sides and exhausted.

This is not the place to present a detailed narrative of the dramatic events of the French and Indian war: the audacious landing of General Wolfe in Gabarus Bay in the full tide of the Atlantic ocean, which determined the fall of Louisburg; the passage of Abercrombie's fifteen thousand men over Lake George and their bloody repulse at the hands of Montcalm's paltry four thousand men at Ticonderoga (July 1, 1758), a reverse which in no way altered the strategic situation; the victorious march of the old, inflexible Forbes, sick to death and carried over the Alleghenies in a sedan chair, to Fort Duquesne, which was rebaptized Pittsburgh "because the spirit of Pitt inspired the enterprise"; finally, the seizure of Frontenac, which cut off Canada from Louisiana. What an amazing change over the preceding years to find the army and navy, Englishmen and colonists, co-operating toward a common end and inspired by the spirit of heroic enterprise! Henceforth Canada was a beleaguered fortress.

Was it possible for France to save Canada? Swivel-chair strategists have so contended. Yet the French cause was lost long before the battle on the Plains of Abraham. It was lost because of the crushing inequality of numbers between the French-Canadian and the Anglo-American forces; because France, while not completely indifferent, was not sufficiently convinced of the importance of Canada to put forth a commensurate effort to save it; because the resolute Pitt was bent on carrying the struggle through to the bitter end; because the American colonies in the north and south, including even the Quakers of Pennsylvania, threatened by the French and Indian menace, responded to the warning of Benjamin Franklin that it was useless to hope for a permanent peace so long as the French were masters of Canada.

In Canada, with its narrow margin of food and other resources, the war created an insupportable situation. It increased the demand for supplies to unprecedented proportions and at the same time caused a sharp reduction in stores already seriously depleted by a succession of crop failures.[38] In the early years of the war military operations were subordinated to agriculture and after 1759 farming was sacrificed to warfare, with results that hastened the final catastrophe. In 1757 the French army could not assemble at Ticonderoga until provisions had arrived from France; it could not clinch its success at Fort William Henry because of the food shortage and the imminent harvest. The stoppage of regular arrivals from France, owing to the British blockade, soon necessitated the rationing of food supplies. Canada, moribund to begin with, was ruined by a corrupt administration. No doubt the decision, intelligence and vigor of the intendant Bigot and his friends of the *Grande Société*, which monopolized all internal and foreign commerce, had some happy effects in the early stages. But their cynical raids on the royal treasury, their undisguised thefts and speculative profits, their systematic depressing of the prices at which the *habitants* were compelled to sell their products, caused ill-feeling and riots and lowered the morale of a people fighting against a superior enemy.

In this colonial society, already suffused with a vigorous Canadian particularism of its own, the French regulars and their officers were regarded as hated and arrogant aliens. Revolted, in their turn, by the universal dishonesty and corruption which they saw around them and impatient of the native militia, which proved refractory to European military discipline, the French officers were inclined to look upon these abuses as something specifically Canadian and to treat the *habitants* generally as provincials and *arriérés*. As the corruption increased, the disgust of the scrupulously honest Montcalm vented itself in the agonized cry, *"Pouah! On suffoque ici."*[39]

Cultured, brave, chivalrous, imaginative, Montcalm represented the highest type of a French gentleman and soldier in the eighteenth century and is rightly regarded as the most luminous figure of the Canadian tragedy. He had been sent out to this savage country to defend a lost cause, only to find himself perpetually hampered by Vaudreuil, the native governor general of Canada, with whom he quarreled over Bigot, over the lack of discipline among Canadian

[38] J. E. Lunn, "Agriculture and War in Canada, 1740-1760," *Canadian Historical Review*, XVI (1935), 130.
[39] A. Lichtenberger, *Montcalm et la tragédie canadienne* (Paris, 1934), 100; J. Tramond in Hanotaux-Martineau, *Histoire des colonies françaises* (Paris, 1929), I, 160.

militiamen, and over the conduct of the war. Montcalm was acutely aware of the critical condition of Canadian affairs. He was in no position to renew his army, while he must expect the Anglo-Americans to increase their forces progressively from year to year. To strike a mortal blow at the English colonies was altogether impossible; all he could do was to postpone as long as possible the inevitable ultimate disaster. Trained in European methods of warfare, to which the war in America tended more and more to approximate, he condemned the profitless futilities of *la petite guerre* advocated by Vaudreuil and demanded a rigidly defensive strategy in the hope that events in Europe might still save the situation. This realistic appraisal of the military situation was his answer to the blithe optimism of Vaudreuil who, ignorant of military affairs, refused to believe in the danger of an English invasion even after the fall of Louisburg.[40] Montcalm and Vaudreuil were at dagger points on every issue of administration and war, a difference which threatened to break into open conflict even in the presence of the enemy. In its efforts to compose this demoralizing strife between the two men, the French government heaped honors upon Montcalm, appointed him lieutenant-general and ordered Vaudreuil to take no decision without first consulting him. But the disagreement between them remained absolute and fundamental.

In the autumn of 1758 Montcalm resolved to send Bougainville to Paris to explain the desperate military situation of Canada and to ask for assistance. He pointed out the overwhelming disparity of numbers and contended that Quebec, far from being a frowning mass of impregnability, bristling with heavy artillery, was actually indefensible.[41] It has become customary to summarize the upshot of the Bougainville mission with the famous remark of Berryer, the minister of marine, that one does not attempt to save the stables when the house is on fire. It is true that the reply of the French crown was that Canada must be left to her own resources. But what more could have been done? It was manifestly impossible to send

40 Capt. Sautai, *Montcalm au combat de Carillon;* T. Chapais, *Le Marquis de Montcalm* (Quebec, 1911); Abbé Georges Robitaille, *Montcalm et ses historiens* (Montreal, 1936); Aegidius Fanteux, "Montcalm," in the *Canadian Historical Association, Annual Report* (Ottawa, 1924); somewhat less useful Abbé H. R. Casgrain, *Montcalm et Lévis* (Quebec, 1891), I, 2.
41 R. Waddington, *Histoire de la guerre de sept ans,* III, 252.

sufficient reinforcements to achieve equality with the English. Had an army of ten thousand men been sent, Canada, already in danger of starvation, could not have fed them. The British naval forces would not have permitted them to arrive, and had they arrived, Pitt would have sent double their number. Neithei Louis XV, nor Belle Isle, nor Choiseul thought of abandoning Canada lightly.[42] Canada was to be saved by the invasion of England. Montcalm was instructed, in case of a catastrophe, that there must be no capitulation, that he must at all costs retain a foothold in the colony, so that the eventual peace negotiations would have to deal with a Canada at least nominally under the French flag. For the rest, Berryer sent three hundred recruits, some technical experts for artillery and two provision ships. But the palm for having provided blockaded Canada with food and other resources for its imprisoned armies belongs to the intrepid and resourceful Abraham Gradis, a merchant of Bordeaux, who refused to suspend his business operations because of the maritime war. His audacity and devotion represented France's will to retain Canada better than did the crown itself.[43]

Meanwhile Pitt had sent out his great expedition against Quebec under Admiral Saunders and General Wolfe.[44] There is no need here to relate the story of the fall of Quebec in the battle on the Plains of Abraham on September 13, 1759, in which both Montcalm and Wolfe lost their lives. The victory of Wolfe's nine thousand men over the fifteen thousand men of Montcalm was due as much to the breakneck audacity of the desperate English general and to the cordial co-operation of Admiral Saunders, as to the divided councils in the camp of the French, where Vaudreuil twice countermanded Montcalm's orders which, had they been executed, might well have altered the course of events.[45] But Canada was not yet won; indeed, Quebec was nearly lost in the winter when, cut off

[42] Abbé G. Robitaille, *Montcalm et ses historiens* (Montreal, 1936), 206.

[43] C. Jullien, *Histoire de Bordeaux* (Paris, 1895), 245; J. de Maupassant, *Abraham Gradis* (Bordeaux, 1917).

[44] R. Wright, *The Life of Major-General Wolfe* (London, 1864); F. E. Whitton, *Wolfe and North America* (Boston, 1929), 223 ff.; F. Parkman, *Montcalm and Wolfe* (Boston, 1884), 2 vols.; E. Salmon, *Life of Admiral Sir Charles Saunders* (London, 1914); G. M. Wrong, *The Fall of Canada* (Oxford, 1914); Mahon, *General James Murray* (London, 1921).

[45] G. M. Wrong, *The Rise and Fall of New France* (New York, 1928), II, 845, 851.

from the sea, its captors were beleaguered by the remaining French army under the command of the capable Levis, who defeated Murray in the second battle of Abraham. But the breaking of the ice brought store ships and relief to the British garrison, and the last hope of France, a fleet of provision ships for her own armies, was intercepted and captured by the British squadrons. The French were compelled to retreat to Montreal. This was the end. Three British armies converged on Montreal, Murray advancing on the left bank of the St. Lawrence from Quebec, Haviland from the south and Amherst from Ontario. Canada was lost and on September 8, 1760, Vaudreuil capitulated.

2. The West Indies

Although the avowed object of the war was the expulsion of the French from North America, Great Britain subdued all the French windward and the neutral islands. It was not, however, until the fall of Louisburg that Pitt and his friend, Beckford, the West India millionaire, settled upon the conquest of Martinique as one of their most cherished plans. For Pitt, ambitious as he was to secure for his countrymen markets from which they had been driven, commercial supremacy in the West Indies was a principal object. The West India interest no longer resisted the annexation of additional sugar colonies as it had done in 1740. This reversal of attitude was due less, as Mr. Namier suggests, to a difference among the West India interest between the "saturated" and the "planters on the make," than to considerations of safety in wartime. Saint Domingue, Martinique and Guadeloupe had excellent harbors to give anchorage to men-of-war and a shelter for swarms of privateers. The people of Martinique, who had the blood of the seventeenth-century filibusters in their veins, alone prized no less than one thousand four hundred English vessels in this war. Barbados and the English Leeward Islands actually suffered from scarcity because of this interruption of trade.[46] These losses will explain the sudden readiness of the legislatures of the British islands to assist in expeditions against the French colonies.

[46] P. Charliat, *Trois siècles d'économie maritime française* (Paris, 1931), 68; R. Pares, *War and Trade in the West Indies* (Oxford, 1936), 221.

The first British success in the West Indies was the conquest of Guadeloupe by Commodore Moore and General Hopson in the spring of 1759. But the strategic importance of Martinique and the difficulty of settling the neutral islands while it remained in French hands rendered the reduction of this island imperative. Choiseul did what he could, even after the disaster of Quiberon Bay, to save it, but when Rodney appeared before the island with a powerful fleet of nineteen vessels Martinique capitulated (February 2, 1762). The other islands, with the single exception of Saint Domingue, fell almost without a struggle.

The terms on which Guadeloupe and later Martinique were asked to surrender stipulated that they would remain wholly French islands under the British flag. The considerable revenues and all the trade went to England, but British planters could not establish themselves there. At once British slave merchants and North American traders hurried their ships to Guadeloupe to take advantage of famine prices for lumber, provisions and slaves. At the peace the merchants of Liverpool alone claimed to have imported more than twelve thousand slaves into Guadeloupe. The rapidly increasing cultivation enabled the planters to increase the produce of the island to more than twice its former volume. The local governor reported that "if kept at the peace, it would add to the security of the leeward islands, increase revenue, lower the price of sugar, supply a great part of the home consumption of coffee, cocoa, cotton, and contribute to the safety of commerce."[47] When it was learned that Guadeloupe was to be returned at the end of the war, Governor Dalrymple, writing to the board of trade, expressed his sorrow that France was to reap all the fruit of British labors, but philosophically consoled himself with the reflection that the islands had been very advantageous to Britain in the meantime.

Guadeloupe was precisely the kind of acquisition which the old English sugar colonies feared most. There was no opportunity for English planters in the island and the London market was flooded with cheap Guadeloupe sugars. There may have been other reasons for the great fall in sugar prices in 1760, but the conquest of Guadeloupe was one of the most important. When the news of the reduc-

[47] K. Hotblack, *Pitt's Colonial Policy* (London, 1915), 55, 61.

tion of Martinique reached London in 1762 the price of sugar fell three shillings, and it was impossible to sell the inferior clayed sugar from Barbados at any price.[48] But whatever the immediate effect on the West India interest, it was held by some of the best informed among English statesmen that without the West Indian conquests England could not have borne the continued expense of the war.

Closely related to the conquest of the West Indies was the fall of the French slave trading stations on the coast of Africa. Already in March, 1757 Pitt sent against Fort Louis on the Gambia River an expedition which made a rich haul in slaves and gum. In the following year he sent Admiral Keppel at the head of an expedition to attack the island of Gorée, which commanded the Senegal trade. Gorée surrendered at discretion and passed into British hands. It was the conviction of Pitt that the exclusion of the French from the coast of Africa would deal a fatal stroke to French commerce and leave it at the mercy of Great Britain. It has already been indicated that the French slave traffic and colonial trade collapsed quickly in the spring of 1757. The economic consequences for Nantes, the great slaving center of France, were disastrous. The wealthy commercial houses of this proud city were bankrupt and its streets were filled with beggars and unemployed sailors. Pitt's African policy achieved its purpose. It raised the price of negroes in the French West Indies to a prohibitive level and weakened the French privateers who manned their ships with slaves. It deprived the enemy of a valuable source of revenue and increased the resources of Great Britain.[49]

3. India

For British naval historians the Seven Years' War in India has become a classic illustration of the relentless pressure of naval superiority in colonial warfare.[50] Their argument, which it is difficult to challenge, runs somewhat as follows: when the news of the

---

[48] R. Pares, *War and Trade in the West Indies*, 481.
[49] Gaston Martin, *Nantes au XVIII siècle, L'ére de négriers* (Paris, 1931), 269.
[50] J. H. Rose in *Cambridge History of the British Empire* (Cambridge, 1929), I, 527; Sir Herbert Richmond, *The Navy in India, 1763-1783* (London, 1931), Introductory chapter.

declaration of war reached India in October, 1756 the French had more than double the fighting force, they held more territory and they disposed of wider political influence among the native princes than did the British. Yet at the end of the war British superiority in both respects was irresistible and their victory crushing. This early French military superiority on land had been acquired in time of peace, when there was no interruption in maritime communications. But as soon as Admiral Watson arrived in Indian waters with a British squadron that advantage vanished. The French political alliances with native princes might be ever so useful in a conflict with Britain, but in the long run they depended on military and financial superiority and neither the one nor the other could be maintained without naval superiority. In short, the power that could transport troops, money and supplies from Europe, while preventing the other from doing the same thing, could be certain of ultimate victory.

But before the war was well under way another material factor in the Indian situation had altered. Robert Clive's extraordinary gift of leadership, his swift intelligence and resolute conduct had made the British the masters of Bengal, the wealthiest province of India. In the absence of a French fleet Admiral Watson was free to carry Clive and his handful of troops to Calcutta, where his first objective was the expulsion of the French from Chandernagor, the granary of the French naval station at Mauritius. An excellent economic strategist, Clive came to the conclusion that the capture of Chandernagor was for the moment more important than the taking of Pondichéry itself, "for without Chandernagor the islands must starve and Pondichéry greatly suffer." The subsequent events in Bengal, the overthrow of the treacherous nawab, Siraj-ud-daula, in the Battle of Plassey, and his replacement by a ruler more amenable to the British, require no extended discussion here.[51] These exploits, which contributed so much to the luster of these memorable years, caused Pitt to describe Clive in parliament as a heaven-born general, as a man who, bred to the labor of the desk,

[51] H. H. Dodwell, *Dupleix and Clive* (London, 1920), 117; by the same author in *Cambridge History of the British Empire, British India* (Cambridge, 1929), IV, 157-165; G. W. Forrest, *Life of Clive* (London, 1918), 2 vols.; M. Davies, *Clive of Plassey* (New York, 1939).

had displayed a military genius which might excite the admiration of the king of Prussia. What Clive did in Bengal, however, was neither novel nor surprising. He had the example of Bussy and Dupleix before him. His control over Mir Jafar, the new nawab of Bengal, was not unlike the policy of the Frenchman Bussy in the Deccan. British troops were the only effective military force in the province and their will was the determining voice in the nawab's councils. In both the Deccan and in Bengal Europeans avoided the appearance of an independent authority and aimed at directing affairs from behind the scenes. In both cases financial difficulties forced the cession of territory whose revenues passed to Europeans. But there was one important difference. The Deccan was to be of little use to the French in the war, while Bengal proved its great value to the British on more than one critical occasion. The war was fought in the Carnatic, which was financially of minor importance and where the British had little to lose and everything to gain. When British funds ran short in Madras, Clive could supply the need from Bengal, while the Deccan was unable to send money to the French in the south. Clive himself, writing to Pitt in January, 1759, put the matter thus:

Notwithstanding the extraordinary effort made by the French in sending Lally with a considerable force last year, I am confident before the end of this they will be near the last gasp in the Carnatic unless some very unforeseen event interposes in their favor. The superiority of our squadron and the plenty of money and supplies which our friends on the coast will be furnished with from this province (Bengal), while the enemy are in total want of everything, without any visible means of redress—an advantage as, if properly attended to, cannot fail of wholly effecting their ruin in that as well as every other part of India.[52]

Yet Clive could not dispense with reinforcements from home. In answer to his urgent appeals Pitt not only sent out a capable soldier in Sir Eyre Coote, but proposed in the house of commons an annual subsidy to the East India Company for the remainder of the war.[53]

[52] Chatham Correspondence, I, 387; Sir Herbert Richmond, The Navy in India, 1763-1783 (London, 1931), Introduction.
[53] B. Williams, William Pitt (London, 1914), II, 26.

The Seven Years' War in India did not seriously begin until the spring of 1758, when d'Aché arrived at Pondichéry with a squadron and reinforcements of four hundred men. The ultimate collapse of French power in India had frequently been attributed to Lally-Tollendal, recently appointed commandant-general of all the French establishments in India, who, though a brave and able soldier, lacked all sense of that delicate statesmanship which the situation required. D'Argenson, who had good reasons to know him, prophesied that if Lally were sent out to India, "Pondichéry will add a civil war within its walls to an external war at its portals."[54] But it must be admitted that the difficult task committed to Lally was rendered insuperable by the terms of his instructions. According to these he was at the same time charged with a reform of the French East India Company at Pondichéry and asked to drive the English out of India, an impossible task for a gifted soldier who was utterly lacking in political talent. His savage sarcasms branded the civilian agents of the company as swindlers and cheats. By his frank disapproval of Dupleix's policy he alienated the natives. He fell out with his officers, who detested him. If he did not have to cope with open rebellion, he was face to face with a passive resistance vastly more dangerous. He was unable to co-operate with Bussy, whose advice he scorned, or with d'Aché, the leader of the squadron, who was as unhappily chosen for his task as Lally for his. Jealous of the least interference with his command, d'Aché was more concerned about the safety of his ships than about French India, which he was sent out to defend.

Lally's initial triumphs, the taking of Cuddalore, Fort St. David and Arcot, were but a prelude to his investment of Madras, which he besieged with a force double that of the defenders. But the British Admiral Pocock, who had succeeded Watson, realizing that Lally's land campaign depended on supplies that came by sea, clung to d'Aché and resolved to force him to a decisive action. He boldly seized a French anchorage at Karikal for a base and did some damage to d'Aché's ships in a second naval encounter. The French admiral, anxious about his communications, then suddenly

[54] A. Martineau in Hanotaux-Martineau, *Histoire des colonies françaises, Inde* (Paris, 1932), V, 222; P. La Mazière, *Lally-Tollendal* (Paris, 1931); Hamont, *Lally-Tollendal*, 61.

abandoned the Coromandel coast and retired to Mauritius on September 3, 1758, not to return for an entire year. From this time forward Lally could no longer count on the complete security of his land operations and stood in perpetual fear lest reinforcements should strengthen the British forces. It was almost useless to attack Madras while Pocock held the sea, so Lally was forced to give up the siege. All he could do was to wait for a change of season, when the autumn monsoon would drive Pocock from the coast to Bombay. During his absence there would be a few months to renew the siege of Madras, but so long as d'Aché lingered at Mauritius, this had to be done by land alone.

Hitherto Lally had not been entirely unsuccessful. With the exception of Trichinopoly, Chingleput and Madras he had swept the English out of the Carnatic. Through no fault of his own he had been compelled to abandon the siege of Madras. To restore his shattered prestige and to subdue Madras, the most vulnerable of all the British posts, he now resolved on a concentration of all the French forces in India. He therefore took the decisive step of recalling Bussy with his seven hundred fifty Europeans from the Deccan and on December 14, 1758 proceeded with the reduction of Madras. He realized that the task must be accomplished with the utmost speed, for there was not money enough for a prolonged siege and if the operations dragged out there was every danger of a return of the English fleet at the end of the winter monsoon. Indeed, Lally had already driven a breach into the wall and had fixed the day of the final attack, when on February 16, 1759 the light squadron of Captain Kempenfelt appeared before the city with supplies and one thousand men. The French troops were so badly paid and so thoroughly demoralized that neither the threats of Lally nor the prayers of civilian agents could persuade them to make another supreme effort. In the meantime Clive sent an expedition against the northern circars under Colonel Forde, who drove the French from that province, retook Masulipatam, and thus deprived Lally, already in straitened circumstances, of another important source of supply.

From this time onward the French game in India was up. The loss of the northern circars, the abandonment of the Deccan, and the relinquishment of the siege of Madras marked the turning point of the war in India. The French still outnumbered the English in the Carnatic, but they were unable to use their troops for lack of funds. These financial difficulties were one of the major causes of Lally's defeat. The ravaged Carnatic could not supply him and the corrupt tax farmers yielded only negligible sums. Distressed Pondichéry did, indeed, receive some assistance from d'Aché, but the latter used up most of the funds intended for Lally by having to go to the Cape, where he had to pay heavily to revictual his ships. No sooner had he appeared on the coast than Pocock forced him into a naval engagement from which he escaped only by withdrawing once more to Mauritius, never to return. Pocock's action was decisive and from this time on nothing could break the English blockade of Pondichéry. The destruction of the French fleets at Lagos and Quiberon Bay and the continued efficiency of Pitt and Anson in European waters made it altogether impossible for Choiseul to send further reinforcements by sea. The arrival from England of Sir Eyre Coote with his regiment enabled the English, now outnumbering the French, to open a campaign which ended in the complete rout of the French at Wandiwash, January 20, 1760, a victory as decisive on land as Pocock's triumph over d'Aché was at sea. The remaining successes were cheaply won. Coote's conquest of the country surrounding Pondichéry struck off the last remaining revenues which the French drew from the occupation of land. Starved out, Pondichéry surrendered on January 16, 1761. When finally Mahé on the west coast fell, the French had lost their last foothold in India.

VI. BETWEEN WAR AND PEACE

When, on October 25, 1760, George II died at Kensington, Pitt was at the zenith of his power. No British statesman had ever carried Englishmen so dramatically from the depths of humiliation to victory in all parts of the world. The most dangerous French battle fleets had been destroyed. Canada, Guadeloupe, Senegal and Gorée had been conquered and Admiral Pocock, who had driven d'Aché from the coast of India, had just anchored in the Downs, bringing with him the news of the decisive victory at Wandiwash. Pitt's continental diversion, the principal justification for the German war, had done its work. His confidence in the economic resources of England was vindicated. The war to conquer commerce and colonies, if it did not pay its own way, was actually a new source of wealth and strength. Though the supplies voted for 1761 amounted to nearly twenty million pounds, nearly twice as much as was voted in 1758, the public loans were quickly subscribed. Agriculture prospered, industries were fully occupied, and trade had never risen so high as during the war. As the boast of Pitt's Guildhall monument put it, "commerce had been made to flourish by war." Shipping gained more than a hundred thousand tons between 1755 and 1763 and the slave trade almost doubled.[55] Yet within less than a year this administration, sure of a parliamentary majority and overwhelmingly popular with the country, was struck down; Pitt, the idol of the whole British empire, the terror of France, was driven from office and his place taken by a swarm of nonentities, royal favorites, the "king's friends," who concluded the peace.

This result was as much due to the intractable, irritable and arrogant genius of Pitt, tinged as it was at times with madness and preventing him from taking account of other people or paying any regard for their wishes and feelings, as it was to the immature and unbalanced obstinacy of George III, the new king. George was resolved to introduce into the cabinet his friend and counselor, Lord Bute, presently the real center of power, in whose abilities he had unlimited confidence. There was nothing in the constitutional practice of the time to prevent the king from dismissing Newcastle, the party manager and head of the political machine, and replacing him by Bute; but Pitt's refusal to serve under him and Bute's reluctance to assume full responsibility for war and peace for the moment prevented the change. Thanks to Newcastle's secret connivance with the king and Bute, however, the latter was brought into the cabinet.[56]

On the surface the coalition of Bute, Pitt and Newcastle appeared

[55] H. Temperley, *Cambridge History of the British Empire* (Cambridge, 1929), I, 501.
[56] L. B. Namier, *England in the Age of the American Revolution* (London, 1930), 181, 332; A. von Ruville, *William Pitt und Lord Bute* (Berlin, 1895), 2; A. von Ruville, *William Pitt, Earl of Chatham* (London, 1907), II, chap. XV; D. A. Winstanley, *Personal and Party Government* (Cambridge, 1910), 19.

irresistible. But even the pressure of the war was not strong enough to reconcile the bitter jealousies and animosities that existed between them. Newcastle regarded Pitt with mingled terror and resentment, and Pitt himself had scarcely a single friend in the cabinet. Pitt's doctrine that he must have full responsibility for the conduct of the war, justifiable enough when the country was in danger, was no longer accepted at court; yet he stubbornly refused to share that responsibility with Bute. Nor was there any agreement between them on the problems of peace and war. Whereas Pitt wanted to continue the war until France agreed to terms which ensured the supremacy of England, Newcastle sighed for a speedy peace at almost any price. Pitt was determined not to assent to any peace which was not made in concert with Prussia, while the other members of the cabinet were not averse to abandoning Frederick. Europe engrossed the thoughts of Newcastle, who looked upon Pitt's colonial expeditions as mere side shows. As for Bute and George III, they had a special program of their own which they intended to execute. They were determined above all to break the monopoly of the Whig party, free the crown from its humiliating subjection to Whig magnates, recover the control of royal patronage and the king's power to choose his own ministers.

This obviously meant that ultimately both Pitt and Newcastle must go, although to attribute to Bute the subtle design to force out first Pitt, the war minister, and then Newcastle, the peace minister, and make peace on his own terms is to credit this showy but ignorant Scot with a political shrewdness which he did not possess. George III and Bute knew that so long as the war lasted they could not dispense with Pitt. For that very reason they wanted to end the war at the earliest possible moment. Such a policy would associate the name of the new king with peace and economy and would at the same time be a bid for power and popularity—and to establish the popularity and credit of the young king was the supreme aim of Bute's life. Like Pitt, therefore, Bute wanted a peace that would redound to the honor of his master. But if, in order to obtain such a peace, the war must be continued, George III and Bute would carry it on anywhere rather than in Germany.[57] George III, who

[57] E. Fitzmaurice, *Life of Shelburne* (London, 1912), I, 102 ff.

"gloried in the name of Briton," had nothing but contempt for Hanover, "that horrid electorate," and Bute, the typical English country gentleman, like the city merchants and the younger generation generally, were strongly opposed to the continental system of the previous generation. They turned to the empire rather than to Europe.

The occasion for Pitt's retirement from office was presented by the peace overtures which Choiseul, anxious to free his country from the strain of a long and unsuccessful war, had forwarded to the English cabinet, overtures with which the question of the Spanish grievances against Great Britain presently became fatefully entangled. Choiseul sincerely wanted peace, and to obtain it he was willing to make heavy sacrifices. But as France was not yet at the end of her resources, there was a limit of concessions beyond which he could not go. From the beginning of his discussions, however, he had two strings to his bow. He wanted peace with England, if the limit of his concessions coincided with what the English ministers were willing to accept, but if he could get no reasonable terms, he would continue the war with the assistance of Spain. In a *mémoire* which he wrote for Louis XV in 1765 Choiseul explained that he expected no success with the dictatorial Pitt, whose position in any case was growing steadily more precarious; that at every stage of the discussion he was alive to the intention of Bute and his party to end the war and destroy Pitt's dictatorship; and that as soon as Pitt had given way to Bute his overtures might serve as a basis for genuine negotiation. Continuing, he wrote, "If on the contrary, we failed in this, my plan was that Spain should be drawn into the war and that France would be able to profit by events which this new complication might produce and repair her losses. Finally, if the event proved unfortunate, I had in view that the losses of Spain would lighten those which France might suffer."[58] In other words, Spain, which had often refused help when France needed it and only offered it now in her own interest when France was bled white by the war, was to be made to pay heavily for assisting. Two months before he sent his overtures to England, Choiseul had informed

[58] Printed in A. Soulange-Bodin, *La diplomatie de Louis XV et le pacte de famille*, 242-243; A. Bourget, *Le Duc de Choiseul et l'alliance espagnole*, 207; J. Corbett, *England and the Seven Years' War* (London, 1907), II, 185.

Spain that he was prepared to sign a Family Compact and had promised to make the satisfaction of Spain's demands on England an indispensable condition of his own peace; if he failed to make such a peace within eleven months, Spain was to declare war on England.

Pitt's blunt and haughty manner did not make him the most suitable negotiator. He was inflexible in his demand for Canada, but his concern for naval power made him attach even greater importance to the Canadian fisheries than to Canada itself. While determined to take enough of Canada to give secure boundaries to the American colonists, he was indifferent as to whether Guadeloupe or Gorée were given up, so long as the St. Lawrence and Newfoundland fisheries remained English monopolies.[59] Choiseul, on the other hand, equally determined on the preservation of French sea power, refused to give up an industry which employed nearly three thousand ships and fifteen thousand Frenchmen, all the more so because the English fisheries yielded considerably less profit and employed only about half the number of men.[60] It is commonly agreed that Pitt's refusal of the Canadian fisheries convinced Choiseul that he must ally himself with Spain and continue the war. In the *Pacte de Famille* of August 15, 1761 France and Spain signed an offensive and defensive alliance by which France engaged herself not to make peace with England until the Spanish grievances had been remedied; in a secret convention Spain promised to declare war on England, if peace were not concluded within eight months. Spain at once began to prepare for war, although the Anglo-French discussions were not broken off until Pitt refused to abandon his Prussian ally and France to abandon Austria.

But why did Spain now throw in her lot with France? So long as Ferdinand VI lived, General Wall sought to realize the policy of his master, Carvajal, "Peace with England and war with all the world beside."[61] This situation changed when Charles III of Naples, whose rigorous application to work and exalted conception of his

[59] Newcastle to Hardwicke, April 17, 1761. P. Yorke, *Earl of Hardwicke* (Oxford, 1913), III, 316.
[60] K. Hotblack in *Transactions of the Royal Historical Society*, Third series, II, 235 ff.; B. Williams, *William Pitt*, II, 84.
[61] J. O. McLachlan, "The Uneasy Neutrality," *Cambridge Historical Journal*, VI (1938), 54-77.

royal office made up for a certain deficiency of intellect, ascended the Spanish throne. Shocked by the weakness of his kingdom, he proposed to raise industry and commerce, restore the army and navy and liberate the Spanish colonies from the yoke of British contraband trade. Although he desired anything but to become a satellite of France, the progress of the war convinced him that French and Spanish interests had become more or less identical, for France could give him security in Italy through the Austrian alliance and in the New World against Great Britain. To the old grievances against Great Britain—the Honduras dispute that had gone on for half a century and more, the Spanish claims to a share in the Newfoundland fisheries, which had lain dormant for fifty years—there were now added the British violations of Spanish neutrality and the outrageous molestations, delaying, robbery, seizure of Spanish merchantmen in European waters by British privateers, which roused national feeling and alienated even the friendly Wall. More alarming still was the complete overthrow of the colonial, commercial and maritime balance by the British conquests in North America and in the Caribbean. Charles III's blood froze at the news of Quebec. In the West Indies Guadeloupe, Martinique, one defense after the other of the Spanish mines in Mexico, was falling into British hands. Already the strongest power in the Caribbean, Britain with her contraband trade in the Spanish colonies and in the Iberian peninsula threatened to reduce Spain to the dependence of Portugal. When Pitt refused even to discuss the Spanish claim to a share in the Newfoundland fisheries, saying haughtily that there would be time enough to deal with this claim when the Tower of London was taken sword in hand, the directors of Spanish policy no longer hesitated to sign the Family Compact.[62]

Whether or not Pitt's information as to the solidarity of the two branches of the House of Bourbon was completely convincing, he was determined to crush them both at a single blow. Since he believed in Spain's intention to fight, he wanted to give her no breathing spell to complete her military preparations. But the evidence of Spanish hostility, which was convincing to Pitt, was considered insufficient by his colleagues and, in the last cabinet meeting

62 B. Williams, *William Pitt* (London, 1914), II, 95.

of October 2, 1761, his demand for an immediate declaration of war was defeated. Pitt resigned. He did so less, as Bubb Dodington suggested, because he could not make such a peace as he had taught the country to expect, then because he believed that it was only by the complete responsibility of the war minister that England could wage a successful war, a theory that now struck Lord Granville, the doyen of the council, as little short of treason.[63] If Bute only a short time later declared war on Spain, he did so because he was afraid of Pitt's popularity and because he did not yet know whether Pitt intended to cause trouble.

When the Anglo-Spanish war broke out in January, 1762 the English fighting machine was in full working order. The hand of the great English minister, though withdrawn from the helm, was still felt in every department of the war. Havana was taken. Admiral Draper, in a side show, took Manila, though the conquest was not known when the peace came. What was new in this war was the effort of the Bourbon powers to set up the beginnings of a "continental system" by sending a summons to Portugal to close her ports to British ships and exclude Englishmen from the Brazil trade. But the Portuguese minister, the Marquis of Pombal, refused, and with the assistance of Count Lippe and the English General Burgoyne broke the offensive of the Spanish invading army. D'Aranda, the Spanish general, was forced to retreat in disgrace.

With the utter failure of the Spanish war machine everywhere, all the hopes which Choiseul had placed on the Spanish alliance vanished. "Had I known," he wrote, "what I now know, I should have been very careful to cause to enter the war a power which by its feebleness can only ruin and destroy France."[64] Once he saw the Spanish colonies in America invaded and conquered and the conquest of Portugal made impossible, he realized that this time the Spanish alliance had come too late. Postponing his projects for revenge, he pronounced himself in favor of immediate peace with

---

[63] Adolphus, *History of England from the Accession of George III* (London, 1840), I, 573; R. Waddington, *La guerre de sept ans,* IV, chaps. 10, 11; on Pitt's last cabinet meeting see H. B. Pemberton, *Carteret* (London, 1936), 326; L. B. Namier, *England in the Age of the American Revolution* (London, 1930), I, 339-343; another version, obviously penned by an enemy of Pitt, is given in the *Annual Register,* 1761, 43-44.

[64] L. Blart, *Les rapports de la France et l'Espagne après le Pacte de Famille* (Paris, 1915), 42.

England in spite of Charles III, who still persisted in demanding from Great Britain concessions which would have been difficult to obtain even had he been victorious.

The reaction of this Spanish war upon Britain's war policy in central Europe was immediate, though scarcely decisive. Lord Bute, now the dominant figure in the cabinet, began by regarding the Spanish and German wars as alternatives, though in the end the Spanish war was the excuse rather than the reason for abandoning the German war and the Prussian alliance. An ignorant tyro in foreign affairs, insular in his outlook and preoccupied with building up the political machine that was to make the crown independent of parliament and political parties, Lord Bute yielded to the rising English detestation of the whole German embroilment and pre-maturely dissolved the military and diplomatic partnership between Great Britain and Prussia before the war had run its full course. Bute and Frederick II soon faced each other with daggers drawn in an acrimonious quarrel. By April, 1762 the breach between Great Britain and Prussia was final and complete. Doubtless, Bute was clumsy, inconsiderate and, from a British point of view, short-sighted, but the charges of his treachery and perfidy against Frederick can no longer be sustained.[65]

The quarrel began when Bute, thinking England allied with a sinking ship, advised Frederick II to make a separate peace with Austria even at the sacrifice of Prussian territory. That Frederick, engaged in a struggle for existence, should regard the cession of any territory as equivalent to annihilation, requires no further explanation here. It was just at this moment, January 5, 1762, that the Empress Elizabeth of Russia died. Profoundly moved at the news, Frederick cried, *"Voilà, grace au Ciel! Notre dos libre."*[66] Indeed, with the accession of the Duke of Holstein-Gottorp to the Russian throne as Peter III the great continental coalition against Prussia went to pieces. This infantile tsar, who distrusted Austria, detested France and hailed the Prussian monarch as his "lord and master,"

---

[65] In an elaborate argument these charges have been made again by Sir Richard Lodge whose *Great Britain and Prussia in the Eighteenth Century* (Cambridge, 1923), 113 ff. can no longer be accepted as a reliable guide. Walter L. Dorn, "Frederick the Great and Lord Bute," *Journal of Modern History*, I (1929), 529-560.

[66] *Politische Correspondenz Friedrichs des Grossen*, XX, 212.

signed immediate peace with Prussia, restored all conquests and placed the Russian army at Frederick's disposal. His sole concern was to assert the rights of his family in Schleswig-Holstein against Denmark.[67] Meanwhile Frederick learned with a start the news of the secret peace overtures of the British ministry to Austria, which appeared to involve Prussian territorial concessions. This surprising information, unhappily, was confirmed by the falsified report of a conversation between Bute and Prince Golicyn, the Russian ambassador at London, to the effect that Bute would force Frederick to make considerable territorial concessions. Thus Frederick believed himself to be in possession of compelling evidence of a diabolical British plot to ruin the Prussian monarchy. Unable to probe the veracity of Golicyn's report, forwarded to him by his friend Peter III, and unconvinced by Bute's personal defense, Frederick had no other alternative but to accept the Russian alliance on such terms as the tsar chose to request. But from the moment when he promised the tsar Prussian military assistance for a war against Denmark, all further hope of co-operation with Great Britain had to be abandoned.

Peter III's stupidity soon stirred up a revolt which cost him his life. He insulted the national sensibilities of the Russian army by his slavish imitation of the Prussian service, the clergy by flouting the orthodox religion, and the following of his wife, Catherine, by the contempt and brutality with which he treated her. With the full knowledge of his wife, Peter was assassinated. When the great Catherine II ascended the throne she revealed in her manifesto of June 28, 1762 to her astonished people and to the world that she had saved Russia from a revolution in religion, in constitution and in foreign policy. But Catherine wanted no renewal of the war with Prussia, still less a war against Austria for Prussian interests, and least of all a war against Denmark for the sake of Holstein.

Utterly exhausted financially and long anxious for peace, Sweden also abandoned the coalition.[68] The continental war now degenerated into a purely dynastic contest between two German rulers. France had no further interest in such a war and Choiseul renewed

[67] J. Krumm, Der Schleswig-holsteinische Gesamtstaat des 18. Jahrhunderts (1934), 16.
[68] E. Amberger, Russland und Schweden, 1762-1772 (Berlin, 1934), 43.

his peace discussions with Bute. Austria, unable to continue the war alone, declared her readiness to discuss terms with Frederick in the Saxon hunting lodge at Hubertusburg.

VII. THE PEACE OF PARIS

The Peace of Paris, so widely condemned in Great Britain and so generally regarded by British historians as falling in its terms far below what their conquests gave Englishmen a right to expect, was signed on February 10, 1763.[69] It is, perhaps, symbolic of the peace as a whole that in this instance the victor, in the person of Lord Bute, actually knocked at the door of vanquished France to reopen peace negotiations. In these negotiations the nimble-witted Choiseul in large measure undid the overwhelming victory of Great Britain by adroitly alternating resolution with timely concession. This veteran diplomat was fortunate in having to treat with an ultra-pacifist like the Duke of Bedford, the British agent in Paris, and a simpleton like Bute, and when for an instant the possibility of Pitt's return to office loomed up, Choiseul declared that he would sooner be condemned to the galleys than deal with the latter. The secrecy in which the discussion of preliminaries was shrouded gave him endless opportunities to play Bedford against Bute and Bute against his colleagues.

In dealing with the British ministers, among whom he encountered the greatest diversity of opinion as to the minimum concessions to be insisted upon from France, Choiseul had all the advantage of having a definite and reasoned idea of French national interest. Since he could not regard this peace as a permanent settlement, he was determined to keep his Spanish and Austrian alliances intact for future use. Accordingly, he announced that he would conclude no final peace without first consulting Spain and, when Charles III revolted against the severe British terms, Choiseul muffled the shock by the voluntary surrender of French Louisiana to

<hr/>

69 H. Temperley, "The Peace of Paris," *Cambridge History of the British Empire* (Cambridge, 1929), I, 492-506; L. B. Namier, *England in the Age of the American Revolution* (London, 1930), I, 331-443; J. Corbett, *England and the Seven Years' War* (London, 1907), II, 327 ff.; L. Pérey, *Le duc de Nivernais* (Paris, 1891); E. W. Lyon, *Louisiana in French Diplomacy, 1759-1804* (University of Oklahoma Press, 1934); J. J. Meng, "Franco-American Diplomacy and the Treaty of Paris," *The American Catholic Historical Society Review*, XVII (1913), 735-744.

his Spanish ally. He was prepared to restore all the conquests made from Britain's German allies, but he declined to return to their owner the Rhenish provinces of Prussia without the knowledge and consent of Maria Theresa.[70] Diplomatic security in Europe, the result of his punctilious fulfillment of obligations to his allies, gave him some compensation for the inevitable colonial sacrifices. As a traditional mercantilist, who valued colonies for their commercial importance, he objected in principle to colonies of settlement in North America and concurred with Voltaire that "France could be happy without Quebec." The surrender of Dupleix's vast empire in India gave him no qualms. All the more did he insist as the irreducible *sine qua non* of peace on the return to France of the Canadian fisheries, the West Indies, Gorée and the French trading stations in India, the commercial core of the old French colonial empire. And, lest these outposts be left at the mercy of British sea power, he began almost at once with a reorganization of the French navy.

The British peacemakers, Bute, Bedford, Egremont, and Grenville, on the other hand, were without exception mere politicians, who were more concerned with their personal safety and popularity than with the economic issues or the strategic problems of imperial defense involved in drafting the terms of the peace. Bute's purview did not extend far beyond the narrow compass of domestic politics and he was completely indifferent to the diplomatic security of Great Britain in Europe. In his precipitous rush to conclude the peace the last British victories came to him as evil tidings, as embarrassing obstacles that interrupted the negotiations. He was so vexed by the victory of Prince Ferdinand over the French at Wilhelmsthal that he addressed to Choiseul a secret letter in which he treacherously begged the French minister to put up a stiff resistance to Prince Ferdinand's army in order that he, Bute, might not be overthrown by the Prussian, that is by Pitt's party in England.[71] He deliberately refused to press Choiseul for the return of the Rhenish provinces to Frederick II. They were, so he is said to have declared in parliament,

[70] A. Schaefer, *Geschichte des Siebenjährigen Krieges* (Berlin, 1874), II, pt. 2, 622.
[71] A. Schaefer, *Geschichte des Siebenjährigen Krieges* (Berlin, 1874), II, pt. 2, 522; P. Yorke, *The Earl of Hardwicke*, III, 369.

"to be scrambled for." Had it not been for the reluctance of Maria Theresa to seize them and the prompt action of the Prussian monarch, a serious difficulty would have arisen. At all events, Frederick II did not owe his recovery of these provinces to the anxious solicitude of his British ally. Not without good reason did Burke later complain that Bute "disgusted every ally we had and from that day to this we stand friendless in Europe."[72]

In the wholesale surrender of conquests which Bute contemplated he abandoned even the pretense of the eighteenth-century principle that no conquests should be restored without an equivalent. With the exception of Minorca, France and Spain had nothing with which to make exchanges. Contemporaries, therefore, accused Bute of "copying the Treaty of Utrecht throughout."[73] At the news of the capture of Havana, however, Grenville and Egremont caused a serious cabinet crisis by insisting upon compensation for its surrender.[74] They went further still. Objecting to Bute's secret negotiations, which frequently left the other ministers in ignorance as to what terms he was offering, they now demanded that the preliminary terms be submitted to parliament for discussion, in the hope, no doubt, of supplanting Bute and placing themselves at the head of a patriotic national party that would draw support from the displaced Whig leaders. Fearful that peace was eluding his grasp and that such a step would lead to extravagant and impossible terms, Bute implored Choiseul to urge Charles III to surrender Florida if he wished to retain Cuba. At the same time he reorganized his cabinet, dropping Egremont, relegating Grenville to the admiralty, where he was harmless, and appointing Fox, a practiced parliamentary manager and debater and the only man who could stand up against Pitt's fire, to defend the peace in the house of commons. Thus fortified, the remaining difficulties were mere bagatelles.

The one important problem of the peace which stirred British public opinion and precipitated a lively debate among a whole army of pamphleteers was the controversy of Canada versus Guade-

[72] E. Burke, "Observations on a Late Publication," *Works* (1852), III, 26.
[73] *Bedford Correspondence*, III, 130-133.
[74] *Grenville Papers*, I, 483 ff.

loupe.[75] Needless to say, the prime objective of the war was to drive the French out of Canada and only the complete French surrender of Canada could cut off at the root the possibility of a recurrence of a similar dispute in the future. But that was more an American colonial than a British problem. For Great Britain the immediate commercial value of Canada, apart from the fisheries, was slight. It was for this reason that Pitt had insisted on a British monopoly of the fisheries. But when the West Indian issue came up for discussion, the restoration of the St. Lawrence and Newfoundland fisheries together with the shelter islands, St. Pierre and Miquelon, had already been agreed upon. So far as Canada was concerned Bedford and many others thought it unwise to remove the French bugbear from the back door of the American colonists, whose doubtful loyalty was already causing some uneasiness in England. If Canada were kept, however, who would guarantee the loyalty of the French-Canadian *habitants*? In any case, an immense army would be necessary to hold so vast a territory. These objections did not apply to Guadeloupe. The trade of this sugar island was much greater than that of Canada and it would produce at once a revenue which would enable Britain to pay at least the interest on the cost of the war. The slave traders were, of course, unanimously in favor of keeping it. The experience of the war had shown that so long as Martinique and St. Lucia remained in French hands, British sugar planters were just as much at the mercy of French threats in time of war as the North American colonists were of the Canadian menace. Above all, the annexation of Guadeloupe would do much to restore the necessary balance between the continental and tropical colonies. North American colonial exporters were compelled to sell their goods to the French as well as the British islands and annexation was the only way to keep this trade within the British empire.

Illuminating as this debate was, it had no influence on the de-

[75] This pamphlet literature has been frequently analyzed. W. L. Grant, *American Historical Review*, XVI, 735-743; C. W. Alvord, *The Mississippi Valley in British Politics* (Cleveland, 1917), I, 49-74; F. Pitman, *The Development of the British West Indies* (New Haven, 1915); R. Pares, *War and Trade in the West Indies* (Oxford, 1936), 216 ff.; for an excellent summary of all the arguments see Hardwicke's letter to Newcastle, April 2, 1762 in L. B. Namier, *England in the Age of the American Revolution* (London, 1930), I, 323-325.

cisions of the ministry. Although public opinion was in favor of keeping the West Indian islands, it was Canada that was retained. Guadeloupe and Martinique were restored; so also was the neutral island St. Lucia, which Choiseul refused to give up because it was necessary to the naval security of the other French Antilles. France ceded the entire North American continent so far as the left bank of the Mississippi, including the right of navigation down that river, and all the other neutral islands in the West Indies. This solution was not wanting in a certain adroitness. It guaranteed the original object of the war, a defensible frontier and peace of mind for the North American colonists, and at the same time provided a fresh field for English capital and enterprise without doing injury to the position of the old English sugar islands in the home market. By accepting these terms, however, Bute surrendered, as Pitt accused him of surrendering and as the War of the American Independence was abundantly to prove, the strategic security of the British West Indies.

The other articles of the peace presented no special difficulties. France restored Minorca and ceded Senegal to Great Britain which, in turn, restored Belle Isle and Gorée, the latter being deemed essential to the French slave trade. In India also Choiseul got what he wanted, the return of the French trading stations on the Malabar and Coromandel coasts and in Bengal. The French agreed, however, to erect no fortifications and to keep no troops in these stations and they acknowledged the British candidates as nawab of the Carnatic and subahdar of the Deccan.

Great Britain and France were already in substantial agreement before Choiseul broke the news of the terms to Charles III of Spain. Since England refused to make peace with France unless Spain made peace at the same time, and since the British terms to France were as generous as those offered to Spain were harsh, Choiseul had the unenviable task of purchasing the British concessions by compelling his Spanish ally to pay heavily for espousing the French cause. Little inclined to make his kingdom pay for the French failure or to play the subaltern role of a docile ally, Charles III made endless difficulties. It was only after Choiseul informed him that if he wished to continue the war he must do so alone that

Charles III yielded, and then only after the cession of French Louisiana with New Orleans.[76] After the surrender of the left bank of the Mississippi to Britain, Louisiana was worth little to France and it was useful to Spain chiefly because its possession would enable her to guard the British approach to Mexico and the treasure colonies. Spain ceded Florida to Great Britain, gave up her claim to a share in the Newfoundland fisheries, agreed to submit the dispute concerning prizes to the British admiralty courts, acknowledged the British right to cut logwood on the Bay of Honduras, and, finally, agreed to renew all commercial treaties.

Lord Bute had triumphed over his enemies at home and this triumph was confirmed on December 9, 1762, when he mustered an overwhelming majority in the house of commons in favor of the peace preliminaries. Fox had conducted his parliamentary campaign with ability and success and there is no reason to believe that the majority was due to government proscriptions and bribery alone. The Whig opposition was weakened by the disunion of its factions, whose leaders for petty and personal reasons were incapable of co-operating. There was something unreal and even ridiculous in the position of Newcastle as the leader of the opposition, after having stood so long for peace at any price. When finally Pitt, tortured with the gout, his legs and thighs wrapped in flannels and his hands covered with thick gloves, arose to deliver his long speech in parliament, he in effect accused Bute of making peace without having reduced France to a second-rate power. But to destroy the French naval training grounds by depriving France of the Canadian fisheries, to retain St. Lucia and Martinique on strategic and Guadeloupe on economic grounds, to keep Gorée and thus exclude France entirely from the slave trade, would have necessitated a continuation of the war. It is impossible to deny that Pitt possessed a profounder insight into the strategic problems of imperial defense than his contemporaries, but, as Burke sarcastically complained, the "Great Commoner" was pre-eminently the spokesman "of a parcel of low toadeaters" (meaning the London merchants) and knew very little of the "great extensive public." Whatever its obvious short-

[76] L. Blart. *Les rapports de la France et de l'Espagne après le Pacte de Famille* (Paris, 1915), 43.

comings, the Peace of Paris secured the original objects of the war and satisfied the reasonable ambitions of most Englishmen who were not prepared to face a war to the knife.

Compared with the colonial and maritime peace the peace between Austria and Prussia was a relatively simple matter. Frederick II categorically refused the mediation of Great Britain and France and signed his own peace with Maria Theresa at Hubertusburg on February 15, 1763, five days after the Peace of Paris. Of the five different plans for peace which Count Kaunitz had in his bag, he was compelled to accept the least favorable, the restoration of the *status quo*. At Hubertusburg Frederick II and Maria Theresa pledged each other mutual friendship and expressed their desire to conclude a commercial treaty. Frederick promised the electoral vote of Brandenburg to Archduke Joseph as candidate for the imperial office. The Empire was included in the peace, but Saxony received no compensation for the extraordinary contributions which for seven years she had paid to Berlin.

Bibliography

Bibliography

BIBLIOGRAPHICAL GUIDES AND WORKS OF REFERENCE

Revised as of January, 1963

A valuable introduction is G. F. Howe and others, *A Guide to Historical Literature* (New York, 1961); another is J. S. Bromley and A. Goodwin, *A Select List of Works on Europe and Europe Overseas, 1715-1815* (Oxford, 1956). For current historical literature in all languages see the periodical *International Bibliography of Historical Sciences* and the appropriate sections of the more specialized *International Bibliography of Economics,* the *International Bibliography of Political Science,* and the *International Bibliography of the History of Religions,* all now published with UNESCO sponsorship. For Germany there is the incomparable Dahlmann-Waitz, *Quellenkunde der deutschen Geschichte,* 9th ed., 2 vols. (Leipzig, 1931); G. Franz, *Bücherkünde zur deutschen Geschichte* (Munich, 1951); the most recent edition of B. Gebhardt, *Handbuch der deutschen Geschichte,* II; and the *Jahresberichte für deutsche Geschichte* (1925 and following years). For Austria there are the comprehensive and judiciously selected bibliographies in K. and M. Uhlirz, *Handbuch der Geschichte Österreichs und seiner Nachbarländer Böhmen und Ungarn,* vols. I-II (Graz, 1927-30); O. Brunner, "Ouvrages sur l'histoire moderne de l'Autriche 1526-1918," *Revue d'histoire moderne,* V (1930), 34-47, 131-142; C. Zíbrt, *Bibliografie české historie,* 5 vols. (Prague, 1900-1912). For France there is the comprehensive but unselective C. Du Péloux, *Répertoire général des ouvrages modernes rélatifs au XVIIIe siècle français (1715-1789)* (Paris, 1926), and, by the same author, *Supplément au répertoire des ouvrages modernes rélatifs au XVIIIe siècle français* (Paris, 1927); P. Caron and H. Stein, *Répertoire bibliographique de l'histoire de France* (Paris, 1923). For Spain there is B. Sanchez Alonso, *Fuentes de la historia española e'hispanoamericana,* 3rd ed., 3 vols. (Madrid, 1952). For Great Britain see S. Pargellis and D. J. Medley, *Bibliography of British History: the Eighteenth Century, 1714-1789* (Oxford, 1951); and C. L. Grose, *A Select Bibliography of British History, 1660-1760* (Chicago, 1939). For Russia R. Kerner's *Slavic Europe* (Cambridge, Mass., 1918) is a selected bibliography in the western European languages; the notes in Akademiia nauk SSSR, Institut istorii, *Ocherki istorii SSSR,* VI-VII (Moscow, 1956-57) provide entry into the Soviet literature before 1956. Besides being the best brief diplomatic history of the period, Max Immich's *Geschichte des europäischen Staatensystems, 1660-1789* (Munich, 1909) contains the most complete collection of the older diplomatic literature. For economic history there are H. Higgs, *Bibliography of Economics, 1751-1775* (London, 1935); W. Sombart, *Die Entstehung des modernen Kapitalismus,* 6 vols. (Berlin, 1927); H. Heaton, *Economic History of Europe,* rev. ed. (New York, 1948); C. Singer and others, ed., *A History of Technology,* vols. III-IV (Oxford, 1957-58); H. Sée, *Histoire économique de la France,* 2nd ed., 2 vols. (Paris, 1948-51); H. Bechtel, *Wirtschaftsgeschichte Deutschlands,* II (Munich, 1952); F. Lütge, *Deutsche Sozial- und Wirtschaftsgeschichte* (Berlin, 1952). The most useful bibliographical manual for colonial history is J. Tramond, Roussier, and Martineau, *Bibliographie d'histoire coloniale* (Paris, 1932); valuable for this period is the *Cambridge History of the British Empire,* 8 vols. (New York, 1929-59). For intellectual and cultural history there are excellent bibliographies in P. Smith, *History of Modern Culture,* II (New York, 1934), 647-676; D. Mornet, *Les origines intellectuelles de la Révolution française,* 5th ed. (Paris, 1954); D. C. Cabeen and J. Brody, ed., *A Critical Bibliography of French Literature. Vol. IV. The Eighteenth Century* (Syracuse, 1951), extensive and detailed; E. Ermatinger, *Deutsche Kultur im Zeitalter der Aufklärung* (Potsdam, 1935), published as a separate volume but part of H. Kindermann's *Handbuch der Kulturgeschichte;* A. S. Turberville, ed., *Johnson's England,* 2 vols. (Oxford, 1933).

A good general history of this period is P. Muret, *La prépondérance anglaise,* 3rd ed. (Paris, 1949), Vol. XI in the Halphen-Sagnac *Peuples et Civilisations* series. This volume is an accurate, scholarly, and sober manual of a traditional kind, often somewhat unimaginative but remarkably free of national bias and embracing the whole of Europe. On certain aspects, notably diplomatic history, it is more detailed than the present volume. The student will cherish the book less for its interpretive power or its grasp of political and military strategy than for the scholarly accuracy of its political narrative. Vol. VI of the older *Cambridge Modern History: The Eighteenth Century* (Cambridge, 1909) contains a number of excellent and informative chapters which still may be read with profit. But the editorial planning of the volume is so faulty that it is extremely difficult to obtain a coherent picture of the leading events of mid-century. The *New Cambridge Modern History* strives with some success for better coherence by ordering the material differently and

generalizing more, and by efforts to place matters in a European scope
insofar as that is possible; it provides less informational detail and next
to no bibliography. R. Mousnier and E. Labrousse, *Le XVIIIe siècle:
révolution intellectuelle, technique, et politique (1715-1815)* (Paris,
1953) successfully incorporates technological and scientific changes. M.
Anderson, *Europe in the 18th Century, 1713-1783* (New York, 1961), is
an excellent brief study with valuable bibliographical notes.

What is attempted in the following pages is not a complete bibliography but a *bibliographie raisonnée,* arranged to correspond roughly to
the chapters of this book. Titles will not ordinarily be repeated.

Chapter I

The most authoritative introduction to the history of international
relations in this period is G. Zeller, *Les temps modernes, de Louis XIV
à 1789* (Paris, 1955), Vol. III of P. Renouvin, ed., *Histoire des relations
internationales.* Some modern re-examinations of the eighteenth-century
principle of balance of power are L. Dehio, *The Precarious Balance*
(New York, 1962); E. v. Vietsch's *Das europäische Gleichgewicht*
(Leipzig, 1942); and the theoretical and bibliographical parts of E.
Gulick, *Europe's Classical Balance of Power* (Ithaca, 1955), which is
mainly devoted to the Congress of Vienna. There are valuable reflec-
tions in G. L. Dickinson, *Causes of International War* (London, 1920);
F. S. Oliver, *Endless Adventure* (London, 1930-1935), 3 vols.; by various
contributors, *Studies in Anglo-French History, Eighteenth to Twentieth
Centuries* (London, 1935); A. Baschet, *Histoire du Dépôt des archives
des affaires étrangères* (Paris, 1875). The second volume of E. Heckscher, *Mercantilism,* 2nd ed. (London, 1955), is more useful for the
seventeenth than for the eighteenth century. Unique in the literature on
the competitive state system are the brilliant and penetrating essays by
Otto Hintze, published or listed in his *Staat und Verfassung* (Leipzig,
1941). Immensely suggestive are the studies by the following German
economists: J. Schumpeter, *Imperialism and Social Classes* (New York,
1951); A. Salz, *Das Wesen des Imperialismus* (Tübingen, 1932); K.
Knorr, *British Colonial Theories, 1570-1850* (Toronto, 1944); R.
Koebner, *Empire* (New York, 1961); W. Sombart, *Krieg und Kapitalismus* (Leipzig, 1913); and Fritz Kern, "Vom Herrenstaat zum
Wohlfahrtsstaat," *Schmollers Jahrbuch,* LII (1928). E. Silberner, *La
guerre dans la pensée économique du XVIe au XVIIIe siècle* (Paris,

1939), emphasizes military aspects of mercantilism; J. Nef, *War and Human Progress* (Cambridge, Mass., 1950), denies that war accelerated economic development. On Ranke's doctrine of the influence of foreign policy on constitutional and social evolution see the comments by the economic historian G. von Below, *Die Deutsche Geschichtsschreibung* (Berlin, 1924).

Chapter II

Otto Hintze never wrote the general comparative history of modern states that would have culminated his studies, but many of his essays may be looked upon as aspects or parts of one; see his *Staat und Verfassung* (Leipzig, 1941), already mentioned. H. Hausherr, *Verwaltungseinheit und Ressorttrennung vom Ende des 17. bis zum Beginn des 19. Jahrhunderts* (Berlin, 1953), is a successful comparative study of the central governments, especially of Prussia and Austria, with less attention to France. Extremely valuable for the administration of government finance are the historical sections of W. Lotz, *Finanzwissenschaft,* 2nd ed. (Tübingen, 1931). A. Goodwin, ed., *The European Nobility in the Eighteenth Century* (London, 1953), is a valuable collection of brief national studies. Max Weber's *Wirtschaft und Gesellschaft,* 4th ed., 2 vols. (Tübingen, 1956), is a systematic and theoretical treatment.

France. In the absence of an adequate modern study of the government and administration of pre-revolutionary France, E. Chénon, *Histoire générale du droit publique et privé des origines à 1815,* II (Paris, 1929), may be recommended at least for its copious bibliographies. There is a growing number of specialized studies. See especially G. Pagès, *Études sur l'histoire administrative et sociale de l'ancien régime* (Paris, 1938); M. Marion, *Dictionnaire des institutions de la France aux XVIIe et XVIIIe siècles* (Paris, 1923); Paul Viollet, *Le roi et ses ministres pendant les derniers siècles de la monarchie* (Paris, 1912); De Luçay, *Les secrétaires d'état depuis leur institution jusqu'à la mort de Louis XV* (Paris, 1881); L. Aucoc, *Le conseil d'état avant et depuis 1789* (Paris, 1876); Louis-Lucas, *Étude sur la vénalité des charges* (Paris, 1883), vol. II; G. Pagès, "La vénalité des offices dans l'ancienne France," *Revue historique,* CLXIX (1932); A. Dussauge, *Le ministère de Belle-Isle* (Paris, 1914); F. Piétri, *La réforme de l'état au XVIIIe siècle* (Paris, 1935); M. Rousselet, *Histoire de la magistrature française,* 2 vols. (Paris, 1957); G. Matthews, *The Royal General Farms in Eighteenth-Century France* (New York, 1958); J. Villain, *Le récouvrement des impôts directs sous l'ancien régime* (Paris, 1952); S. McCloy, *Government Assistance in Eighteenth Century France* (Durham, 1946). On the *parlements,* E. Glasson, *Le parlement de Paris* (Paris, 1901), vol. II; R. Bickart, *Les parlements et la notion de souveraineté nationale au XVIIIe siècle* (Paris, 1932); V. de Marcé, *Le contrôle des finances* (Paris, 1928); R. Villiers, *l'organisation du parlement de Paris et des conseils supérieurs d'après la réforme de Maupéou* (Paris, 1937); *Remontrances du parlement de Paris au XVIIIe siècle,* ed. by Flammermont (Paris, 1888-1898), 3 vols.; P. Beik, *A Judgment of the Old Regime* (New York, 1944); F. Ford, *Robe and Sword* (Cambridge, Mass., 1953). The best studies on the intendants are those of the Russian scholar P. Ardascheff, *Les intendants de province sous Louis XVI* (Paris, 1909), and his article "Les intendants de province, etc.," *Revue d'histoire moderne et contemporaine,* V (1903); invaluable also is the scholarly biography by M. Lhéritier, *Tourny, intendant de Bordeaux* (Paris, 1920), and A. Rebillon, *Les états de Bretagne de 1661 à 1789* (Paris, 1932). F. Ford's unique *Strasbourg in Transition, 1648-1789* (Cambridge, Mass., 1958), written as a description of the impact of French annexation on the old imperial city, contributes significantly to more general questions of French government and society under the Old Regime.

Spain. The standard work on Spanish institutions in the eighteenth century is Desdevises du Dezert, *L'Espagne de l'ancien régime* (Paris, 1897-1904), 3 vols., revised and republished under the title "Les institutions de l'Espagne," in *Revue Hispanique,* LXX (1927); A. Ballesteros y Baretta, *Historia de España y su influencia en la historia universal,* 2nd ed., IX (Barcelona, 1958); R. Altamira, *Historia de España y de la civilización española* (Barcelona, 1935); A. Ferrer del Rio, *Historia reynado de Carlos III° en España* (Madrid, 1856), vol. I; F. Albi, *El corregidor en el municipio español bajo la monarquía absoluta* (Madrid, 1943); A. Girard, *La répartition de la population en Espagne dans les temps modernes* (Paris, 1929); H. Berindoague, *Le mercantilisme en Espagne* (Paris, 1929); R. D. Hussey, *The Caracas Company* (Cambridge, Mass., 1934); A. Rodriquez Villa, *Patiño y Campillo* (Madrid, 1882); C. Kany, *Life and Manners in Madrid, 1750-1800* (Berkeley, 1932); A. Domínguez Ortiz, *La sociedad española en el siglo XVIII* (Madrid, 1955); J. Sarrailh, *L'Espagne éclairée de la seconde moitié du XVIIIe siècle* (Paris, 1954).

Austria. Starting-point for study of the constitutional evolution of the German Empire after the Peace of Westphalia is F. Hartung's brief

Deutsche Verfassungsgeschichte vom XV. Jahrhundert bis zur Gegenwart, 7th ed. (Stuttgart, 1959). On the lesser German states, see F. Carsten, *Princes and Parliaments in Germany from the Fifteenth to the Eighteenth Century* (New York, 1959); H. Rall, *Kurbayern in der letzten Epoche der alten Reichsverfassung, 1745-1801* (Munich, 1952); and the specialized material cited in B. Gebhardt, *Handbuch der deutschen Geschichte,* II. On Austria proper there is the excellent J. Redlich, *Das österreichische Staats- und Reichsproblem* (Vienna, 1920), vol. I; W. Schüssler, *Das Verfassungsproblem im Habsburger Reiche* (Stuttgart, 1918); K. Springer, *Grundlagen und Entwicklungsziele der österreich-ungarischen Monarchie* (Vienna, 1906). Older but still valuable manuals are A. von Luschin, *Österreichische Reichsgeschichte* (Bamberg, 1896), and I. Beidtel, *Geschichte der österreichischen Staatsverwaltung* (Innsbruck, 1896), vol. II. Most important for the central government are the volumes in the *Die österreichische Zentralverwaltung* series (Vienna, 1907 and later years). Quite the best study on Bohemia in English is Robert Kerner, *Bohemia in the Eighteenth Century* (New York, 1932), written as a companion volume to H. Marczali, *Hungary in the Eighteenth Century* (Cambridge, 1910). The best general history is A. Rezek, J. Svátek, J. Prášek, *Dějiný Čech a Moravy nové doby, 1648-1815* (Prague, 1932); from the German point of view B. Bretholz, *Geschichte Böhmens und Mährens* (Reichenberg, 1924), 4 vols.; E. Denis, *La Bohême depuis la Montagne Blanche* (Paris, 1930), 2 vols. On Hungary there is, besides the brief but scholarly F. Eckart, *Short History of Hungary* (London, 1934), A. Domanovzky, *Die Geschichte Ungarns* (Munich, 1923). In Magyar the standard work is B. Hóman and G. Szekfü, *Magyar történet* (Budapest, 1928-1934), vols. IV-VII. The more recent *Magyarország története,* Vol. I, Part 2 (Budapest, 1958), was published by the Hungarian government for university use. See also F. Valjavec, *Geschichte der deutschen Kulturbeziehungen zu Südosteuropa,* 2nd ed., III (Munich, 1958); and E. Link, *The Emancipation of the Austrian Peasant, 1740-1798* (New York, 1949). For Italy see F. Valsecchi, *Le riforme dell'assolutismo illuminato negli stati italiani, 1748-1789* (Milan, 1955); by the same author, *L'Italia nel settecento dal 1714 al 1788* (Milan, 1959); L. Bulferetti, *L'assolutismo illuminato in Italia (1700-1789)* (Milan, 1944); E. Rota, *Le origini del Risorgimento (1700-1800),* 2nd ed., 2 vols. (Milan, 1948).

Prussia. Much the best political as well as constitutional and administrative history of Prussia is O. Hintze, *Die Hohenzollern und ihr Werk*

(Berlin, 1916), a work belied by its royalist title. A brief introduction is G. Schmoller, *Preussische Verfassungs-, Verwaltungs-, und Finanzgeschichte* (Berlin, 1921). For a discussion of the older literature on Frederick the Great and the Prussian bureaucracy see my articles in the *Political Science Quarterly*, vols. 46 and 47 (1931, 1932). Essential to a grasp of the constitutional evolution of Prussia are L. Tümpel, *Entstehung des Brandenburgisch-Preussischen Einheitsstaats im Zeitalter des Absolutismus* (Berlin, 1915), and O. Hintze, "Preussens Entwicklung zum Rechtsstaat," *Forschungen zur Brandenburgischen und Preussischen Geschichte,* XXXII (1920). By no means negligible is H. Mirabeau, *De la monarchie prussienne* (London, 1788), 7 vols, on which see H. Reissner, *Mirabeau und seine Monarchie Prussienne* (Berlin, 1926). Of fundamental importance on Prussian administration is the vast document publication begun by G. Schmoller, *Acta Borussica, Denkmäler der preussischen Staatsverwaltung im 18. Jahrhundert* (Berlin, 1892-1936). In addition to the separate divisions devoted to the grain trade, commercial policy, monetary system, the silk and woolen industries, the section *Die Behördenorganisation und die allgemeine Staatsverwaltung,* 15 vols., is easily the most important. In addition to the studies indicated above E. Wolff, *Grundriss der preussisch-deutschen sozialpolitischen und Volkswirtschaftsgeschichte* (Berlin, 1909); H. Rosenberg, *Bureaucracy, Aristocracy, and Autocracy: the Prussian Experience, 1660-1815* (Cambridge, Mass., 1958).

Russia. Among the general works on eighteenth-century Russia the following are the most serviceable: P. Milioukov, M. Kizevetter and others, *Histoire de Russie* (Paris, 1932), vol. II; K. Stählin, *Geschichte Russlands seit den Aufängen bis zur Gegenwart,* III (Stuttgart, 1930); V. Gitermann, *Geschichte Russlands,* II (Zürich, 1949); V. O. Kluchevsky, *A History of Russia* (New York, 1960), vol. IV. The standard general Soviet history in 1962 is that published by the Akademiia nauk SSSR, Institut istorii, *Ocherki istorii SSSR,* VI-VII (Moscow, 1956-57), ed. A. I. Baranovich and others, the notes to which serve as an entry into more specialized Soviet literature, though much of this has been superseded by monographic work published since 1956; a solid older Marxist history is M. N. Pokrovsky, *History of Russia from the Earliest Times to the Rise of Commercial Capitalism* (New York, 1931). A good general history is M. Florinsky, *Russia: a History and an Interpretation,* I (New York, 1953); on the middle of the century G. Vernadsky, *History of Russia,* 4th ed. (New Haven, 1954), and B. Pares, *History of Russia,* rev.

ed. (London, 1955), are less informative. The best study of the reign of Elizabeth is K. Waliszewski, *La dernière des Romanov* (Paris, 1902); see also F. Ley, *Le maréchal de Münnich et la Russie au XVIIIe siècle* (Paris, 1959). Profound and informative is Boris Brutzkus' "Die historischen Eigentümlichkeiten der wirtschaftlichen und sozialen Entwicklung Russlands," *Jahrbücher für die Kultur und Geschichte der Slaven*, X (1934); also G. Sacke, "Adel und Bürgertum in der Regierungszeit Katharinas II von Russland," *Revue belge de Philologie et d'Histoire*, XVII (1938). On Russian economic history see J. Kulisher, *Russische Wirtschaftsgeschichte* (Jena, 1925), vol. I, and "Die Kapitalistischen Unternehmer in Russland, etc.," *Archiv für Sozialwissenschaft und Sozialpolitik*, LXV (1931); B. Gille, *Histoire économique et sociale de la Russie* (Paris, 1949), and the important Soviet study by P. I. Lyashchenko, *History of the National Economy of Russia* (New York, 1949). J. Blum, *Lord and Peasant in Russia* (Princeton, 1961), is a fundamental historical analysis of the serf problem. See also M. Tugan-Baranowsky, *Geschichte der russischen Fabrik* (Berlin, 1900), and especially D. Gerhard, *England und der Aufstieg Russlands* (Berlin, 1933), which is excellent on the foreign trade of England and Russia.

Great Britain. No English historian has ever discussed the contrasting constitutional evolution of England and the states of the Continent more effectively or brilliantly than Ernest Barker, *National Character and the Factors in its Formation*, 4th ed. (London, 1948). Vols. X-XII of the most authoritative work on English constitutional and legal history, Sir William Holdsworth, *History of English Law* (London, 1922-1938), 14 vols., deal with the eighteenth century. On the position of the crown under the Hanoverians R. H. Gretton, *The King's Majesty, a Study in the Historical Philosophy of Modern Kingship* (London, 1930); R. Lucas, *George II and His Ministers* (London, 1910). On the British cabinet E. H. Turner, *The Cabinet Council of England* (New York, 1932), vol. II; W. Hasbach, *Die parlamentarische Kabinets-Regierung* (Stuttgart, 1917). For the composition of parliament see A. S. Turberville, *The House of Lords in the Eighteenth Century* (London, 1927) and the pioneer analysis of L. B. Namier, *Structure of Politics at the Accession of George III* (London, 1929), 2 vols., and by the same author, *England in the Age of the American Revolution* (London, 1930). On the party system, besides the brief essay by G. M. Trevelyan, *The Two-Party System in English Political History* (Oxford, 1926), see the brilliant study of Keith Feiling, *The Second Tory Party, 1714-1832* (London,

1938); W. T. Laprade, *Public Opinion and Politics in Eighteenth Century England* (New York, 1936). On local government no country has anything comparable in thoroughness and clarity to Sidney and Beatrice Webb's *English Local Government from the Revolution to the Municipal Corporations Act,* 9 vols. (London, 1906-1929); see also the work by the Austrian historian J. Redlich, *Local Government in England,* ed. by F. Hirst (London, 1903), 2 vols.; John and Barbara Hammond, *The Village Labourer,* 2 vols. (London, 1948); G. Slater, *The Growth of Modern England* (London, 1933).

Chapter III

Alfred Vagts, *History of Militarism,* rev. ed. (New York, 1959), is vastly superior in grasp and scholarship to P. Schmitthenner, *Krieg und Kriegführung im Wandel der Weltgeschichte* (Potsdam, 1930). Although open to criticism on many points Hans Delbrück, *Geschichte der Kriegskunst* (Berlin, 1920), vol. IV, is still most valuable. The best history of military literature is still Max Jähns, *Geschichte der Kriegswissenschaften* (Berlin, 1891), vol. III. On the social structure of armies see H. Speier, "Militarism in the Eighteenth Century," *Social Research,* III (1936). The best study on the French army is the superb and scrupulously honest A. Dussauge, *Études sur la guerre de sept ans, le ministère de Belle-Isle* (Paris, 1914), which, though unfinished, is one of the profoundest studies of mid-century France generally. Admirable for its clarity, though useless for the navy, is Col. Réboul, *Histoire militaire et navale* in G. Hanotaux, *Histoire de la nation française* (Paris, 1925), vol. VII; L. Tuetey, *Les officiers sous l'ancien régime, nobles et rôturiers* (Paris, 1908); L. Mention, *L'armée sous l'ancien régime* (Paris, 1900); L. Susane, *Histoire de l'ancienne infantérie française* (Paris, 1849), is still excellent. R. Quimby, *The Background of Napoleonic Warfare: the Theory of Military Tactics in Eighteenth-Century France* (New York, 1957), explores military doctrine to argue that Revolutionary and Imperial methods were not so revolutionary after all.

The only complete documentary history of the Prussian army is General C. Jany, *Geschichte der Königlich-Preussischen Armee* (Berlin, 1928), whose second volume is also the most comprehensive history of the wars of Frederick II. The best analysis of the structure of the Prussian army is E. Dette, *Friedrich der Grosse und sein Heer* (Halle, 1914); K. Demeter, *Das deutsche Offizierkorps* (Berlin, 1930); W. Goerlitz, *History of the German General Staff, 1657-1945* (New York, 1953).

On Prussian recruiting see W. Schultz, *Die preussischen Werbungen unter Friedrich Wilhelm I und Friedrich dem Grossen* (Berlin, 1887); H. Höhne, *Die Einstellung der sächsischen Regimente im Jahre 1756* (Halle, 1926); P. Losch, *Der Soldatenhandel* (Kassel, 1933).

Official military histories have at best a relative value. In working with them it is best to remember the ironical comment of the old General von Moltke that such histories contain the truth, sometimes nothing but the truth, but never the whole truth. This applies to: *Die Kriege Friedrichs des Grossen,* ed. by the German General Staff (Berlin, 1890-1896), I, 1-3; II, 1-3; *Die Kriege unter der Regierung der Kaiserin-Königin Maria Theresia: Österreichischer Erbfolgekrieg 1740-1748,* published under the direction of the Imperial Military Archives (Vienna, 1896-1914), 9 vols.; General C. Pajol, *Les guerres sous Louis XV* (Paris, 1881-1889), 7 vols.

On the constitutional position of the English army see J. S. Omond, *Parliament and the Army* (Cambridge, 1933). Sir J. W. Fortescue's *History of the British Army,* II (London, 1899), is written without knowledge of the structure and organization of continental armies. This cannot be said of E. M. Lloyd, *Review of History of Infantry* (London, 1908). There is much good information in E. H. Skrine, *Fontenoy and Great Britain's Share in the War of the Austrian Succession* (1906); Evan Charteris, *William Augustus, Duke of Cumberland* (London, 1914-1925), 2 vols.; Beckles Wilson, *Life and Letters of J. Wolfe* (London, 1909); W. Wood, *Winning of Canada: Chronicle of Wolfe* (Toronto, 1915).

A. T. Mahan stimulated interest in naval strategy by his *Influence of Sea Power upon History, 1660-1783* (Boston, 1889), but it was not until Admiral Sir Herbert Richmond published his thorough and authoritative *The Navy in the War of 1739-1748* (Cambridge, 1920), 3 vols., that all aspects of naval warfare, including commerce, were considered. See also his *National Policy and Naval Strength and other Essays* (London, 1928), and his *Statesmen and Sea Power* (Oxford, 1947). G. Marcus, *A Naval History of England,* I (London, 1961), is a brief narrative with valuable bibliography. For naval statistics see R. Beatson, *Naval and Military Memoirs of Great Britain* (London, 1804), 6 vols. Sir W. L. Clowes, *The Royal Navy* (London, 1897-1903), 7 vols., gives information about the constitutions of the fleet, pay, prize money; better in many respects is D. Hannay, *Short History of the British Navy* (London, 1909), vol. II, and particularly his *The Sea Trader* (London, 1912), which is as useful for economic as for naval history. Other important studies are E. C.

Millington, *Seamen in the Making, A Short History of Nautical Training* (London, 1935); A. T. Mahan, *Types of Naval Officers* (Boston, 1901); M. Lewis, *England's Sea-Officers* (London, 1939); W. H. Hodges, *Select Naval Documents* (Cambridge, 1922); J. Charnock, *History of Marine Architecture* (London, 1802), vol. III; G. E. Manwaring, *The Flower of England's Garden* (London, 1936); J. R. Hutchinson, *The Press Gang* (New York, 1914). Useful are the following biographies: Sir John Barrow, *Life of Lord Anson* (1839); B. Tunstall, *Admiral Byng* (London, 1928); D. Ford, *Admiral Vernon and His Times* (London, 1907); M. Burrows, *Life of Hawke* (London, 1883).

The best histories of the French navy are R. Jouan, *Histoire de la marine française* (Paris, 1932), vol. I, and the admirable J. Tramond, *Manuel d'histoire maritime de la France des origines à 1815,* new ed. (Paris, 1947); more detailed but somewhat less useful is G. Lacour-Gayet, *La marine militaire de la France sous le règne de Louis XV* (Paris, 1910); on Cardinal Fleury's support of the navy see A. M. Wilson, *French Foreign Policy during the Administration of Cardinal Fleury* (Cambridge, Mass., 1936); for a critical analysis of French naval strategy see R. Castex, *Les idées militaires de la marine du XVIIIe siècle* (Paris, 1911), and Léon Vignols, "La course maritime," *Revue d'histoire économique et sociale,* XV (1927).

Chapter IV

Although few episodes of European history have an ampler literature than the War of the Austrian Succession, much of it is of secondary importance to the student who desires a conspectus of the war as a whole, because it is written on the basis of one particular set of archives or with one of the belligerents in view without reference to the others. There are two notable exceptions to this all but general defect, if it is a defect: Fritz Wagner, *Kaiser Karl und die Grossen Mächte* (Stuttgart, 1938), which in its broad European base and solid documentary foundation supersedes most of the works on the earlier phases of the war, and Paul Vaucher, *Robert Walpole et la politique de Fleury, 1731-1742* (Paris, 1925), which in its concluding chapters rises to a European outlook. To these may be added the thorough but tedious Sir Richard Lodge, *Studies in Eighteenth Century Diplomacy, 1740-1748* (London, 1930), the largest portion of which is devoted to the preliminaries of Aix-la-Chapelle. Because of this national character of the literature it is most convenient to consider it by countries. Also, general national histories not already cited for earlier chapters will be mentioned here.

Austria. Together with the handbook of K. and M. Uhlirz, mentioned above, H. Hantsch, *Die Geschichte Österreichs,* 2nd ed., II (Graz, 1953); H. Kretschmayr, *Geschichte von Österreich* (Vienna, 1936); F. M. Mayer, R. Kaindl, H. Pirchegger, *Geschichte und Kulturleben Deutschösterreichs,* 5th ed., II (Vienna, 1960); W. Coxe, *History of the House of Austria* (useful because of the diplomatic documents at the disposal of the author), (London, 1820), vol. IV, present serviceable general histories. A. von Arneth, *Geschichte Maria Theresias* (Vienna, 1863-1879), 10 vols., is the most completely documented work on the reign, but often no more than a transcript of the documents. Far more readable and excellent on foreign affairs is E. Guglia, *Maria Theresia* (Munich, 1917), 2 vols.; most satisfactory of all is the penetrating and concise H. Kretschmayr, *Maria Theresia* (Gotha, 1925); see also G. Gooch, *Maria Theresa and Other Studies* (London, 1951); popular but useful is K. Tschuppik, *Marie Thérèse* (Paris, 1936); G. Turba, *Die Grundlagen der Pragmatischen Sanktion* (Vienna, 1911-1912), 2 vols., is a conclusive study. Emphasizing Austria's relation to Germany the brilliant work by H. von Srbik, *Deutsche Einheit* (Vienna, 1937), vol. I. For the Austrian Netherlands H. Pirenne, *Histoire de Belgique,* vol. V, is essential (vol. III in the beautifully illustrated 1948-52 Brussels edition), as is H. Übersberger, *Österreich und Russland* (Leipzig, 1906), for foreign affairs. The *Algemene geschiedenis der Nederlanden,* VII-VIII (Utrecht, 1953-55), ed. J. v. Houtte and others, includes the present Benelux countries.

Prussia. The most important printed sources on Prussia under Frederick the Great are: *Oeuvres de Frédéric le Grand,* ed. by J. D. E. Preuss (Berlin, 1846-1857), 30 vols.; his diplomatic correspondence published under the title *Politische Correspondenz Friedrichs des Grossen,* ed. by J. G. Droysen, M. Duncker, G. B. Volz (Berlin, 1879-1938), 45 vols.; G. B. Volz, *Die politischen Testamente Friedrichs des Grossen* (Berlin, 1920); G. B. Volz, *Friedrich der Grosse und Wilhelmine von Bayreuth, Ihr Briefwechsel* (Leipzig, 1926), 2 vols.; *Preussische Staatsschriften aus der Regierungszeit Friedrichs II,* ed. by J. G. Droysen and R. Koser (Berlin, 1877-1892), 3 vols. In spite of its weakness on many points R. Koser, *Geschichte Friedrichs des Grossen,* 7th ed. (Berlin, 1921-1925), 4 vols. (vol. IV contains the most complete bibliography), is still the standard biography. More accurate on the youth, the intellectual development and diplomacy of Frederick is A. Berney, *Friedrich der Grosse, Entwicklungsgeschichte eines Staatsmannes* (Tübingen, 1934). One of the best portraits is Wilhelm Wiegand, *Friedrich der Grosse* (Bielefeld, 1902); brilliantly written though not differing essentially from Koser's interpretation is G. Ritter, *Friedrich der Grosse,* 3rd ed. (Heidelberg, 1954); Onno Klopp, *Friedrich der Grosse* (Vienna, 1868), is quite the ablest hostile portrait. Chapter XV of G. Gooch's *Frederick the Great* (London, 1947) will serve as an introduction to the historiographical controversies over Frederick; other scholarly English studies are those of F. W. Reddaway, *Frederick the Great* (London, 1902), and F. Veale, *Frederick the Great* (London, 1935); Norwood Young's *Frederick the Great* (London, 1920) is a war book; C. Easum, *Prince Henry of Prussia, Brother of Frederick the Great* (Madison, Wis., 1942), discloses unusual and fascinating material; Thomas Carlyle's *History of Frederick II Called the Great* (London, 1873), 10 vols., is still valuable as a personal portrait but almost useless for statesmanship, diplomacy, and warfare; Ernest Lavisse, *Le Grand Frédéric avant l'avènement* (Paris, 1893), is a work of great literary beauty and sound scholarship, but L. Paul-Dubois, *Frédéric le grand d'après sa correspondance politique* (Paris, 1903), is the most adequate general French study. The most serviceable studies on the intellectual development of Frederick II are: E. Henriot, *Frédéric II et Voltaire* (Paris, 1927); F. Meinecke, *Machiavellism* (New Haven, 1957); Werner Langer, *Friedrich der Grosse und die geistige Welt Frankreichs* (Hamburg, 1932); W. Dilthey, "Friedrich der Grosse und die deutsche Aufklärung," *Gesammelte Schriften* (Berlin, 1927), vol. III. C. Grünhagen, *Geschichte des ersten schlesischen Krieges* (Gotha, 1881), 2 vols., is still the most complete and scholarly study of the Silesian War; to this must be added G. B. Volz, "Die Politik Friedrichs vor und nach seiner Thronbesteigung," *Hist. Zeitschr.* CLI (1935); G. Roloff, "Friedrich und das Reich, etc.," *Forsch. zur Brand. und Preuss. Geschichte,* XXV (1913); R. Becker, *Der Dresdner Friede und die Politik Brühls* (Leipzig, 1902).

France. H. Carré, *Le règne de Louis XV (1715-1774)* (Paris, 1911), vol. VIII, part 2 in the Lavisse *Histoire de France.* is generally regarded as the standard history of this period, but while excellent on domestic affairs it presents only an inadequate summary of foreign and colonial affairs. These gaps may be filled by P. Rain's *La diplomatie française d'Henri IV à Vergennes* (Paris, 1945), and by the materials cited for Chapters VI, VII, and VIII, below. P. Gaxotte, *Le siècle de Louis XV* (Paris, 1933), Eng. trans. *Louis XV and His Times* (Philadelphia, 1934), is a brilliant and often powerful study of domestic affairs but abounds in puerilities on foreign affairs. As a defense of Louis XV the book over-shoots the mark. The same may be said of P. de Nolhac, *Louis XV et Marie Leczinska* (Paris, 1902); *Louis XV et Mme. de Pompadour* (Paris, 1904); Mme. de Saint-André, *Louis XV* (Paris, 1921). Important for a study of Louis XV is the *Correspondance du duc de Noailles et de Louis XV*, ed. by Rousset (Paris, 1865), 2 vols. The most informative printed source on French diplomacy is the *Recueil des instructions données aux ambassadeurs et ministres de France depuis les traités de Westphalie jusqu'à la Révolution française*, 25 vols. (Paris, 1884-1929), notably the volumes for Austria, Spain, Bavaria, Prussia and Holland, but they also have their limitations. The chief value of the thorough Maurice Sautai, *Les préliminaires de la guerre de la succession d'Autriche* (Paris, 1907), and his *Les débuts de la guerre de la succession d'Autriche* (Paris, 1910), lies in the fullest statement of diplomatic events and the copious reprinting of documents and memorials; Alfred Baudrillart, *Philippe V et la cour de France* (Paris, 1890-1901), 5 vols., is the most scholarly diplomatic study of this period and is of permanent value. The most ambitious attempts to write the dramatic history of this decade from the point of view of French diplomacy are the numerous works of the Duc de Broglie, *Frédéric II et Marie Thérèse, 1740-1742* (Paris, 1883), 2 vols.; *Frédéric II et Louis XV, 1742-1744* (Paris, 1885), 2 vols.; *Marie Thérèse impératrice, 1744-1746* (Paris, 1888), 2 vols.; *Maurice de Saxe et le marquis d'Argenson, 1746-1747* (Paris, 1891), 2 vols.; *La paix d'Aix-la-Chapelle, 1748* (Paris, 1891). Broglie has frequently been charged with an anti-Prussian animus. While this is true, his works remain the fullest documentary account of French diplomacy in these years. Other impor-tant works are E. Zévort, *Le marquis d'Argenson* (Paris, 1880); J. Colin, *Les campagnes de maréchal de Saxe* (Paris, 1900); H. Camon, *Maurice de Saxe, maréchal de France* (Paris, 1934); Spenser Wilkinson, *The Defense of Piedmont* (Oxford, 1927); Marquis d'Argenson, *Journal et Mémoires inédits*, ed. E. Rathéry (Paris, 1859-1867), 9 vols.; D. Carutti, *Storia del regno di Carlo Emanuele III* (Turin, 1859). For the maritime and colonial war, outside the works which will be reviewed in another connection, see P. Crepin, *Mahé de la Bourdonnais* (Paris, 1922), and L. Roubaud, *La Bourdonnais* (Paris, 1932); P. Charliat, *Trois siècles d'économie maritime française* (Paris, 1931); J. Vinson, *Les français dans l'Inde* (Paris, 1894).

Great Britain. The most complete history of this period is W. E. H. Lecky, *History of England in the Eighteenth Century* (London, 1899-

1901), 7 vols., which, however, is more useful for cultural history than for political and diplomatic history since it is not based on an extensive investigation of original sources. Brief but comprehensive in scope is Basil Williams, *The Whig Ascendancy*, 2nd ed. (Oxford, 1962); for this period I. S. Leadam, *Political History of England* (ed. W. Hunt and R. L. Poole), vol. IX (London, 1909), is still useful but largely antiquated. Printed correspondence and memoirs by contemporaries there are in great profusion: *The Bedford Correspondence* (London, 1843), 3 vols.; *Grenville Papers* (London, 1852), 4 vols.; *Private Correspondence of Chesterfield and Newcastle, 1744-46*, ed. by Sir R. Lodge (London, 1930); *Memoirs and Correspondence of Sir Robert Murray Keith* (London, 1849); A. Bisset, *Memoirs and Papers of Sir Andrew Mitchell* (London, 1850), 2 vols.; *Private Correspondence of Sir Benjamin Keene*, ed. by Sir R. Lodge (London, 1935); the Trevor, Hare, and Onslow Papers in *Royal Historical Manuscripts Commission, Reports*, vols. IX and XIV (1895); Lord Hervey, *Some Materials towards Memoirs of the Reign of George II* (London, 1931), 3 vols.; Bubb Dodington's *Diary* (1784). Useful biographies are: W. Coxe, *Memoirs of Sir Robert Walpole* (London, 1798); W. Coxe, *The Pelham Administration* (London, 1829); S. R. Stirling Taylor, *Walpole and his Age* (London, 1931); N. W. B. Pemberton, *Carteret, the Brilliant Failure of the Eighteenth Century* (London, 1936); A. Ballantyne, *Lord Carteret* (London, 1887); B. Williams, *Carteret and Newcastle: a Contrast in Contemporaries* (Cambridge, Engl., 1943); P. Yorke, *Life and Correspondence of Philip Yorke, Lord Chancellor Hardwicke* (Oxford, 1913), 3 vols., is especially valuable for foreign affairs and often expands into a history of the period; E. Fitzmaurice, *Life of Shelburne* (London, 1912).

There is no comprehensive study of British foreign policy for these years. For the Spanish War of 1739 the exhaustive and definitive Richard Pares, *War and Trade in the West Indies* (Oxford, 1936), supersedes all previous studies, even the capital study by Paul Vaucher, mentioned above; Sir R. Lodge, *Great Britain and Prussia in the Eighteenth Century* (Oxford, 1923), suffers from the same defect which mars so much of Droysen's work, since the author consults only English diplomatic sources; more useful is A. W. Ward, *Great Britain and Hanover* (Oxford, 1899); E. Charteris, *Cumberland* (London, 1913), is valuable for the later phases of the Austrian Succession War; see also P. Geyl, *Willem IV en England tot 1748* (Leyden, 1927); D. B. Horn, "Saxony in the War of the Austrian Succession," *Eng. Hist. Review*, XLIV (1929). On the English trade war and privateering W. B.

Johnson, *Wolves of the Channel* (London, 1931); C. E. Fayle, "Economic Pressure in the War of 1739-1748," *Journal of the Royal United Service Institution,* XLIII (1923); C. Wright and C. E. Fayle, *A History of Lloyds* (London, 1928).

Chapter V

An adequate bibliography on the Enlightenment would require another volume, and every brief selection suffers to some degree from arbitrariness, to which this one is no exception. More extensive bibliographies are the third volume of G. Lanson's *Manual bibliographique de la littérature française moderne* (Paris, 1925); and D. C. Cabeen and J. Brody, ed., *A Critical Bibliography of French Literature,* IV (Syracuse, 1951). The most heroic effort to discuss the movement in all its various aspects is P. Smith, *History of Modern Culture* (New York, 1934), vol. II. No other work presents such a comprehensive picture. More concerned with political thought than with larger philosophic and religious aspects is the extremely intelligent book of Kingsley Martin, *French Liberal Thought in the Eighteenth Century,* 2nd ed. (London, 1954). Among general works F. Lange's *History of Materialism,* 3rd ed. (London, 1925), though to some extent antiquated, is still useful. Daniel Mornet's brief *French Thought in the Eighteenth Century* (New York, 1929) is often feeble but generally serviceable. Had Mornet taken more trouble to study his economic and social history he might have avoided some of the worst errors in his otherwise excellent *Les origines intellectuelles de la Révolution française, 1715-1787,* 4th ed. (Paris, 1947). No one has sketched this social background of the movement more brilliantly than B. Groethuysen, *Die Entstehung der bürgerlichen Welt- und Lebensanschauung in Frankreich,* 2 vols. (Halle, 1927-30), unless it be the more modern P. Sagnac, *La formation de la société française moderne,* II (Paris, 1946); more specialized treatments are E. Barber, *The Bourgeois in Eighteenth-Century France* (Princeton, 1955); F. Ford's *Robe and Sword* and his *Strasbourg in Transition,* already mentioned; M. Glotz and M. Maire, *Salons du 18e siècle* (Paris, 1945); and R. Picard, *Les salons littéraires et la société française, 1610-1789* (New York, 1943); H. Laski, *The Rise of Liberalism* (New York, 1936), unhappily does nothing more than to sketch the economic background, although his introductory essay in F. Hearnshaw, *The Social and Political Ideas of Some Great French Thinkers of the Age of Reason* (London, 1930), is wide enough in its scope. Unsurpassed for logical acumen and keen analysis are the relevant chapters of George H. Sabine,

A History of Political Theory, 3rd ed. (New York, 1961). Carl Becker's adroit *Heavenly City of the Eighteenth Century Philosophers* (New Haven, 1932) is a stimulating essay, but occasionally repeats outworn romantic and Hegelian formulas; C. Frankel, *The Faith of Reason* (New York, 1948), is a more sympathetic and probably more balanced judgment; H. Vyverberg, *Historical Pessimism in the French Enlightenment* (Cambridge, Mass., 1958), points to another dimension; on the idea of nature see B. Willey, *The Eighteenth Century Background* (London, 1940).The profoundest and keenest philosophic analysis of the entire movement is that of Ernst Cassirer, *The Philosophy of the Enlightenment* (Princeton, 1951); a striking contrast with Cassirer is A. Cobban, *In Search of Humanity* (New York, 1960), which means something quite different by "the Enlightenment"; yet another contrast is P. Hazard, *European Thought in the Eighteenth Century* (New Haven, 1954).

On the scientific background of the Enlightenment there is the authoritative and thorough A. Wolf, *A History of Science, Technology and Philosophy in the Eighteenth Century,* 2nd ed. (New York, 1952), which, however, is anything but perspicuous; W. Whewell, *History of the Inductive Sciences* (London, 1857), 3 vols.; F. Dannemann, *Die Naturwissenschaften in ihrer Entwicklung,* 4 vols., 2nd ed. (Leipzig, 1920-23); H. Butterfield, *The Origins of Modern Science* (London, 1949); A. Hall, *The Scientific Revolution* (Boston, 1954); C. Singer, *A Short History of Scientific Ideas to 1900* (Oxford, 1959); R. Mousnier, *Progrès scientifique et technique au XVIIIe siècle* (Paris, 1958); P. Brunet, *L'introduction des théories de Newton en France au XVIIIe siècle* (Paris, 1931); P. Brunet, *Les physiciens hollandais et la méthode expérimentale en France au XVIIIe siècle* (Paris, 1926); P. Brunet, *Maupertuis* (Paris, 1929); Hélène Metzger, *La doctrine chimique: Newton, Stahl, Boerhaave* (Paris, 1930); D. Mornet, *Les sciences de la nature en France au XVIIIe siècle* (Paris, 1911). For the influence of Cartesian philosophy on the *philosophes* see G. Lanson, *Études d'histoire littéraire* (Paris, 1929); A. Vartanian, *Diderot and Descartes* (Princeton, 1953); on exotic literature the works of G. Atkinson, *Les rélations de voyages du XVIIe siècle et l'évolution des idées* (Paris, 1923) and his *The Extraordinary Voyage in French Literature from 1700 to 1720* (Paris, 1922); G. Chinard, *L'Amérique et la rêve exotique dans la littérature française* (Paris, 1913); H. N. Fairchild, *The Noble Savage* (New York, 1928); J. L. Myres, *The Influence of Anthropology on the Course of Political Science* (Berkeley, 1914).

On the Enlightenment and Biblical criticism, theology and religion, there exists an impressive literature: above all the admirable K. Aner, *Die Theologie der Lessingzeit* (Halle, 1929), and the works of Ernst Troeltsch, *Gesammelte Aufsätze zur Religionssoziologie und Geistesge-schichte* (Tübingen, 1925), vol. IV; by the same author, "Religion-swissenschaft und Theologie im 18. Jahrhundert," *Preussische Jahr-bücher*, vol. 114 (1903); by the same author, *Protestantismus und Kirche in der Neuzeit* (Berlin, 1922); on the side of Catholic defense A. Monod, *De Pascal à Chateaubriand, les défenseurs françaises du Chris-tianisme* (Paris, 1916); on liberal Catholicism R. Palmer, *Catholics and Unbelievers in 18th Century France* (Princeton, 1939); P. Alatri, *Profilo storico del cattolicesimo liberale in Italia nel settecento* (Palermo, 1950). On the French materialists there are, besides the work of F. Lange, *History of Materialism* (London, 1925), and Cassirer's penetrating analysis: R. Boissier, *La Mettrie* (Paris, 1931); René Hubert, *D'Holbach et ses amis* (Paris, 1928); W. H. Wickwar, *Baron D'Holbach* (London, 1935). On English deism the classic work of Leslie Stephen, *English Thought in the Eighteenth Century*, 3rd ed. (London, 1949), 2 vols., is still unapproached; see also J. M. Robertson, *A Short History of Free-thought* (New York, 1906), 2 vols.; Mark Pattison, *Essays and Reviews* (1861); Norman Sykes, *Church and State in England in the XVIIIth Century* (Cambridge, 1934). On David Hume: R. W. Church, *Hume's Theory of Understanding* (London, 1935); R. M. Laing, *David Hume* (London, 1932); John Laird, *Hume's Philosophy of Human Nature* (London, 1932), and the popular biography by J. Y. T. Greig, *David Hume* (New York, 1931).

On Diderot and the Encyclopedists there are, besides the older work of John Morley, *Diderot and the Encyclopedists* (London, 1878), and Ducros, *Les Encyclopédistes* (Paris, 1900), 2 vols., excellent studies by René Hubert, *L'esprit des sciences sociales dans l'Encyclopédie* (Paris, 1923); J. Le Gras, *Diderot et l'Encyclopédie* (Amiens, 1928); E. Weis, *Geschichtsschreibung und Staatsauffassung in der französischen Enzyklopädie* (Wiesbaden, 1956); the superlatively attractive studies by Jean Thomas, *L'humanisme de Diderot* (Paris, 1933), and H. Gillot, *Denis Diderot* (Paris, 1937); B. Groethuysen, "La pensée de Diderot," *La Grande Revue*, vol. LXXXII (1913); J. Luc, *Diderot* (Paris, 1938); by the Russian historian I. K. Luppol, *Diderot* (Paris, 1936); P. Hermand, *Les idées morales de Diderot* (Paris, 1923); A. Wilson, *Diderot* (New York, 1957); J. Oestreicher, *La pensée politique et économique de Diderot* (Vincennes, 1936).

Among the countless works on Voltaire it is difficult to select representative studies, but outstanding are: John Morley, *Voltaire,* 4th ed. (London, 1882); R. Aldington, *Voltaire* (London, 1925); Georg Brandes, *Voltaire* (New York, 1934), 2 vols.; A. Noyes, *Voltaire* (New York, 1939); P. Gay, *Voltaire's Politics: the Poet as Realist* (Princeton, 1959); in French G. Lanson, *Voltaire* (Paris, 1906); G. Pellissier, *Voltaire philosophe* (Paris, 1908); A. Bellesort, *Essai sur Voltaire* (Paris, 1925). For Voltaire and religion there is above all L. Torry, *Voltaire and the English Deists* (New Haven, 1938), and his *The Spirit of Voltaire* (New York, 1938); A. R. Morehouse, *Voltaire and Jean Meslier* (New Haven, 1936); J. R. Carré, *Réflexions sur l'anti-Pascal de Voltaire* (Paris, 1935). For Voltaire's historiography there is the delightful volume by J. B. Black, *The Art of History* (New York, 1926); Karl Ritter, *Entwicklung der Geschichtswissenschaft* (Munich, 1919); E. Fueter, *Geschichte der neueren Historiographie* (Berlin, 1911); A. von Martin, "Motive und Tendenzen in Voltaire's Geschichtsschreibung," *Hist. Zeitschr.,* vol. 118 (1917); J. Brumfitt, *Voltaire, Historian* (London, 1958).

For the social sciences of the Enlightenment there are, besides René Hubert's study on the social sciences and the *Encyclopédie,* indicated above, M. Leroy, *Histoire des idées sociales en France,* I, 2nd ed. (Paris, 1946); J. B. Bury, *The Idea of Progress* (London, 1920); H. J. Laski, *Studies in Law and Politics* (New Haven, 1932); H. Sée, *L'évolution de la pensée politique en France au XVIIIe siècle* (Paris, 1925); M. E. Carcassonne, *Montesquieu et le problème de la constitution française* (Paris, n. d.); J. Dedieu, *Montesquieu* (Paris, 1913); R. Shackleton, *Montesquieu; a Critical Biography* (London, 1961); S. Cotta, *Montesquieu e la scienza della società* (Turin, 1953); the analytical and systematic W. Stark, *Montesquieu: Pioneer of the Sociology of Knowledge* (London, 1960); G. Weulersse, *Le mouvement physiocratique en France de 1756-1770* (Paris, 1910), 3 vols.; G. Weulersse, *Les physiocrates* (Paris, 1930); A. Oncken, *Geschichte der Nationalökonomie* (Leipzig, 1920), vol. I; R. Gonnard, *Histoire des doctrines économiques* (Paris, 1930).

For Rousseau there are biographies by M. Josephson, *Jean-Jacques Rousseau* (New York, 1931), and C. E. Vulliamy, *Rousseau* (London, 1931); D. Mornet, *Rousseau, l'homme et l'oeuvre* (Paris, 1950); F. Green, *Jean-Jacques Rousseau; a Critical Study of His Life and Writings* (New York, 1955); Irving Babbitt, *Rousseau and Romanticism* (Boston, 1919); E. H. Wright, *The Meaning of Rousseau* (New York, 1929); C. H. Hendel, *Jean-Jacques Rousseau, Moralist* (New York, 1934), 2 vols.; René Hubert, *Rousseau et l'Encyclopédie* (Paris, 1928); G. Lanson, "L'unité de la pensée de J.-J. Rousseau," *Annales de la société de Jean-Jacques Rousseau* (1912); A. Cobban, *Rousseau and the Modern State* (London, 1934); H. Höffding, *J.-J. Rousseau's Philosophy* (New York, 1933); E. Cassirer, *The Question of Jean Jacques Rousseau* (New York, 1954); W. Ziegenfuss, *Jean Jacques Rousseau; eine soziologische Studie* (Erlangen, 1952); R. Derathé, *Le rationalisme de Jean-Jacques Rousseau* (Paris, 1948); A. Schinz, *La pensée de J.-J. Rousseau* (1929), 2 vols.; P. M. Masson, *La religion de J.-J. Rousseau* (Paris, 1916), 3 vols.; C. E. Vaughan's introduction to *The Political Writings of Jean-Jacques Rousseau* (Cambridge, 1915), 2 vols.

For the emotional revival in French, English and German literature: P. Trahard, *Les maîtres de la sensibilité française au XVIIIe siècle,* 4 vols. (Paris, 1931-1933); A. Monglond, *Histoire intérieure du préromantisme français, de l'abbé Prévost à Joubert* (Grenoble, 1929); E. Gosse, *History of Eighteenth Century Literature* (London, 1889); W. L. Phelps, *The Beginnings of the English Romantic Movement* (New York, 1893); A. Dobson, *Samuel Richardson* (London, 1902); Paul Dottin, *Samuel Richardson* (Paris, 1931); *The Cambridge History of English Literature: The Age of Johnson,* vol. X (New York, 1933); J. Texte, *Rousseau et les origines du cosmopolitanisme européen* (Paris, 1895); E. Schmidt, *Richardson, Rousseau und Goethe* (Berlin, 1895); A. Eloesser, *Die deutsche Literatur vom Barock bis zu Goethes Tod* (Berlin, 1930).

On Pietism and Methodism there is R. Knox, *Enthusiasm* (Oxford, 1950); A. W. Nagler, *Pietism and Methodism* (Nashville, 1918); O. Uttendorfer, *Zinzendorfs Weltbetrachtung* (Berlin, 1929); O. Pfister, *Die Frömmigkeit des Grafen Zinzendorf* (Berlin, 1925); K. Pinson, *Pietism as a Factor in the Rise of German Nationalism* (New York, 1934); *The Journal of John Wesley,* ed. N. Curnock (London, 1909-1916), 8 vols.; C. E. Vulliamy, *John Wesley* (London, 1931); S. G. Dimond, *The Psychology of the Methodist Revival* (London, 1926); F. C. Gill, *The Romantic Movement and Methodism* (London, 1937).

The most serviceable general history of eighteenth-century art, valuable particularly for its superb illustrations, is Max Osborn, *Die Kunst des Rokoko,* in the *Propyläen-Kunstgeschichte* (Berlin, 1929), vol. XIII. For a fuller discussion see René Schneider, *L'art français au XVIIIe siècle* (Paris, 1926); Louis Gillet, *La peinture aux XVIIe et XVIIIe siècles* (Paris, 1913); E. and J. de Goncourt, *L'art du XVIIIe siècle* (Paris, 1906), 3 vols.; L. Hautecoeur, *Greuze* (Paris, 1913); for art criticism and

Diderot's *salons* see H. Gillot, *Denis Diderot* (Paris, 1937); C. Justi, *Winckelmann und seine Zeitgenossen* (Leipzig, 1898), vol. I; Austin Dobson, *William Hogarth* (London, 1907). P. Lavedan, *Histoire de l'urbanisme*, II (Paris, 1941), is an illustrated history of urban design.

Chapter VI

The problem of the position of the colonies in the various national economies of this age of mercantilism is receiving increasing attention; and the problem of colonial trade is inseparable from the general problem of all foreign trade. For reasons of space the author has had to renounce a complete and full analysis of this important problem, necessary as it might otherwise appear. See especially for France J. Lacour-Gayet, ed., *Histoire de commerce*, VI (Paris, 1951); L. May, *Histoire économique de Martinique* (Paris, 1930); Gaston-Martin, *Nantes au XVIIIe siècle* (Paris, 1928); Gaston-Martin, *Nantes au XVIIIe siècle: l'ére des négriers, 1714-1774* (Paris, 1931), one of the most important studies on the mid-century; see also his more general *Histoire de l'esclavage dans les colonies françaises* (Paris, 1948); T. Malvézin, *Histoire du commerce de Bordeaux* (Bordeaux, 1892), vol. III; E. Garnault, *Histoire du commerce Rochelais au XVIIIe siècle* (La Rochelle, 1891), vol. III; Paul Masson, *Histoire du commerce français dans le Levant au XVIIIe siècle* (Paris, 1911); A. M. Wilson's chapter on the commercial expansion of France in his *French Foreign Policy During the Administration of Cardinal Fleury* (Cambridge, Mass., 1936), 290-317; and the materials on the French colonial system and on specific colonial areas cited below.

For the economic and commercial history of Great Britain in the middle decades of the century there are above all the works of E. Lipson, *Economic History of England, The Age of Mercantilism*, III, 3rd ed. (London, 1943); T. Ashton, *An Economic History of England*, III (London, 1945); the somewhat less useful W. Cunningham, *Growth of English Industry and Commerce, Modern Times*, pt. II (Cambridge, Engl., 1917-1919); and Paul Mantoux, *The Industrial Revolution in the Eighteenth Century* (London, 1935); C. R. Fay, *Great Britain from Adam Smith to the Present Day*, 5th ed. (London, 1950); E. A. J. Johnson, *Some Origins of the Modern Economic World* (New York, 1936); though dealing chiefly with the period after 1763, of interest for these years are J. and B. Hammond, *The Rise of Modern Industry*, 7th ed. (London, 1947), and *The Village Labourer, 1760-1832*, new ed. (London, 1920), also *The Town Labourer, 1760-1832,* new ed. (London, 1920); D. G. Barnes, *History of the English Corn Laws, 1660-1846* (New York, 1930); L. Harper, *The English Navigation Laws* (New York, 1939); H. Sée, *Modern Capitalism* (London, 1928); E. L. Hargreaves, *The National Debt* (London, 1930); J. Clapham, *The Bank of England,* I (Cambridge, Engl., 1944); C. Wilson, *Anglo-Dutch Commerce and Finance in the Eighteenth Century* (Cambridge, Engl., 1941); K. Davies, *The Royal African Company* (London, 1957); M. Wilbur, *The East India Company* (New York, 1945); L. Sutherland, *The East India Company in Eighteenth-Century Politics* (New York, 1952); Lillian Penson, *The Colonial Background of British Foreign Policy* (London, 1930); J. B. Botsford, *English Society in the Eighteenth Century as Influenced from Oversea* (New York, 1924); G. Unwin, *Studies in Economic History* (London, 1927); H. Heaton, *Economic History of Europe,* rev. ed. (New York, 1948).

Studies on the French colonial system in the eighteenth century are generally less satisfactory than those on the British colonial empire. A. Girault, *Les colonies françaises avant et depuis 1815,* 6th ed. (Paris, 1943), is a brief manual. There are some useful comments in Chr. Schéfer, *La France moderne et le problème colonial* (Paris, 1907), and C. L. Lokke, *France and the Colonial Question* (New York, 1932); H. Priestley, *France Overseas through the Old Regime* (New York, 1939), is a survey based on secondary sources; G. Frégault, *François Bigot,* 2 vols. (Montreal, 1948), is about the last intendant of New France; extremely useful is L. E. Wroth and G. L. Annan, *Acts of the French Royal Administration concerning Canada, the West Indies, Guiana and Louisiana* (New York, 1930); the best analysis is that of J. Tramond in his section on the French West Indies in Hanotaux-Martineau, *Histoire des colonies françaises* (Paris, 1929), vol. I. See also J. Tramond, *Le régime commercial des Antilles au XVIIIe siècle* (Paris, 1904); J. Saintoyant, *La colonisation française sous l'ancien régime* (Paris, 1929), vol. II; and G. Hardy, *Histoire sociale de la colonisation française* (Paris, 1953). For Great Britain A. Keith, *Constitutional History of the First British Empire* (Oxford, 1930), is invaluable for the constitutional relations between the colonies and the mother country; see also O. M. Dickerson, *American Colonial Government, 1696-1765* (New York, 1962), and G. L. Beer, *British Colonial Policy, 1754-1765* (New York, 1907). Far the most comprehensive analysis of the British empire in the middle of the eighteenth century is L. Gipson's monumental series bearing the general title *The British Empire before the American Revolution,* begun in 1936, of which vols. I-VIII treat this period. F. Verneau, *Il conflitto anglo-francese da Luigi XIV alla Pace di Vienna (1660-1783)* (Bologna, 1939), concentrates on imperial rivalries; G. Graham, *Empire of the North Atlantic,* 2nd ed. (London, 1958), describes the Franco-British struggle for North America from a British viewpoint. For the economic structure of the British empire there is C. R. Fay's brief *Imperial Economy* (Oxford, 1934); J. F. Rees' brilliant chapter "Mercantilism and the Colonies," in *Cambridge History of the British Empire* (Cambridge, 1929), vol. I; C. M. MacInnes, *An Introduction to the Economic History of the British Empire* (London, 1935); by the same author, *England and Slavery* (Bristol, 1934).

At the head of any list of books on the West Indies, whether French or British, in this period there should be the careful and remarkably thorough Richard Pares, *War and Trade in the West Indies, 1739-1763* (Oxford, 1936), which covers every phase of the conflict between Great Britain and France. For the French Antilles, besides the works already mentioned: L. Vignols, *Les Antilles françaises sous l'ancien régime* (Paris, 1928); M. Satineau, *Histoire économique et sociale de Guadeloupe* (Paris, 1928); A. Martineau, *Trois siècles d'histoire antillaise* (Paris, 1936); on the commerce between Bordeaux and the Antilles S. Denis, ed., *Nos Antilles* (Paris, 1935); C. A. Banbuck, *Histoire politique, économique et sociale de la Martinique sous l'ancien régime* (Paris, 1935); P. de Vaissière, *Saint-Domingue* (Paris, 1909). For the British West Indies see F. Pitman, *The Development of the British West Indies* (New Haven, 1917); A. Burns' brief *History of the British West Indies* (London, 1954); W. J. Gardner, *History of Jamaica* (London, 1873). There is still no study on the economic aspects of the English slave trade comparable to Gaston-Martin's study mentioned above. Useful, however, are W. H. Wyndham, *The Atlantic and Slavery* (Oxford, 1935), and Eliz. Donnan, *Documents Illustrative of the History of the Slave Trade to America,* vol. II (Washington, D.C., 1931); see also L. Peytraud, *L'esclavage aux Antilles avant 1789* (Paris, 1897); E. C. Martin, *British West African Settlements* (London, 1927).

H. H. Dodwell's brilliant and thoughtful study *Dupleix and Clive* (London, 1930) discusses every aspect of the Franco-British conflict in India; see also *The Cambridge History of India* (Cambridge, 1929), vol. V; Sir William Hunter, *History of British India* (London, 1900), 2 vols. Among the many works on Clive, G. W. Forrest, *Life of Clive* (London, 1918), 2 vols., and Mervyn Davies, *Clive of Plassey* (New York, 1939), stand out. On the French East India Company there is the informative

W. H. Dalgliesh, *The Perpetual Company of the Indies in the Days of Dupleix* (Philadelphia, 1933). The most authoritative and complete life of Dupleix is A. Martineau, *Dupleix et l'Inde française* (Paris, 1920-1929), 5 vols.; see also Martineau's single volume *Dupleix, sa vie et son oeuvre* (Paris, 1931); Virginia Thompson, *Dupleix and His Letters* (New York, 1934); still useful is P. Cultru, *Dupleix* (Paris, 1901); on Bussy there is A. Martineau, *Bussy et l'Inde française* (Paris, 1935).

Among the countless works on British North America it is necessary to mention here only H. Osgood, *The American Colonies in the Eighteenth Century*, vol. IV (New York, 1924); E. C. Kirkland, *A History of American Economic Life*, 3rd ed. (New York, 1951); *Cambridge History of the British Empire* (Cambridge, 1929), vol. VI. For French Canada there is G. M. Wrong, *The Rise and Fall of New France* (Toronto, 1929), 2 vols.; more useful is J. Tramond, *Le Canada après le traité d'Utrecht*, in Hanotaux-Martineau, *Histoire des colonies françaises* (Paris, 1932), vol. I; a good economic study on French Canada is L. Vignols, "La mise en valeur de Canada à l'époque française," *Revue d'histoire économique et sociale*, XVI (1928); H. A. Innes, *The Fur Trade in Canada* (New Haven, 1929); J. W. Jewdwine, *Studies in Empire and Trade* (London, 1923); Firmin Roz, *Vue générale de l'histoire du Canada, 1534-1934* (Paris, 1934); G. Goyau, *Les origines religieuses du Canada* (Paris, 1924); E. Lauvrière, *La tragédie d'un peuple, histoire du peuple acadien de ses origines à nos jours* (Paris, 1922); G. Frégault, *La civilisation de la Nouvelle-France (1713-1744)* (Montreal, 1944); C. W. Alvord, *The Illinois Country, 1673-1818* (Springfield, 1920); Heinrich, *La Louisiane sous la compagnie des Indes* (Paris, 1907); G. Oudard, *Vieille Amérique, la Louisiane au temps français* (Paris, 1931).

Chapter VII

A colorful discussion of the controversy over responsibility for the outbreak of the Seven Years' War is H. Butterfield, *The Reconstruction of an Historical Episode: the History of the Enquiry into the Origins of the Seven Years' War* (Glasgow Univ. Publ., 1951), which probably overstates the role of Russia. Russia's role is the subject of W. Mediger, *Moskaus Weg nach Europa* (Brunswick, 1952), which, taken with M. Braubach's *Versailles und Wien von Ludwig XIV bis Kaunitz* (Bonn, 1952), has rendered much of the old debate irrelevant. R. Waddington, *Louis XV et le renversement des alliances* (Paris, 1896), is probably the most serviceable of the older studies. The most valuable printed source collections are Frederick's *Politische Korrespondenz* and G. Küntzel and G. Volz, ed., "Preussische und österreichische Acten zur Vorgeschichte des Sieben jährigen Krieges," *Publikationen aus den K. Preussischen Staatsarchiven*, LXXIV (Leipzig, 1899). British foreign policy in the critical spring and summer of 1756 is reasonably clear. In T. W. Riker's *Henry Fox* (Oxford, 1911), vol. I, and Evan Charteris, *The Duke of Cumberland and the Seven Years' War* (London, 1925), we have excellent studies on the growth of the war party and on the foreign policy of Newcastle. D. B. Horn, *Sir Charles Hanbury Williams and European Diplomacy* (London, 1930), is a scrupulously accurate and scholarly study from the British position; it is less informed and less reliable in continental matters.

On the Austrian chancellor Kaunitz there is the admirable study by G. Küntzel, *Fürst Kaunitz-Rittberg als Staatsmann* (Frankfort, 1923); H. Schlitter, ed., *Correspondance secrète entre Kaunitz-Rietberg, ambassadeur impérial à Paris, et le baron de Koch, secrétaire de l'impératrice Marie-Thérèse, 1750-1752* (Paris, 1899); J. Khevenhüller-Metsch, *Tagebuch* (Vienna, 1914). On Frederick's policy see G. Küntzel, "Die Westminsterkonvention," *Forsch. zur Brand. und Preuss. Geschichte*, IX (1897); less scholarly is F. Wagner, *Friedrichs des Grossen Beziehungen zu Frankreich und der Beginn des Siebenjährigen Krieges* (Hamburg, 1896); H. Delbrück, "Der Ursprung des Siebenjährigen Krieges," *Preussische Jahrbücher* (1895), 79; E. Daniels, "Friedrich der Grosse und Maria-Theresia," *Preussische Jahrbücher* (1900), 100.

For French foreign policy before the outbreak of the war see the Braubach and Waddington volumes mentioned above; also P. de Nolhac, *Madame de Pompadour et la politique* (Paris, 1928). Prusso-French relations on the eve of the war still await a definitive study.

Chapter VIII

The most serviceable general reference work on the Seven Years' War is Richard Waddington, *La guerre de sept ans* (Paris, 1899-1915), 5 vols. This magnificent study, useful for diplomacy as well as for military history, is a monument of independent, exhaustive research and sanity of judgment. No account of battles and naval operations is more complete or more reliable. Following a chronological procedure M. Waddington relates the history of the war as a succession of incidents, which unfortunately destroys the unity of the war and makes it impossible to envisage the larger strategical problems. On a more restricted scale Sir Julian Corbett, *England in the Seven Years' War* (London, 1907), 2 vols., discusses the strategy of naval operations, though neither so successfully nor so thoroughly as Admiral Richmond has done for the War of the Austrian Succession. Yet this work has never been superseded. Somewhat antiquated as a result of these studies but the only complete history of the war (Waddington's was never completed) is A. Schaefer, *Geschichte des Siebenjährigen Krieges* (Berlin, 1867), 2 vols.

The best general account of the continental war by a military expert is General Curt Jany's *Geschichte der Königlich-Preussischen Armee* (Berlin, 1928), vol. II; see also his "Der Siebenjährige Krieg, ein Schlusswort zum Generalstabswerk," *Forsch, zur Brand. und Preuss. Geschichte,* XXXV (1932). On the controversy concerning the strategy of Frederick the Great one should consult Otto Hintze, "Delbrück, Clausewitz und die Strategie Friedrichs des Grossen," *Forsch. zur Brand. und Preuss. Geschichte,* XXXIII (1921), and Hans Delbrück, *Friedrich, Napoleon, Moltke* (Berlin, 1892); also Delbrück's *Geschichte der Kriegskunst* (Berlin, 1920), vol. IV, 415 ff.; A. v. Schlieffen, *Friedrich der Grosse als Feldherr* (Berlin, 1913); far the most brilliant and incisive discussion is that by K. Lehmann, "Ermattungsstrategie oder Nicht," *Hist. Zeitschr.,* vol. 151 (1934); among French works the best is R. Sauliol, *Frédéric le Grand, le campagne de 1757* (Paris, 1934); H. Bonnal, *De Rosbach à Ulm* (Paris, 1903). For Prussian government finance during the war see A. O. Loehr, "Die Finanzierung des Siebenjährigen Krieges," *Numismatische Zeitschrift,* vol. 58 (1925); O. Hintze, *Die Hohenzollern und ihr Werk* (Berlin, 1916), 377; H. Mauer, *Die private Kapitalanlage in Preussen im 18. Jahrhundert* (Berlin, 1921).

Of William Pitt there are many biographies: O. Sherrard, *Lord Chatham,* 3 vols. (London, 1952-1958), is authoritative; readable and brilliant is Brian Tunstall, *William Pitt, Earl of Chatham* (London, 1939); generally sound but prone to cover up the weakness of the great commoner is Basil Williams, *The Life of William Pitt, Earl of Chatham* (London, 1914), 2 vols.; extremely valuable is Kate Hotblack, *Chatham's Colonial Policy* (London, 1917); *Correspondence of William Pitt with Colonial Governors,* ed. J. S. Kimball (New York, 1900), is invaluable for understanding Pitt's work as war minister; see also J. D. Griffith Davies, *A King in Toils* (London, 1938).

For the Duke of Choiseul there is *Mémoires du duc de Choiseul,* ed. F. Calmette (Paris, 1904), on which see P. Muret, *Revue d'histoire moderne et contemporaine,* VI (1905); Ch. Filon, *L'ambassade de*

Choiseul à Vienne en 1757-1758 (Paris, 1872); Soulange-Bodin, *La diplomatie de Louis XV et le pacte de famille* (Paris, 1894); A. Bourget, *Études sur la politique étrangère du duc de Choiseul* (Paris, 1907); Louis Blart, *Les rapports de la France et de l'Espagne après le pacte de famille* (Paris, 1915).

On the fall of Canada, besides the works already mentioned, F. Parkman, *A Half-Century of Conflict* (Boston, 1892), 2 vols., and *Montcalm and Wolfe* (Boston, 1884), 2 vols.; A. Lichtenberger, *Montcalm et la tragédie canadienne* (Paris, 1934); M. Sautai, *Montcalm au combat de Carillon* (Paris, 1909), a military study; T. Chapais, *Le Marquis de Montcalm* (Quebec, 1911), one of the best studies; Abbé Georges Robitaille, *Montcalm et ses historiens* (Montreal, 1936), more than a historiographical essay; Beckles Willson, *Life and Letters of James Wolfe* (New York, 1909); F. E. Whitton, *Wolfe and North America* (Boston, 1929); G. M. Wrong, *The Fall of Canada* (Oxford, 1914); R. Mahon, *General James Murray* (London, 1921). For the West Indies in the Seven Years' War, R. Pares, *War and Trade in the West Indies* (Oxford, 1936), is the most satisfactory military and economic study. For naval operations in Indian waters during the Seven Years' War see the penetrating introductory chapter of Sir Herbert Richmond's *The Navy in India, 1763-1783* (London, 1931); M. Davies, *Clive of Plassey* (New York, 1939), and the works by Dodwell and Forrest, indicated above; the best French account is A. Martineau in Hanotaux-Martineau, *Histoire des colonies françaises, Inde* (Paris, 1932), vol. V; P. La Mazière, *Lally-Tollendal* (Paris, 1931).

On the outbreak of the Anglo-Spanish war and the fall of Pitt see F. Rousseau, *Règne de Charles III d'Espagne, 1759-1788* (Paris, 1907), vol. I, and J. O. McLachlan, "The Uneasy Neutrality," *Cambridge Historical Journal,* VI (1938); J. Adolphus, *History of England from the Accession of George III* (London, 1840), vol. I. For the dissolution of the Anglo-Prussian alliance W. L. Dorn, "Frederick the Great and Lord Bute," *Journal of Modern History,* I (1929); J. Krumm, *Der Schleswig-holsteinische Gesamtstaat des 18. Jahrhunderts* (Glückstadt, 1934); E. Amberger, *Russland und Schweden, 1762-1772* (Berlin, 1934).

For the Treaty of Paris there is Z. Rashed, *The Peace of Paris, 1763* (Liverpool, 1952); the admirable discussion by H. Temperley in *Cambridge History of the British Empire* (Cambridge, 1929), vol. I, and L. B. Namier's comments in *England in the Age of the American Revolution* (London, 1930), vol. I, 331-443; L. Pérey, *Le duc de Nivernais* (Paris, 1891); E. W. Lyon, *Louisiana in French Diplomacy*

(Norman, Okla., 1934); C. W. Alvord, *The Mississippi Valley in British Politics* (Cleveland, 1917), vol. I, 49-74; F. Pitman, *The Development of the British West Indies* (New Haven, 1915); for the Peace of Hubertusburg, C. Beaulieu-Marconnay, *Der Hubertusburger Friede* (Leipzig, 1871).

Index

INDEX